2005

IN THE SHADOWS OF HISTORY

More praise for *In the Shadows of History*

"Chet Cooper's winsome, self-effacing memoir contains as many insights as a dozen dry policy tomes. He was a witness to most of the great events of the second half of the twentieth century, and his view of them is remarkably clear. His humanity and sense of humor will make you smile as you learn."

—Sanford J. Ungar
President, Goucher College

"Fine material for historians, but will such an obscure figure interest the recreational history buff? Happily, yes, for Cooper's ironic sensibility endows his account—at least of his formative years—with readably breezy self-deprecation. . . . Cooper's memorable memoir is replete with pungent observations of CIA chiefs, cabinet secretaries, and British prime ministers."

—*Booklist*

IN THE SHADOWS OF HISTORY

FIFTY YEARS BEHIND THE SCENES OF COLD WAR DIPLOMACY

-CHESTER L. COOPER-

FOREWORD BY ROBERT MCNAMARA

Prometheus Books

59 John Glenn Drive
Amherst, New York 14228-2197

Published 2005 by Prometheus Books

Inquiries should be addressed to
Prometheus Books
59 John Glenn Drive
Amherst, New York 14228–2197
VOICE: 716–691–0133, ext. 207
FAX: 716–564–2711
WWW.PROMETHEUSBOOKS.COM

09 08 07 06 05   5 4 3 2 1

Library of Congress Cataloging-in-Publication Data

Cooper, Chester L.
    In the shadows of history : fifty years behind the scenes of cold war diplomacy / Chester L. Cooper.
        p. cm.
    Includes bibliographical references and index.
    ISBN 1-59102-294-0 (hardcover : alk. paper)
    1. Cooper, Chester L. 2. Politicians—United States—Biography. 3. United States. Dept. of State—Officials and employees—Biography. 4. United States—Foreign relations—1945–1989. 5. Cold War—Diplomatic history. I. Title.

E840.8.C669A3 2005
327.73'009'045--dc22

                                                                2005005104

Printed in the United States of America on acid-free paper

To Orah, 1917–2002

And for Joan and Ron;
Sue and Tom;
Elizabeth, James, and Annah

CONTENTS

8   CONTENTS

FOREWORD

C het Cooper first came to Washington in the summer of 1942 and, except for the time spent in the infantry and the Office of Strategic Services and in several official tours abroad, has lived and worked in our nation's capital ever since. He knows not only where the proverbial bodies are buried, but also who buried them. During his career, he developed an uncanny skill in distinguishing which orders from On High made sense and which made sense to ignore—and has been able to survive. Even though Chet has subsequently held many important posts in the field of international affairs and, later, in global environmental policy, Vietnam has never been far from his concerns. Indeed, he describes the American experience in Vietnam as his "albatross."

At the Department of State, Chet and his boss, Ambassador Averell Harriman, kept alive the flickering hope for a negotiated peace in Vietnam even during the period when the Hanoi leadership and the Johnson administration seemed unable to agree on any step, however minimal, that might lead to talks. Harriman and Cooper, the two would-be peacemakers, were persistent, stubborn, and innovative in pursuit of their elusive goal.

Many deputies and special assistants in the White House, State Department, and Pentagon spend their careers inconspicuously dealing with day-to-day issues that may never reach their principals' desks. Many others spend months, even years, shouldering heavy burdens for their exhausted, over-

9

committed bosses during times of dangerous crises. Over the course of half a century, Chet Cooper has been one of those.

Thinking back, there are three such occasions that come immediately to mind. One occurred before my time in Washington, and two happened while I was there.

In the summer of 1956, Col. Abdul Nasser, Egypt's charismatic, popular, anti-Western leader, seized the Suez Canal. The canal had long been a jewel in England's imperial crown and was a valuable commercial and strategic shortcut from Europe to the Middle East and Africa. President Dwight D. Eisenhower and Secretary of State John Foster Dulles were outraged, but strongly opposed a military response by Britain and France. Nevertheless, a few months later, Britain and France, together with Israel, attacked Egypt. Washington all but broke off relations with its three allies and regarded the British role, especially, as a betrayal.

Chet Cooper, then deputy to the senior CIA man in London, had established close and trusting relations with his British and diplomatic colleagues. Secretary Dulles charged Chet with maintaining a link between the American embassy and the British defense, diplomatic, and intelligence establishments and handling all US-British issues too urgent or delicate to put on hold until relations were reestablished. For almost two weeks, on a twenty-four-hours-a-day, seven-days-a-week basis, Chet kept the tattered special relationship intact.

Another incident, one which I got to know firsthand, took place at the climax of the Cuban Missile Crisis in October 1962. In preparation for President John F. Kennedy's television announcement that the United States was going to blockade Cuba until and unless the Soviet Union removed its nuclear missiles from the island, the president and his advisers decided to brief the leaders of key American allies and reveal to them the highly secret missile photographs. Former secretary of state Dean Acheson would go to Paris and see Charles de Gaulle, Chet would go to London and brief Prime Minister Harold Macmillan, and others would go to Bonn and Ottawa.

The prime minister requested that the leaders of the opposition Labour Party also be briefed in order to obtain parliamentary support for Kennedy's blockade action. Washington told Chet to go ahead. Then, later that afternoon, there was a call from Downing Street. The prime minister, anxious to outflank the loud and growing "Ban the Bomb" sentiment in England, requested that Chet give the British press a briefing just prior to Kennedy's speech and show the photos, the only documentation that Soviet missiles were, indeed, in Cuba. Time was slipping by. Chet sent an urgent message to the president's advisers relating Macmillan's request and giving them two hours to respond with a go/no-go reply. At 11:30 PM London time, a half hour before Kennedy was to speak, there was still no reply—which, considering our frenzied activity in the White House at that point, should not have been surprising.

In any event, Chet made the decision. It was "go." He briefed the defense correspondents of a dozen British newspapers and the BBC. US Ambassador to Britain David Bruce told Chet it went well, and Chet dashed to his nearby hotel to hear the speech and then went to bed after a long, hectic day.

According to Chet, he was awakened by two outraged calls. Pierre Salinger, the president's media assistant, and Arthur Sylvester, my public affairs assistant, both promised dire retribution on Chet's return to Washington. Chet later told me that instead of trying to go back to sleep, he dressed and prowled the streets, waiting for the first editions of the London papers to appear.

All the papers, from the stately *Times* to the tabloids, and even the normally anti-American *Guardian*, supported Kennedy and the notion of a blockade. The word from Downing was warm and appreciative. Chet returned to Washington a day or two later. All was forgiven.

Effective deputies are not simply policy implementers; they are also initiators, even innovators. Thus, during the worst years of the war in Vietnam, Chet, together with Assistant Secretary of State William Bundy, conceived and put forward the Phase A–Phase B negotiations formula (the invisible swap of a halt to Hanoi's infiltration of its troops into South Vietnam for a halt to the US bombing of North Vietnam, to be followed by negotiations). This formula (obviously oversimplified here) served as the core of the American negotiation position until 1968 and is still part of the lore of the experience in Vietnam. Here, Chet well describes the roller-coaster tale of Phase A–Phase B.

These are just a few examples of Chet Cooper's readiness to stretch the boundaries of a deputy's role. Nor is he the only example of how—in Washington, at least—those who rarely, if ever, receive their fifteen minutes of fame often influence, shape, and even determine America's national security and foreign policies.

Years later, when Chet became involved in international environmental issues and enlisted me in the effort, our professional association developed into close friendship. As years have folded into decades, I am proud that, together, Chet and I are still on the same team and, hopefully, fighting the good fight.

—Robert S. McNamara

PREFACE

The story I am about to tell is drawn from the vantage of my role as a middling official in Washington's national security community and subsequently in international environmental think tanks. Despite a presence close to Washington thrones, however, I am unable—even if I chose to—to reveal new juicy gossip; either I was not paying attention, or whatever tidbits I gathered up have long since become known. In the course of my long career as deputy or special assistant to, of, or for somebody or something, however, I have learned a few things of interest from my station to the rear and left of center stage, or sitting just above or below the salt at official lunches and dinners.

Stints in the US infantry, the Office of Strategic Services (OSS), the CIA, the White House, the Department of State, and a variety of defense, foreign policy, and environmental institutes have been my lot. Thus, for almost six decades, I have been a participant in, or a witness to, a great drama—America's global experience. My professional life has been spent in the shadows of history.

At the outbreak of World War II, I was deputy for research to a formidable woman, a pal of Franklin Delano Roosevelt, who headed the mid-Atlantic regional office of a temporary establishment, the Defense Health and Welfare Agency. (David Rockefeller was the *real* deputy—I was twenty-four, he was twenty-five.) Many years and several deputyships later, I worked for McGeorge Bundy at the White House and later for Ambassador

at Large Averell Harriman at the State Department. I held five more deputyships until a few years ago, when, in my eighties, I became a deputy emeritus. However immodest it may sound, in the course of time I had become a
Mother of All Deputies.

What do deputies do? A deputy prepares the path forward, cleans up the
mess left behind, and ties up the loose ends. He writes and rewrites draft
communiqués, agendas, speeches, and news releases, frequently on his way
to international conferences, and often corrects them on his way back to
Washington. A deputy must be adept at stroking and sweet-talking angry colleagues and irate bosses who feel rebuffed or ignored by those at higher
levels. In short, deputing is an art.[1] A seventeenth-century Jesuit had it right:
"When you counsel someone you should appear to be reminding him of
something he had forgotten, not the light he was unable to see."[2]

Being a deputy was fun. Sometimes. At least my life has not been dull.
My time in the OSS was, in retrospect, a hoot. My close exposure to the Suez
war (actually, *too* close; I was the only American casualty) and the Polish and
Hungarian uprisings (all of which ended sadly) were wrenching and traumatic, physically and emotionally challenging.[3] The French-Indochina War
and America's Vietnam War were frustrating and maddening,[4] the Cuban
Missile Crisis was truly scary, and a kaleidoscope of revolutions, coups, and
insurgencies kept me from daydreaming at work and sleeping at home.

During the latter half of the twentieth century and the first few years of
this one, Washington's foreign policy officials, congressional leaders, their
deputies, and their advisers have spent time and energy in the cauldron of foreign revolutions and coups, cold and hot wars, guerrilla and civil wars, international terrorism, and nuclear blackmail and proliferation. Presidential aspirations have been met or shattered; government careers have escalated or
plummeted; health and family lives have been victims, while pundits, talk-
show hosts, and armaments lobbyists and peddlers have prospered.

In the face of this, one could rightly assume that today's policymakers
have become wiser than those of the past; they must have learned *something*
from the tension and turbulence of the post–World War II period. Maybe. But
from what we can see with a naked eye, probably not. The Bush II administration was convinced at its outset that it had nothing to learn from its predecessor—even if its officials had bothered to find out. And, of course, Bush's
predecessor refused to acknowledge that his antecedent could contribute any
advice of value. And his predecessor . . . In short, Washington politicians and
policymakers, largely by choice or absentmindedness, remain bereft of what
could have been learned from yesterday's experience. Of course, each outgoing administration jealously guards its records, but, still, there are enor-

mous and easily accessible holdings at the National Archives, and witnesses to the recent past are readily available.

In *The Tempest* Shakespeare reminded his audience that "what's past is prologue," and the Archives building in Washington tells us this at its entrance. But is anyone listening? G. W. F. Hegel, the nineteenth-century German philosopher, may well be right: "What experience and history teach us is . . . that people and governments never have learned anything from history."[5]

If Hegel had lived in Washington a century and a half later, he could have indulged in an even more lugubrious lament. In this most politicized city, at this most politicized time, history as we know it barely exists. Present incumbents erase yesterday in favor of today and, for a fresh incumbent, history starts on the day he first struts into office. For better or worse, however, history—or a particular slice of it—has been my constant companion, my shadow, over a long procession of yesterdays.

I am struck by how little past mistakes and triumphs have influenced the United States' approach to current opportunities and challenges. Yet all is not lost. While there is no substitute for the new kids on the block having to be exposed, firsthand, to relevant documents and seasoned witnesses, historians and memoirists can do much to bridge the past and the present. I have tried to build such a bridge in what follows.

*   *   *

Before embarking on the story I have to tell, a caveat emptor, so to speak, seems appropriate. It has to do with my recall of conversations with various bosses, colleagues, and associates. When I have used quotation marks, the material is based on actual notes or what I am confident is a reasonably accurate account. I have also used quotation marks when the material is obviously grossly improbable. When a conversation actually occurred, but memory of its color and precise contents is vague, I have not used quotation marks.

NOTES

1. Deputies in the government, I suspect, are now a different breed. In olden times (*my* times), a deputy was usually *the* deputy, who was directly responsible to *the* boss. Government agencies now have such officials as "deputy associate deputy secretary," "principal assistant deputy undersecretary," "deputy deputy assistant secretary," and "deputy associate deputy administrator." Following a decision up the chain of command must now be a lifetime job.

2. Bathasar Gracian, *The Art of Worldly Wisdom*, trans. Christopher Maurer (New York: Doubleday Currency, 1992), p. 4.

3. Chester L. Cooper, *The Lion's Last Roar: Suez 1956* (New York: Harper & Row, 1978).

4. Chester L. Cooper, *The Lost Crusade* (New York: Dodd Mead, 1970).

5. Joseph McCarney, *The Routledge Philosophy Guidebook to Hegel on History* (London: Routledge, 2000).

ACKNOWLEDGMENTS

I and this story owe much to many. Farley Chase, then an associate of literary agent Ronald Goldfarb, patiently and skillfully saw my way through the prepublisher thickets. Andrew Malone, honor student, guardian of proper English prose, music critic, and bird-watcher, slaved away in good cheer as he translated my impenetrable handwriting into readable form. The enterprise prospered from his skills.

Susan Cooper and Joan Gould, daughters and best of friends, kept the darkness of sudden aloneness at bay. Susan read the entire manuscript and provided not only perceptive criticism, but also ready access to experts at the National Archives. Joan introduced me to the British Archives and unearthed golden documents.

At the National Archives, I was fortunate to gain the assistance and earn the friendship of superarchivist John Taylor, who knows everything about almost everything. John is the benefactor of countless authors and scholars in the field of foreign affairs. Richard Smith, Michael Hussey, and Mat Nathanson deserve laudatory mention and many thanks for the photographs and maps they located and provided.

I must acknowledge the generous and knowledgeable help of my grandson James Duesterberg, who treated me to a course in Computer 101, typed a chapter's worth of pages, and gave me the benefit of his critical eye and constant support.

Elizabeth Malone, in her quiet, constructive way, helped me through rough moments during the recent past, not only in the course of writing this book, but in many other ways as well.

Paulette Wright's tolerance for my inability to deal with twenty-first-century office technology has saved many a day. Her smile and her skills have helped enormously in getting this book from me to you.

William Walker, an "adopted son" and master of many arts and several sciences, employed his blue pencil liberally to identify misspellings, unclear references, and unnecessary commas.

John Levenson helped me sort out some complicated family relationships and saved me from potential anguish.

Meghann French copyedited this work with care and diplomacy. Editor Mary A. Read of Prometheus Books was helpful, patient, and a good "boss."

Giving birth to a book involves more than composing and editing. Emmy Concepcion's concern, care, and cooking did much to keep my spirits up and my home inviting. She made a nontrivial contribution to the task of authorship.

LIST OF ABBREVIATIONS

ABM   Antiballistic Missile

BBC   British Broadcasting Corporation

CIA   Central Intelligence Agency

DOD   US Department of Defense

DOE   US Department of Energy

IEA   Institute for Energy Analysis. A think tank in Oak Ridge, Tennessee.

IIASA   International Institute for Applied Systems Analysis. An East-West research group on environmental, energy, and resource issues based in Laxenburg, Austria.

JCS   Joint Chiefs of Staff. Senior and staff representatives from the army, navy, air force, and marines.

NGO   Nongovernmental organization. A nonprofit policy research think tank officially accepted to attend, unofficially, at international conferences.

NIH   US National Institutes of Health in Bethesda, Maryland

NSC   National Security Council. The president's national security advisory group, staffed in the White House.

NWC   National War College. The US military's highest and most prestigious educational institution, based at Fort McNair in Washington, DC.

ONE   Office of National Estimates. A small group of Central Intelligence Agency analysts preparing classified analyses and reports for high-level government security officials and the president.

OSS   Office of Strategic Services. A World War II clandestine operations, propaganda, and analysis organization. The predecessor of the CIA.

PNNL   Pacific Northwest National Laboratory in Richland, Washington. An environmental laboratory under the Department of Energy. Originally charged with developing scientific and technological approaches to cleaning up the radioactive waste from the nearby Hanford plutonium processing plant. Now also focuses on a broad array of global environmental issues.

SCUA   Suez Canal Users' Association. An organization proposed in 1956 by Secretary of State John Foster Dulles. He hoped it would resolve the impasse over the Suez Canal. (It did not.)

WWICS   Woodrow Wilson International Center for Scholars in Washington, DC. The memorial to President Wilson established in 1970. Provides yearlong fellowships to approximately thirty scholars from the United States and abroad. A Washington center for intellectual discussions.

I

IN THE BEGINNING

I t was an early lunch in Whitehall; nevertheless, Her Majesty's short, portly foreign secretary was noticeably in his cups. (Not unusual—indeed, this situation was likely to blossom during the course of the day. It normally did.) He somewhat shakily lifted his glass to the US ambassador at large. In rich, plummy tones he offered his congratulations for "having the wit to appoint my old friend as your special assistant."

The ambassador at large was stone-cold sober (also not unusual—he always was, even after indulging a bit). He rose, looked down from his six feet at the foreign secretary, and, with a steady hand, raised his glass. "Sir," he said all too frostily, "congratulations are not in order, but gratitude might well be. I took your friend off the street just to save the world from another book."

Now, thirty-five years and a few books later, both Secretary George Brown (with whom I had had a long and rocky relationship) and Ambassador at Large Averell Harriman (who was by then my model and my mentor/tormentor) have long since passed away. As I embark on this enterprise I can see Brown's mischievous smile and, more especially, Harriman's disapproving eye.

"You should take some time, Guv, to write your memoirs," I had admonished Harriman on several occasions. "People should not write their memoirs until they are on their deathbed," Harriman would snort. "Please don't raise the subject again."

Well, Guv, you waited too long, but I shall not. Time is slipping by quickly.

*   *   *

My grandchildren, and their parents before them, have often asked, "Papa, what is it that you actually *do*?" In moments such as these I have envied doctors, lawyers, police officers, teachers, violinists; they know what they are, they know what they do. As for me, I've never been quite sure. Write? Travel? Negotiate? Conspire? Plan? All—or none—of the above? In desperation, I have resorted to a "Well, you see . . . ," performed a helpless shrug, organized a sheepish grin.

Surely, this is a piece of unfinished business that needs some attention. It is high time to give Elizabeth, James, and Annah a thoughtful, straightforward answer as to what I do and what I did. In the process, perhaps I will find myself the wiser. It may even be that recalling my mishmash of an education and my zigzag, nonlinear so-called career will, unlike the pudding Winston Churchill's hostess once provided him, turn out to have a theme.

The story I wish to tell covers many decades and many places. Yet it must start sometime, somewhere. There is no more logical takeoff point than at the beginning. So . . .

*   *   *

The beginning occurred in a middle-class suburb of Boston soon after World War I. Although there were still a few well-to-do Irish Catholic families in Roxbury when I was growing up—the Nunn kids, for example, lived nearby in an imposing green-shuttered white house with a large front lawn—almost all of the children I played with and most of my schoolmates in the nearby Garrison School were Jewish.

What I recall of my childhood and adolescence seems hardly the stuff of high drama. Remaining in the sieve of my memory is a mélange of tranquil, restless, anxious years spent in a quiet, homogenous community in the warm embrace of a patient mother and a not-so-patient father. There was also Mitchell, my younger brother, whose presence in this early period frequently involved more agony than ecstasy, but who soon became my best friend. Compared to many of my contemporaries, I had an easy ride, but there were still some sharp angles and rude bumps along the way between infancy and manhood. Looking back now, some still haunt me.

We lived on the first floor of an ample duplex house within walking distance of the Garrison School, Franklin Park, a synagogue, some shops, and a bank. A few blocks away was the trolley stop from which my mother and I would rattle our way downtown. There I had my all-too-frequent visits with our dentist, Dr. Fritz, who unfailingly removed and waved his set of false teeth as a warning to errant young patients. Mother's reward for my being brave was an ice cream at Thompson's Spa and a small purchase at Jack's Joke Shop. Then there was the usual detour to Filene's Department Store or S. S. Pierce's Groceries. Other downtown excursions were entirely pain free: to the Public Gardens for a ride on the swan boats; family strolls up Newbury Street, window-shopping the art, antique, and Brooks Brothers stores; and on to supper (not dinner) at Schrafft's.

School in those early days was, by and large, a pleasant experience, in contrast to the dozen or so years yet in store for me. Our principal, Miss Keyes, was a prim middle-aged gentlewoman who wore her hair piled high and was never without a lace neckpiece that seemed to be nailed to her flesh. Miss Keyes and I remained on good terms throughout our kindergarten-sixth-grade relationship. She told my mother she appreciated the way my neckties always matched my shirts. So it was that, whatever my grades in conduct or arithmetic, I carried my class flag at assembly. As I advanced in years, I became a recess monitor. (This responsibility would hold me in good stead years later when I was a military policeman, ad interim, on a troop ship.)

The young teachers—Misses Connelly, Kelly, Wilansky, O'Reilly, et al.—seemed terrified of Miss Keyes. A perceptible wave of tension accompanied her frequent and unannounced appearances in the classrooms. By far, the favorite teacher of the sixth-grade boys was Miss Kelly, who was barely out of school herself. Boogy August was in part responsible for her popularity; he claimed he saw her bloomers one day when he looked up the stairwell as she leaned against the rail on the second-floor landing. They were pink, he smirked.

Despite the moral support of Miss Keyes, I was, even then, hardly a star pupil; on the other hand, my brother was, much to my anguish. Miss Donnelly, who came to the house on occasion to tutor me, told my parents that "Chester is a dreamer. This may not be a bad thing, mind you." No matter. The teachers at the Garrison School exposed me to Christmas carols, the Pledge of Allegiance, the Lord's Prayer, and English grammar. I was none the worse for any of this.

*   *   *

My parents had a warm, caring relationship. Instances of angry words and serious tension between them were rare, and their long, serene marriage set a good example for Mitch and me.

I remember my father as a perfectionist—or, to put it more gently, as a man with high standards of beauty and quality. Although my mother did some of the family shopping, my father insisted on buying our fruit (from John-the-fruit-man), flowers (Carbone-the-florist), and meat (Altar-the-butcher). His suits were, of course, impeccably tailored (Faber-the-tailor). In the spring, he (and Delmonico-the-gardener), meticulously planned and planted the flowers and vegetables.

In due course, my father became a person of consequence, although he started out humbly enough. He was an excellent fly fisherman, a knowledgeable antiques collector, a generous supporter of a dozen charities, and an honored friend of both our mailman and the president of the now-defunct New York, New Haven and Hartford Railroad.

Dad was too involved in his business and community activities to spend much "quality time" with Mitch or me. But, whether or not I realized it at the time, he was a good friend and wise counselor. He took me fishing on Cape Cod and in Maine, to wrestling matches, to the occasional ballgame, and to the circus (I was in love with the circus then and am still). We attended many elegant antique auctions in Connecticut and Rhode Island (when estates were put to the hammer to pay taxes), and many less impressive ones in the Boston area where Hale-the-auctioneer presided.

Dad was proud of my brother and me—extravagantly so, embarrassingly so. He must have bored relatives, friends, and acquaintances to tears with exaggerated accounts of our every modest accomplishment. (My mother, on the other hand, was circumspect and more discriminating, although no less proud when pride was due.)

It was not until I was six or seven years old that I learned that my father had heart trouble. We were at a small resort hotel one winter when, in the dead of night, a fire broke out. My brother and I awakened to the sound of shouting and the smell of smoke. Firemen had broken the window to our second-floor room and were urging us to climb down their ladder. My mother lifted Mitch, I was close behind, and then I heard my father shout, "Help! I'm a sick man!" I realized later that we had taken this vacation because Dad was recovering from another heart attack. His cardiac problem was a constant source of worry. When I was eleven or twelve, I remember looking anxiously down our street on my way home from school each day to see if Dr. Richmond's car was, once again, parked outside our home.

An important element of his therapy, an antidote to the stress of his business, was his appreciation and knowledge of eighteenth-century English and American antiques and his love of fine art. Although Dad had excellent taste, he made his share of mistakes. So it was that his office was crowded with stuff bought on impulse and exiled by my mother. Many decades later, some of this banished stuff (including a thirty-six-inch Buddha) now resides in my office, having been exiled yet again, this time by my wife. (Now I am concerned about the eventual fate of these weekday companions.)

If my father was impatient of delays, inefficiency, incompetence, fools, and mediocrity, my mother was the essence of tolerance and tranquility. Like my father, however, she had impeccable taste and high standards with respect to her appearance, her home, and the values of her children. "Mother" to her children, "Nana" to her grandchildren (never "Mom" or "Grandma"), she was a quiet and private gentlewoman, content in her own company. She was also a discriminating collector of old porcelain and silver.

Mother was a steadying influence over her dynamic husband, her high-strung younger son, and her restless older one. She was beloved by her daughters-in-law and her grandchildren—as much a friend and confidante as she was a Nana. I can't remember Mother ever being seriously ill until shortly before her death at age ninety.

Mother's family was large and suffocatingly close. Two sisters had married two brothers and several members of the flock lived in adjoining houses. Memories of my late childhood are frequented by the strife created and fueled by a bitter, tempestuous aunt.

Like many wars, the *causa bellum* of the one in my mother's family has been lost in the mist of decades past. Nonetheless there was much "collateral damage" which left my parents, my brother, and me in its wake. The events of these dark years still intrude, now and then, in my dreams.

*   *   *

I know little about my parents' early years; Mitch and I have often berated ourselves and each other for our lack of interest, even curiosity. I do know that soon after my father arrived in Boston from Europe, he and his brother David owned a small dry goods shop. And I know that after graduating high school my mother was a secretary to the soon-to-be Hollywood mogul Lewis B. Mayer. And that pretty much sums it up.

Dad came from a musical family. His father, a vain and irascible man, had been a cantor and a composer of sorts. An aunt told me that my grandfather had studied with Tchaikovsky, but I put that claim in the same dubious category as her conviction that the Coopers (originally "Copernic") had an ancestor named Copernicus.

Uncle Dave sang for a short time in the Metropolitan Opera chorus, and his daughters sang in various choirs and choruses in and around Boston. Uncle Ben was a better-than-average violinist and played in informal quartets with members of the New York Philharmonic. I suspect that the opportunity to use one of Ben's four Stradivarius instruments may have had something to do with their readiness to include him.

My mother's family had immigrated to America a generation before my father's. Two of her brothers were engaged in local politics and the law, and two were on the periphery of the entertainment business. I remember a vaudeville actress (Nan Halperin) and a child movie star (Deanna Durbin) who made occasional visits in the 1920s.

Margaret McManus was the fifth member of our household. She came to us fresh from Ireland's County Sligo. I can't remember my childhood before she arrived. Margaret was beautiful, her complexion was porcelain-like, and she had waist-length auburn hair. She was graced with a wonderful laugh, a rich brogue, and a fearful temper. If, in her opinion, Mitch or I were "bold" or "saucy," we would be treated to a "box" on each ear. When we were older, we retaliated with such bold and saucy tactics as setting off Mitch's metronome (he was a hopeless piano student) and hiding it in the recesses of a dark closet or under her bed.

Margaret supervised Mitch's piano practice, pronouncing his efforts "miserable, miserable, Mitchell. For the love of God, I don't know why your mother is throwin' good money after bad." And evening after evening, she listened to me rehearse my Bar Mitzvah speech: "Not so fast, there, darlin'. And for the love of God, stop scratchin' yourself. Now start again, the place where you thank your grandfather." During this period there were many winter evenings where her two sisters, Bridget and Agnes, and her brother, Joe, gossiped about the "old country" and drank endless cups of tea in the kitchen. Joe played the accordion and Bridget taught me to dance a passable jig.

Margaret also served as an occasional, involuntary audience for rehearsals of "Chet Cooper and His Melodians," a group my mother referred to as a "musical aggravation." Although the Melodians, for which I was the impresario and drummer and Lenny Bernstein an occasional pianist, were but a pimple on Boston's cultural face, we were, as such ensembles go, in some demand at local weddings, anniversaries, and Bar Mitzvahs. In all modesty, we played a mean "Tiger Rag" and a mournful "Stormy Weather." The highlights of our two-year career were a summer gig at a respectable roadhouse and a dozen or so weekend nights at a squalid, run-down nightclub. At the latter establishment, to my surprise, I noticed the frequent presence of one or another of my allegedly respectable uncles or older cousins. They seemed to have a good time and be none the worse for their experience.

In due course, I discovered a hitherto unknown conspiratorial quality in my mother. As I set forth for my gig one Friday night, I overheard her on the telephone: "Joe, tonight it's your turn to go to the Red Rose and keep an eye on Chester." It may have been Cousin Sam or Uncle Ellis to whom my father observed that it cost him more to clean my tuxedo than I earned from wearing it.

When Margaret married, she promptly sent to Ireland for her younger sister, Mary. Mary was not Margaret. She was far from comely. She was constantly angry. She had a fiery temper that was easily ignited and difficult to quench. Mary tolerated our family, and vice versa, for seven turbulent years. In the summer of 1939 she decided to go back to Ireland for a visit. Although she hadn't become a citizen, she refused to believe, despite my family's warnings, that if war broke out she would be unable to return to America. Stuck in Ireland, she spent her remaining years in County Sligo complaining of her ill fortune.

*   *   *

Looking back, I realize that despite many friendships made in my Boy Scout troop, school, and the Chieftains Sport and Social Club, I was an unsettled, private, and introspective kid. I found pleasure in the solitude of long walks through nearby Franklin Park or along the beach where we had a summer house. (The house was named "Mitches," which was a source of worry to me. Was he the favorite son? If not, why didn't my parents name the house "Chesmitch." After all, I was three years older than Mitch.)

I was a fair athlete and a middling student. (Mitch was a rotten athlete, but a good student.) Indeed, it was not until I was well along in my university studies that my records contained more than an infrequent B, let alone a rare A. Only literature and history seemed to get my juices flowing. Chauncey Hall, a science-focused prep school, and MIT provided few such courses. My great achievement—my fifteen minutes of fame—occurred during the second year at MIT when, much to the astonishment of myself, my parents, and the mathematical genius Prof. Norbert Weiner, I pulled off a solid, golden B in Advanced Calculus.

It was not only my inauspicious and desultory educational experience that clouded my teenage years. There was an ever-present anxiety about anti-Semitism evident at home and rampant in Europe. The ineffable Father Coughlin ranting his vicious anti-Semitic diatribes from his diocese in Detroit, the unspeakable treatment of the Jews in the Soviet Union, and the even more horrid events in Germany kept me awake wondering what the future held for me and my family.

In those days I was constantly on edge about any real or imagined anti-Semitic slander. Any newspaper or magazine article in which the capital letter *J* appeared immediately caught my eye; it was with a sigh of relief that the word in question turned out to be John, or Jersey, or Jackson. I seethed with anger over any misdoing by someone with a Jewish name. I remember walking to High Holiday services with my parents and Mitch and finding that the entrance to our temple was guarded by a line of policemen. Once inside, my father steered us away from the pews near the stained glass windows, lest one of the hoodlums who had been jeering at us outside threw a rock.

Overlaying all this was the Great Depression. My father had had his own troubles shortly before the stock market crash in October 1929. At the time of one of his heart attacks, he had sold whatever stocks he had and had borrowed on his life insurance. Our family had cut back on all but the necessities. By 1931, however, Dad had started a new venture—an enterprise that provided warehousing and other services for automobile dealers throughout New England.

The effects of the Depression were ubiquitous. Well-spoken men in soiled and tired three-piece suits sold apples or pencils on windy street corners. Elderly couples braved long lines at soup kitchens. The single mother of one of my Chieftain friends "entertained" men in the late afternoons (Hank used to delay returning home to avoid his mother's guests). Our next-door neighbors lost their home and moved, with their married children, into an unheated summer cottage. In her small kitchen, my father's sister baked bread, which I delivered to customers in the neighborhood. The FDR Memorial bordering Washington's Tidal Basin has several reminders of this period, but I wonder whether any of them is meaningful to subsequent generations.

Uncle Ben Cooper remained unscathed. He had invented a remote counting device that was being installed on the burgeoning toll roads and bridges throughout the country. He was a bachelor and, as his favorite nephew, I was designated his "heir apparent." Since my parents detected little promise in any other line of endeavor (despite the fame of "Chet Cooper and His Melodians"), a guaranteed career in engineering, especially in the midst of the Depression, seemed worth the cost of sending me to Chauncey Hall.

*   *   *

Chauncey Hall was then located on Boston's Copley Square near the Public Library. The headmaster, a bald, nearsighted, pipe-smoking, owl-like, Dickensian figure, murmured after my father extolled my virtues at the admissions interview that I "didn't have the look of a horse thief" and welcomed me to three years of unmitigated drudgery.

Each Friday morning, I awaited, together with other less-than-first-rate students, a call from the headmaster—a call automatically triggered by any grade on any subject that was lower than the grade on that subject the week before.

"Well, Cooper," the interrogation would begin, "I see that you squeezed out a B-minus in trigonometry this week. I am correct, am I not?"

"Yes, sir, that is correct, sir."

"But last week your work in trigonometry was judged a B. Is this not so?"

"Yes, sir, that is correct, sir."

"How do you explain this decline, Cooper?"

"I do not know, sir."

"I *do* know. In the course of a week, you have become either stupid or lazy. Either way, I expect that this worrisome matter will be taken care of next week."

"Yes, sir. It will be. Thank you, sir."

One way or another, and despite what must have been a record-breaking low score on the Latin College Board exam, I was admitted to MIT in the class of 1939. Depressed in the face of this outlook, I began searching for an exit, or at least a detour. I had long loved the ocean, and a berth on a merchant ship seemed attractive, but in those Depression days gaining membership in the Maritime Union was almost impossible. I wanted to join a kibbutz in Palestine until I saw some pictures of people farming in the hot sun of a barren desert. I thought about applying for a job in the Ringling Brothers, Barnum & Bailey Circus band (seriously—I still do), but I didn't know how to get myself down to their winter quarters in Sarasota. I decided to enlist in the Loyalist Army during the Spanish Civil War until I discovered that the Abraham Lincoln Brigade had been taken over by the Communists.

During this difficult period, my mother was both a saint and a genius. "If that (whatever it was) is what you really want to do, Chet, I think you should give it a try. But for goodness sakes, let me help you pack so at least you'll take along enough socks and underwear." My father, on the other hand, would explode in exasperation and frustration whenever I announced a new career aspiration. "The circus!!! Is that why you went to Chauncey Hall? To play the drum in a *circus*?"

No matter. I went to MIT as programmed. Except for mathematics, I managed during my first two years to enroll in the lean menu of what most of my fellow students referred to as "crap courses"—English Literature, Economics, Social Psychology (which MIT then dubbed "Human Engineering"), and History. By the end of my sophomore year, reality dawned: The honeymoon was over. I now confronted the grim prospect of having to master Mechanical Drawing, Physics, Thermodynamics, and Chemistry. For someone with my eclectic intellectual taste and limited talent, these courses would involve a great deal of sweat, little pleasure, and virtually every waking hour. It would now be all work and no play. And I would always be a square peg trying to fit into a round hole.

I finally grew up. I made two consequential decisions:

1. I would not spend the next two years learning Mechanical Drawing or any reasonable facsimile thereof;
2. I would not go into the engineering business with Uncle Ben or anyone else.

So it was good-bye, MIT; good-bye, dean's list (yes, I had made the dean's list!); good-bye, gym team; good-bye, chorus line in the annual Tech Show; good-bye, ROTC band. Hello, New York University.

*   *   *

I cannot say that my short educational career at New York University was a source of either fond memories or a splendid education. On the other hand, living in Greenwich Village provided wonderful memories and a modest portion of maturity. McSorley's Saloon on the East Side was the source of good conversation and ample ale. A variety of cheap restaurants on Eighth Street (including a second-day hamburger joint—lunch, twenty-five cents) offered nourishment, if not ambience. The Irving Place burlesque theater near Gramercy Park and the weekend sidewalk exhibits on Washington Square provided dubious entertainment and a dollop of culture. (My favorite artist, a self-styled "modernist," promoted a new medium—a combination of mustard, ketchup, and glue.) Not to be overlooked was the Italian winery on Bleecker Street with its cellar full of giant barrels of sour-smelling fermenting grape juice. ("Very good," my fellow connoisseurs and I solemnly pronounced in the back room as we took frequent advantage of Mr. Bari's hospitality and drained several paper cups of the stuff.) To give NYU its due, it was there that I enrolled in several courses in economics and economic history and discovered I was capable of collecting clusters of As.

During my university years, I spent several summers working at a boys' camp near Skowhegan, Maine. I was something called a Trip Counselor. There were climbs up Mount Katahdin, canoe trips on Moosehead Lake, horseback treks along back roads to Waterville, and visits to paper mills, shoe factories, and logging camps. All this came to an explosive end in the camp's closing week of 1939. War broke out in Europe and the warm sun of late August disappeared beneath chilly, dark clouds.

*   *   *

England and the English have long fascinated me—English literature, thanks to the Boston Public Library; English furniture, silver, and porcelains, thanks to my parents; English history, thanks to a lonely liberal arts professor at MIT. My newfound interest in economics kindled a long-smoldering determination to take a graduate degree at the London School of Economics. By the winter of 1940 the war in Europe dashed all such hopes, so, after another summer in Maine, I was off again to New York City.

Soon after I returned to New York, I ran into bright, smiling Diana Something, who had been the dramatics counselor at camp. She was at a drama school and was doing a bit of acting. We spent many pleasant evenings attending the theater (second balconies) and enjoying inexpensive Greenwich Village restaurants. The relationship ended still in the platonic stage when, as naive as I was, it occurred to me that she was making a none-too-subtle effort to recruit me into the Communist Party. "You won't have to give your real name," she assured me. (Many years later, when, by chance, we met on a beach in Long Island, she apologized for her "stupidity." She said she had left the party soon after our last conversation.)

I enrolled at both Columbia University and New York University and moved from a squalid room near Washington Square into a clean, sunlit one uptown at International House near the Columbia campus. Space was available there for an American student because so many young people from Europe and Asia had to cancel plans to study abroad.

My change of residence was welcome from an intellectual as well as a geographic point of view. Close contact with foreign students was a broadening experience, especially for someone whose travel outside the United States had been limited to an overnight stay in Quebec. Of course, the war cast a pall over every social gathering. Conversations focused on Japan's crimes in China and Germany's in Europe. The radio in the student lounge was constantly tuned to the news.

*   *   *

Classes uptown at Columbia and downtown at NYU, together with a research job for one of my professors (at thirty-five cents an hour), kept me on the run. Nevertheless, I found time for courting. Her name was Orah.

I first saw Orah at the start of my second semester at Columbia. She was having dinner in a nearby restaurant with a friend from my camp days. I invited myself to join them. Although my friend pointed grudgingly to an empty chair, his guest was amused. She was lovely! Smiley! Classy! Smart! A week later, on the first day of the Monetary Theory class at Columbia, I saw her walk into the lecture hall. I made sure to sit next to her when the class met again. I never became an expert in monetary theory (my attention was diverted elsewhere), but I am grateful to Professor Angell, nonetheless.

At lunch soon after, Orah asked me where I came from. "Boston," I replied with pride. "Why?"

"Well," she said, "I wondered, because you talk funny."

I was outraged. "People from Boston are universally known to speak well. Everybody knows that. But you talk through your nose. Where are *you* from?"

"Cleveland," she said haughtily.

I discovered several weeks later that Orah had told me the literal truth, but she was referring to Cleveland, North Dakota, not Cleveland, Ohio. (On our honeymoon, we passed through her Cleveland—a grain elevator, a general store, a post office, a railroad siding, and a few score houses.)

Our courtship days were characterized by neither leisure nor peace of mind. Orah worked at Macy's Department Store on Saturdays and Thursday evenings, and my job at the university was time consuming, if not demanding. We were both anxious to get our graduate degrees as quickly as possible, and we squeezed in our fair share of study; whatever time we could spend with each other was precious.

Orah and I were engaged in the autumn of 1940, and married in June 1941. War with Japan or Germany, or both, hovered close and menacing. We rarely mentioned it, but we each knew that our life together would soon be drastically changed.

*   *   *

My days at the Garrison School typically began by pledging "alleginz" to the flag and mouthing "America the Beautiful." (My teachers tended to discourage me from singing—"Just say the words softly, Chester. That will do.") And then Miss Donnelly, or Miss Skelly, or Miss Devlin would remind us how thankful we should be to be living in bountiful America, especially now that the war—the War to End All Wars—had been fought and won.

In 1941, hardly fifteen years later, on a Sunday afternoon of a chilly, damp early December day, Orah and I were at the Metropolitan Museum. The artifacts of ancient Egypt, especially the steles with their mysterious and exquisitely carved hieroglyphs, held us in thrall until it was time to meet friends who were picking us up for dinner.

Their car was waiting on Fifth Avenue just outside the museum entrance. As we walked down the steps toward them, we sensed that something was wrong—very wrong. Jeanette and Henry were ashen, tight-lipped, grim. An awful, dreadful reality dawned; war had begun. Dinner was silent and solemn.

In January 1942, my uncompleted PhD in urban land economics shelved for the "duration," I was summoned to Albany. There I was assigned to a task force under Lt. Gov. Charles Poletti whose mission it was to cope with the tide of workers and their families flooding into newly established defense plants and expanded military bases. Orah soon began work in the state's Office of Price Administration. Not very long after, as a budding infantryman, I was learning to shoot a rifle, aim a bazooka, and thrust a bayonet. So much for Misses Donnelly's, Skelly's, and Devlin's comforting views of the future.

*   *   *

Unlike Orah, who, for a few years, had had a part-time job at Macy's, I had only some trivial summer jobs and some slave labor at the university before arriving at the State House in Albany. My assignment to the lieutenant governor's office was my first honest-to-goodness professional job. I was now earning a salary (three thousand dollars a year) rather than an hourly wage. To add to my self-pride, I had my own desk, swivel chair, and wastebasket.

I had barely settled into the windowless office I shared with two other young task force recruits and a grumpy veteran civil service clerk when I was summoned to the Capitol Building across the street. Surely, I grumbled, the lieutenant governor could have given me time to catch my breath. Yet I was anxious to meet Charles Poletti and forgave him for his impetuosity.

During the prewar Depression years, Poletti was regarded by the press, New York politicians, and the state's Democratic voters as the bright young hope to succeed Gov. Herbert Lehman—and after that, even to achieve a high Washington post. As it turned out, however, none of this was in his cards. He blew it. As a military government officer, he squandered a promising postwar career for a mess of pottage. He paid a consequential price for his black-market activities in Italy. There is an electric power station named after him in the Borough of Queens, but, beyond that, Poletti left no conspicuous footprints on either the state or national scene.

So much for Poletti; now back to me. To my disappointment, it was not the lieutenant governor who sought my presence. It was a clerk in the personnel office. Who, he asked, was to be the beneficiary of my retirement policy? Retirement! Did either Governor Lehman or Poletti really think I planned to sit on that squeaky chair, at that small desk, beside that dented wastebasket, in that dark, dreary office for the next forty years? Then I realized that, with Hitler's shadow looming larger each day, my shelf life in Albany would be measured in months, not decades. I gave him Orah's name and retreated across the street.

Despite the image of a seasoned and clever professional—and a married one, to boot—which I tried to project, I obviously did not fool the sour clerk assigned to my group. To him, I was still a raw, wet-behind-the-ears neophyte in the world outside academe. For the first couple of weeks he grudgingly guided me through the terra incognita of Albany's bureaucratic and political life. He provided two pieces of advice which I still recall.

On a day I was scheduled to see a member of the assembly about a problem in his constituency, my mentor grabbed my arm as I was leaving the office. "Listen, son," he whispered, "when you see this guy, or any of these guys, don't say, 'Pleased to meet you.' Say, 'Pleased to *see you again*.' Throw him a little off balance—know what I mean?" The ploy turned out to be even more useful in Washington than it was in Albany.

Then there was his admonition when, passing my desk, he saw me reading a newspaper. "Listen," he scolded, "don't *ever* let anyone see you reading a newspaper during office hours unless you're holding a pencil—make it a red one. Then it won't make any difference what you're reading—comics, sports page, anything—with a pencil, people will think you're doing research." This advice did much to improve the quality of my working life over many decades. I've passed it down to several generations of favored and grateful young colleagues.

I spent much of my time on the task force negotiating, pleading, and groveling. Overcrowded and understaffed schools and hospitals and under-staffed and poorly equipped public service providers had not only become a threat to the health and safety of defense-related communities, but were also beginning to affect the defense effort itself. Every mayor of every commu-nity with an aircraft plant, a munitions factory, or an army camp needed (or claimed to need) more hospital beds, temporary classrooms, nurses, teachers, policemen, housing, another fire engine—you name it. I was learning on the job, writ large. Gloversville, Farmingdale, Utica, Port Henry, and a dozen other New York towns I had never heard of before were becoming familiar overnight destinations.

Whether I significantly advanced the war effort in the course of the six months I spent in Albany, I hesitate to say. My moment of glory stemmed from a rough correlation I had worked out between the number of people in a particular expanding community and the volume of garbage collected (there were no garbage disposals in those days). It was a primitive formula that provided a rough-and-ready weekly local census. Aside from this no-brainer, I cannot recall anything I did that was worthy of either censure or approbation. No matter—I was, of a sudden, plucked out of Albany and dis-patched back to New York City. A grander assignment awaited.

*   *   *

In the summer of 1941, President Roosevelt had established a new emer-gency governmental body: the Federal Defense Health and Welfare Agency. How I wound up in the headquarters of its Mid-Atlantic regional office, I have never discovered. But in the late summer of 1942, I became chief of research (with an office that had a window). I was now on leave from New York University to New York State, and from New York State to the federal government. I forget who was paying me, and I don't recall being asked to designate a beneficiary for a federal pension.

My boss, Anna Rosenberg, provided an introduction to a whole new world. Thus far, the women in my life—my wife, mother, teachers, girl-friends, classmates—had been affectionate, caring, and nonthreatening. Mrs. Rosenberg may well have been an affectionate, caring, and nonthreat-ening woman, but she did not waste such qualities on the likes of me. Stuffed into her short, slim frame was a fiery, explosive, hyperenergetic, for-midable temperament.

During World War I, Anna had been a volunteer nurse. After the war, she organized the Future Voters League, and campaigned for women's voting rights. She was active in the New York State Democratic Party, an ardent New Dealer, and a friend of Franklin Roosevelt. There was, I later discovered, a Mr. Rosenberg, but he never seemed to emerge from Mrs. Rosenberg's domineering shadow.

My memory of her is one of constant motion and high emotion. When she scurried down our office corridor, the odds were favorable that a storm was brewing; I, or one of my colleagues, was in trouble. Thankfully, the clickity-clack of her high heels on the stone floor and the clanging of her earrings, bracelets, and necklace gave ample warning of her approach. I still recall the desperate attempts to compose myself for the awful moment when she would burst into my room, and then my relief when I heard the tempest strike somewhere to my right or left.

Mrs. Rosenberg's deputy, and my immediate boss, was a newly minted PhD from the University of Chicago. He was a year older than I, mild and courtly, cordial, but somewhat distant—a striking contrast to the bombastic, overpowering, and earthy Anna. Except for the expensive cut of his wardrobe, there was little about David Rockefeller to suggest a particularly intimate relationship to Standard Oil.

Early in my Anna Rosenberg incarnation, I discovered that the small town of Port Henry, New York, was on our urgent to-do list. Port Henry had become familiar to me during my brief tenure in Albany. Its iron ore deposits were not large enough to be important in times of peace, but they were too significant to ignore in times of war. The iron mines had reopened earlier that year and the town was facing a flood of would-be miners and their families. Health and social services, nurses, teachers, policemen, and housing were desperately short.

When the town's problems came up at a staff meeting, I told Mrs. Rosenberg of my earlier visits there, and that I had already met with Port Henry's mayor and other local activists to make a start on dealing with the worst of their problems. Anna ordered David and me to drive up for a current firsthand look. (Later that day, I purchased a cheap map of northeast New York, but David had already purchased a smaller one that cost twenty-five cents less. Shades of John D.)

Port Henry's mayor looked weary and was much less jovial than when I had last seen him. The burdens of office were beginning to show. "Mr. Mayor," I said, "after I met with you last summer, I arranged some help. Mr. Rockefeller and I want to talk to you about what you now need most and then see what we can do about it."

The mayor looked up at me and winked. "How are ya, Mr. Rockefeller?"

he hooted at David. "Pleased to meetcher." He put one thumb under each of his suspenders, stretched them out, and hollered, "I'm Mae West."

It took a few minutes to straighten out the mayor and soothe David, but, in the end, we had a productive conversation. Back in New York City, we were able to expedite the delivery of his most urgent requirements.

Once a month, in the Hotel Astor ballroom, Mrs. Rosenberg assembled the movers and shakers from the swollen towns and expanded military establishments in New York, Pennsylvania, New Jersey, and Delaware. Anna and her senior staff sat at a table on the stage; the dozens of industry representatives, admirals, generals, and local and state officials arranged themselves in rows throughout the huge room. On each side of Anna, and within easy reach, were two telephones, one black, one red. She used the standard black one constantly to badger her secretary, who was minding the fort back at the office. The red phone, according to Anna, was a direct line to the White House.

An important item on the agenda of every meeting was a status report of every requirement or request that had been raised at previous meetings. It was awaited with trepidation not only by her staff, but also by even the most senior civil servants and hardened military officers.

"David," she would say, "where's our list? Okay. Now, Admiral, last month you promised you would soon have more dependents' housing available at your Navy Yard. Yes?"

"Well, Mrs. Rosenberg, you see—"

"Not yet, Admiral. Am I seeing the housing?"

"Well, no, Mrs. Rosenberg. There's a problem. We can't get enough lumber."

Anna snatched the red phone. "Anna Rosenberg here. Is he there? Franklin? It's Anna. Fine. You? Good. Listen. Admiral Smith of the Navy Yard says ——. Good, Franklin. Thanks. See you soon. Bye."

In the several meetings I attended, I was unable to ascertain whether the red phone was actually connected to any terminal, let alone to one at the White House. Nonetheless, the missing lumber, the elusive plumbing, or the scarce medical supplies somehow soon appeared where needed.

Soon after World War II, Anna became the first civilian to be granted the prestigious Medal of Freedom, and in the early 1950s she was the first woman to be appointed an assistant secretary of defense. At the Pentagon, she played an instrumental role in integrating the army, navy, and air force. (I recall a trip she made to Korea during the Korean War. In Seoul, a reporter asked her how many black soldiers were fighting there. I can just picture her withering look when she said she neither knew nor cared how many *black* soldiers were there; as far as she was concerned, there were only *American* soldiers there.)

*   *   *

I had volunteered for the navy soon after Pearl Harbor when I was in Albany, but was rejected—flat feet and nearsightedness. It was clear, nonetheless, that my civilian days were numbered. We decided to move to Washington. Orah, with her graduate degree in economics, found a job in one of the war agencies within forty-eight hours of our arrival. As for me, I would soon be welcomed by the infantry, flat feet and eyeglasses notwithstanding.

Charles Poletti, Anna Rosenberg, David Rockefeller, and I had expended considerable energy, ingenuity, and sweat over the past many months helping communities deal with the strain on their transportation facilities, housing stock, school systems, health facilities, social services, and public safety concerns. But while we were preoccupied in the Northeast, who had been addressing those problems in the nation's capital? Apparently, nobody. Everything the natives and migrants in Port Henry had to put up with—the stresses, the shortages, the frustrations—was magnified in the swollen, bursting neighborhoods of Washington, DC.

The ubiquitous inconveniences and the daily hassles did not come as a surprise to us; we knew that our move to the wartime nation's capital would hardly be a pleasant experience. But there was another dimension, to some extent unexpected, that was troubling.

Washington had grown in many ways since Roosevelt's administration and the advent of the New Deal in the early thirties. Yet, a decade later, it was still a small Southern town in outlook, culture, and mindset. Even in government cafeterias, including those of the new war agencies, blacks and whites were separated. The "back-of-the-bus" syndrome was not strictly observed in Washington, but was enforced across the Potomac River in Virginia. Washington's one theater, the National, refused admission to blacks. It employed a "color expert" (himself a person of color) to stand next to the ticket collector and identify any would-be theatergoer who possessed a modicum of the wrong pigment.

The struggling National Symphony Orchestra, under the baton of an earnest, long-suffering conductor, had to be content with a short season and a scanty complement of musicians retired from other orchestras or barely out of a conservatory. Performances (for whites only) were held in the city's only adequate auditorium, the DAR's Constitution Hall, where the acoustics were atrocious.

Washington did have two important art galleries—the Corcoran, a hallowed institution then across from the White House on Pennsylvania Avenue, and the new National Gallery, housed in a gracious classical building not far from the Capitol on Constitution Avenue. When we moved to Washington the gallery was already several years old, but its collection was still sparse. For many years, it was referred to as the Mellon Gallery. (Andrew Mellon was the most prominent and generous of the early patrons.) With the growth of the collections and the increase in donors, the official name, the National Gallery, took hold.

For several months Orah and I camped out in a procession of rented rooms in various sections of the city. As a consequence, we became all too familiar with Washington's restaurant offerings. Eating out three meals a day became a monotonous and tiring chore, especially since the choice of cuisine was limited and we had to rely on the city's inadequate and overcrowded public transportation wherever we went. There were three French restaurants: Napoleon's, La Salle du Bois, and Chez François (the best of the three, and one of the few restaurants in Washington where one could meet nonwhite friends). Scholl's cafeteria was a reliable standby and provided good, inexpensive, simple food. The Romanian Inn (complete with a gypsy fiddler), a few Italian restaurants, a Russian nightclub called the Troika, and a dozen restaurants in Chinatown helped relieve a fairly steady dinner diet of fried chicken, collards, and sweet rolls.

Each day presented its own challenges, particularly during the time when we lived in rented rooms. Breakfast, lunch, and dinner usually entailed torturous bus rides. Dealing with laundry, dry cleaning, shoe repair, cavities, concert tickets, prescriptions, and bank deposits was frustrating and time consuming. July and August in Washington before the days of air conditioning were miserable and enervating; salt pills, electric fans, and iced tea were constant companions. Both at work and at home, heat exhaustion and fainting were occupational hazards. War or no war, a combination of high temperatures and high humidity signaled the closing of government offices.

The daily commute was a gut-wrenching experience. Poorly ventilated and mechanically unreliable buses were operated by exhausted, nerve-racked, and inexperienced drivers. It was by no means rare to witness a driver stop his vehicle halfway into town and dash off screaming, "I quit! One of you drive this goddamn bus!" Nor was it uncommon for veteran passengers to guide a newly hired driver along his designated route.

Then, of course, there were the rank-and-file "natives," primarily clerks and minor bureaucrats, some of whom dated from before the First World

War. They made no effort to hide their resentment of the "pushy" newcomers from the South and the "arrogant" ones from the Northeast who spoiled their once-relaxed city. On another, more elevated level of society, resentment against the auslanders was also deep and rampant. The correspondent David Brinkley, who even then must have been well connected, reports on the Cave Dwellers, "the earliest residents of the city, mostly rich. . . . Their city . . . had been taken over by a lot of pompous, ill-dressed, argumentative New Dealers, some of whom didn't even shave every day. Just invite one of them—and he would arrive for dinner smoking a pipe. As for the Cave Dwellers, they were beneath the notice of both Eleanor and Franklin, and of the earnest young engineers and economists wrestling with steel priorities, rubber substitutes and price controls."[1]

*   *   *

In my quest for employment between Anna Rosenberg and the army, I was interviewed by John Blandford, the stately director of the National Housing Agency. The session seemed to go well, although Blandford and, especially, his prim deputy perceptibly iced up when I mentioned that I had been working for Anna Rosenberg in New York City. No matter—Blandford took me on.

Orah and I each had two jobs. During the day we put in long hours at our respective offices. In the evening we searched for a place to live. We were so desperate that Orah set morals aside and offered the manager of a well-located apartment house a bribe of five dollars to put us on the waiting list. The manager was shocked—after all, her going rate was at least one hundred! Meanwhile, we were staying with a friend in his crowded quarters, and our situation was getting critical.

Each day I rose at dawn to read the classified ads. One day, after a dozen fruitless telephone calls, I succeeded in finding a furnished room downtown that had not yet been snatched up. Instead of going to my office, I dashed to the advertised address. An ample woman with a pronounced Italian accent showed me a comfortable and clean room. The rent was outrageous, but that was par for the course. Finally, I thought, we would have a decent place to stay until an apartment became available.

I agreed to her terms. As I was leaving, the woman tugged at my sleeve. "You're not Jewish, are you? I don't rent to Jews."

"No," I lied. "Are you Italian?"

"Yes, from Naples," she smiled.

"Well, I'm sorry, but I don't want to live with an Italian."

It was a difficult trade-off, but I felt I came off well, even though we were, so to speak, still out on the street. My landlady manqué almost certainly rented the room to someone more suitable within the hour. We, on the other hand, were unable to find anything as pleasant as the room I had thrown away. A few months later, however, by a stroke of luck (and without a bribe), we moved into an "efficiency" apartment on Sixteenth Street that would be our home for the next four years.

Yet all the crowding, the inconveniences, the unfriendly locals were just background noises; America was at war, after all, and Washington was a command center. The worrisome reports from the various theaters of battle, and a pervasive sense of foreboding, dominated every waking hour. For the past two years, the news had been bleak. The Nazis had torn up and swallowed much of Western Europe, advancing deep into Russia and the Ukraine. The Japanese overran much of Southeast Asia and China. Compared to the plight of people elsewhere, life in Washington was a picnic. No one I knew, or knew of, complained. No one quit his or her job (except for bus drivers stretched beyond their limit) and went home.

*   *   *

Winston Churchill's courage and oratory during this dark period lifted the spirits of the despondent and inspired hope among the imprisoned and those desperately hanging onto their freedom. Some of his wartime speeches still haunt my memory. In the desolate spring of 1940, on the eve of France's surrender when Britain would be left to fight alone, he broadcast these spine-tingling words: "We shall not flag or fail. We shall go on to the end. . . . We shall fight on the beaches, we shall fight on the landing grounds, we shall fight on the fields and in the streets, we shall fight in the hills; we shall never surrender."[2]

Franklin Roosevelt, already more frail than his countrymen suspected, held hope aloft during the woeful hours after Pearl Harbor: "We are going to win the war and we are going to win the peace that follows. And in the difficult hours of this day—and through the dark days that may yet come—we will know that the vast majority of the members of the human race are on our side. Many of them are fighting with us. All of them are praying for us. For, in representing our cause, we represent theirs as well—our hope and their hope for liberty under God."[3]

("Where are today's giants, who are today's heroes?" my children have often asked. If there are any in the audience, will they please step forward?)

*   *   *

The draft board's "Greetings" arrived in due course. Soon after, I boarded a bus to Fort Meade, Maryland, with a small satchel of toilet articles and a book or two. Within hours I was treated to a GI haircut and fitted out with a new wardrobe. ("How do you like your clothes, pal?" the wise guy supply sergeant asked. "Too big or too small?")

I doubt that any wartime recruit in any army anywhere is prepared for that first night in the barracks. As for me, lying on my cot and listening to "Taps," I felt more alone than I ever felt before, or have felt since. Orah was only twenty miles away, but already seemed out of reach. A familiar book had just closed; a strange new one had just opened.

NOTE

1. David Brinkley, *Washington Goes to War* (New York: Knopf, 1988), p. 19.
2. Martin Gilbert, *Churchill: A Life* (New York: Henry Holt, 1991), p. 656.
3. Franklin D. Roosevelt, *The War Message* (Philadelphia: Ritten House, 1942), pp. 30–31.

2

"THIS IS THE ARMY . . ."

ABOUT SELECTIVE SERVICE, AKA THE DRAFT OR CONSCRIPTION

Conscription—the process by which US military services, primarily the army, met their manpower needs in wartime—was first introduced during the Civil War. At this time a conscript could buy his way out for three hundred dollars or induce another man to serve as his substitute—hardly effective or honorable. World Wars I and II were fought largely by conscripts. In the Vietnam War the army relied on the draft to fill its ranks. In the Iraq war the burden is borne by regular volunteers, reservists, and National Guard troops.

The draft system was basically a lottery. On or near his eighteenth birthday, every male had to register at a local office of a federal agency. Unless he was physically handicapped, in ill health, or mentally unstable, or had special (designated) dispensation, he was assigned a lottery number. If and when his number was drawn (the drawings during World War II were made once a month) he was required to report to a nearby military center. His call to arms came in an official personal letter that started with "Greetings." During World War II eleven million men were thus greeted.

Not long after Pearl Harbor Day (December 11, 1941), I volunteered for the navy. I had always liked the sea, and during one of my restless periods in my late teens I made a desultory effort to get a job on a freighter or passenger ship. I flunked the physical exam at the local navy recruiting station—

nearsightedness and flat feet (until then I had thought the army did all the marching). In due course I received my greeting; the army (infantry) seemed glad to see me despite my physical imperfections.

The draft arrangements instituted during the Vietnam War in the early 1960s clearly discriminated against the poor and socially disadvantaged and as a result exacerbated political unrest. In 1973 the draft was abolished in favor of an all-volunteer army.

*   *   *

America has been described as a "melting pot"—an amalgam of religions, economic backgrounds, ethnic groups, skin colors, educational attainments. By and large, I have found this to be so—except for B Company at Fort McClellan Basic Training Center in Alabama.

I and a couple of other auslanders wound up in B Company quite by accident. We were initially assigned to A Company, which was made up of recruits from nearby Washington and Baltimore. A Company was over-manned, however, and B Company lacked a full complement. At Fort Meade, and during my brief original posting at Fort McClellan, I met several congenial Washingtonians. I did not welcome being transferred, but no one had asked for my opinion.

Most of my new barracks-mates turned out to be "Pennsylvania Dutchmen" drawn from the hosiery mills and the farms of Lancaster County. ("Outten de lights!" and "Shutten de door!" were common demands in the barracks.) The depression in the thirties had hit their communities hard, and high school was a luxury their families could not afford; young boys had to do their share to put food on the table. Many of my buddies-to-be were barely literate.

I was an unfamiliar specimen to them. They were an alien breed to me. Neither they nor I had ever seen the likes of each other. It took a while, but the barriers finally broke down. During precious free hours we would have a beer or a meal together at the Service Club. I helped several of them write letters home, and I read the letters they received; they helped me learn to take a rifle apart and then clean and reassemble it. Before we went our several ways four months later—some later to survive, some not—they and I had gone through a strong bonding process.

Life for an infantryman-to-be involved fourteen hours or more a day in kaleidoscopic activity—dawn inspection, calisthenics, a run-through on the obstacle course, a lecture on venereal disease or nose picking (a good time to catch up on sleep, especially when the unfortunate lieutenant-lecturer dimmed the lights for his much-too-graphic slide show), and then an hour of drill. A quick lunch and then rifle practice, a six-mile march, and a class in map reading—all this accompanied by Captain Greeley's screams ("Get your ass moving, soldier!"), dutifully echoed by Drill Sergeant Ball. Before we "outtened de lights," we cleaned our rifles, shined our shoes, and, on occasion, had enough remaining energy left to write a letter home.

There have been only a few people in the course of my life whom I have actively disliked. Captain Greeley and Drill Sergeant Ball rank high on this short list. I detested them during the Fort McClellan days and detest them heartily still. Their job, I realize now, and I think I knew even then, was to manufacture soldiers out of civilians, but notwithstanding that, they clearly relished their roles as all-powerful tyrants.

Greeley had flunked out of flying school, according to our first sergeant (who didn't like Greeley either, probably for more justifiable reasons than I). Rain or shine, in the heat or in the cold, he strutted around the B Company area wearing his old flight jacket instead of standard infantry garb. The possibility that I would wind up under his command in combat was the stuff of nightmares. (The reverse, as I will disclose, was the theme of many a sweet dream.) I eventually discovered that his gung-ho image and just-let-me-at-'em posturing were hollow; he was an emperor without clothes. One day, during the lunch break on maneuvers, I overheard him tell his executive officer that he had just gotten orders to join a regiment in Europe after the current training cycle. He admitted that he was scared stiff and would try to stay on at McClellan. I never discovered—or cared—if he succeeded.

The macho, loudmouthed Drill Sergeant Ball, the bane of B Company's every waking hour, also turned out to be a tin hero. His denouement in my eyes occurred early one morning when the company, laden with sixty-pound packs, trench tools, and M-1 rifles, was setting off on yet another marathon march up and down the hills of northern Alabama. For some reason, I had to dash into the orderly room before we marched out. There I saw Ball stuffing his backpack with about a dozen rolls of toilet paper, in place of the heavy gear the rest of us were schlepping. I stared at him. He glared at me. He was clearly unsure whether I would keep his secret. (He had a right to be concerned.) Luckily for both of us, there were only a couple more weeks to go before we would see the last of each other.

But there are pleasant postwar dreams: Captain Greeley is in a starring role. He appears in my elegant office, hat in hand, on bended knee, with tears streaming. He begs me for a job, any job. I look haughtily down at him (in my dreams, at least, he was shorter than I). I remind him that the army is short of infantry men, and that the recruiting center is nearby. Another nice dream stars Drill Sergeant Ball. For a reason that tends to vary from night to night, I order him to do two hundred push-ups. Standing over him, I yell: "83, 84, 85, 76, 77, 68, 69 . . ."

After seventeen weeks, if only to spite Greeley and Ball, my barracks buddies and I wound up as reasonably acceptable "grunts." We were proud of ourselves and each other. A few days before the training cycle was over, our regiment marched in review before Fort McClellan's commanding general.

"We paraded today," I wrote Orah, "the 34-year-old barber whose wife and kids have left him, the young coal miner, the truck driver—the one whose 16-year-old daughter is pregnant, the hosiery mill hands, the husky farm kids, the guy they just let out of the stockade, the street-smart Baltimore bookie who boasts of two ex-wives, the teacher, the former cop, the short-order cook, the radio announcer. All of us are soldiers now. Remember Irving Berlin's song, 'This is the Army, Mr. Jones'?"

*   *   *

Our shipping-out orders came on our final day at McClellan. Most of the GIs in B Company were being dispatched to Europe. By some quirky shake of the dice, however, my orders sent me in the opposite direction; together with a few other B Company alumni, I was slated to be an infantry replacement for the Mars Task Force in Burma. A day or so later, I was home in Washington on a two-week furlough, proudly sporting a rifleman's badge, hard muscles, and the blue cap trim of an infantryman.

Furlough over, I bade Orah and my parents good-bye and journeyed by plane to Chicago, then by troop train to a camp in northern California, to another one in Washington State, to a staging area, and, finally, to the port of embarkation in California. Much of this time was spent ladling out mashed potatoes and meat loaf behind long food counters at giant mess halls, painting and then repainting temporary barracks, standing guard over something or someone, marching to and fro, and reading and writing letters. The war seemed to be going along, for better or worse, without me.

I was not forgotten or mislaid, however; ship-out day came in due course. Two thousand men and perhaps a hundred women were crammed aboard the troopship at Long Beach, California. As we trudged up the gangway, a band on the dock played the "Colonel Bogey March," since familiar from the movie *The Bridge over the River Kwai.* (We didn't realize it then, but many of us were headed in the direction of that bridge.) As the ship inched away from the pier, hundreds of women leaned from windows of factories and offices along the shore, shouting, waving, blowing kisses. If any of us hadn't yet realized the epic drama of the moment, that sentimental, noisy good-bye surely brought it home.

I found my steel cot somewhere in the nether regions of the ship's hold. It was three up on a stack of five, with another five cheek by jowl. I could have touched eight other GIs—if I were of the mind to do so—without getting out of my cot. There were about two hundred of us in the compartment, and, as days folded into weeks, the smell ripened and persisted, even when we were out on deck. There are still moments when I think I catch a whiff.

A latrine, with saltwater showers and semisalt cold-water taps, adjoined our sleeping area. From Long Beach until we reached Bombay, exactly a month later, the toilet would play host, twenty-four hours a day, to a continuous crapshoot and a marathon poker game. Some of the low rollers and even a few of the high rollers must have taken time off to sleep and eat, but I can't vouch for that. What I can say with assurance is that, since washing was a residual claimant on their time, they all contributed generously to the stench in our compartment.

After I hoisted my duffel bag up to my cot and had a few minutes to look around, I realized with a sense of foreboding that here, in this crowded space, the army had either decided to conduct an experiment or found it necessary to maximize available space. There was a mix of black and white soldiers. Nothing in my Washington or Fort McClellan experience made me sanguine about the next several weeks. I had been assigned to military police duties for the length of the voyage and was sure that I would find myself in the thick of ugly racial arguments, possibly even violence. My principal responsibility, however, involved standing at the entrance to the officers' comfortable ward room and keeping my fellow GIs, white and black, from lingering to stare, jeer, or curse as they filed past the open door twice a day on the way to and from their own jammed, stand-up mess hall. (I must admit to only partial success.)

Happily, concerns about tension and friction in our compartment were unfounded. Common sense prevailed. Phrases like "I'm sorry," "Sorry, fella,'" "'Scuse me," "My fault," and "Thanks, Sarge" could be heard many times a day. Whether this was true in other compartments of the ship (or, indeed, whether the mixture in our compartment was unique) I don't know, but goodwill and prudence defused what, at that time and in other circumstances, could have been some nasty confrontations.

Our course during most of the voyage hovered near the equator. We were not in convoy and had no escorts. A few antiaircraft and antisubmarine weapons on board presumably would get us through. Oppressive tropical heat, a widespread bout of seasickness (thanks in part to the unfriendly Australian Bight), several general quarters alarms (my compartment was so deep in the ship's bowels that I never got close to an open deck before the antiaircraft guns became silent and the all-clear was sounded), and endless boredom were our constant companions.

A stop at Melbourne, Australia, for water, fuel, and provisions provided a brief respite from the monotony. None of the "passengers" was allowed to go ashore. Nonetheless, standing at the ship's rail and bantering with the Aussie longshoremen was a welcome diversion. The best moment came when it was time to cast off. After more than two weeks at sea, the ship had arrived high in the water. By the time it had taken on its supplies, our vessel had lowered several inches into the sea. Three mammoth steel hatches that had been opened from the hull onto the wooden pier were now well embedded in the wooden planks. Despite the heaves and shoves of a score of longshoremen, the hatches were impossible to close. Expectations were high that we would be spending the remainder of the war in Melbourne Harbor.

Our ship's captain, apparently both desperate and embarrassed, summoned the senior army officers, who summoned the captains and lieutenants, who summoned the regular and temporary military police. The game plan was to rock the ship from side to side while the men on the pier strained to close the hatches, inch by inch, until they could finally be secured.

Over the PA system came the order for all aboard to dash to the port rail. Then, at the sound of the ship's horn, everyone aboard was to dash to the starboard rail. And so forth. And so back. My responsibility was to stand precariously on a stanchion and gesticulate wildly to all the jeering GIs within my sight as to which side of the ship they were supposed to run to at any given moment. It was a hilarious and by no means well-choreographed exercise. But, in due course, the hatches were shut, the lines were cast off, and India bound we sailed.

One steamy, tedious day followed another. My routine was always the same. First, an early morning scramble to find whatever space in the latrine was unoccupied by the crapshooters and the poker players. Then to my duty station outside the officers' ward room. After the interminable line of soldiers had filed to and from breakfast in the mess hall, I was free to enjoy my own morning repast—powdered eggs, powdered milk, and Wonder Bread, the first of two meals each day. Finally, a climb up to an open deck to escape from the smells below, but usually too late to find sitting space in the shade.

We were well into the Indian Ocean when the late-afternoon torpor was broken by an announcement on the ship's PA system: "Rosh Hashanah services will be held at 1930." Someplace deep in the hold, about a hundred officers, GIs, sailors, marines, and Red Cross ladies gathered to pray on the eve of the Jewish New Year. There was no chaplain, but a tall, gaunt (by this stage of the voyage, of course, everyone was gaunt) marine sergeant led the service. There were some, but not enough, prayer books, and no Holy Ark. Nonetheless, my grandfather would have been deeply moved by the fervor of the prayers that night and on the following morning.

We landed in Bombay on day 31 and left the ship the next morning. In a letter to Orah I described my first sight of India, gained from a perilous perch on the rail. "I had a difficult time trying to convince myself that I wasn't dreaming. Threading their way through the noisy chaos on the dock were a half-dozen anemic-looking cows. Hundreds of Indian coolies were milling around. Some wore ragged, voluminous garments, which completely enveloped their bodies, others wore only loincloths which exposed, for all to see, their miserably thin arms and legs. Most were barefoot. All wore turban-type rags. (There was something about even a makeshift turban which gave those poor chaps an air of majesty.) Many workers were actually pushing moving railway cars around the dock. If they weren't displaying enough motivation, a dozen or so better-clad, officious-looking Indians wielded heavy canes to liven up their pace."

*   *   *

That raw initial impression of India—the crowding, poverty, reliance on muscle rather than machinery, sticks striking bare backs—would, in time, be countered by more visceral and more gentle experiences. Nonetheless, that first dockside scene long evoked India for me.

We had an hour or so to luxuriate in the British army washrooms adjoining the pier before being assigned to cars in the waiting troop train. I had the first good look at myself in more than a month. The moustache that I had nourished in the hope and expectation that I would emerge from the ship looking like that other Cooper—Gary—was a great disappointment; I turned out to be the twin of Groucho Marx. A hasty shave returned matters to the status quo ante.

My former shipmates and I, somewhat cleaner and less odiferous, piled into our designated third-class carriages and settled down for what lay in store: a stop-and-go five-day crawl across the breadth of India. Our destination turned out to be a military replacement depot east of Calcutta, in what is now Bangladesh. The railway cars were primitive: wooden benches, no lights, and many tiny animals. Except for the steel baggage/freight carriage that had miraculously been assigned to me and eight others, the other GI-occupied cars were antiquated wooden ones that were so rickety I wondered whether they would last the journey.

Much of our car was taken up with boxes, crates, and bags, and our personal space was consequently limited. Yet our situation was relatively comfortable. There were four benches and a closet with a hole in the floor. The open windows gave us whatever breeze was available. We slept one on each bench, one on each of two luggage racks, and two on the floor. Luckily, someone had to be on guard at night, so we didn't have to face the problem of where the ninth man would sleep. Food was a simple matter: We each had several cartons of K rations, and we could usually find hot water for our powdered coffee or tea at a nearby canteen or station when our train stopped, as it frequently did, to make way for other, apparently more important ones.

I have returned to India on many occasions since then, but that first journey across the subcontinent was the most memorable of my trips. Staring out at the villages and towns when we were in motion, or wandering through them during the long waits for a change of locomotive or for higher-priority traffic to pass (and all other traffic, passenger or freight, was higher priority) was a fascinating experience for someone who had barely traveled beyond America's northeast coast. I especially remember one particular evening, just after dark. The train was on a siding, as usual, waiting for an express to pass. Since we had no lights, and thus couldn't read or write, I had stretched out on my bench neither asleep nor awake when I heard the tinkling of what must have been hundreds of bells. In the dim light of a half-moon I could make out a single-file line of ox-drawn carts, several score of them, laden with farm produce (rice, probably). They were following a narrow path along the railway tracks. The only noises to be heard were creaking wagon wheels, the music of the bells around the necks of the oxen, the whack of a club on the back of a lagging team, and unintelligible snatches of quiet conversation. Like the scene on the Bombay dock, this episode comes to mind whenever I think of my first days in India.

The frequent pauses in each day's journey promised to provide a chance to eat our rations comfortably, free from the shake and rattle of the moving train. But, during the first day, no sooner would I break open a K ration package than dozens of sorrowful-looking children and adults reaching out for food would appear at the open carriage windows or door. I found myself hungry that first night, having given away a large share of my day's allotment. From then on, I traded the noisy jostling of the moving train for a meal of sorts in relative peace.

During one of our longer stops I had a chance to chat with the train's conductor, a rotund Anglo-Indian, who gave me my first lesson in India's class structure. "Look around you if you ever get to a city here," he said. "You'll observe the same occupational and social divisions we have on the railway. Here, the engineer is usually British, almost always a Scot. The conductor, that's me, is an Anglo-Indian—my mother is Indian, my father was a British shopkeeper. The coal wallah is an Indian, a low-caste Indian. Now if you go to a restaurant in town, you'll see that the manager is British, the cashier is an Anglo, the kitchen and dining room staff are Indian, again, low caste. It's hard for any of us to move up, or even down, in status. This is especially true for Anglo-Indians; we fit only a very narrow slot." I wanted to hear more, but the engine whistle blew and he trotted up and down the track hustling his passengers aboard.

During the long train journey, and frequently during the many weeks that preceded it, I thought of the waste of time and the undoing of many months of training that had typified my (and probably a hundred thousand others') experience since I had left B Company in June. It was now September and much of my intervening time had been spent hanging around mess hall kitchens, performing what was euphemistically described as "latrine duty," pacing on guard, slapping paint, or digging postholes—all to little purpose. There had been no rifle practice, no serious physical exercise, no forced marches, no maneuvers. I had lost weight at sea and was sure I had lost strength and skills as well. I wondered how effective a rifleman replacement I would now be. But I was not being paid to think.

*   *   *

In due course we reached our destination, an ugly, dusty village about thirty miles east of Calcutta and the home of a makeshift US Army camp, Kanchapara (or, as many came to call it, "Camp Shapiro"). The camp made Fort McClellan seem like Newport or Palm Beach. There was not a permanent building, not a tree, not a shrub in sight. It was brown ground, tan tents, khaki uniforms. An occasional drooping American flag added a touch of color. So did the eyes of every GI and every officer—yellow with streaks of red, thanks to the required daily doses of quinine pills to keep malaria at bay.

Very much like my month on the troopship, there was nothing—
nothing—to do. Even KP duty would have been a relief, but that was
reserved for local Indians. Luckily, there was an occasional day pass to Calcutta, reached on the back of a truck driven at death-defying speed through
crowded villages by some crazed GI who made it a point of honor never, ever
to give way to anything—animal, vegetable, mineral, and especially to a
vehicle racing toward us. It was amazing that people in the villages en route
hadn't banded together one dark night to set our camp afire.

My exposure to Calcutta, and my subsequent train ride from Calcutta to
New Delhi, comprised a course in Another World 101. Somewhat insulated,
as I was, from the most brutal efforts of America's Great Depression, I had
nevertheless witnessed (it was impossible not to) the bread lines, soup
kitchens, and shantytowns that pockmarked that era. None of this prepared
me, however, for the miasma of desperate poverty that seemed to infect so
much of Calcutta—families who lived their lives from birth to early death
on filthy streets; ubiquitous, aggressive, horribly maimed beggars; and,
worst of all, ragged children who would run up and grab the legs of American or British soldiers, shrieking, "Daddy! My daddy!" until they were
shaken (or kicked) off.

The Red Cross lounge or the dining room of an "Other Ranks [i.e.,
enlisted men] Only" hotel offered a place to write letters or vary one's diet.
The conspicuously rich Indians dining in the better restaurants with their
entourages of women, children, and retainers provided color and a brief look
at another Calcutta.

English soldiers and policemen were, of course, much in evidence, but
so were English civilians—the officials, bureaucrats, clerks, wives, gov-
ernesses, shopkeepers, and camp followers. They were choosy, of course, as
to where they walked (I admit I would have been, too, if I had known
enough) and seemed to my jaundiced eye unaware of or immune to the
smells, noise, clutter, dung, and poverty, or, for that matter, American GIs. I
had no occasion to meet any of these people, but I decided not to like them.
(Not long after, however, I became close friends with some British soldiers
there, and ten years later, in London, I got to know and admire many former
members of the Indian Civil Service.) I concluded that living in a British
ghetto must have uncovered and exaggerated the most unpleasant personal
qualities of the colonialists—which is probably the only conclusion I drew
during my early weeks in India that I still believe may be true.

During virtually every day I spent in Calcutta, there was some form of
riot: Muslims versus Hindus, petty thieves versus petty shopkeepers, pro-

nationalist students versus the police. Beneath the blanket of resignation and fatalism there was a seething restlessness.

Back at the Kanchapara depot, too, the natives were restless. There was no question that our final assignments would, in due course, be revealed. But when? Where? To what unit? Almost every GI in the camp was a replacement for someone or something—as a loader, truck driver, or armed escort on the murderous Burma Road, or as an engineer, medic, artilleryman, or rifleman for one of the hard-pressed battalions fighting in Burma. Since casualties in every category were running high—from dysentery and/or malaria and/or enemy fire—the replacement market was brisk. It was no wonder that a sense of foreboding laid heavily over the hot, still tents of Kanchapara.

I had been at the depot for a couple of weeks when, as I was ambling list-lessly (the normal style of movement there) toward my tent after morning roll call, I was hailed by a corporal I hadn't seen before. I could tell immediately that he was not one of us layabouts. His uniform was neatly pressed, he was carrying a clipboard, and he seemed to be in a hurry—sure signs that he was a headquarters clerk. "Some guy said you're Cooper. Are you?" He looked at my name tag. "Okay, I guess you are. The adjutant wants you. C'mon." I went, not without some morbid curiosity. Adjutants tended to mean trouble for a GI awaiting orders.

"What's your serial number, son? Right. Okay." The major pointed to a sheet of paper on his desk. "This came from CBI Headquarters. You've been assigned to OSS. You're supposed to move out ASAP."

"Sir, what and where is OSS?"

The major shrugged. "I dunno, soldier, but it says here you have to volunteer."

"Whatever it is, major, it's got to be better than this. I volunteer."

He grinned. "You're probably right, soldier. It has to be better than this. We'll cut your orders. You're going to Delhi. That's all I know. Come back before lunch."

*   *   *

I don't think I have an especially delicate constitution, but being in the midst of mobs of people has always made me feel uncomfortable. Even at football games I seek to come before or after an audience surge to the entrance or the exit. The month at sea, when it was literally impossible to stand, sit, walk, or lie down without being trampled on or pushed or touched and the several days with eight others in the cramped space of the baggage car had made me feel edgy. The crowded villages adjoining the camp and the jammed streets of Calcutta made me yearn for a few square feet of empty space. But Calcutta's railway station pushed me to the limit of *compis mentis*.

Wave upon wave of people with an assortment of bundles and children were advancing to or receding from the train platforms. I had my heavy army duffel bag and a small satchel that I was desperately trying to retain as I was shoved, pulled, pushed, and tugged in the general direction of the trains. The heat and the humidity and the noise virtually finished me off. Then, out of nowhere, a Royal Air Force sergeant major shouted above the din: "Where yer goin', chum?"

"Delhi, Sergeant," I hollered. "If I ever find the train."

"So am I. Follow me. I know this place." He carved his way through the crowd and we were soon on the platform where the overnight train was waiting. "What kind of ticket d'you have?" He looked at it and shook his head. "It's the bloody intermediate class. You don't want that. It's steerage. Come with me, chum. I'll fix it."

I followed him into a second-class sleeping car. It had six comfortable-looking bunks that could be curtained off for privacy. Three Indians, two in European slacks and shirts and one in a dhoti, were already on board. The conductor came through to check our tickets. He looked at mine and then at me. "This is a second-class carriage," he smiled, "and you have an intermediate ticket."

My sergeant friend came to the rescue. "It's OK. You see, he's with me." The conductor shrugged and left.

It turned out that Tony, the sergeant major, had been in the RAF since 1939, and had been in India since early 1941. (Four years after our train journey, I got a letter from him; he was hoping to be demobilized within a few months. By then, I had been a civilian for more than a year.) He planned to go to university after the war and get a degree in economics, and then either teach or go into politics. He wound up teaching in the Midlands.

The train and the debate seemed to start at the same time. Two of the Indians were fluent in English. Indeed, one had gone to university in Scotland and was a lawyer. The other was in the textile business. I never did discover who the third man was, or whether English was his second language as well; he went immediately to his bunk and drew the curtains.

The issue, naturally enough, was India's postwar future. The debate was wide ranging: India's precolonial history, the sins versus the virtues of the British view of India, the Hindu-Moslem problem, Gandhi versus Churchill, civil rights, British discrimination against the Indians, and Indian discrimination against Indians (the caste system). Most important was the matter of the subcontinent's independence. My new friend was an articulate, well-read, highly vocal, and nonapologetic defender of British colonial policy, despite the fact that he was an enthusiastic member of the Labour Party. The argument went on most of the night. Neither side gave in, but the three men parted friends. As for me, I had my first lesson in British Colonial Policy 101.

As Tony and I went our separate ways, having exchanged home addresses and vows to keep in touch (and we did until he died, many years later), he clapped me on the back and said, "You know, I could have argued either side of the bloody question."

So it was that, two days after I received my orders, I found myself in New Delhi's main railway station once again in the midst of a milling, suffocating mélange of saris, dhotis, pantaloons, British army uniforms, bare-bottomed children, and a score of downcast, manacled Japanese POWs. I edged as close as I could to the information counter where I was told I would be met.

As I look back now, I realize that almost everything consequential that has happened to me as an adult, aside from being a husband and a parent, started from the moment when another sergeant, a smiling GI, shoved his way through the crowd. "Hi, are you Mr. Cooper? OK? Let's go. The jeep is triple-parked." It took a minute for the words "Mister" and "jeep" to register. I hadn't heard "Mister" in more than a year and I hadn't gone from A to B on anything but my feet, a ship, a train, or a truck for many months.

With horn hooting, brakes squealing, wheels skidding, and sergeant cursing, we made our way, crawling and careening, through streets spilling over with people, carts, cows, camels, oxen, ponies, cars, and bicycles. We wound up, at last, on a shaded lane, well away from the hustle and bustle of the main road. "Here you are. Good luck." The sergeant pointed to a large European-style house, waved a "So long," and drove off.

3

THE VOLUNTEER

ABOUT THE OFFICE OF STRATEGIC SERVICES (OSS)

In the summer of 1941 the United States confronted two ominous threats—war in Europe and war in Asia. The British had been fighting the Nazis for two years; the Chinese had been fighting the Japanese for six. President Roosevelt, as part of his effort to prepare the United States for what appeared to be inevitable hostilities, established a temporary "defense" agency, the coordinator of information (COI). This group, which turned out to be the great-grandfather of the Central Intelligence Agency, set in train America's tentative, primitive engagement in the "black arts"—spying, propaganda, dirty tricks, and guerrilla warfare. To head this enterprise Roosevelt appointed decorated World War I general, prominent Wall Street lawyer, and Republican politician manqué William "Wild Bill" Donovan.

The COI had a short shelf life; six months after America went to war the agency was disbanded. The information and some of the propaganda activities, as well as many of the prestigious authors, playwrights, and journalists, were transferred to the new Office of War Information. The secret, less straightforward, mischievous responsibilities were passed on to something called the Office of Strategic Services (OSS) headed by Donovan.

The mandate of the OSS, announced the president in June of 1942, was short, if not sweet:

1. To collect and analyze such strategic information as may be required by the US Joint Chiefs of Staff.

57

*2. To plan and operate such special services as may be directed by the
   Joint Chiefs of Staff.*

The general's task would have been difficult in any case, but was made
more so by Washington's entrenched bureaucracy, which felt threatened by
the new, brash kids on the block (their *block*) who had an aggressive, street-
smart boss with access to a big budget and who apparently would operate
under few if any constraints. Nonetheless, Donovan and his jaunty, high-born
senior staff and don't-give-a-damn cocky majors, sergeants, and civilians not
only survived, but thrived. The one person who mattered, the commander in
chief, approved of, indeed even liked, what they were doing.

The OSS made its most impressive contribution in Europe when, especially
in occupied France and the Balkans, it took a significant toll on Nazi activities.
The FBI director prevented the OSS from operating in Latin and South America
and Chinese intelligence chief Tai Li hampered OSS activities in China.

As will be evident from the tale that follows, my direct contact with General Donovan was limited to a couple of salutes and one presentation of
arms. Nonetheless, his informal, can-do, non-chickenshit approach was
familiar to everyone under his command even from a distance of twelve thousand miles.

What follows in the next two chapters is but a miniscule slice of the OSS
story, in which I played a miniscule part. Nevertheless, this experience not
only shaped my life, it may well have saved it.

*   *   *

The OSS jeep careened around the corner onto a quiet, deserted street.
I hoisted my duffel bag and made my way along a path to a stout door
reinforced with steel rods. Two fierce-looking Sikh guards stood passively on
either side of the door. I had sudden doubts about the wisdom of my volun-
teering, and then a realization that it was too late for second thoughts. I
pushed the bell and shouted my name into a telephone on the door. After a
minute or two I found myself within the OSS confines.

A sailor (what was a sailor doing in the middle of India?) sat at a beaten-
up wooden table in the hall. He asked for my orders, checked them against a
list he took out of a drawer, and gestured toward a corner where I could stow
my stuff. He pointed to a sign-up sheet that, so far as I could tell, had only
two other names on it, and then led me into a nearby room crowded with

desks, files, wall charts, boxes, and people in army and navy uniforms. "Cooper," he announced to no one in particular. He may have been splendid at swabbing decks, but he was rotten at conversation.

A stocky navy lieutenant grudgingly parted company with a pile of paper, shook my hand, and shoved a chair in my direction. "Welcome aboard," he said. "Look, things are pretty messy around here, and I'm busy. Do you have a clue what this is all about?" I shook my head. "Well, I'll give you the ten-minute, quick-and-dirty treatment."

"Delhi," he said when he concluded his briefing, "is the OSS headquarters for the China-Burma-India theater. Our branch—what's your name again? Chet? Okay, Chet, our branch is based in this house. We're renting it from a British dentist—for much too much money. I know. I was a real estate agent before the war."

This turned out to be the sum total of my official orientation to the United States Office of Strategic Services. Whatever else I learned came my way in bits and snatches over the subsequent months.

On the assumption that one of the "messy" matters included in the lieutenant's responsibility was personnel, I asked how long I would be in New Delhi, and where I'd be going from there, if anywhere. He was sure that I wasn't assigned to the New Delhi headquarters, since that would be on his watch. That meant that I would probably be on my way out as soon as a message arrived from Washington—probably in several days. He didn't yet know where, but guessed it would be "over the hump" to China. "Meanwhile," he suggested, "find an empty berth in one of the enlisted men's bedrooms upstairs. When you come back I'll give you some papers to autograph and material to look over. Sit any place you can find a chair."

It was clear that neither the lieutenant nor any other present resident of the dentist's house knew what to make of a GI who appeared on short notice from an infantry replacement depot. He told me, with a slightly superior air, that they were used to dealing with people who had been recruited stateside and who had been carefully interviewed, psychologically tested, put through survival training, and then fully briefed.

"Well, then, how did *I* wind up here?" I asked. He wasn't sure, but heard that the OSS was having difficulty getting troopship slots to Asia because of competing priorities in North Africa and Europe. He guessed that the OSS had recently resorted to recruiting a few army people already in Asia whose credentials were based on information available in Washington. There were no briefings, no survival courses, no interviews, no psychological tests, he said with a note of disapproval and a shrug.[1]

There was little I could do in Delhi to wage war against the Japanese. Everyone in the house was, or thought he or she was, too busy to bring a transient neophyte up to speed. Someone did give me a cursory security briefing, however, and someone else handed me a few telegrams and reports to read. I found a Chinese language book on an abandoned desk, and this occupied me a few hours a day. For much of the time, however, I wandered around the city. Yet again, I was engaged in the now-familiar exercise of hanging around.

One rainy day, my do-it-yourself Chinese lesson was interrupted by a Sikh security guard, who whispered that an Indian gentleman had asked to see me and was waiting at the entrance outside. Since I knew no one in Delhi—or India, for that matter—I was sure there had been some mistake. It was no mistake; I had a mysterious, inexplicable visitation from a slight, middle-aged man in a white dhoti, carrying a briefcase and a large black umbrella. He looked earnestly at me through thick spectacles and asked, "Mr. Cooper?" I nodded. He handed me his card. "If you ever have need of my services here in the city, please call." He offered a hint of a bow and disappeared into the rain. Once back inside, I looked at his card. Under his name was printed: "BA Oxford (Failed). Subscriber to the *New York Times*." Who sent him, why he came to me, or how he knew my name, I never discovered.

My ventures around the city and my Chinese language study soon came to a close. About ten days after I arrived, I was on my way to China—and this without the need to call on the services of my failed Oxonian friend.

*   *   *

The twelve-seat China National Airways plane took off in the chilly dawn from an airfield in Northern India. My fellow passengers included a few Free-French army officers, three or four Chinese carrying battered suitcases ("contrebandiers," one of the Frenchmen whispered), and a silent, grave American civilian, who, it later turned out, was head of the OSS China research group in Washington and was to spend a few days at the OSS detachment in Kunming.

I was handed a parachute (which no one explained how to use) and a sandwich, and my name was checked off. That was the sum total of China Airways' pretakeoff preparations. Two insouciant, gum-chewing pilots in uniforms I didn't recognize motioned us to climb aboard. We fastened our seat belts, and off we went.

I later learned that flying over the Himalayas courtesy of the US Army

Air Corps was an entirely different matter. This involved preboarding instructions and a solemn briefing, including how to don a parachute. Each passenger was then given a survival kit, maps of the area, and a silk to-whom-it-may-concern message in a half-dozen local languages promising a reward for assistance to and the safe return of lost or stranded US personnel. I was unaware of all this, of course, on the day of my happy-go-lucky flight with China Air.

After a few hours of stomach-churning climbs and heart-stopping dives, we landed on the runway at the Fourteenth US Air Corps (aka the "Flying Tigers") base in Kunming. I clambered, somewhat unsteadily, off the plane to the sound of an air-raid siren. I spent the next fifteen minutes in a rice paddy ditch bordering the tarmac.

*   *   *

My first impressions of China, no less than those of India, involved a culture shock and a few surprises. After the melancholy faces of Calcutta and Delhi, Kunming seemed a smiling city despite its poverty, widespread opium consumption, corruption, and thousands of war refugees. Most Chinese I confronted seemed ready to laugh with or at me (although they may, at the same time, have been muttering something obscene in Chinese). I have often wondered about the genetic, historical, religious, and environmental explanations for the differences between the two peoples. Surely India's century-long colonial experience must have had some bearing on the dissimilarity.

One surprise was my ability to communicate in French with many Chinese in the city. The French had a long-standing economic and political presence in Kunming, largely due to the city's proximity to French Indochina. It was also the northern terminus of the Indochina Railroad, which had long provided Kunming with its most available point of access to the outside world. The dining room in the Hôtel du Commerce, still in operation when I arrived, provided a welcome and exotic change from the nondescript meals in our camp (Julia Child's presence notwithstanding; her culinary skills had not yet surfaced) and the Chinese food in town. The hotel bar was a gathering place for Free-French officers, many of whom, I suspect, were gathering information on the activities of Indochinese nationalists and Communists who had sought safety from the Japanese occupation of Vietnam, Laos, and Cambodia. Combinations of Chinese, Vietnamese, and French civilians with no obvious occupation huddled in corner tables over copious amounts of tea or cognac and endless cigarettes. Things and information of value were obviously being bought and sold, but it was hard to tell buyers from sellers. I'm sure the local American presence was among the matters of interest.

Mountainous Yunan Province in southwest China, and particularly its capital city of Kunming, was traditionally a haven or a place of exile for political troublemakers, mavericks, and suspect intellectuals. It was China's Siberia—a place both difficult to get to and difficult to leave. Until air travel within China became available, communication between Kunming and much of the rest of China involved traveling to a Chinese coastal port, sailing to a Vietnamese port, and then taking a train from Saigon or Hanoi to Kunming. It was a long, unpleasant and costly journey.

Despite Kunming's remote location, or perhaps because of it, the local university had an excellent reputation throughout China. By the time I arrived in Kunming, it was a hard-pressed host to several refugee universities from the east coast whose faculties and students had trekked hundreds of miles westward, carrying their books and laboratories, in the face of the Japanese occupation.

Kunming's location beyond the easy reach of China's prewar capital, Nanking, in central China, and even of its wartime capital, Chungking, in southwest China, was a mixed blessing. On the one hand, the university and the city's residents were virtually free from the social, economic, and political meddling of China's corrupt and inefficient national government. On the other, they were subjected to the venal and equally corrupt provincial governor, Lung-Yun, an archetypal warlord. He not only ignored the central government, but his provincial army was not loath to do battle with Chiang Kaishek's troops. Worst of all, he had a monopoly on Yunan's ubiquitous and highly profitable opium trade, and openly permitted, if he did not actually encourage, opium use throughout his realm.[2]

The OSS compound was on the outskirts of the city center, about a mile or two from the crumbling city wall. The establishment consisted of a large villa (probably rented or bought from a prosperous local official) and two or three small outbuildings original to the site. The OSS had added a few hastily constructed structures, including a latrine, a mess hall, and a warehouse. We lived in several tent-barracks. In the middle of the compound was a stretch of bare ground, and in the center of this space was a flagpole. Surrounding the whole was a stone wall about seven feet high.

The day-to-day administration of our detachment was headed by a colonel who, in real life, had been a New York lawyer. His preoccupation (largely frustrated here) with military spit and polish was more suited to the trainees of Fort McClellan than it was to the assorted oddball practitioners of "strategic services" under his command in Kunming.

A few officers and ten or so GIs, several of them former National Guard junior noncoms, comprised the rest of the detachment's headquarters unit. Except for two Chinese-American security captains and the mess officer, I'm not quite sure what the other officers did. The noncoms ran the motor pool and presided over the warehouse. Their first sergeant, theoretically at least, was in charge of all the OSS GIs. He had the thankless, hopeless task of subjecting a hodgepodge collection of linguists, forgers, cartographers, historians, photographers, artists, economists, explosives experts, and former gentlemen of leisure to some semblance of military discipline. One of my tentmates confessed that the only thing about army procedures he was sure of was to salute with his right hand.

It would have been asking too much of anyone, let alone our short-tempered, edgy and unhappy first sergeant, to shape up such a raucous mob to the satisfaction of the colonel. To add to his problems, many (by means fair or foul) had been presented with or had otherwise obtained enough stripes and graduate degrees along the way to regard themselves as above being pushed around by former National Guard types. (It would not be unjust to say that whatever else it was, this OSS contingent was tainted with more than its fair share of social and intellectual elitism.)

I arrived at the compound when, early each morning, the first sergeant was still attempting to assemble the twenty or so OSS GIs, who he assumed were his military responsibility, around the flagpole to engage in a roll call, mild calisthenics, and gentle drills. Few showed up. Fewer still engaged in either the exercises or the drills. A particularly frustrating moment for him occurred one morning when, in preparation for a VIP visit, he ordered "the troops" to form up at one end of the compound and walk slowly forward while picking up the cigarette butts and scraps of paper that littered the ground (shades of Fort Meade and Fort McClellan). He was greeted for his pains by hoots of laughter and shouts of anger. The hoots came from the OSS contingent; they didn't do litter. The shouts came from the detachment's Chinese coolies; they regarded the discarded cigarette butts as legitimate gleanings. (The first sergeant was probably unaware that the butts were the makings of born-again cigarettes that found their way, under such brand names as Ostrich or Lucky Stripes, onto the stalls of Kunming's street markets. Actually, he rarely strayed beyond the compound's borders.)

Although morning formations and drill were pretty much shrugged off, procedures in the event of air-raid sirens were taken seriously. In local GI parlance, the warnings escalated from "One Ding Bao" (Japanese planes had taken off and were flying west) to "Two Ding Bao" (Japanese planes were headed toward Kunming) and "Three Ding Bao" (Japanese planes were getting close). "Ding Bao" was the trade name of a vodka produced by White Russians somewhere nearby. The numbers signified the quality of the vodka. Thus, number one was produced yesterday; number three, the premium brand, was at least two weeks old.

At the sound of a Two Ding Bao, Kunming's inhabitants headed out of the city. Since our compound was on one of the few roads leading into the countryside, warning alarms and all-clear signals were quickly followed by a stream of people moving past the compound from and back to town. The GIs were posted along the compound's outside wall and at the entrance to make sure that unfriendly folk or even the enemy did not enter under cover of the passing crowds.

I and a few other honest-to-goodness soldiers among the OSS GIs, together with the former National Guardsmen from the headquarters unit, were posted, carbines ready, at the gate. Having had a week or so of impromptu Chinese language study, I felt confident enough during my first air-raid duty to shout, in Chinese, to the hurrying passersby, "Keep going down the road!" Much to my satisfaction, the Chinese looked at me, smiled, and waved. After the all-clear I was heartily congratulated by several officers and fellow GIs for my language skill. The moment was spoiled, however, by one of our Chinese linguists, who took me aside later and whispered that I had really been shouting, "Where is the restaurant?" He promised to exchange his secrecy for a carton of cigarettes.

*   *   *

My brief effort to teach myself Chinese made me realize, not for the first time in my life and unfortunately not for the last, that a little knowledge could be a dangerous thing. So when one of my fellow OSSers told me that he had found a Chinese teacher, a Miss Wu, who would instruct a group of us at her home, I was an eager and early candidate. This turned out to be a pleasant, albeit short-term, educational venture.

Miss Wu was a classy lady as well as a patient and competent instructor. She proudly pointed out, early on, that she was Manchu rather than Chinese. We were more impressed, however, by her striking good looks than by her ancestry. She was tall, slim, and carefully and artfully made up: The slit along the side of her silk cheong sam seemed, to me at least, to reveal an especially generous length of thigh.

No matter. She was a good teacher, and the four of us in her class—a future general counsel in the State Department, a future assistant secretary of state, a future senior Foreign Service officer, and a future senior CIA officer—made encouraging progress and basked in her smiling approval. Our lessons turned out to be recreational as well as informative; Miss Wu's gentleman friend, who obviously was prospering in the black market, hosted some awesome banquets, and our after-class conversations became increasingly lively and wide ranging.

Before long, however, trouble appeared in our private little oasis of culture and cuisine. Just as we were about to set out for an evening class, one of the security officers summoned the scholars into his office, closed the door, and informed us that Miss Wu was a spy—a beautiful spy, a charming spy, but a spy nonetheless. Her companion was not only a black-market maven, but her spy boss.

We assumed the captain meant they were Japanese spies. Perhaps he did. Perhaps he did not. He wasn't specific. Perhaps he didn't know himself who Miss Wu and her friend were spying for (if anyone, or if they had more than one customer). After all, Kunming was chock a block full of spies, aside from those in the OSS. There were spies reporting to Gen. Tai Lee, Chiang Kaishek's secret service chief. In addition, there were Chinese Communist spies, Free-French spies, US Army spies, US Navy spies, and USSR spies. And let us not forget the Japanese spies. Anyway, whether our esteemed teacher was any of these, or none of these, or all of these, school was now over. Life in Kunming just didn't seem the same.

*   *   *

In those early months, relations between OSS officers and enlisted men tended to be informal and frequently topsy-turvy. (In two cases, enlisted men and officers had recently been university classmates.) Not long after I arrived, I found myself heading a group of two civilians, two captains, a lieutenant, and a few enlisted men. (My reputation as a senior, albeit intimidated, aide to Anna Rosenberg must have preceded my appearance in Kunming.) In due course, and sadly, the command ladder was sorted out. Officers were officers; enlisted men were not. Regardless of rank, however, we were all on a first-name basis—except for the colonel.

Our group was, in effect, a miniature think tank: two economists, a geologist, a former banker, a geographer, a China scholar, and a couple of lawyers. Our task was to provide OSS Headquarters in Washington with information and analyses regarding the political, economic, and security situation in Japanese-occupied areas. I remember, especially, the study we did (for which we received commendations) of China's raging inflation and another of a stretch of China's east coast as a possible staging area for the invasion of Japan.

Although I called our ex-banker Scottie instead of Captain Blackwood, rank still had its privileges. It made no difference to him, but it did to the colonel. My letters home were censored by Scottie. He used one toilet, I used another. We ate at designated tables. Visits to town were segregated—officers on even-numbered dates, enlisted personnel on odd—an arrangement often breached by a simple exchange of insignia.

Civilians were given the same treatment as officers, a matter of scorn and annoyance, especially when two civilians (former missionaries, no less) sold us their monthly whiskey ration at a profit. (GIs could get beer, but not liquor.) Among the dozen civilians in the detachment were a few women—a linguist, a photographer, and the aforementioned Julia Child, who spent her days as head of the unit's files.

Rank aside, transacting any business in town involved nontrivial logistical and financial preparations. Americans were forbidden by the Chinese government to use US currency in dealing with Chinese, a considerable nuisance since the inflation of China's currency had become out of control. The black-market dollar-yuan exchange rate was one to many thousands—and escalating daily. The government in Chungking also refused to print money in denominations of more than one hundred yuan, so even a minor purchase necessitated carrying enormous bundles of money. If three or four of us went to a restaurant, one had to travel ahead by rickshaw with a satchel or two bulging with one hundred-yuan notes.

One of my principal tasks in Kunming involved interrogating Chinese refugees who, by foot, wagon, rickshaw, and truck, found their way to southwest China from Japanese-occupied cities and towns to the east. My partner in this enterprise was, as I, a sergeant and a budding economist. Since the Chinese professors, writers, and scientists on our interview roster would hardly bother discussing serious matters with common soldiers, Joe and I took turns at promoting ourselves. For Professor Chin, I would wear my regular uniform and drive Joe, now resplendent in borrowed major's insignia, and his "client" to a restaurant or teahouse where he did his interrogating. For Doctor Chiang, Joe, back in his sergeant's attire, would drive, and I, now a "lieutenant colonel," would host and interrogate. We were not above hamming it up: "Be a good chap, Sergeant, and collect my laundry," or "Cooper, pick us up in two hours," or "It's OK, Sergeant, get yourself a bit of lunch if you get hungry."

Another task, one already mentioned, was both more challenging and more consequential: to assess the prospects for success of a major US military landing on the beaches of Chechiang Province, on China's east coast. (The Chechiang landing was being considered by the war planners as a possible final stepping stone for the United States' invasion of Japan itself.) Our group was charged with collecting, translating, and scrutinizing whatever information on the area we could find—maps, old national and provincial surveys, soil samples, photographs, anything we could glean from our interrogation of refugees from the province and on-site reports from local agents. (A photographer sent out by our group was discovered in the area and shot by a nearby Japanese army unit.) In a recent exploration of old OSS/China files at the US National Archives, I discovered a report to Washington from one of our senior officers commending Joe and me for having worked thirteen hours a day, seven days a week for several weeks on this project.

*   *   *

One afternoon in early 1945, as I was walking across the compound, I noticed several diminutive men in loose black trousers and jackets. They were escorted by a few OSS officers, one of whom later told me that they had been meeting with "Annamite" guerrillas. A man called Ho Chi Minh and three of his followers were soliciting OSS assistance for their anti-Japanese guerrilla activities in Vietnam. Altogether, they made a few more visits, but in the end they succeeded in obtaining only encouraging pats on the back, a few pistols, and some rounds of ammunition. In a few years, Ho Chi Minh would dominate my waking hours and cause me many sleepless nights.

Another visit, more important to us at the time, was one in the spring of 1945 by the head of the OSS, Gen. William "Wild Bill" Donovan. Donovan was no run-of-the-mill World War II temporary soldier. He had been awarded the Congressional Medal of Honor in World War I, served as an assistant attorney general, and in 1932, the year Franklin Roosevelt swept into the White House, had been the Republican nominee for governor of New York. Donovan, then a senior partner in a prestigious New York law firm, was appointed to head the OSS by Roosevelt in June 1942. Soon after, many of his younger law firm associates found themselves serving in the OSS under Wild Bill.

Despite his distinguished World War I military record, Donovan was more a civilian in uniform than a hard-bitten general. He took a jaundiced view of efforts to transform OSS detachments into spin-offs of standard army units. "If OSS is going to be like the army," he is reported to have said, "we don't need OSS." Evidently our colonel was unaware of Donovan's feelings; in preparation for the general's visit, we were put through several military drills. Our first sergeant was in his glory. For many of our number, this was their maiden voyage into "Left-right!" "'Tenshun!" and "At ease!" On one occasion, a recent arrival barely missed shooting the man next to him when he accidentally fired a bullet at the order "Present arms!" From that moment on, all ammunition was confiscated.

The word got around our barracks that Donovan had a reputation for pausing at random as he strode past a line of enlisted men and engaging in the following dialogue:

"All well, Soldier?"

"Yessir."

Then, turning to his aide, "Promote that man."

No wonder, then, that on the morning of Donovan's visit, the detachment's two-score GIs lined up more or less smartly with their empty carbines more or less properly presented. For me, at least, it turned out to be a morning well spent; without further ado, the general made me a staff sergeant. (Two privates became corporals.)

$$*   *   *$$

A week or so after my well-deserved, if sudden, promotion, my fortunes took another abrupt turn. This time fate was nudged not by a message from the War Department to a remote and dusty camp near the Burma border, but by a toss of a coin in a local Chinese restaurant.

In the informal environment of the OSS compound, I had become friendly with two captains, both of whom had long backgrounds in China. Captain Stelle, a PhD from Harvard, was the son of a highly respected missionary family. Captain Sargent, a PhD from Columbia, had taught at a Chinese university. In military parlance, we frequently "fraternized" and ignored the officer–enlisted man procedure for visits into town.

One afternoon in the early spring of 1945, the two suggested I join them that night for dinner. I borrowed one of Clyde Sargent's shirts and one of Charlie Stelle's caps, and off we went. It became clear after we sat down at the table that this would not be just a social occasion. Each had been given orders a day or so before to head a small special unit north and east of Kunming, and each was trying to recruit me.

Clyde's group, "Project Eagle," would be attached to the Korean Provisional Army. This OSS unit was a newborn product of Chinese-American-Korean geopolitics. Clyde's mission had three objectives: to assist the recently established provisional army in seducing Koreans to desert from nearby Japanese units; to train the young provisional army recruits in the black arts of intelligence; and to infiltrate the trained recruits (by then, second lieutenants) back into Japanese-occupied Korea.

Charlie had been ordered to establish a small group that would serve as an OSS liaison to Communist Party chairman Mao Tse-tung's headquarters in the caves of Yenan, about 150 miles due north of Sian.

Their question: "Which unit would you like to join? It has to be one or the other."

My response: "Tell me more."

Their response: "We don't know much more. We'll find out after we get there."

My response: "Either. Both."

The choice was made for me by a coin toss. Sargent won. So did I; within a decade, the ineffable Sen. Joseph McCarthy destroyed the careers and ruined the lives of several Americans who had served in the US liaison missions to Mao's headquarters.

A couple of weeks later, I hitched a ride on a small transport plane to Kweilin and then sweet-talked my way past the all-powerful, puffed-up sergeant who allocated the scarce space available for American military personnel on the feeble, rickety train north. The railway tracks had been torn up twenty-five miles or so south of Sian, but I got a truck ride into the city. I checked into the small OSS base, and later that day was offered a jeep ride to the Korean Provisional Army headquarters, about thirty miles into the western desert.

*   *   *

Our village, Tu-ch'iao, had a noble provenance. Fifteen hundred years before it had been an overnight resting place for the courts of the T'ang and early Han dynasties on their annual treks from their permanent capital in Sian to their summer capital in the foothills of Tibet.

The Eagle team was located in the courtyard of a Ming Dynasty temple. The Korean army camp was dotted with scores of small tents for the new officers-to-be, a few larger ones that served as classrooms, and a makeshift drill field. The camp was located at the edge of the village, within walking distance of the Eagle quarters. The temple was in reasonably good condition despite its age; the dry desert air saw to that. We had our meals, planning sessions, and card games at a table in front of the room-length platform on which eight giant, ferocious porcelain gods kept watch over us. Clyde had his "command post" in the corner of the temple. The communications equipment and generator were located in a nearby shed. The kitchen was in a lean-to attached to the temple. A primitive latrine was at the far edge of the temple yard. (In due course, this latrine would be replaced by an edifice breathtaking in its elegance and technological sophistication.)

On a clear day we could see in the distance the outlines of a few pyramids, the tombs of some early Han emperors. Although the pyramids were three-sided rather than the four-sided ones of ancient Egypt, from across the desert, they evoked the pictures of Egypt in my school geography books. Passing nearby in a jeep one day, the tombs seemed to be relatively intact, although they had been looted over many centuries. Nonetheless, as late as the 1940s, the Chinese had few clues as to the awesome treasures that were hidden there. But ten years later, when local farmers were digging a well, they uncovered the first of thousands of larger-than-life terra cotta infantry and cavalry figures. Once again, they would see the light of day, after being buried for more than two millennia. Many years later, Orah and I visited them in their own museum and saw a small sample of them later in Washington's National Gallery.

Our OSS contingent consisted of Clyde (newly promoted to major), a communications officer, two explosives specialists, an executive officer, a weapons instructor, and an operations officer (the newly minted staff sergeant) who was to hold the job until the arrival of an experienced, commissioned officer, who never, in fact, showed up. The "operations center" consisted of a small table in my tent on which were piled some old maps, not very accurate order-of-battle reports of the Japanese units across the nearby Yellow River, a few pages of instructions from Kunming, and the Korean training schedules—the stuff of young Project Eagle.

Within hours of my appearance at Tu-ch'iao, Clyde stripped off my new staff sergeant's stripes and promoted me—temporarily, unofficially, surreptitiously, and illegally—to captain. And now that I was a "captain" in the OSS, I would hold the equivalent rank of colonel among the Koreans. (If only Captain Greeley and Sergeant Ball could see me now! It would be better still if they showed up as members of my staff—if I had had a staff.) A sergeant, Clyde explained, would cut no ice with the Korean officers or even the Korean trainees, who had been given the rank of officer-candidates. This gave me neither surprise nor offense; the past several months had inured me to both.

"Captain Cooper," Clyde grinned, "you're now a member of Project Eagle's second echelon. I trust you can cope with your new responsibilities." What Major Sargent did not say, nor did he need to, was that the third echelon of his command consisted entirely and exclusively of George, the cook.

Ah, yes, George the cook. He was a Greek who had jumped ship in Shanghai and somehow made his way to Sian. Meanwhile, Clyde had been sending messages hither and yon requesting a "GI cook." I gather GI cooks were either nonexistent or much in demand. Anyway, the logistics people in Sian discovered George and sent him our way. The problem was that Clyde was not only a gourmet, but was himself a gourmet cook. (Some time after the war, he conducted gourmet Chinese cooking lessons.) George, with the help of a willing but feckless young Korean, nonetheless did the best he could—which may have been barely adequate for the deckhands on a Greek freighter.

*   *   *

The Korean Provisional Army was the grandiose name of the minuscule, unarmed, and untested military force of the star-crossed Korean Provisional Government. The Provisional Government, in turn, was, despite a thick overlay of cosmetics, a cover for the Chinese national government's ambitions to control a postwar Korea. It existed under the paltry, self-serving patronage and unyielding thumb of Generalissimo Chiang Kai-shek, president of China.

Kim Ku, president of the Provisional Government, and his cabinet were aging patriots who opposed the Japanese occupation of Korea after its losing war against Japan in 1910. Following their fruitless efforts within Korea, they fled to China via Manchuria in the 1920s and 1930s. The Provisional government was established in 1944 to ensure that the government of postwar Korea would owe its allegiance to Chiang Kai-shek. I suspect Project Eagle was cobbled up in part as a sop to Chiang, and in part to put down a marker representing American interest in the course of events in northeast Asia.

President Kim Ku and his entourage traveled from their modest headquarters in Chungking to Project Eagle in the early summer. The visit challenged George's primitive culinary talents, to say nothing of the virtually nonexistent skills of the timid, frightened young boy General Lee had sent over to help in the kitchen. The "banquet" we planned was the least of our concerns, however. The visit required diplomatic skills and political savvy well beyond the experience and ken of the members of Project Eagle. As a consequence, the time Kim Ku and his cabinet spent with us was awkward, even painful. On the night of our makeshift feast, Clyde did what he could to pull together something of a ceremony, but the Korean dignitaries were unable to rise to even our modest effort. They lumbered through a well-worn choreography, treated us to limp handshakes, and tortured us with interminable speeches, which were adequately translated (I'm guessing here) by one of General Lee's aides. I envied those who fell asleep during dinner.

After our guests departed, we gathered around the table in the temple for a postmortem. It was a grim session. What concerned us was not whether the Koreans were satisfied with their visit and their American liaison team, but what *we* had seen and heard that evening. Did it make much sense, we wondered, for the United States to rely on these tired, isolated, heartsore, unworldly men to run what was bound to be a strife-torn, poor postwar Korea?

Why did the OSS, for that matter, get involved in Chiang's geopolitical game? Washington, after all, was grooming its own postwar Korean leader, US-educated Syngman Rhee, who had been biding his time in Honolulu. Perhaps, we surmised, Project Eagle, aside from a small genuflection to Chiang Kai-shek, represented an American hedge in the unlikely event that Kim Ku actually came out on top when push came to shove after the war. (In fact, Kim Ku was murdered on the eve of the 1948 presidential election. His assassin was never apprehended and Syngman Rhee was unopposed.)

It turned out that we needn't have worried about Kim Ku's reaction to his visit. Not long after he returned to Chungking, he sent a message to General Donovan: "I am satisfied with the work and cooperation between General Lee Bum Suk [the commander of our Korean officers-to-be] and Captain [sic] Sargent. I hope you can give them all guidance possible."[3]

General Lee was a different kettle of fish. He had been an anti-Japanese guerrilla during several years of the Japanese occupation of Korea and then, like Kim Ku and many others, fled to China via Manchuria. Soon after he arrived in China, he was sent to Whampo, Chiang Kai-shek's former military academy, and in the course of time he became a general in the Chinese army. Lee was about fifty years old, much younger than Kim Ku and his other political bosses. He looked and behaved like a character from central casting for a grade B, made-in-Bombay movie. Unlike the officials of the provisional government, he was neither heartsore nor tired. He did not walk; he marched. He did not nibble; he devoured. He did not sip; he gulped. He was short, ramrod straight, trim, bald, and energetic. He cultivated a thin, neat mustache. His revolver, swagger stick, and menacing German shepherd dog were ubiquitous accompaniments during his every waking hour.

The Korean officer trainees numbered about three hundred. They had at least a high school education, were in good physical condition, and had been culled from a much larger group of deserters from the Japanese army. Those who were not selected for training were sent off to a Chinese prisoner-of-war camp, a fate less onerous, I am sure, than being the lowest of the low in Japanese army units.

The officer candidates came to the Eagle training center from their menial stations in the Japanese army and were well aware of the perks and privileges enjoyed by commissioned officers. Early on, they decided it was beneath their newfound dignity to make their beds; that was a job for coolies. Within a half hour, however, they were spending a long, hot morning jogging in an endless circle around the dusty drill field. Eventually, they were ordered back to their tents, where they did, indeed, make their beds, and stood at attention until all three hundred of them had been subjected to a meticulous inspection by the general himself. End of rank/privileges problem.

Meanwhile, General Donovan was continuing to make his way around the various OSS units in China. About a week after I joined the Koreans, and two weeks after Wild Bill's visit to Kunming, he dropped in on us. The seven Eagles, the Greek cook, and General Lee lined up in front of the temple to greet him. He paused in front of me as he strolled past. "You look familiar. Haven't I seen you recently?"

"Yes sir. Cooper, sir. In Kunming, sir."

He looked at General Lee standing nearby and lowered his voice.

"I promoted you, didn't I? Sergeant, wasn't it?"

"*Staff* Sergeant, sir," I murmured.

"Well," he winked, "you've made great progress since we last met, Captain. Congratulations."

*   *   *

Early that summer, we were joined by a Chinese doctor, Hou Bao-chang. He had been Clyde's colleague at a university on China's east coast, where he was dean of the medical school. He had joined the university's trek west to Chengtu, a picturesque city one hundred miles southwest of our village. Clyde had wrangled a summer job for Hou as Eagle's medical officer.

Dr. Hou was the first Rockefeller Fellow from China, and received his medical training at the University of Chicago in the early 1920s. While none of us was seriously ill or injured during Dr. Hou's stint with Project Eagle, we benefited mightily from his ability to bargain with the villagers of Tu-ch'iao for the finest fruit, the best chickens, the largest eggs at the cheapest price. Our cuisine also improved; the doctor was a splendid chef, and George a willing student.

What I treasured most, however, was Dr. Hou's wisdom and companionship. He was a talented raconteur, a patient listener, and a strong bridge between our two cultures. It became a regular evening routine for several of us to sit around the table in the temple entranced by his stories of rural life, his recounting of the springtime journeys of the Han courts through our village on their way northwest to their summer capital, and his tales of peccadilloes of rulers past and present. In the uncertain light of our kerosene lamps the towering Ming gods seemed to be among Dr. Hou's audience; I wonder whether they were checking on the political correctness or verisimilitude of his tales. (Orah and I saw much of Dr. Hou in Washington after the war. He became a close friend, virtually a member of our family. The zealots of China's Cultural Revolution had much to answer for when they caused his death.)

There were other good moments that summer. On a clear, moonlit night in the temple courtyard, one of General Lee's aides accompanied his wife on a rickety upright piano as she sang several Schubert lieder. (Where his piano or, for that matter, where his wife came from, I don't know.) And then there were the long walks at dawn, or at sunset, through the desert to the place where a stream splashed its way toward the Yellow River.

Our daytime hours that July and August were marked by alternating periods of optimism and anxiety. According to the Eagle instructors and the few Korean officers on General Lee's staff, the trainees were making progress in learning and applying the black arts. But serious problems arose after they completed their training and became bona fide second lieutenants. At this point, they were scheduled for infiltration back into Korea. Like the policemen in *The Pirates of Penzance*, however, they were more inclined to march hither and yon boasting of their potential feats than they were to actually set off and perform them. Many simply went AWOL on their way to Korea. Operations officer notwithstanding, there was little I could do to actually deliver them to their appointed station.

Another source of concern was the presence of the Japanese across the Yellow River. Every few weeks or so there were rumors that they were preparing to make the crossing and head toward Sian. The seven of us, even buttressed by George, General Lee, and his Korean trainees, hardly presented an obstacle to a Japanese assault. We were low-hanging fruit that would be picked off within the first hour of their march. Moreover, I can reliably report that Project Eagle's operations officer had no foolproof Plan B!

*   *   *

Despite Kim Ku's message to General Donovan reporting satisfaction with Project Eagle, we were treated, in mid-July, to a sudden, unwelcome change of command. A somewhat unsteady Lt. Col. Walter Bride arrived on a day's notice from Chungking via Sian to take over from Clyde, who would remain as the project's deputy commander. (This, of course, automatically demoted me to the third echelon.)

According to the colonel, he had been transferred to give Project Eagle a "shot in the arm." While a shot may have been needed, he had not been transferred solely for this purpose. We learned later that, probably as a result of Donovan's visit to Chungking, Bride had been sent our way to remove him as far as possible from China's capital. Our village was thirty miles away from the nearest bottle of whiskey, and Bride's obstreperous presence would be less embarrassing in our remote Ming temple than it apparently was in wartime China's capital city.

Bride pretty much kept to himself, and was strangely quiet, for a couple of weeks. We joked that he was brooding about how to deliver his "shot in the arm." We were right. As it turned out, however, it was not a joking matter. In due course, he announced at dinner that we would soon be parachuting into Korea to free American prisoners of war. There was complete silence. Looking around at his seven incredulous subordinates, he slammed his hand on the table. "Sergeant, or Captain, or whatever the hell you are," he pointed at me, "you're the operations guy, right? Get us moving." He rose and weaved his way back to his tent. An hour or so later, I gathered my wits and courage and decided that he and I needed a little chat.

"You know, Colonel," I said (not sure that he *did* know), "at least a couple divisions of Japanese are based in Korea and these haven't seen any action. They probably don't even know that Japan is getting beaten." Bride shrugged.

I said I'd try to obtain some recent order-of-battle information on Japanese troops in Korea. I would also try to find out approximately how many US POWs were there, and where they were. But, I said, I didn't think any OSS people in Chungking, Delhi, or Washington, or even in the army's G-2, could give us much useful stuff very soon.

Bride was not focusing. In fact, he seemed even further out of the picture than he was an hour earlier (bourbon?). "Lishen, Cooper, what we'll do is we'll jump into the capital. Whasa capital? Take 'em by surprise. Right? Our names on headlines or on tombstones. Right?"

I mumbled something to the effect that I wasn't crazy about either a headline or an epitaph, but I'd work on the problem. The problem was that it really *was* a problem. Intelligence on the situation in Korea was sketchy. Even the stuff from our trainees who had managed to get back to Korea was of little help. Aside from the lack of adequate, reliable information, none of us had ever jumped out of a plane. No matter; even if we had been veteran paratroopers, it was unclear what we would do after we touched ground intact—if, indeed, we did. Nor was it clear how a lone US military transport plane would be received as it crossed the Yellow Sea into Japanese airspace. Prospects looked nasty to everyone, except our new commanding officer. He seemed above, under, or far out of it all. Was I scared? Yes.

A couple of days before we were scheduled to perform our bit of derring-do, a courier from the OSS group in Sian drove into the temple grounds with mail and some spare parts for our communications equipment. I hastily dashed off two notes: one to Orah (Soon be off for a while—can't say where—don't know for how long—Good-bye—love you), and one to the OSS colonel commanding in Kunming (I know this is way out of channels, but senior guy here is off his rocker—we're going to be jumping into Korea—not sure where—no one knows how to jump—no clue whereabouts US POWs—want you to know what happened to Eagle project). The courier promised to get both letters out as soon as he got back to Sian. He kept his promise.

The initial attempt to launch the headline-or-tombstone rescue mission aborted. The pilot of the plane Bride managed to con out of someone in Sian (I did not have the clout, let alone the appetite, to pull off the deal) was not unaware of the incongeniality of flying alone in a small transport plane across the Yellow Sea. He must have given this some sober thought; as he taxied toward the small band of Eagles waiting on the tarmac, he turned his aircraft a tad too sharply and smacked his left wing against the side of the hangar. "Sorry about that, colonel, y'all will need another airplane and another crew. Good luck."

On the following day, the Eagles tested their carbines and revolvers in case it would be necessary to ward off an attack by a few Japanese battalions, and once more lined up on the tarmac. A new, more innocent pilot hurled the group aloft. But the enterprise ended in a limp anticlimax. The plane miraculously landed safely on a Japanese airstrip in Korea (no one had jumped) and hastily took off when two Japanese army officers said they had no authority to receive the Eagle group. They suggested that our merry group get the hell out (or words to that effect). Just as the plane headed back over the Yellow Sea, a message came over the radio from OSS Headquarters in Kunming. The plane was to return immediately to Sian. (In the end, I was neither court-martialed nor decorated for venturing out of channels. But I lived to tell the tale.)

Orah probably had the worst experience of anyone involved in the episode. She had returned home from work one evening just as the phone rang. "Mrs. Chester Cooper? This is Western Union. Are you alone? No? Your sister is with you? Good. Please sit down." At this point she slumped to the floor and handed the phone to Rita. "Mrs. Cooper, the telegram reads— I'm afraid it's bad news—'Chet's grandfather died this morning. We'll call about funeral arrangements. Aunt Celia.' Would you like it delivered?" (My grandfather was eighty-five years old.)

Once back at camp, Colonel Bride disappeared with no more notice than when he arrived. (Two years later I read, in a CIA telegram from Manila, that our former colonel, now a hustler, had gotten involved there in some hefty bribery deals. Some time after, Bride died under mysterious circumstances in Thailand.)

It was now early August. Clyde and General Lee were working out their plans and schedules for the month's training. Their session was interrupted when our communications officer burst into the temple waving a sketchy report. A monster bomb had been dropped on a Japanese city. There were enormous casualties. We spent the rest of the morning standing around the radio shack. Armed Forces Radio took pains to qualify the story about the bomb and repeatedly stressed Washington's warnings that the war was by no means over; hard fighting was still expected.

*   *   *

A few days later, it was my turn to do the mail-and-errand run into Sian. Dr. Hou, who had opened a street clinic in the village and needed to replenish some medical supplies, came along. After we had finished our errands and had lunch, Dr. Hou took me to a calligraphy museum nearby. We were examining some beautifully chiseled, perfectly balanced Chinese characters on a large stone stele near the entrance when a small boy grabbed Hou's arm. He was jumping up and down and shrieking with excitement. Hou listened, smiled, patted the boy's head, put his arm around me, and said quietly, "The war is over."

I had come full circle. In December 1941, at a museum in New York looking at a stele with Egyptian hieroglyphics, I learned of Japan's attack on Pearl Harbor. In August 1945, at a museum in Sian looking at a stele with Chinese calligraphy, I learned of Japan's surrender.

NOTES

1. After the war I learned that one of Orah's colleagues at the War Production Board in Washington, in due course, was recruited by the OSS and gave my name to his superior, who, in turn, started the wheels turning.

2. Soon after the war, his son opened a Chinese restaurant in Washington.

3. National Archives, record group 226, entry 154, box 167.

4

ORAH, HERE I COME!

ABOUT WAR AND PEACE

The war in Europe ended on May 7, 1945, with Hitler's suicide and the Nazi surrender. Fighting continued in Asia until August 15, 1945, when Japan accepted defeat. For several years after the fighting, Germany and Austria were occupied by American, British, French, and Soviet troops; Japan was occupied by American forces, while Manchuria was occupied by Soviet soldiers as a reward for the Soviet Union's declaration of war against Japan a week or so before Japan surrendered.

I returned to the United States in the latter part of November 1945 and was demobilized soon after.

The wartime alliance between Britain and the United States on the one hand and the Soviet Union on the other began to fray soon after V-J Day and then degenerated quickly into what became known as the cold war.

* * *

In one role or another, I have done a fair amount of marching. I was a Boy Scout and a member of my school's drum and bugle corps and MIT's ROTC band. And, lest you forget, I was an infantry trainee. And, of course, I marched in numerous graduation ceremonies (usually to the ponderous beat of Elgar's "Pomp and Circumstance"). But nothing, parade-wise, can compete with the chaotic, joyous torchlit procession I graced on the night of V-J Day in 1945. With only a few hours' notice, two thousand Chinese soldiers, a dozen or so local dignitaries, and three score Americans assembled and then threaded their way through the ancient, narrow streets of Sian. Together with the laughing, weeping, shouting crowds of onlookers, we ducked and dodged strings of firecrackers tossed from storefronts and overhanging windows. ("Wouldn't it be just swell if, after two years with the trigger-happy Chinese Army, I lost an eye from a V-J Day firecracker," a grinning GI hollered.)

In the dim, flickering light I saw a small boy riding piggyback on Clyde's shoulders. Within minutes I had my own little rider. A giggling young mother had handed her to me and was now trotting alongside. "Are you talking to me, the kid, or yourself?" Clyde yelled. "Myself," I shouted. I had been reciting a private mantra. "Orah, here I come. On my way home. Here I come. I'm on—"

As it turned out, three months would pass before I was actually "on my way." Evidently, the OSS's Kunming headquarters, Gen. Bill Donovan, and President Truman had pretty much forgotten the existence of Project Eagle. Both the War Department and Donovan's Washington headquarters seemed to have other, more consequential matters on their minds: helping (in the end, to no avail) Chiang Kai-shek win the race between his Nationalist forces and Mao Tse-tung's Communist Fourth Army for control over areas in central and east China being vacated by the defeated Japanese; disarming, guarding, and repatriating Japanese troops throughout China; and dispatching American sailors, marines, and soldiers from Pacific outposts, the European theater, and the United States for occupation duty in Japan. So, incongruous and incredible as this may seem, six OSS officers, one OSS staff sergeant, and a Greek cook ambling around China's western desert did not warrant much attention by the top brass in either Kunming or Washington during the late summer and early autumn of 1945.

During this period, our communications with Sian and Kunming, to say nothing of letters to and from home, had become infrequent and sporadic. Fuel for our three jeeps and our portable generator had run low. Trips to Sian were saved for occasional, necessary runs. By and large, we were pretty much left to our own resources. Nevertheless, we neither were nor felt deprived. The days were crisp and bright, the nights were cool. We dined well on the village's ample harvest of fruit and vegetables and on local chickens and fish. The Japanese across the Yellow River were no longer a concern. We rarely saw General Lee and his new young lieutenants, who were preoccupied with plans and arrangements to return to their emancipated homeland. In short, our life was serene. And boring.

Dr. Hou, concerned about our idle hands and our growing impatience to get home, urged us to bestow a legacy on our village hosts. And so was born the Grand Eagle Latrine. He selected a gently sloping site a few hundred yards from the temple and then designed a concrete structure consisting of three sections. The first, the highest on the slope, was a shower room, where two large oil drums on the roof released sun-warmed water when tipped by a yank on an attached chain. Next, there was a washroom containing two metal cooking pans resting on a wooden bench, which were filled by dipping water from another former oil drum. Finally, there was the toilet salon, the most elaborate of all the compartments. It was fitted out with two surprisingly comfortable old inner tubes. Outside, at the lower end of the small building, there was a depository for night soil, which was collected each evening by a local farmer.

The construction of the actual building was left to laborers from the village who finished the job in four days. (Why not? In Kunming I had seen an airport runway and a hangar completed within two weeks—and this without any machinery.)

The Eagle Latrine's interior decoration turned out to be a labor of love, if not taste. The full strength of our complement set to work to contrive handlebars for the showers, toothbrush and soap containers for the washroom, and reading racks for the toilets. Somehow, somewhere, Dr. Hou found a few containers of red, black, and gilt paint. Every drop was applied enthusiastically and without restraint to every flat surface. When finally finished, the interior of Eagle Latrine, especially in the warm glow of candlelight, looked like a reasonably respectable stateside Chinatown nightclub.

Our enterprise was not only a sanitary, technological, and artistic success, it also provided a healthy, if zany, diversion for eight restless souls. The edifice was not universally admired, however. Some time after our grand opening (Dr. Hou was invited to take the first shower, and Clyde had the first pee), a colonel based in Sian, who had long been curious about the OSS-Korean project in the boonies, ventured out to take a look. He spent an hour with us while we briefed him. Before returning to Sian, he asked me if he could use our latrine. I proudly led the way, and then waited by his jeep to see him off. As he climbed in and settled himself, I heard him mutter to his driver, "Jeez, you should have seen that. These guys have been out here too long!" (Oh well, *de gustibus non disputandum est*.)[1]

During those weeks of waiting, I began to worry about what civilian life would have in store. What would I be equipped to do? An army brochure I had picked up in Sian noted that former infantrymen would be qualified to work as policemen, night watchmen, physical trainers. There was no mention of economists or teachers. Could I compete with those who, at home, had been honing their professional skills over the past few years? Could Orah and I get along on her salary until I found a job?

Dr. Hou and I had a long talk about my postwar future one night. He had, by now, become my confidante and counselor. "Chet," he said, "don't be in a hurry. Happiness, success, fame, money at thirty mean little; they can quickly disappear. But if you can feel fulfilled and at peace when you are sixty, you will have led a successful life." (I discovered the wisdom of his remark many decades later.)

A few days before I left Project Eagle for Kunming, and then home, Dr. Hou and I managed to take one of our jeeps for a ceremonial final day in Sian. We arrived early at a restaurant famous for its Peking duck. We selected our dinner from a flock of fat, force-fed creatures waddling around in a pen beside the restaurant. With the victim's identifying metal insignia in hand, we went to several antique shops in search of some small pieces of old porcelain I could take home for Orah. Later that afternoon we returned to the restaurant and devoured the crisp, golden-brown remains of our chosen fowl. Over cups of warm rice wine we made a pledge: At our next dinner together, whenever and wherever that might be, we would replicate this farewell meal in Sian. It was a pledge that Orah would come to regret.

*   *   *

Much had changed at the headquarters in Kunming. The compound had been spruced up, the OSS complement had grown much larger, and the former air of informality had been replaced by one of brisk purposefulness. The first sergeant and the colonel were in their element—even if the detachment's mission was now to break camp rather than wage war.

Some things remained the same, however. Jerry, the cheerful houseboy, continued to bustle around making beds and sweeping the tents. Apparently, he was still impressing the girls in town with the importance of his responsibilities at the Americans' camp. His windowpane eyeglasses and impressive array of fountain pen tops, protruding conspicuously from a jacket pocket, projected, with some success, the image of a young, scholarly professional. I noticed, however, that the GIs were now more guarded in their banter with him. There were hardly any more cute references to bringing Jerry back with them to Seattle, or Detroit, or New York. Indeed, there seemed to be a tacit recognition that this joke may have already gone too far. In fact, it had gone *much* too far, but we wouldn't realize this for another couple of weeks.

The timing of a GI's departure for home was based on a point system heavily weighted by his length of overseas service. My friend Joe and I had relatively high scores, so once back in Kunming, we were not destined to remain there very long.

As I joined the rank of soldiers on the Fourteenth Air Force tarmac waiting to board the Calcutta-bound transport plane, I saw, to my horror, that Jerry was standing nearby clutching a battered suitcase. Someone had said, once too often, that Jerry could join him in America once the war was over. A corporal from the OSS team who had more guts and compassion than I could summon up asked each of us for a few dollars. He then went over to Jerry, put his arm around his shoulder, whispered something, gave him whatever money he had collected, patted him on the back, and walked, head down, back to his place in line. As the plane taxied down the runway, my last sight of Kunming through the plane window was a dolorous one: Jerry was standing alone, clutching his suitcase, as he watched the plane head south and east.

Within twenty-four hours I was back in Kanchapara. It was now a holding area for happy troops on their way to Fargo, Baltimore, or Atlanta, rather than to a replacement depot for apprehensive men on their way to the Burmese jungle or the Burma Road. The long rows of tired tents, the flag hanging limply from the pole outside headquarters, and the ramshackle mess hall were pretty much as I had remembered. But there were no more obligatory quinine tablets (and therefore no more bloodshot eyes and yellow complexions). The mood throughout the camp was relaxed rather than grim. The war was over. We won. Cold Coca-Cola flowed freely. We were going home.

More than a thousand of us left Calcutta on the troopship SS *Patrick*. This time there were no practice abandon-ship exercises and no actual alarms. Weather and sea behavior permitting, there were no restrictions about wandering around the enlisted men's open decks. And, this time, we had three meals daily instead of two. Of course, the craps and poker players continued to have priority places in the latrines.

*   *   *

We were at sea for three weeks and a bit. Most of the journey was uneventful and tedious. A brassiere hanging from the lookout mast provided an hour of entertainment early on, and there was an occasional impromptu jam session, and a couple of fights. But other than that, the first two weeks or so were occupied by gazing out to sea, dozing in the hot sun, and a few chores that couldn't be avoided but were performed in a half-hearted, desultory way.

One break in our routine occurred in the harbor of Columbo, Ceylon (now Sri Lanka). As our ship inched its way to the dock to take on provisions and fuel for the remainder of the journey, a British troopship, headed toward the open sea, passed close by.

"Where were ya?" yelled a GI standing at the rail.

"Burma. Where yer headed?" a Cockney voice shouted.

"Home!" came a loud chorus from the *Patrick*. And then, "Where y'all goin'?" from a leather-lunged corporal.

"Bloody Vietnam!"

Then came an exchange of parting shots that would have made the diplomats in both the State Department and the Foreign Office cringe.

"Limey bastards!"

"Bloody Yanks!"

It occurred to me that most of the troops aboard that British troopship had probably been in Asia for at least three years. Why weren't *they* going home? What would they be doing in Indochina? I discovered the answers not very long after. By that time I, too, was heavily engaged in Vietnam.

Ten days after the encounter with the British, the *Patrick* steamed from the Red Sea into the Mediterranean through the Suez Canal.

*   *   *

When I was at the Garrison Elementary School I became aware, even in those tender years, of Britain's extensive global power—or, anyway, its global influence. On every classroom wall hung a map of the world. Even an eight-year-old could see that pink—the color designating British rule—was dominant on every map. Pink spread over much of Africa and covered the whole of the Indian subcontinent; Malaysia was pink and so, too, was a large part of the Middle East and some of the Caribbean; Canada was pink and so were Australia and New Zealand. A critical communications link in this vast pink domain was the Suez Canal, which, cutting through Egypt's narrow isthmus, was a strategic and trading shortcut between Britain and India, the jewel of the empire.

Seeing the canal, to say nothing of passing through it, was a spine-tingling experience. English history and literature represented a considerable portion of my educational diet at school in Boston. Even as a boy, I had a nodding acquaintance with eighteenth-century English furniture, porcelain, and silver. Much of my disposable time at high school and college, and too much of my homework and studying time, was spent on repeated trips to see *How Green Was My Valley*, *Mutiny on the Bounty*, *Goodbye, Mr. Chips*, and the like. I had then hoped to take a graduate degree at the London School of Economics, but Hitler forced me to abandon that plan. It is fair to say that I was then—and am even now—an unabashed Anglophile.

If I had had the gift of prescience, I would have realized that my journey home, with its fleeting exposure to Vietnam and the passage through the Suez Canal, foretold much about my life-to-be. Even if I had had this insight, however, it would have been brushed aside. All I cared about then was that each day at sea shortened the distance between Orah and me.

*   *   *

Hardly had the *Patrick* left the tranquil Mediterranean and entered the less friendly Atlantic when a storm struck. For several days, the ship lurched and lunged, pitched, tossed, and creaked. Seasickness spread like a plague. Just the thought of food was enough to trigger nausea. Even if the queasiness could be willed away, the dizzying trek through long passageways and up and down companionways to the mess hall made the strongest stomach rebel.

All open decks now became off-limits, but every morning the ship's crew retrieved sick men and an occasional woman curled up in wave-washed corners. They had obviously been desperate for fresh air; once out, they were too weak to make the hazardous trek back to their bunks. After a few days, however, the hazards topside seemed an even trade with the constant moans and sour smells belowdecks.

This time my shipboard duties (at least until the storm) consisted of chipping and painting the decks and lugging provisions from the hold to the kitchen area. Joe, poor guy, had KP duty for most of the voyage. I can still see his face, green and distorted, as he gamely ladled out mashed potatoes and creamed chicken to whomever among us managed to clamber or crawl his way to the mess hall. And I can still hear the sound of the hundred steel cots in our compartment banging and clanging as the ship laboriously ascended, hesitated for a moment, and then skidded down the giant waves and smashed into the sea.

The storm-tossed *Patrick* would have been well behind schedule in any case, but we were further delayed, according to a bo'sun, because a nearby merchant ship radioed that it had engine trouble and might need assistance. The *Patrick* circled steadily for many hours, but finally received a signal that the problem had been solved. We continued on our impatient way west. Finally, in a cold, misty November dawn, our ship approached New York Harbor. A call from the bridge brought most of those who were not still debilitated by seasickness dashing up to the open decks.

By seven o'clock, the outline of the Statue of Liberty was discernible through the murk. Home! Minutes later, I discovered that my left fist was clamped shut. It would be several weeks before I could use my hand without difficulty. Some form of hysteria, one doctor said.

We disembarked to the sound of an army band and the welcome of scores of smiling Red Cross ladies dispensing milk (*real*, not powdered) and doughnuts. The only jarring note was the long line of ambulances that had been summoned to deal with our injured or dehydrated casualties.

Buses took us to Fort Hamilton in Brooklyn. After a day or two of "processing," a change into winter khakis, two weeks' leave, and more "processing," we were on our way to becoming civilians. One of the last steps in the transformation was a speech by a suspiciously solicitous and unctuous master sergeant urging the ex-GIs to join the army reserve. He had only modest success. As I was leaving the room, he drew me aside. "You ought to sign up, Sergeant. That way, if there's another war, you'll protect your rank." It was a no-sale.

*   *   *

Orah and I returned to Washington after an emotional Thanksgiving in New York with our families. I reported to what I had thought was OSS Headquarters, but learned that the OSS had been recently abolished. Something called the Strategic Services Unit (SSU) was in its place. There didn't seem to be much difference. Someone there suggested I "stay in touch."

What has been described as the "knifing of OSS" was more a process than an event. It started as early as 1942, when the OSS had hardly emerged from its womb, and continued until October 1945. So it was that, in addition to Japan and Germany, General Donovan had to fight off two domestic enemies. The Federal Bureau of Investigation (FBI) and the Army Intelligence Staff (G-2) regarded the OSS as a snotty new kid trespassing on their sacred turf. To complicate General Donovan's efforts, the far Right in Congress and the right-wing press characterized the OSS as a "Super Gestapo." Surprisingly enough, however, it was not any of these groups that delivered the final blow. Rather, according to author Thomas Troy, the coup de grâce came from an unlikely, and possibly unwitting, source—Harry Hopkins, Roosevelt's, and later Truman's, special adviser.[2]

The SSU was an ephemeral organization, a placeholder until the White House, State Department, and Pentagon were able to decide what, if anything, to do with the resources and accumulated expertise of what had been the OSS. A first order of business was to face up to the retention or disposal of thousands of OSS military and civilian personnel. As it happened, most were released or left on their own accord to take up their former jobs or seek new careers in law firms and universities, or on Wall Street and Main Street. Those who remained were recruited for or assigned to one of three organizations: former OSS analysts were encouraged to join a new Office of Intelligence and Research in the Department of State; those who had intelligence or reporting experience were interviewed for assignments to a new, independent establishment, the Central Intelligence Group (CIG); and those who had been engaged in what was euphemistically termed "operations" were beckoned to a new Office of Special Operations.

At my checkout interview, it was suggested that my experience in China would be of value to the CIG. Was I interested? The answer was a tentative yes. But could I know more about it? "Not yet," I was told. "Be patient. The wheels grind slowly here. Don't call us. We'll call you."

Christmas came and went. The old year folded into 1946. Fort McClellan, India, China, and the OSS were now well behind me, but I still had no idea of what lay ahead. What I *did* know was that I had to find a job. And soon. But where? For whom? Doing what? There was no word from the shadowy CIG. I decided to pick up my reemployment rights in the wartime housing agency. It would be only a holding position—temporary employment in a temporary organization. Thankfully, Orah still had her job with a White House group, so we had some sense of security. But I was restless, nervous, anxious. Dr. Hou's point about the shallowness of success at thirty and the robustness of success at sixty was all to the good, but thirty was already on the horizon and success at any age seemed nowhere in sight.

*　　*　　*

As it happened, I had another opportunity to discuss the thirty-sixty homily with Dr. Hou. He called me from San Francisco that spring. We were both so excited that it was hard to sort out just what had brought him to America and what he would be doing here. He was finally able to speak rationally, and I could finally bring myself to listen carefully. It turned out that, thanks to his efforts to keep the Eagles healthy and sane, Washington had awarded him a fellowship in the United States. He would be able to catch up on the medical advances made during the years China was at war. He had arranged to spend several months at the Walter Reed Army Hospital in Washington, and another several months at Johns Hopkins Hospital in Baltimore. He was scheduled to arrive in Washington within a few days.

Orah, who, by now, felt as if she had long known Hou Bao-chang, whispered, "Tell him he can stay with us until he gets settled." I shook my head; we were still in the one-room "efficiency" we had found before I left for the army. But she won. For a week or so, Dr. Hou lived with us, sleeping on a borrowed cot behind a borrowed screen. I had forgotten our pledge in Sian, but during that week he reminded me of it.

At the time, virtually every Chinese restaurant in Washington served only Cantonese food. Since Peking duck was a rare North China delicacy, Dr. Hou volunteered to prepare the promised dinner in our apartment. Orah, innocent of the recipe and preparation process and relieved that she would not have to do the cooking, readily agreed. We invited Clyde Sargent (now working with a relief agency), Charlie Stelle (now at the State Department), Orah's sister, Rita, and her husband, Bud, for the following Sunday evening. Hou would devote Saturday to shopping and preparation. It was then that Orah had premonitions of what was in store.

Hou wanted to buy a live duck and execute and defeather it in the kitchen. That way, he pointed out, he would not bruise the skin—essential if the duck was to be properly prepared. But Orah stood firm. No live duck, no defeathering—dead or alive—in our small kitchen. Hou wanted to line the oven with charcoal to provide the desired amount of heat. Again, Orah was decidedly uncooperative. No charcoal; the gas oven would have to do.

Somewhat disappointed, Dr. Hou and I went off to find a dead, defeathered, undressed, fat female duck. We went to several butcher shops before Hou was satisfied. Then to Chinatown for the appropriate sauces, vegetables, and pancake supplies. (This was before the days when all this would be available at a nearby supermarket.) Next stop was a Chinese liquor store for several bottles of rice wine. Finally, we had to find the glass tube that was to be inserted between the duck's outer (with luck, unblemished) skin and inner fat. It was now late Saturday afternoon, and the medical supply stores were closed. But we managed to get what we needed from the pharmacy at George Washington University Hospital.

By late Saturday night, Hou had cleaned out the duck, blown into the glass tube to inflate it, and persuaded Orah to (sort of) agree to hang the football-shaped fowl, head down, from the shower rail so it could drain and dry overnight. He then undertook other preparations for the next day and, with Orah, more or less cleaned up the mess in the kitchen. This accomplished, he joined us for a midnight snack at a nearby hamburger joint.

The dinner on Sunday night was a huge success. The duck and its accoutrements were a triumph, adequate quantities of martinis and rice wine were consumed, and Dr. Hou, justifiably, felt that we had redeemed our Sian pledge. The downside was that it took many days before Orah restored the kitchen to its pre–Peking duck condition, and a week before the stench in the bathroom, and especially in the shower, disappeared.

*   *   *

Aside from his medical studies, Dr. Hou had another mission to perform in America—a mission that became obvious as soon as he unpacked. Carefully wrapped were a few dozen pieces of jade and porcelain and several scrolls. Orah and I were sure that they were his own, but we nodded understandingly when, with some embarrassment, he explained that they belonged to "friends" who were in difficult straits because of the many years of chaos, war, and inflation. "As a favor to them" he hoped to sell the pieces to an American collector.

My parents had taught me something about American and English antiques. Now I was about to begin a course in Chinese Antiques 101. For the next several weekends, I accompanied Hou on visits to curators, dealers, and academic specialists. In addition to the Smithsonian museums in Washington, our travels took us to Philadelphia, New Haven, New York, and Boston. At our first session (Washington's Freer Gallery) the curator told us that the pieces in the collection were fine examples and were almost certainly genuine. But there was a "but"—if they were to be sold as originals, rather than good copies, each piece would have to be accompanied by a guarantee of authenticity signed by a recognized expert. Dr. Hou—and certainly I—had not realized that without such authentication, the vases, figurines, and carvings would attract fashionable interior decorators looking for bargains rather than affluent private collectors or museums.

Would the Freer curator be willing to certify their age? No, nor did he think any other experts would do so. The art of fakery had been so perfected in China that certification of authenticity for commercial purposes was extremely risky. If it later turned out that Hou's pieces were fakes, even old and good fakes, the authenticating expert could be held liable. Without careful testing and reliable provenances, he said, he and his fellow experts would be taking a big chance.

In the end, we were able to dispose of virtually all the pieces. A friendly New York dealer was in contact with Senator Thomas Francis Green of Rhode Island. The senator was an avid, if not the most discriminating, collector of Chinese jades and porcelains. He agreed to buy most of the lot. He paid less than what it was probably worth, but well above interior decorator prices. My father bought some of the rest. (Those pieces are now in my own modest collection.)

At the time, Green probably held the age record in the Senate. Not long before he died I found myself standing beside him at a Dutch Embassy cocktail party. He was consulting his pocket diary.

"Are you looking to see where you are going next, sir?" I asked. "I'll be glad to drive you."

"No, son, I'm not planning to go anywhere but home after this, and I know how to do that. I'm just trying to remember where I am now."

The senator left an enormous legacy of Chinese snuff bottles, vases, tea caddies, porcelain and jade figures, scrolls, and goodness knows what else. Until not so long ago, a Washington auction house was still including some of the senator's collection in its periodic estate sales.

*   *   *

At the urging of Orah and Dr. Hou, I had begun to think about an important piece of unfinished business. Actually, I had hardly exchanged my army uniform for a civilian suit when the ghost of my aborted PhD began to haunt me.

When I left New York University in 1941, I was led to believe that all that stood between Mr. Cooper and Dr. Cooper was my unfinished PhD dissertation. During the war, however, the university had moved the goalposts. According to the graduate dean, my department chairman (since retired) had been too permissive. I now needed several more credits. No, I could not take the courses at a university in Washington; it had to be their courses on their property. No, they could not make exceptions because of the war; we were now at peace, and rules are rules. After my aborted pre–Pearl Harbor dissertation and my completed comprehensive exams, the academic skies looked dark. Unless I found a job in New York, finishing my degree would mean commuting there twice a week. It was thanks, but no thanks. However, fourteen years, two dissertations, and a few more comprehensive exams later, I was finally awarded a PhD by the American University in Washington.

More important than a doctorate in the winter of 1946 was a job. I went to New York to explore two leads. One was at Bankers Trust Company, where a former professor was a senior vice president. He turned up an opening there for a junior economist, but warned me that the bank's salaries were much lower than what I had hoped to earn, and that living costs in New York were high. Bankers Trust was a nonstarter.

The other possibility seemed much more attractive. Like my experience years before with the Washington landlady, however, I had the prize within my grasp and then threw it away. An introduction to the president of the Research Institute of America, a business consulting and advisory company, had been arranged by a friend who had rejoined the firm after his military service. The institute was just staffing up after its wartime doldrums. The omens looked good.

The head of the company, Leo Cherne, was a brilliant, multitalented economist. My interview with him went so well that he made me an offer on the spot. The institute had just opened a Washington office headed by an economist named William Casey. "Bill is a smart, energetic guy who, like you, was in OSS." Cherne mentioned a generous salary and promised to call Casey to say I would be joining him shortly. I felt relieved of a heavy burden. We shook hands and that was that. Or so it seemed.

Just as I got up to leave, Cherne banged his hand on his desk. "Gee, Chet, I almost goofed. I hired a personnel officer a week ago and I've been forgetting to put her in the hiring loop. She'll sulk for a week unless you go to her office and tell her you'll be joining Casey in Washington. She'll insist you take some kind of a Mickey Mouse test. Don't worry, I've taken it. So has your friend Henry. Sorry, but I've got to humor her along."

The woman gave me some papers to sign and handed me three blue books each containing about twelve pages. She showed me into a small cubicle. "Start with book 1. A bell will ring in three minutes. Go directly to book 2, and when the next bell rings after three minutes go directly to book 3."

Book 1 was a piece of cake, yet I was only half finished when a bell rang. Not good. I began to perspire as I grabbed book 2 and raced forward to deal with somewhat more complicated questions. Once again, the bell sounded before I made much of an inroad. By now my heart was pounding and I was getting panicky. I snatched book 3 and tried to compose myself as I scribbled madly in an effort to make some respectable progress. Yet again I lost the battle. But, just as the bell rang, Ms. Personnel opened the door and said, "You can turn to book 2 now."

"Book 2!" I screamed. "I'm well into book 3! Three bells have rung—or am I going nuts?"

"Oh," she murmured sweetly, "it's the sunlamp on the other side of the screen. People are supposed to turn over when the bell rings after a minute. And please don't shout."

I cast reason, prudence, and self-interest aside. I stood up, put on my jacket, and, with as much dignity as I could summon, announced that I didn't want any further exposure to either her blue books or her sunlamps.

This was not my last encounter with Leo Cherne. Ten years later I was at the Tokyo airport waiting to board a plane to Washington. I was standing near a man who looked vaguely familiar. He approached me with a quizzical smile. "Hi, my name is Leo Cherne and I think we've met. Aren't you someone—Cooper, right?—I hired several years ago? It *was* you, wasn't it? What happened? Bill Casey kept waiting for you, but you never showed up." Evidently Ms. Personnel had been so shaken by my behavior that she forgot to tell Cherne that I had fled.

*   *   *

Leo was a man of many talents and deep passions. He was a first-class sculptor and, during the midsixties, spent many hours in my White House office in between sessions of sculpting a bust of President Lyndon Johnson. (I am the proud owner of a Cherne bust of Abraham Lincoln.) I also was to see him occasionally in his capacity as chairman of the International Rescue Committee, a group that helped artists, musicians, writers, and scholars flee from foreign tyrants. He died too young.

As for Bill Casey, I was probably luckier than I deserved. Casey was as difficult and arrogant as he was brilliant. When President Ronald Reagan appointed him director of the CIA, he regarded himself as above the restrictions that guided his fellow government officials and civil servants. His principal accomplishment (to put it delicately) was the orchestration of the Iran-Contra caper in the mid-1980s. He died before the curtain closed on that comedy of errors.

Soon after my heroic act of principle in New York, my temporary job in Washington had come to an end. Meanwhile, a new government agency with a vaguely familiar ancestry was in the process of gestation. Was I interested in employment? My contact was uncommunicative about the nature of the organization and professed ignorance about the nature of the job. She simply asked me to fill out a long security form and an employment application. Of course, I had my own suspicions about both the organization and the job; the group that talked to me persuasively but guardedly in late November 1945 had apparently finally gotten its act together.

On the home front, Orah was pregnant. We decided to take a long summer vacation while I was still a free man. Sometime in September, I learned that my neighbors had been questioned by the FBI. Apparently my employment application was being reviewed. But the watchwords from Washington were still: Be patient. Keep in touch.

Soon after New Year's in 1948 I was employed, not by the Central Intelligence Group, but by its more consequential new successor, the Central Intelligence Agency.

NOTES

1. For those whose Latin has become rusty: "There is no accounting for taste"— or something to that effect.

2. Thomas F. Troy, "Knifing of the OSS," *International Journal of Intelligence and Counterintelligence* 1, no. 3 (1986): 95–107.

5

ENTER THE ALBATROSS

ABOUT THE NATIONAL SECURITY COUNCIL

The National Security Council (NSC) and the Central Intelligence Agency were created by the National Security Act of 1947. The NSC was composed of the president, the vice president, the secretaries of state and defense, and what is now the Federal Emergency Management Agency. The director of the Central Intelligence Agency and the chairman of the Joint Chiefs of Staff were advisers to the National Security Council. At various times presidents made ad hoc appointments to the council (John F. Kennedy appointed his brother Bobby, who was then head of the Justice Department).

The NSC staff is now headed by the president's assistant for national security affairs (who, under George W. Bush, is Stephen Hadley). Under President Richard Nixon and his assistant, Henry Kissinger, the NSC staff expanded substantially from less than a score of specialists. It is now a fairly substantial presence in the country's national security community.

The council's responsibilities include the coordination and planning of defense activities. I was one of the CIA's staff assistants to the NSC in 1953 and 1954, the CIA's liaison to the NSC staff in 1963, and a member of the NSC staff from late 1963 until mid-1966, when I jointed the Department of State.

*   *   *

In the CIA's early years, and probably even now, candidates for employment needed all the staying power they could muster. The odds were (are!) high that many of them would toss in the towel, accept other jobs, or die of old age between the time an anonymous caller told them they were being "processed" and the time those who had been accepted and were still ambulatory walked through the agency's door. In my case, I was told to "be patient" in late August 1946 and then, at last, to "come to work" in early February 1948. In between, I hung around (shades of the army), did some teaching, and became, despite my caller's admonition, increasingly impatient.

My group at the newly minted Central Intelligence Agency inhabited a ramshackle World War I temporary building on the edge of the Potomac River, where the Kennedy Center now stands. We were close to Washington's only brewery and down the hill from the headquarters of the navy's medical corps. On my arrival, I was anointed chief of the China Branch of the Far East Division of the Office of Research and Reports of the Directorate of Intelligence of the Central Intelligence Agency. (In Washington, the longer the title, the less important the job.)

Our division chief was a short-tempered, underqualified navy captain who, a few years before the war, had served as the American naval attaché in Tokyo. When displeased, his face would darken and twitch—an early warning to batten down the hatches. In extremis, he would throw his eyeglasses at the unfortunate subordinate whose attitude, appearance, or performance displeased him. Nonetheless, I regarded him with some (guarded) affection; he was transparently unsuited for and unhappy with his job, but showed up gamely every day to deal as best he could with his personal and professional demons.

One clue as to the source of his irritability came to light a few days after the birth of my first child. At lunch he proposed a toast. As we raised our glasses, he asked, "What's the girl's name?"

"Joan," I said. "Joan Lawrence Cooper."

"To Joan! How wonderful to have such a simple name," he murmured. He swallowed his drink and signaled for another. "I can't tell you what it's been like to be Ethelbert Wall II. I've been teased, tortured, and haunted since I was five years old." By now, the rumors of his tendency to weep after a sip or two of alcohol were amply verified.

"That must have been tough," I sympathized. "What did you name your son?"

Now the tears began to flow in earnest. "Ethelbert Wall III."

Ethelbert II retired to his mink farm in Virginia a few months later. I forget who succeeded him, but, in a year or so, I succeeded whoever that was. My own tenure in that post was brief.

*   *   *

In the formative years of the National Security Council, the various civilian and military agencies comprising the national intelligence community were a disparate group of rivals competing for White House attention and growing budgets. The army (G-2) and navy (Office of Naval Intelligence, ONI) had long histories, but were staffed by officers who were regarded as lesser beings within their services. This was probably even more the case with the air force, a new postwar service where pilots, not desk jockeys, reigned supreme. The State Department's Office of Intelligence and Research, largely staffed by former OSS Research and Analysis academics, was looked down upon, even distrusted, by the military intelligence folk and, to some extent, by the old-line foreign service officers. For its part, the CIA was, in the eyes of G-2 and ONI, a newcomer morphed from the heartily disliked OSS. The agency acquired clout only after Gen. Walter Bedell Smith, one of the army's most admired and feared senior generals, was appointed director in 1950. In the higher reaches of the intelligence community, however, the CIA was still only one voice in Babel.

Needless to say, this lugubrious state of affairs hardly served either the president or the National Security Council very well. A lean and inadequate NSC staff did what it could to make silk purses out of the sows' ears the intelligence agencies dumped at the White House door.

It did not take long for Director Smith and his new deputy director, Allen Dulles, an able Wall Street lawyer and a superstar former OSS operator, to seize the problem. Their consultant in this enterprise was Harvard professor William Langer, the eminent historian (and a leading authority on American ducks) who had headed the Research and Analysis Branch of the OSS. Late in 1950, they set in train a better way. The national intelligence process was conceived and launched.

The Office of National Estimates (ONE) was responsible for integrating data and information—classified and unclassified—from a wide variety of sources: from secret agents' reports to newspaper articles, from foreign broadcasts to foreign codes—as well as reviewing the contributions submitted by the other members of the intelligence community.

The ONE staff consisted of about twenty specialists and experts drawn from within and outside the agency. It had the task of pulling the relevant information together and preparing a draft national intelligence estimate addressing trends and developments around the world that were, or should have been, of concern to senior US officials and the president. The draft would then be reviewed by the Board of National Estimates, a group of "elders"—a few university professors, a couple of senior CIA staffers, two generals, an admiral, and a representative from the private sector.

After two merciless interviews, one by Harvard Professor Langer (on leave to chair the board and direct the office), the other by Professor Sherman Kent from Yale (the vice chairman of the board and deputy director of the office), I was appointed to head the Far East Division on the ONE staff. Both of my new bosses had been senior officials in the OSS. Both were highly regarded scholars. Both provided me with a first-class, if harrowing, post-postgraduate education.

The board review subjected the young members of the staff, who, at this point, were already edgy and exhausted from late nights of reading, drafting, and redrafting, to a combination of a PhD examination, a taste of the Spanish Inquisition, and a dollop of Chinese (or Baghdad-type) torture. The staff draft was treated to generous helpings of suggestions, criticisms, and rewrites. Some board members would have carefully read the staff draft; some would have given it a mere glance. Some could always be counted on for important, substantive questions and contributions; others would typically argue about the tense of verbs and the placement of commas.

The board review completed, the manicured, pedicured, and shampooed draft estimate would be circulated to the several intelligence components—state, army, navy, air force—of the National Security Council. These people—some smart, a few dumb—would add to, subtract from, or simply object to the document on a line-by-line basis. Finally, the CIA's director would pass on it and, occasionally, add his views, after which we staff members would draw a deep breath; go out for a hearty, wet lunch; and settle down for the next journey to hell and back.

There were three associates on my substaff: a specialist on Japan and Korea, one on China, and one on Southeast Asia. When push came to shove, however, the four of us covered all issues of concern throughout the vast, troubled Asian region. Life for our small band was frenetic (as much, if not more so, as for those focusing on the Soviet Union). We presided over the rout of Chiang Kai-shek's nationalist army, its escape to Taiwan, and the subsequent high tension between the nationalists and Communists on either side of the Taiwan Strait. In the meantime, there was the war in Indochina between the French and the Vietnamese, soon to be overshadowed by the North Korean invasion of South Korea and the dispatch of US forces. Just to make matters interesting, there were also such sideshows as the Communist-led Huk Bala Hup rebellion in the Philippines, an insurgency in Malaysia, and a succession of coups in Indonesia, Thailand, and Burma. To keep us off the streets in the event of a quiet moment, the birth pangs and early years of the US-sponsored government in Japan involved careful watching and frequent reporting.

On the domestic front, Orah, Joan, and I had moved into our new house in the autumn of 1951, and Susan Louise graced our family soon after. There were now four of us. Life at home—to the extent I could share in it—was full and sweet.

*   *   *

Bill Langer and Sherman Kent were demanding bosses. Their boss was even more so. General Smith had been Eisenhower's chief of staff during World War II. He had a sharp mind, an acid tongue, a pair of ice-cold eyes, and an ulcer—a formidable arsenal. "Beware of the Tongue and the Look," a friend who had served under Smith during the war warned me. His warning was apt and timely, but ignored—which is how and why I became an occasional target of, or a witness to, the general's sarcasm and wrath during the years to come.

In the spring of 1952, I received my first Purple Heart. The general was scheduled to brief the National Security Council on the situation regarding the Taiwan Strait at eleven o'clock one rainy morning. I was to show up at the White House with a large, detailed map of Taiwan, the strait, and the East China coast at 10:40 and assist the general in his briefing. A van was to fetch me and the two cartographers who had the secret map in their care at 10:15. The cartographers arrived on time, but there was no van. Nor was there one at 10:20 or 10:25.

A telephone company pickup truck was parked near the entrance. In desperation, I accosted the driver. I explained that I was engaged in a project of great national importance, and this was a matter of personal life or death. Could he take us and the map to the White House as fast as he could go? The driver grinned and nodded. I sat in front and the two cartographers climbed in the back, protecting the map from the pouring rain with their raincoats. Off we sped. Breathless, heart pounding, palms sweating, I was outside the Cabinet Room at 11:55, inside the room at noon, and out by 12:30.

I rode back to CIA with the general, who seemed satisfied with the briefing. Encouraged by what seemed to be his benign mood, I told him of my hair-raising dash to the meeting. "Perhaps you could write a note to those cartographers, sir. I really felt sorry for them. They got soaking wet trying to protect the map from the rain."

Smith unleashed both the Look and the Tongue. "Cooper," he said in a soft, menacing voice, "never mind worrying about those people. You should have been worrying about me. You were almost late!" End of discussion.

*   *   *

Constant crises in Asia left little time for much of a personal life. Except for fleeting glimpses of Joan and Susan, I felt both deprived of family time and guilty for not having more. Although Orah and I managed to have dinner together no matter how late I arrived home, the children were asleep when I left in the morning and asleep when I returned at night. Weekends were abbreviated; vacations were few and short, but sweet and savored. By the summer of 1952, I was coming close to being a physical and intellectual basket case. But rescue was at hand.

In September my various CIA bosses shoehorned me into the National War College for a ten-month stint. I found myself in the company of army, air force, and marine colonels and navy captains who were slated for promotion to flag rank. I was told (warned?) that I was the youngest student, one of few civilians, and certainly the first former enlisted man to attend this most elite of the military training institutions. No matter. I decided that if I could take on infantry basic training, General Smith, and the Board of National Estimates, the War College would be a piece of cake.

The National War College (now a component of the National Defense University) is located at the southeast end of Washington's Fort McNair. The fort has a venerable history. Four coconspirators in Lincoln's assassination were hanged on a site across the road from the present Officer's Club. In 1901 Dr. Walter Reed discovered a vaccine for yellow fever at the hospital on the post. (His discovery came none too soon; the disease was ravaging the military and civilian workforce constructing the Panama Canal.) The famous architect Stanford White designed the handsome War College building. (He was later shot by the jealous husband of Evelyn Nesbit, a naughty nightclub tease who did her tantalizing shtick from a trapeze). Fort McNair has long been the home of the army's honor guard ("The Old Guard"), which was formed in the late eighteenth century and, on special occasions, parades in wigs and Revolutionary War uniforms.

The perimeter of the fort on the bank of the Potomac River is lined with senior officers' quarters, and, on the opposite side, with noncommissioned officer accommodations. Tennis courts, a modest golf course, and a swimming pool provide sport and recreation for the fort's residents. A post exchange and a military stockade are tucked away in an inconspicuous corner.

I looked forward to spending ten months there instead of in the old, too-hot or too-cold "Tempo E." Moreover, I would have a chance to read widely and to listen to lectures on issues of political and national security concern. The guest lecturers, two or three a week, promised to be people of considerable importance and impressive experience. Adding frosting to the cake was the prospect of having a great deal of free time. I could now have dinner and spend weekends and national holidays with my family. Orah, Susan, Joan, and I could even go off somewhere for a Christmas vacation. And in the offing was a ten-day trip to Europe for a series of NATO briefings.

The time at McNair proved to be an intellectual feast and a physical respite. My tenure also provided two unanticipated bonuses, one ephemeral, the other of long-term value.

Before I actually started my War College year in September 1952, I had somehow squeezed out time to muddle my way through the two courses and the exams that had been left over from my aborted prewar effort to earn a PhD. The relatively relaxed schedule I was about to enjoy offered an opportunity to move forward on the one academic obligation still outstanding, the dissertation.

In the course of my work at the CIA and my exposure to the National Security Council during my pre–War College years, I had become interested in the concept of "strategic importance." What did it truly mean? What did the strategic importance of a foreign country imply in terms of an American commitment? What were the factors that determined whether country X was or was not of strategic importance to the United States? The term seemed to mean different things to different people; as in the case of many other matters discussed by high-level people at high-level meetings, this one was fuzzy and undefined.

There were then about fifty sovereign countries constituting "the world." (There were more than 160 as of 2 PM, May 15, 2005.) Thirty-five or so were deemed to be "strategically important," "of great strategic importance," or "of vital (or critical) strategic importance" by one or more of the armed services, the State Department, the office of the secretary of defense, or the CIA. It seemed to me that if any country were "strategically important" to the United States, some nontrivial economic, military, and political commitments had to be involved. After all, threats to a "strategically important" country should not be regarded as a spectator sport. Could the United States actually meet its formal and implied obligations to all "strategically important" countries spread across the world?

This seemed worth exploring. I decided to make it the subject of my War College final essay and, later, of a more ambitious PhD dissertation. I would first examine the conceptual issue and then use a particular country as an example. Burma seemed especially interesting. It was not terra incognita to me, and could be an intriguing case study since the army and the State Department regarded it as strategically important, but the navy, air force, Department of Defense, and CIA did not. How did, would, or should the National Security Council go about reconciling these views?

To make short work of the haggling and the frustration I endured in the course of the following year, I will simply report that the National War College liked the term paper; the CIA would agree to my turning it into a dissertation, but only if I eliminated the sensitive Burma case study; the university would agree to my subject and approach, but only if I included the interesting Burma case study. So back to square one—where the matter rested, half alive, half dead, for another six years.

The second bonus gleaned from my War College experience proved to be a winner. A dozen or more of my classmates rose to high rank in the 1960s, just about the time I was appointed to the National Security Council staff at the White House a decade later. During the years when I needed all the help and information I could get from the Pentagon, one of my NWC chums had become chief of the army staff; another, the commandant of the Marine Corps; and still another, the deputy chief of naval operations. Several other classmates wound up in top command or staff positions in Germany and Vietnam or at NATO headquarters. This web of contacts turned out to be the most valuable gift I received during my tenure at Fort McNair.

Our trip to northern Europe that spring involved two or three days each in Paris, Berlin, Copenhagen, and London. This was my maiden voyage to Europe, and now, fifty years later, I still recall my sense of anticipation as the plane took off from Andrews Air Force Base. The excitement on the part of several of my fellow travelers, however, substantially exceeded my own. Theirs took on a shrill, fevered pitch just as we headed north and east; they had forgotten to hand over their car keys to their wives, a bit of absentmindedness that necessitated a dozen hasty, indiscriminate purchases of Chanel perfume or Hermès scarves within hours of our arrival in Paris.

Two memories of that trip remain vivid: In Berlin there was the frequent sight of children and old men and women, some maimed, some whole, sorting out rubble for usable bricks, bits of salvageable hardware, and, even more important, some coins or jewelry. In Oxford, where I dashed as soon I could flee yet another military briefing in London, I reveled in the sense of history and learning evoked by the handsome, ancient colleges.

*   *   *

The time at Fort McNair was over all too soon. In June 1953 I "graduated" and returned to real work. Meanwhile, Dwight Eisenhower had defeated Adlai Stevenson to win the presidency, John Foster Dulles had succeeded Dean Acheson as secretary of state, Bedell Smith had left the CIA to become undersecretary of state, and Allen Dulles had been promoted to replace Smith as director.

Eisenhower inherited a world in turmoil. France was trapped in an unwinnable colonial war in Indochina. The United States and South Korea, together with a few allies, were fighting a costly war against both the North Koreans and Chinese in Korea. There were also dangerous confrontations with the Soviet Union in Europe, particularly in connection with the worrisome Berlin situation. The cold war was becoming colder and more warlike every day. Everywhere, the Soviet bloc and the Western allies were engaged in a zero-sum political and economic game; a mishap, or accident, or embarrassment for one was an advantage for the other.

A miasma of foreboding permeated much of Washington life, both inside and outside the halls of government. The government had begun to practice mock emergency operations for "essential personnel." Many of my neighbors in Chevy Chase built bomb shelters in their backyards. As I examined a map of Washington one day in the early fifties, I realized to my horror that our new house was well within the dangerous radius of "Ground Zero." Orah and I promptly stored water, medicines, food, and blankets in our basement.

During this period, while Joan and Susan cowered under their little desks during their school's air-raid drills, I spent several three-day practice emergency exercises behind heavy steel and well-guarded doors in a man-made, air-conditioned cave about an hour's drive from Washington. There we would go through mock communication exchanges, prepare "evaluations," participate in war games. In reality, of course, these exercises, to say nothing of Joan and Susan's, were feckless. One only had to drive home in a rainy evening rush hour to realize the chaos that would accompany an emergency evacuation of Washington. (This is at least as true today as it was then.)

Moreover, there were many "essential personnel" such as myself who, in the event of a genuine impending disaster, would head home to try to protect their families, instead of fleeing to their emergency underground stations fifty miles away.

The tensions in America and the concerns about attacks from abroad bred and nurtured anti-Communist campaigns at home. Wisconsin's senator Joseph McCarthy basked in the limelight of his indiscriminate and usually inaccurate accusations. His diatribes and investigations gathered momentum in an atmosphere of tolerance, if not approval, on the part of some of his congressional colleagues, several members of the conservative press, and the extreme right wing among the general population. Life in Washington in those days was not a barrel of laughs.

*   *   *

During this period, Western military alliances, on the one hand, and the Warsaw Pact and the Sino-Soviet bloc, on the other, dominated the global political map. Except for Sweden and Switzerland, Eisenhower and Dulles recognized no "neutrals"; either a country was our friend or the friend of our friend, or our enemy or the friend of our enemy. Such countries as India, Egypt, Yugoslavia, and the two score others who professed to be "non-aligned" were regarded as (and, more often than not, actually were) tools, or sycophants, or allies of the Soviet Union and Communist China.

By the time of Eisenhower's inauguration, the US defense budget had grown from $15 billion to $50 billion. Foreign assistance programs had reached $8 billion. Within the Pentagon, the army, navy, air force, and marines each jockeyed for a larger share of the defense budget. The CIA and the State Department were also participants and contenders in the struggle for responsibility, money, and recognition.[1]

Eisenhower, by both personal inclination and professional background, abhorred fuzzy lines of communication, sloppy staff work, and overlapping responsibilities. Crisp, clear, and well-defined were his watchwords. By the time he moved into the Oval Office, however, the country's national security responsibilities had evolved from primarily military defense to a much broader, less clear-cut set of considerations. America was facing a growing array of international concerns, opportunities, and obligations. In particular, the Communist takeover of mainland China, the increased international influence of the Soviet Union, and the bellicose diplomacy and propaganda coming from the Sino-Soviet bloc called for a more robust and muscular foreign policy. This was exemplified by the new secretary of state, John Foster Dulles. It was his and the president's view that the National Security Council's composition, organization, and staffing would have to reflect and respond to a more hostile and complicated world.

By the early summer of 1953, six months into his administration, Eisenhower's National Security Council had been restructured and revitalized from the loose institutional arrangements and the doldrums of the last year or so of the Truman period. A small, newly motivated NSC staff was established under Robert Cutler, the president's special assistant for national security affairs. He provided improved communication between the council and its members, orchestrated meeting schedules and agendas, and had close access to Eisenhower.

Cutler was one of the most colorful persons in the new NSC community. He was a stylish Boston banker and had been on Eisenhower's staff during World War II. A bachelor, he lived during the week at the posh Metropolitan Club, within easy walking distance of the White House and biking distance of Rock Creek Park. Since Cutler's dinner hour of choice was 8:30, his weekly meetings, scheduled for two o'clock, consisted of leisurely, sometimes interminable gossip, jokes, and reminiscences before he felt the need to turn to the agenda items. (Many of Cutler's jokes were raunchy, but since there were no women at any level of the NSC then, and for a long time later, neither he nor we were embarrassed.) I was a regular junior attendee at these meetings; Wednesday night dinners in Chevy Chase were frequently on hold until 9:30.

Two new bodies were formed as part of Eisenhower's more structured NSC. In preparation for the council's meetings, a planning board, made up of senior officials with policy planning or research responsibilities (e.g., the head of the Policy Planning Staff of the State Department and the assistant secretary for international security affairs of the Defense Department), developed briefing papers and draft policy documents tied to the NSC's upcoming agenda items. Following the NSC meetings, an operations coordination board, consisting of senior officials charged with implementation responsibilities (e.g., relevant assistant secretaries of state and the director of the Office of Civil Defense) were charged with putting NSC decisions into effect and monitoring their progress. The CIA's deputy director of intelligence was a member of the planning board; the deputy director of operations was a member of the coordination board.

On my return to the CIA from Fort McNair in July 1953, I was reassigned to the ONE staff. In addition, I was appointed as an assistant to the

CIA's deputy director for intelligence in his NSC planning board role. My colleague in the NSC assignment was the smart, admirable William Bundy.[2]

With the planning board assignment, I became involved in Soviet and Middle East concerns in addition to my usual worries about the increasingly ominous developments in Korea, Indochina, and China/Taiwan. Adding seasoning to the stew was the fact that I was now directly responsible to two bright, energetic, and frequently contending bosses: Bob Amory, the deputy director for intelligence, and Sherman Kent, who had succeeded William Langer as ONE's director.

My experience, however lowly, on the planning board was valuable and fascinating, not only because it provided an exposure to world problems outside Asia, but also because it gave me an early education in Interagency Bureaucratic Machinations 101; relations among the various components of the national security community were by no means warm and cozy.

Complicating the challenges of Berlin, Indochina, and Korea, the new administration was faced with a budget crunch. This, I discovered, provided an opportunity to kill ideas, proposals, or programs that any policy planning board member or staffer thought were inadvisable, stupid, or simply invasions of one's own turf. Thus, if someone at the table proposed a program of foreign assistance that went counter to someone else's interests or judgment, all one had to do was smile, nod, and say, "That sounds okay, but how much will it cost?" Whether the answer was $52.28 or $525,280, one would draw a deep breath, look around the room, and roll one's eyes. That tended to be the end of that. Of course, I was not the inventor of this tactic, nor its only practitioner. Indeed, I, too, had many occasions to lick my wounds.

*   *   *

A mile or so up Pennsylvania Avenue, Senator McCarthy was wreaking havoc at the State Department, where John Foster Dulles was an indifferent spectator. McCarthy cast a wide net, but came up with few big fish. Nonetheless, the toll on the morale and the cost in lawyers' fees, time, stress, and family life was enormous for scores of government staffers. In due course, McCarthy turned his attention to the army. In a fit of mental instability or inebriation, he went so far as to question the loyalty of Gen. George Marshall, the World War II chief of staff and former secretary of state, and of Gen. Johnny Johnson, my War College classmate and later the army chief of staff. McCarthy's outrageous overreach at last encountered opposition. He quietly dropped his accusations, the first sign that the emperor had no clothes.

It would be CIA Director Allen Dulles, however, who made it abundantly clear that McCarthy was, for all practical purposes, stark naked. In his final throes, McCarthy set his sights on the CIA, which, he professed, was populated with many Communist agents. His target there was my friend and NSC staff partner, Bill Bundy. Bill was being vetted for a special security clearance, one needed for his work on NSC issues. McCarthy's investigators discovered that Bundy had contributed $200 to help the former State Department employee Alger Hiss fund his defense against charges of being a Communist agent. This, of course, made Bill a prime suspect in the Communist conspiracy. McCarthy summoned Bill to Capitol Hill for a confrontation.[3]

I was innocent of any of this until the day McCarthy planned Bill's capture. Early that morning I talked to Bill about a matter to be discussed at an NSC meeting a few hours hence. We met for ten minutes or so, and I then returned to my office to prepare some notes. In due course, I telephoned Bill to ask him to join me and see what I had just prepared. His secretary answered the phone.

"Ask Bill to stick his head in my door. He'll know why," I said.

"I'm sorry, Chet, he's not here today."

"What do you *mean*, 'He's not here'? I saw him less than an hour ago!"

This time her voice, ordinarily gentle and pleasant, had an uncustomary edge—"Chet, he's *not* here, *hasn't* been here, and will *not* be here for a few days."

"Where is he?"

"I don't know. In fact, I told you all I *do* know—or *want* to know."

What she did not know, but what I soon discovered, was that one of McCarthy's minions had been on his way over to the CIA to serve Bundy a subpoena. Horrified, I wrote a hasty note of resignation to Allen Dulles, to take effect on the day Bill would be required to subject himself to the senator and his meretricious aides. I needn't have bothered. When Allen Dulles heard that McCarthy was now after the CIA, he informed the senator that only he himself, and not any of his subordinates, would answer to the senator. When he was told that Bundy was about to be subpoenaed, he had him spirited away to a CIA safe house somewhere in the Virginia countryside.

Dulles reported all this to the National Security Council, after first discussing the situation with Vice President Richard Nixon. Nixon, Eisenhower, and the other NSC members, including the thus-far craven John Foster, endorsed Allen's action. In a day or two, McCarthy caved in. Bill was back at his desk. I still had a job.

*   *   *

Meanwhile, Communist governments abroad were not idle. The Soviet Union was ratcheting up tension in Berlin, tightening its grip on Eastern Europe, and seducing the leaders of the self-styled "unaligned nations." The fighting in Korea was continuing with heavy losses on both sides; a clear-cut victory for South Korea, the United States, and their UN allies seemed highly unlikely. The situation in Indochina was deteriorating; only the most starry-eyed optimists could see any satisfactory way out for the French. For his part, Secretary Dulles was speaking loudly and waving a big stick at the Communist bloc and the so-called neutralists. The cold war was getting colder each week.

By late 1953 the French situation in Vietnam was desperate and Paris was pressing for an international conference to settle the war. The British lent their encouragement to the idea; the Soviet Union, China, and the People's Republic of Vietnam in Hanoi were apparently not opposed. President Eisenhower and Secretary Dulles, however, were dead set against holding, let alone attending, such a meeting. Their objection was based, in no small part, on their abhorrence of the Chinese Communists, who, they knew, were bound to play a conspicuous role in any international conference dealing with Asia.

There was yet another issue which troubled the president and his secretary of state: Although the United States had provided the French with substantial amounts of arms and equipment early in their campaign to restore their pre–World War II position in Indochina, there was, by now, an unspoken but perceptible American reluctance to pull Paris's colonialist chestnuts out of the fire.

The international conference notion, however, had a flip side as far as the administration was concerned. A conference on Asia might provide Washington with a face-saving way out of the costly stalemate in Korea—an unpopular military and political situation in which American casualties were alarmingly high and prospects for a clear-cut victory increasingly dim.

In the end, a compromise of sorts was cobbled up. The United States would agree to participate officially in a meeting in Geneva to consolidate a cease-fire in Korea. At such a conference, a Chinese presence would be appropriate, since Washington regarded China (as it regarded North Korea) as a belligerent. The United States would then attend a follow-up conference on Indochina, but would not regard itself as an official, formal, honest-to-goodness participant, regardless of what other attendees might think.

Both Allen and John Foster Dulles thought the US delegation should have a direct link to the CIA in Washington, whether the United States turned out to be an official or unofficial participant. I was chosen. So it was that, on a brisk sunny day in the spring of 1954, I arrived in Geneva. I did not realize it then, but what was to become my personal albatross had just landed perilously close by.

NOTES

1. Robert H. Johnson, "The National Security Council: The Relevance of Its Past to Its Future," *ORBIS* 12, no. 3 (Fall 1969): 709–35.

2. In due course, Bundy became deputy assistant secretary of defense, assistant secretary of state, and then editor of *Foreign Affairs*, the prestigious journal of the Council on Foreign Relations.

3. Hiss professed his innocence, but was tried, found guilty, and—still professing innocence—served a jail sentence. In the aftermath of the breakup of the Soviet Union, however, Russian intelligence officials confirmed that Hiss had indeed been a Soviet spy.

6

GENEVA AND MANILA
SUNNY SKIES, GATHERING CLOUDS

ABOUT NATO, THE EDC, AND SEATO

The North Atlantic Treaty Organization was established in 1948—a cold war response to the growing Soviet threat to Western Europe in general and West Germany in particular. Each member of NATO (fourteen originally, and fifteen several years later when West Germany joined) contributed military units to a NATO force under the command of an American general. NATO was originally based in Paris, but in 1966, at French request, it moved from Paris and found a new home in Brussels, Belgium. At the same time France removed its forces from NATO's command, although it maintained its political and economic link with the organization.

The European Defense Community (EDC) was originally proposed by French statesman Jean Monnet in 1950. The idea was originally a product of French fear of German rearmament and to a somewhat lesser extent was a reflection of Monnet's concern for the development of a unified Europe. The notion of an integrated European army eventually including German units and subordinate to the NATO command was debated for a few years by the major Western European countries and the United States (which strongly supported the enterprise). By 1952, however, the French had become ambivalent because of renewed concern about German rearmament and their sensitivity to a laundry list of real and imagined sins of omission and commission by the United States and Britain. By the midfifties the EDC had died.

The Southeast Asia Treaty Organization (SEATO) was born in 1954 in Manila, shortly after the adjournment of the Geneva Conference on Indochina. It was convened in haste by John Foster Dulles, who had been calling for "united action" against Communist inroads in Asia. Dulles apparently thought that SEATO would develop into a robust bulwark along the lines of NATO. However only two genuinely Southeast Asian nations—the Philippines and Thailand—responded to the call. The only purpose SEATO was to serve was as a rationale used by President Johnson for the dispatch of American troops to Vietnam. SEATO disappeared from the international scene in the mid-1970s.

*   *   *

I was entranced with Geneva, if not with its aloof and smug inhabitants. The city was bursting with the promise of a glorious spring. The lake was sparkling under a bright sun. Window boxes in virtually every building were sporting bright red geraniums, the parks were dotted with tidy and colorful plantings, and the sidewalks adjoining the cafés were adorned with gay umbrellas and freshly painted tables and chairs.

For the participants in the international conference on Indochina, however, Geneva's beauty would extend only to the door of the Palais des Nations. Inside the conference center—once the site of the ill-starred League of Nations—ugly sores would soon appear, sores that would scar many of the participating nations for years to come.

The American delegation was headed by a reluctant, wary secretary of state, John Foster Dulles. He had not wanted to come and he was unhappy that he had. He arrived the day after I. His welcome to Geneva, unlike mine, was marked by a gray sky and a chilly wind—an omen of things to come? As opposed to his brother Allen, John Foster, at least to those outside his inner circle (if, indeed, he *had* an inner circle), was cold, hulking, and gruff.

A former American ambassador has recalled his early impressions of the secretary: ". . . a forbidding figure indeed—stern, unsmiling, and seemingly oblivious of the young staff officers who were ever-present to do his bidding."[1] Around this time a record on which the comedienne Carol Burnett warbled an aria entitled "I Fell in Love with John Foster Dulles" had a modest but selective sale in Washington. I suspect the former ambassador was the proud owner of one. So was I.

Dulles suffered and sulked through the initial phase of the conference which dealt with Korea. Soon after the opening ceremonies of the Indochina phase, however, he handed the baton to Undersecretary Bedell Smith (yes, the former CIA director) and dashed back to the more congenial atmosphere of Foggy Bottom. Our delegation, more than two hundred strong, included political, military, and intelligence representatives, communications technicians, marine guards, and secretaries.

It was no secret, even within the rank and file of the American delegation, that President Eisenhower and his secretary of state had little taste for what was in store. But regardless of how Washington regarded the Indochina part of the enterprise, the United States would obviously have to play a leading role during the Korean negotiations; an early armistice in Korea was a high priority for the Eisenhower administration. This segment was expected to be (and, in the event, was) relatively short. It was the Indochina discussions that promised to be long, acrimonious, and politically awkward for Eisenhower and Dulles.

There would be, first of all, the nagging presence of the Chinese. The conference would mark the Beijing government's debut on the international stage. China was expected to field a delegation of at least three hundred. The attendance of Zhou Enlai, the Chinese foreign minister, and John Foster Dulles at the same meeting carried troubling possibilities; any semblance, even the wisp of a hint of a signal, that Washington intended to recognize the Chinese Communists was anathema to the Eisenhower administration.

To reduce the perception that American participation in the conference implied a softening of Washington's refusal to recognize Beijing, members of the US delegation were forbidden any contact—oral or physical—with the Chinese. (I did not witness this, but some of my delegation colleagues reported that Zhou Enlai, upon finding himself in close proximity to Dulles, extended his hand in greeting, but that Dulles turned away.)

To complicate matters further, Soviet foreign minister Vyacheslav Molotov would be sharing the chairmanship of the conference with Anthony Eden, Great Britain's foreign secretary. On an official level, this combination could not have been more galling for Dulles. On a more personal basis, Eden's presence, especially as cochairman, would pose additional difficulties. Dulles thoroughly disliked Eden—and vice versa. Both had had key roles during the birth of the United Nations in San Francisco in the spring of 1945. Working with each other turned out to be a source of agony rather than ecstasy. As time went on and their contact increased, their mutual dislike flourished.

Relations between Dulles and Eden were further strained during the US election campaign in 1952. Eden foolishly wrote to Eisenhower, his World

War II comrade, urging him not to appoint John Foster secretary of state. Ike, of course, shared Eden's letter with Dulles. One way or another, Dulles probably made sure that Eden knew that he knew of the letter.

In his memoir, Eden noted that his "difficulty in working with Mr. Dulles was to determine what he really meant and in consequence the significance to be attached to his words and actions. . . . A preacher in the world of politics, Mr. Dulles seemed sometimes to have little regard for the consequences of his words."[2]

According to one of Dulles's aides, Eden and Dulles "just weren't on the same beam. . . . Just personality-wise, they weren't destined to work together. . . . [Eden's] calculated lazy manner . . . wasn't Dulles' dish of tea."[3]

The two men were, in fact, an odd couple. Eden was the model diplomat, straight out of a Hollywood movie—privileged background, trim of figure, military-style moustache, highly decorated World War I veteran, elegant dress, impeccable manners. But—there is always a "but"—he was also physically frail and temperamentally high-strung.

Even if all other considerations could have been put aside, the increasingly desperate situation of the French army in Indochina cast a deep shadow. In France itself, the political situation was fragile, and the French people were fatalistic. Nothing short of a complete Communist military and political victory seemed in store. To be a witness, let along a party, to such an outcome was abhorrent to both Eisenhower and Dulles. They were convinced that nothing good would emerge from the Indochina talks at Geneva. Dulles instructed his undersecretary to maintain a low, uncommitted stance.

*   *   *

I arrived in Geneva fitted out with a staff of four. Jean, our communications technician, had a smile as bright as the sun. Joan, my secretary and general assistant, was blessed with impeccable French, awesome clerical and editorial skills, and a formidable backhand on the tennis court. A young woman whose name I have forgotten, if I ever knew it, practiced something called "content analysis," which I assumed was one of the black arts. And then there was Vladimir.

Vladimir was, he said, from a noble White Russian family. And, he said, he was Allen Dulles's official Russian and French interpreter. And, he said, he was well connected to the social elites of Georgetown, the Hamptons, and, yes, Geneva, too. Vladimir had convinced Allen Dulles (who, he said, was a personal friend), and Allen, in turn, had convinced John Foster, that Vladimir could lip-read Russian. Vladimir promised that "together with Chet Cooper," he would inform the senior members of the delegation as to what Foreign Minister Molotov and his deputy, Andrei Gromyko, might be whispering to each other during the proceedings. This, of course, would permit John Foster and Bedell to anticipate Soviet behavior and tactics.

Even before the conference began, however, I decided that, however talented Vladimir might be in the Russian lipreading department, he was destined to be a heavy burden to carry, a thorn in my side, a nontrivial—excuse the expression—pain in the ass. With extravagant rhetorical flourishes, he informed me soon after his arrival that he did not like his hotel room. He also confided that he did not like the hotel food. In fact, he did not like the hotel. Finally, the CIA's per diem allowance was inadequate to meet his needs.

I gave Vladimir's whining short shrift, but we reached a modus vivendi—if he would take his medicine like a big boy, I would later tell his good friend Allen Dulles what a good sport he had been to put up so bravely with the discomfort and unpleasantness of one of Geneva's most luxurious establishments. In the event, it soon turned out that Vladimir was not able to lip-read the whispered Molotov-Gromyko conversations—not unless I arranged for him to sit chock-a-block alongside the Soviet delegation (which meant shoehorning him in with the Poles) or provided him with opera glasses to train on the two Soviet grandees.

The Vladimir problem was solved after about a week or so. Among the many things about the hotel that hardly measured up to his royal standards was the laundry service. I discovered that, in his despair, he had sent his soiled shirts and underwear back to his Georgetown laundress—not by mail, but in the delegation's diplomatic pouch. So it was *dosvedanya*, Vladimir. Home, too, went Ms. Content Analysis. The CIA contingent now consisted of Jean, Joan, and me. Of course, there was another, less conspicuous, agency representative in Geneva—and a good thing, too. Charlie Cooper, a spookish chap, had long been assigned to the consul general's office as assistant consul, or something. I was also relieved to see my OSS friend Joe in the State Department group; we had been a good OSS team in Kunming, and now would be in Geneva, as well.

*   *   *

Before I had left Washington, I was given my own spookish assignment: to find out, one way or another, if the legendary Vietnamese Communist leader Ho Chi Minh was still alive, and if he was, to determine whether he was still actually the head of the Vietnamese Communist Party. The covert folk at the agency seemed reluctant to trust an egghead from the Office of National Estimates with such a sensitive mission, but since I was the only CIA staffer accredited to the conference, and since they did not want to compromise their own Charlie Cooper, they had no other option.

As it happened, this was just the right job for an egghead. Soon after the conference started I had lunch with a congenial member of the conference secretariat. I told him of my longstanding interest in Vietnam and asked if I could see the exchange of correspondence between the secretariat and the Viet Minh delegation. He replied that this wasn't a problem, so long as I could read French. An hour later, in the secretariat office, I discovered that the invitation was addressed to His Excellency Ho Chi Minh in Hanoi and that the acceptance came from Ho. My friend assured me that the UN secretariat had no doubt, on the basis of previous contacts, that the signature was truly Ho's. My satisfaction of "mission accomplished" was tempered, however, by the realization of how little Washington then knew about Vietnam.

In any case, whatever kudos I awarded myself were soon forfeited. A few days after General Bedell Smith took over from John Foster Dulles, I was summoned to Smith's office. "Cooper," he said, "Allen Dulles told me, as I was leaving Washington, that anything I needed from CIA you would provide."

I nodded and gave him a hearty, "Yes, sir!"

"Well, I want to find out whether the Viet Minh people here are reporting to the Chinese or the Sovs. Put a tail on the Vietnamese and let me know where and how they spend their time."

It took a moment for me to catch my breath and then to curse Allen Dulles. "Well, sir, as you may remember, I'm *Chet* Cooper—the Office of National Estimates." (It was all too evident that Smith did *not* remember.) "I don't do things like that. You need *Charlie* Cooper. He's chief of station here. You can reach him through the consulate."

Smith treated me to a bravura version of the Look. I crawled off.

The following day, Charlie called. "Hey, Chet, your friend the general is mad as hell. He wants to see you."

"What's wrong?"

"Well, his secretary called me to his office. He needs something he called an 'estimate' from headquarters. He wants to know what the Chinese might be planning to do in Indochina. I said I wouldn't know how to go about doing that, and told him to call you. You better get up to see him pronto. And good luck."

I approached the general with wariness and—I admit it—fear. He barely gave me a chance to step into his office. "Listen! Cooper! Did what's-his-name tell you I want an estimate on Chinese intentions toward Indochina? Well I do. So get it. Fast. And another thing—Krishna Menon, the Indian foreign minister, is coming to my suite upstairs to talk about the conference. I want my sitting room bugged. And I want *you* to do it. No more Gilbert and Sullivan stuff. Understand?" His eyes locked onto mine, but there was also a trace, a mere ghost of a smile—or was this just wishful thinking?

Anyway, I nodded, mumbled, "Yes sir!" and ran out. I told Jean to send a message to Sherman Kent, director of the Office of National Estimates, asking for a fast-track estimate. That done, I dashed over to Charlie to tell him to bug Smith's room and, subsequently, to undertake whatever other chores Smith threw at me that were beyond, beneath, or above my pay scale or my capabilities.

Just for the record, I should report that the senior members of the Vietnamese Communist delegation were spending time with leaders of both the Chinese and the Soviet delegations, sometimes separately, sometimes together. I should also note that, more than forty years later when I was reminiscing with former Hanoi government officials, they reminded me that "meeting" with the Chinese or the Soviets was one thing, "reporting" to them quite another. They stoutly maintained that they were then, and still are, independent of both.

Aside from dealing with Bedell Smith's numerous, urgent, and varied requirements, I had a problem with Secretary Dulles's admonition to avoid any contact with the Chinese. Early in the Korean sessions I spotted a familiar face among the Chinese delegation. A former classmate and friend from MIT was in the third row of their section, not far from Foreign Minister Zhou Enlai. A year or two before, I had heard that he was in the American Department of the Chinese Foreign Ministry. I knew from his slight nod when we passed each other at the conclusion of the first session that he had recognized me.

Several days later, by sheer chance, we happened to be alone in the elevator going from the Palais' ground floor up to the conference room. We embraced, exchanged a couple of sentences, and then swapped our grins for dour expressions as the elevator door opened. We never had another opportunity to encounter each other.

Of the dozen or so delegations at the Indochina phase of the conference, the small Viet Minh group especially interested me. Conspicuously rich Geneva, with shops overflowing with consumer goods, streets absent of military uniforms but chock-a-block full of brightly lit cafés and nightclubs, must have given them (along with most members of the Soviet and Chinese delegations) a severe culture shock. Many of the Vietnamese Communists probably came to Geneva within a few days of hiding in the jungle or in the back alleys of Hanoi. Now, hastily dressed in ill-fitting Western clothes, they were being driven about Geneva in large automobiles and were sitting in the same room with the capitalist Americans, British, Canadians, and even their enemies, the French.

To be sure, the security officers in all the Communist delegations tried to minimize the possibilities of infection by the capitalist bug. There were evening classes and sing-alongs, late-afternoon group walks, supervised games, and certainly no solo explorations of the city, or meals in cafés, or unsupervised shopping.

Early on, it was both amusing and poignant to witness the open curiosity with which the Vietnamese, Soviet, and Chinese delegations regarded each other, and especially how they regarded the Americans, British, and French. The dapper Anthony Eden, the forbidding Bedell Smith, and the increasingly anxious French were particular targets of their stares. As the days folded into weeks, however, even the most junior Vietnamese had gained enough confidence to hand copies of Pham Van Dong's speeches to General Smith with about the same amount of fear and trembling I would have displayed.

*   *   *

The Korean phase of the conference was pretty much cut and dried, although it was enlivened by polemics from Zhou Enlai, and from Molotov on the days he was not in the chair. (When he was chairing the meeting, however, he comported himself well indeed.) For their part, the North Koreans, by choice or by direction, played only a bit role.

Much of this time was given over to the military modalities of an armistice. This meant, of course, that the dozen or so military and civilian representatives from the United States delegation and the Korean army officers from both north and south had much of the responsibility. They seemed to make rapid progress, perhaps because most of their deliberations took place in small working groups.

The Korean discussions ended on May 7 with an armistice agreement July 1953—a fragile agreement, to be sure, but an agreement nonetheless. Or so we thought. Serious political problems in connection with the POW issue had been either swept under the rug or set aside. They would come back soon enough to complicate the implementation of the armistice agreement. In fact, more US and allied troops were killed or wounded in the period between the "armistice agreement" and the end of the war in July 1953 than between the outbreak of the war and the so-called armistice.

From the point of view of international peace, the Korean War was actually much more dangerous than the colonialist-nationalist conflict in Indochina. In Korea, after all, American forces were directly engaged with Communist Chinese as well as North Korean troops, and there were common borders between the Soviet Union and both China and North Korea. It was only in Korea that the cold war had actually turned hot. Nonetheless, the specter of a Communist victory in Indochina hung low and threatening over the Korean discussions.

*   *   *

Washington's concern about Indochina had little to do (despite the allegations and convictions of the Viet Minh) with a desire to help the French maintain their colonial position, or to substitute an American colonial presence. Instead, two different considerations were at the root of America's interest in assisting France.

The first was to forestall yet another Communist victory in Asia. China had fallen to the Chinese Communists only a few years before, and a decisive anti-Communist victory in Korea was not in prospect. A real or apparent Communist triumph in Indochina would not only be a devastating blow for Paris, but would also be a serious setback for Washington.

The second consideration stemmed from Washington's desire to bring France into the European Defense Community (EDC), the anti-Soviet military organization then under discussion in Washington and in Western Europe capitals. With a large part of its army and some of its air force committed to the war in Vietnam, and with other units deployed in North Africa, however, France's military establishment was hard-pressed, even without assuming additional responsibilities in Europe. Aware of this, Washington had agreed to assist France politically and militarily in Indochina in exchange for Paris's participation in the EDC (soon to become NATO).

The US-French bargain was not without opposition in Washington. Several State Department officials familiar with Southeast Asia were troubled by a conspicuous American association with France's attempt to retrieve its pre–World War II colony. There was a strong constituency arguing that World War II should have put an end to meretricious colonial attitudes and policies; self-determination should be one of the lofty aims of the victorious allies.

France, however, lost little time in asserting its prewar claim to Indochina.[4] The British troops I had seen in the harbor at Colombo in November 1945 were on their way to Vietnam to help France reestablish its colonial regime. By 1947, however, it became clear that the times and the growing nationalist strength in Vietnam called for Paris to provide the Vietnamese with the appearance—but, *certainment*, not with the reality—of an independent government.

The principal player in this French farce was the almost-forgotten, dissolute emperor Bao Dai, who had abdicated his royal responsibilities a decade before. Bao Dai was coaxed out of his paradise of wine, women, and thongs in Hong Kong for discussions in Paris about assuming leadership of an "independent" Vietnam. Once in France, the emperor proved to be both physically aloof and politically astute. He led the French on a merry chase for almost three years. Finally, in 1950, the French signed an agreement giving the reincarnated emperor and his kingdom the trappings of independence. French advisers would sit close by, of course, and French officials would maintain control over defense and foreign affairs.

The United States government, despite the objections of several French and Asian specialists in the State Department, recognized Bao Dai as head of the "independent" Vietnamese government. The emperor chose a cabinet of courtiers and mediocrities and installed himself in his former palace in Hue, the old royal capital. The burdens of his daily grind were alleviated by the attentions of a young lady, delicately described by Stanley Karnow as a "spectacular French blond courtesan"[5] who, in addition to her other duties, became a ubiquitous member of the emperor's kitchen cabinet. Needless to say, Vietnam's new thin and tattered veil of independence did little to satisfy the ardent, aggressive followers of Ho Chi Minh. In due course, the emperor resigned as prime minister, although he held onto his emperorship, and presumably his courtesan, when he retired to the pleasures of southern France.

*   *   *

By early 1954, even before the Geneva Conference convened, both the French and the non-Communist Vietnamese had lost whatever remaining patience and confidence they had in Bao Dai. If a non-Communist post-French Vietnam were to have any prospect of viability, a strong, incorruptible prime minister had to be found. The Americans just happened to have such a candidate on the shelf. His name was Ngo Dien Diem.

In the course of little more than a decade, Diem, who had been ensconced in Catholic retreats in America and Europe, was installed as prime minister of Vietnam in 1954, and then murdered by officers of his own army in 1963. Diem first caught the eye of prominent American Catholics in 1952, when he went into voluntary exile from Vietnam. He became a virtual recluse in Maryknoll seminaries in New Jersey and New York State. On occasion he emerged to lecture at obscure academic meetings, or to touch base with Vietnamese in the United States, seeking their support for his return to Vietnam in some important capacity.

In 1953 he left for Europe. He wanted to be closer to the large, influential Vietnamese community in France, and especially to his politically active brother, Ngo Dinh Nhu. There, in the quiet of a Belgian monastery, he bided his time.

On the eve of the Geneva Conference it was clear to the Vietnamese nationalists, the French, and the Americans that a new prime minister was needed. Bao Dai, still the emperor, agreed with Diem's American and Vietnamese supporters that Diem was the most suitable candidate. Although the French were unenthusiastic, hoping for someone more pliable, the deal was made and Diem arrived in Saigon in late June.[6]

*   *   *

Paris, recognizing defeat, declared Vietnam genuinely and completely independent on May 6, 1954. The French colonial presence came to an end after ninety years. But the war was not quite over. There was still the matter of extricating thousands of regular and Foreign Legion troops from the besieged bastion Dien Bien Phu, the major remaining French outpost in Vietnam.

The French delegation was seated next to the Americans in the Palais des Nations. On May 8, just as the Korea discussions were coming to a close, I saw a man walk quickly down the aisle and hand a note to French foreign minister Georges Bidault. Bidault paled and whispered to his senior aide. His aide dashed from the hall. I scribbled a sentence, "Dien Bien Phu has fallen," and passed it to General Smith.

Dien Bien Phu was not just another French military outpost in an isolated valley on the Laos border (see map). It was a major bastion, manned by thirteen thousand soldiers and containing vast amounts of military equipment. Its mission was to prevent the Viet Minh from overrunning Laos. By late 1953, however, the fort had assumed a symbolic role; it represented France's resolve not only to guard the borders of Laos, but also to maintain a strong foothold in Vietnam. Senior French generals were convinced that Dien Bien Phu was

Dien Bien Phu on the Vietnam-Laos border.

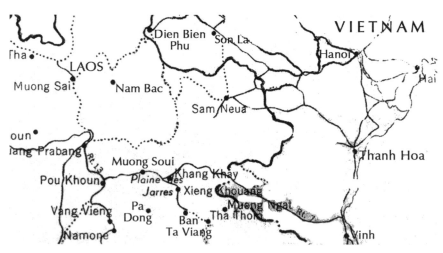

Source: US National Archives

impregnable. (The lesson of the Maginot Line in 1939–40 was apparently ignored.)

Gen. Vo Nguyen Giap, commander of the Viet Minh forces, decided that Dien Bien Phu was where his army would make a concerted assault against the French forces. For several months in late 1953 and early 1954, his forces streamed into positions around Dien Bien Phu. By spring, fifty thousand Viet Minh troops surrounded the fortress from positions above the valley and in foxholes and tunnels along the fort's perimeter. They intercepted supplies, gunned down French patrols, and strafed incoming aircraft. Rain and fog during the winter further hampered French supply efforts.

So desperate was the French position that senior officials in Washington—Secretary of State Dulles, Vice President Nixon, and chairman of the Joint Chiefs of Staff Adm. Arthur Radford—were considering sending US bombers, and possibly US troops, to relieve the trapped French forces. There were rumors that even atomic bombs were on their list.

In a speech presaging what was later to come, Nixon told the American Society of Newspaper Editors on April 17 that "the United States, as a leader of the free world, cannot afford further retreat in Asia. It is hoped the United States will not have to send troops there, but if the government cannot avoid it, the Administration must face up to the situation and dispatch forces."[7]

President Eisenhower, however, left little doubt about his opposition to sending American bombers, let alone troops, to assist the French at Dien Bien

Phu. "I couldn't think of anything probably less effective than in a great big jungle area and with a besieged fortress, trying to relieve it with air force."[8]

*   *   *

Since early 1954 Eisenhower and Dulles had been agonizing about how to save Dien Bien Phu and thus the French position in Indochina. French support for the EDC as well as a rollback of the Communists in Asia was at stake—or so the White House, the State Department, and the Pentagon firmly believed.

As spring approached, the French situation at Dien Bien Phu became increasingly worrisome. It soon became clear that the fortress, its thousands of defenders, and its valuable materiel were all in danger. The only salvation was massive American assistance. Dulles and Radford were inclined to involve the United States. (Even employing nuclear weapons was considered.) Eisenhower was opposed to using US ground troops or air units. At the very least, he insisted, other Western countries, particularly the British, would have to join in the enterprise. And that explains why Radford and his aide were having dinner at Chequers, the British prime minister's country retreat, on April 26, 1954.

Radford was on a sales mission: If the British and the Americans did not rush large amounts of aid to the besieged garrison, according to Churchill's assistant, who took the notes, the French defeat would be a "turning point in history." The government of Prime Minister Joseph Laniel would be replaced by a neutralist one, Paris would not ratify the EDC, and "NATO itself might well be destroyed."

According to the notes of the meeting, Radford was seriously concerned that if Indochina fell to North Vietnam's Communist army, much of Southeast Asia, Australia, New Zealand, and Japan would soon follow (the "dominoes"). More than that: countries of the Near East and Africa were vulnerable. Radford then reached the top (or the bottom) of his liturgy: "This was the moment at which to make a stand against the Chinese." The admiral opined that "the Russians, who were frightened of war, would not openly go to the aid of the Chinese." If the British "cooperated over this the United States would be willing to help [the British] in other spheres."

Churchill, who, according to the record at least, remained civil throughout, responded by informing his dinner guest that the British "could not allow ourselves to be committed . . . to a policy which might lead us to destruction, the more so when we believed that the action which the Americans now proposed was almost certainly to be ineffective. We could do nothing to save Dien Bien Phu and the French would realize that they had not the strength to hold down all of Indochina. . . . The loss of the fortress must be faced." When the British studied the results of the Geneva Conference, they would consider the situation in consultation with the United States.

Radford may not have been the ideal choice for this mission, but at least Churchill (and we) gained an insight as to high-level American strategic thinking during the midfifties.[9]

With the fall of Dien Bien Phu, the French bargaining position tumbled from minuscule to virtually nonexistent.[10] Foreign Minister Bidault confessed to Anthony Eden that his hand consisted of "a two of clubs and a three of diamonds."[11]

The Indochina discussions droned on with interminable speeches, vitriolic tirades, and mischievous interventions. Adding to the delay, the conference was frequently interrupted by time-outs and recesses as delegates caucused or went back to their capitals for consultation and instructions.

When it became clear that the conference was likely to extend well into June, Orah, Joan, and Susan joined me in Geneva. Their arrival made me much more tolerant of delays and interruptions; in fact, now that they were with me, the longer the conference lasted, the better. We had rented an apartment overlooking the lake and Mont Blanc, the children were attending a Swiss school and learning French, and our weekends were unfailingly pleasant—much more so than the discussions at the Palais.

As June was drawing to a close, one could sense frictions among the Communist delegations. Molotov was obviously calling the signals, both in his role as cochairman and as head of the Soviet delegation. Zhou Enlai, a skilled diplomat within the Sino-Soviet bloc, seemed anxious to establish his own identity as a player on the international stage.

Pham Van Dong and his Viet Minh delegation were conspicuously unhappy about the course of the proceedings. After all, they had come to Geneva as the clear victor, and yet their influence was eroding day by day in the face of Soviet and Chinese concerns for their own, broader interests. More than four decades later, officials in Hanoi would bitterly refer to Geneva 1954 as a betrayal and a sellout, not by their adversaries in America, Britain, and France, but by their comrades in China and the Soviet Union.

To me, at least, all this was interesting, but by no means worrisome. What was both interesting *and* worrisome was the tension between the British and the Americans—especially between Dulles (and, soon, Smith) and Eden. From Dulles's press conferences in Washington (which, typically, were conducted without advance notice to Eden) and from the communications between the

State Department and the delegation, it became clear that Eisenhower and Dulles were ready to see the conference break up without an agreement.

Distrust of Anthony Eden escalated after he made a speech in London, where he had gone for consultations in late June. He implied that a solution to the Indochina problem might follow the lines of the Locarno Pact, a series of agreements following World War I in which the European countries guaranteed the peace in Europe. Dulles regarded this as a signal that Eden was prepared to invite China and the USSR to share power in Southeast Asia with the UK, the United States, and France. To the secretary and the president this was another, flagrant indication that Eden would go to any lengths to secure an agreement, any agreement, in Geneva. The American delegation was told to be ready to pack.

Meanwhile, the French parliament was becoming increasingly impatient and restless about the snail's pace of the negotiations. On June 17, Prime Minister Joseph Laniel was succeeded by Pierre Mendes-France. Mendes-France was not just another off-the-peg wannabe premier. He was a socialist, a Jew, and a proactive, courageous personality. He had been a vocal opponent of French policy in Indochina for several years and was a savvy politician. (Come to think of it, not *altogether* savvy; one of his early moves as premier was to try to substitute milk for wine as France's national drink. He failed.)

On June 21, barely a few days after he took office, Mendes-France announced that he would resign unless the negotiations in Geneva resulted in an agreement by midnight July 21. Mendes-France's threat had nontrivial implications for several of the key delegations. The prospect of renewed political instability and chaos in France was decidedly unwelcome to the Americans, British, and Canadians. The notion of a socialist premier in France raised hopes (which, as it turned out, were false) in Moscow, Warsaw, and among the Chinese and Viet Minh of increased Communist influence in Western Europe. In short, from his ornate office in Paris Mendes-France, together with, as we will see, a small and almost forgotten Asian delegation, became the most influential actors in Geneva's Palais des Nations.

Early on, the notion of dividing Geneva into Communist and non-Communist zones hovered over the deliberations. There were, after all, two precedents for a solution along these lines: in Germany and in Korea. More powerful impetus was given to this idea because, for both the same and different reasons, China and the Soviet Union found merit in the partition solution.

It was generally accepted that the Americans would replace the French as the dominant influence over whatever non-Communist regime took power in Vietnam after the conference. Indeed, individual Americans, including the

Kennedy family and powerful cardinals, had been lobbying on behalf of Ngo Diem Dinh since May. Surely, when the partition issue rose in discussions in Moscow, Beijing, and Hanoi, and among the Communist delegations in Geneva, the role of the United States would have had to be reckoned with.

The geopoliticans in Moscow had their own perspective on this outcome. To them, Communist control over all of Vietnam would provide the Chinese with a foothold in Southeast Asia, a prospect that was by no means congenial. American influence over a part of Vietnam was better, in their calculations, than Chinese influence over the whole country.

To the Eisenhower administration, the desired solution would be a political and military defeat for the Viet Minh and a consequent setback for the Sino-Soviet bloc in Southeast Asia. Even the hawkiest of the hawks, however, including John Foster Dulles himself, had to realize, albeit grudgingly, that a north/south, Communist/non-Communist partition of Vietnam was inevitable given the dolorous current situation. Of course, in the light of Dulles's earlier instructions to the US delegation, the Americans would do little overtly to help achieve such a solution.

For Great Britain, particularly for the exhausted, nerve-racked Anthony Eden, virtually any solution short of complete submission to Communist demands had attraction. Eden had had more than enough of Dulles's negative criticism and meddlesome obstruction. More important, perhaps, was his anxiety to have a Geneva agreement to his credit as he impatiently stood by waiting for Prime Minister Winston Churchill finally to announce his retirement (which, in the event, was still two years away).

The French, as A. J. Langguth has noted, "fared better as negotiators than as warriors."[12] With Bidault's "two of clubs and three of diamonds," the French came out of their debacle in Vietnam better than the Viet Minh, who had come to Geneva with several aces, kings, and queens.

Before he left for Switzerland, Pham Van Dong must have been confident of a favorable outcome. After all, the Viet Minh were, by then, dominant in much of Vietnam, the French political situation and bargaining power were frail, and the non-Communist Vietnamese were demoralized and ineffectual. Primarily preoccupied with their own political and strategic priorities, however, the Soviets and Chinese gave their Vietnamese comrades short shrift.

Perhaps more than any other senior person in Geneva, Zhou Enlai could be regarded as the godfather of the partition solution. Once he advanced the idea, it achieved enough momentum that by early July, it was not a question of *whether* there would be a partition, but *where* the dividing line in Vietnam would be.

In my conversations in Hanoi decades later, I tried but was unable to learn what inducements Molotov and Zhou made in order to get Ho Chi Minh's acquiescence to a dividing line well above what Hanoi expected (and probably, all things considered, deserved). Perhaps the former Viet Minh officials and my new friends didn't know. In any case, Pham Van Dong and his boss, Ho Chi Minh, must have been beckoned or pushed up the garden path, where they were forced to accept a division along the thin neck of Vietnam at the seventeenth parallel. With this agreement, the Viet Minh based in Hanoi and the Vietnamese non-Communists based in Saigon would each control half the country.

Zhou Enlai, together with Molotov, had a keen interest in maintaining a socialist premier in Paris. As the critical date, July 21, neared, and as an agreement was still uncertain, Molotov took charge. The key delegations, except for the Americans (who refused to participate), assembled at his villa for a showdown session. It was there that partition along the seventeenth parallel was decided and rammed down the throats of the Communist Vietnamese. To sweeten the pot a bit for them, an election for a national government of Vietnam was scheduled two years hence. (Pham Van Dong argued for six months; Mendes-France argued for no elections. Neither got his way, but in the end, it didn't make any difference, since the election was never held.)

In the late evening hours of July 20, the draft agreement, together with the exhausted delegates, was ready to be put to bed. The deadline was within reach. But the feisty, tiny Cambodian delegation had not yet been able to register the fact that, deadline or no deadline, Mendes-France's premiership notwithstanding, they were not ready to sign up. Molotov, the chairman, wearily and patiently went over their numerous objections, some trivial, some consequential. Time ticked by. A few minutes before midnight, some genius set back the ornate clock on the wall of the conference hall. By fair means or foul, the deadline was (sort of) met.

The next day the agreement was signed by all except the South Vietnamese and the Americans. The conference ended with little ceremony. Anthony Eden, among others, looked back on this experience without nostalgia: "I had never known a conference of this kind. The parties would not make direct contact and we were in constant danger of one or another backing out the door."[13]

Each of the new Vietnams went home to fashion a whole country out of its half. The French managed to withdraw from their former colony with a fig leaf of dignity, only to become soon embroiled in—and lose—another ugly war in Algeria. The United States lost no time in persuading its not-altogether-enthusiastic allies to join a "united front" to resist further Communist expansion in Southeast Asia.

*   *   *

Even in northern Europe, August 1954 was reasonably fine—"partly cloudy," as the weatherman would say. Orah and I looked forward to a holiday. Joan and Susan were not due back at school until early September. And our new Volkswagen Beetle was roomy enough for a longish journey through Western Europe, providing we stowed our luggage on the roof and the two kids respected their territorial boundaries in the back seat. There was every sign of a bon voyage.

Outside of Switzerland, the scars of war were still evident wherever we traveled. Bombed-out buildings, men and women with missing limbs, and food shortages were graphic reminders that World War II was but yesterday. During my National War College trip a year or so before, I must have been so involved with briefings, honor guards, and welcoming dinners that, in effect, except for sights of ruined Berlin, I had traveled in a well-insulated cocoon. Now, driving from town to town, walking the city streets, I had a totally different experience.

The bitter memories and the horrid legacies of the war remained fresh and stark throughout France, England, and the Low Countries. Americans were welcome; our VW, which I had bought in innocence or stupidity, was not. The truth dawned one evening after a long drive, when I drove up to an attractive Dutch hotel about twenty miles from Amsterdam. The doorman approached and said in German, "We have no rooms. The hotel is full."

As if on cue, four-year-old Susan cried out, "Oh, Daddy, I'm so tired!"

The doorman suddenly became all smiles. "Americans! Welcome! I'll park your car and take care of your luggage." And he added to Susan, "We have a nice room, especially for you."

We wound up our holiday in England and sailed home from Southampton. Although Orah and I did not know it then, our family would be disembarking at Southampton a year later, almost to the day, for a three-year stay in London.

*   *   *

Neither President Eisenhower nor Secretary Dulles felt comfortable with the outcome of the Geneva talks. Indeed, anticipating a Communist military victory in Indochina and a political victory in Geneva, Dulles had been urging "united action" to halt, by military means if necessary, a southern thrust by the Communists in Asia. Hardly had the British, French, and other non-Communist delegations returned home when Dulles called for a meeting to develop a plan to achieve this. I was soon on my way to the Philippines to participate in the birth of the South East Asia Treaty Organization (SEATO).

A nonstop trip by air from Washington to Manila now takes about seventeen hours. The journey in the late summer of 1954 was by no means nonstop. My Northwest Airlines flight left National Airport and landed in Chicago. From Chicago we flew to Seattle, and then to Anchorage, and then to Cold Bay, Alaska, and then to Hokkaido, and then to Tokyo, and then to Hong Kong, and then to Singapore, and then, finally, to Manila—five days and four nights, ten breakfasts, three lunches, and two dinners later.

The flight was delayed twelve hours at a spartan naval air station in Cold Bay, about as far out on the northern edge of the United States as you can get without wading in the Pacific Ocean. Apparently, the plane had left Anchorage without enough fuel to reach the regular refueling stop in the Aleutians. It was Sunday, and the navy commander did not have authority to refuel a commercial airliner that just happened to drop by. No one at the Pentagon could be reached to give him an okay, and no one could be reached at Northwestern's headquarters in Seattle who could solve the problem. The passengers and crew bunked up in the bachelor officers' quarters until the matter was finally sorted out.

I arrived at the delegation's hotel in Manila in less-than-mint condition. Early the next morning, I crawled across the street to check in at the embassy. Aside from a monstrous case of jet lag, I had been visited by bedbugs during the night. Even at eight o'clock, it was beastly hot and beastly humid, and I was encased in the nonporous embrace of a vintage 1954 wash-and-wear shirt and jacket I had taken to Geneva. My spirits were not lifted by an encounter I had with a ragged ten-year-old boy outside the embassy. He grabbed my arm and shouted, "Change money?" I shook my head. "Nice girl?" I shook his hand off my arm. "Nice boy?" The air conditioning of the embassy barely helped me to face the day.

*   *   *

Just as the Americans were reluctant to go to Geneva, the British (perhaps, in part, because Eden was in no mood to be at Dulles's beck and call) required considerable prodding to attend the session in Manila. In the end, Eden agreed to send a small delegation, although he himself stayed home.

Dulles did decide to attend; after all, it was his idea. He originally envisioned a treaty for Southeast Asia roughly along the lines of the North Atlantic Treaty Organization. Whatever starch, teeth, and credibility such an organization might have had, however, was removed when, on the eve of the conference, President Eisenhower insisted that American ground forces would not be part of any military deal reached in Manila.

In a sense, the meeting in Manila brought to mind the nightmare that haunts every ambitious hostess. It was a party to which no one (or hardly anyone) came. Only two bona fide Southeast Asian nations attended: Thailand and the Philippines. The other partygoers consisted of Britain, grudging and skeptical; France, anxious to atone for its parliament's recent rebuff of the European Defense Community; Pakistan, eager to court the United States for military and economic assistance; the two stalwarts Australia and New Zealand; and, of course, the United States. This made a grand total of seven.

After a few preliminary working group meetings to address the sins of omission and commission in the American draft text (which I had helped to prepare and which, truth to tell, arrived in Manila barely half-baked), the plenary meeting opened on September 6. The session was marked by listless, unfocused discussion, and the meeting wound up its thin agenda the following day. The pact was christened the Southeast Asian Treaty Organization, or SEATO. (Its original name was rejected after a member of the Thai delegation passed me a note warning that its acronym was a dirty word in Thai.) During the final moments I was reminded of Mark Twain's assessment of the accomplishments of his Confederate militia company: "What could you expect of them? . . . Nothing. . . . That is what they did."[14]

The only consequential provision emerging from the SEATO pact was a protocol to the effect that the countries of Indochina were specifically included in the provisions of the treaty. Thanks to this, SEATO turned out to be useful for Lyndon Johnson, who, years later, cited the treaty as a rationale for US military action in South Vietnam.

International conferences tend to wind up with ceremony, whether or not much has been accomplished. The SEATO meeting ended with a grand flourish—a fiesta at the Malacanang Palace.

Secretary Dulles was seated at the head table, clad in a traditional Filipino sheer tropical dress shirt, which wasn't quite his style—and it was evident from his discomfort that he knew it. Together with others from the US delegation, I (in my wash-and-wear jacket and shirt) sat at a table close to the entrance in the event that the heat, or the possibility of more interesting entertainment elsewhere, necessitated an unobtrusive getaway.

Fate dictated, however, that I remain to the bitter end and watch enviously as several of my colleagues melted away. I had barely finished the first course when a young man from the CIA's communications center rushed over to me and handed me a note: "Chinese Communists currently bombing offshore islands Quemoy and Matsu. Threatening to bomb Taiwan itself. Inform Secretary ASAP."

I told the messenger to let me know of any further developments. Then, much to her surprise, I swept up Dulles's secretary, Phyllis, and we danced our way to where Dulles was sitting. There, we performed a passable rhumba in place while I whispered the news. He scribbled a note on his placecard: "Keep me informed and see me tomorrow at eight." Phyllis and I danced off. There were no more messages, but I went to the communications center on my way back to the hotel. A few more bombs were unloaded on the offshore islands, but this seemed to be nothing to bother the secretary about that night.

The next morning Dulles sent me off to Taiwan. I was to look at the situation, talk to US and Chinese nationalist military and civilian officials, visit military installations, and return to Washington in several days with a report on whether I thought Chiang Kai-shek could hold out against an attack from the mainland long enough for US assistance to arrive.

I wasn't sure why Dulles singled me out for this errand. To be sure, I was a former infantry corporal, OSS staff sergeant, and National War College graduate. Nevertheless, my vast expertise on the tactics and strategy of defending an island from attacks by sea had become a bit rusty.

I spent about a week in Taiwan. I met with our embassy and CIA folk, with President Chiang's generals, colonels, a few lieutenants, and Madame Chiang. I had a look at an air base, several coastal defenses, and the garrisons on Quemoy. I had some good Chinese meals, did a bit of shopping, and experienced no bombing attacks. I concluded that the Communists were trying to score points during the Manila meeting (which Beijing had referred to as "an aggressive move"). From what I could see and hear, I reported that, if necessary, Taiwan could hold out until expeditious US aid was made available. Then I went home.

NOTES

1. Robert Hopkins Miller, *Vietnam and Beyond* (Lubbock: Texas Tech University Press, 2002), p. 21.

2. Anthony Eden, *Full Circle: The Memoirs of Anthony Eden* (Boston: Houghton Mifflin, 1960), p. 124.

3. Quoted in Leonard Mosley, *Dulles* (Boston: Dial, 1978), p. 354.

4. The United Kingdom, Holland, and Belgium also claimed their prewar colonies.

5. Stanley Karnow, *Vietnam: A History* (New York: Viking, 1983), p. 181.

6. For a more complete account of Ngo Dinh Diem and his appointment as prime minister, see Chester L. Cooper, *The Lost Crusade: America in Vietnam* (New York: Dodd Mead, 1970), pp. 120–28.

7. *New York Times*, April 17, 1954, p. 1.

8. As quoted by Melvin Gurtov, *The First Vietnam Crisis* (New York: Columbia University Press, 1963), p. 136.

9. For a fuller account of the Radford-Churchill meeting on April 26, 1954, see British National Archives, Ref: FO 3711 112057.

10. For a fuller account of the battle of Dien Bien Phu and the leading French military officers involved, see Karnow, *Vietnam*, pp. 189–98.

11. Eden, *Full Circle*, p. 124.

12. A. J. Langguth, *Our Vietnam: The War 1954–1975* (New York: Simon & Schuster, 2000), p. 79.

13. Eden, *Full Circle*, p. 144.

14. Mark Twain, "The Private History of a Campaign That Failed," *The Family Mark Twain* (New York and London: Harper Brothers, 1935), p. 1283.

7

EDEN AND DULLES

NEVER THE TWAIN...

ABOUT THE BRITISH INTELLIGENCE COMMUNITY

This chapter deals to a large extent with my close contact with the British intelligence community during the latter part of the 1950s. It is dotted with acronyms which, although defined in the abbreviations, deserve at least some modest explanation here. There are some overall similarities between the British organization and our own, but once one probes beyond some overall generalities confusion quickly sets in. We do, after all, have two different types of government.

At the pinnacle of the British intelligence community (setting aside the cabinet and the prime minister) is the Joint Intelligence Committee (JIC). The JIC is chaired by a senior foreign office official and is made up of the chiefs of the various elements of the community—the Foreign Office, the military intelligence branches, the Joint Intelligence Board, MI6, MI5, and the GCHQ. (Be patient; the initialized groups will be dealt with momentarily.)

The Joint Intelligence Committee does not supervise its constituent bodies, but incorporates their information and views in papers prepared for selected Cabinet members and the prime minister. The committee is served by a Joint Intelligence Staff (JIS) made up of bright representatives from the members of its parent body, the JIC.

MI6, together with MI5 and the GCHQ, has long been known (from usage rather than for security reasons) by its initials. MI6 is roughly equiv-

alent to the operations and secret intelligence segments of CIA. Until rela-
tively recently, the director of MI6 was an unknown ghostlike figure outside
British intelligence. When I was in London he was a cultured, broadly read
graduate of Oxbridge.

MI5 is Britain's counterintelligence agency, combining some of the
activities of our Federal Bureau of Investigation and the counterintelligence
groups of the CIA. Unlike MI6, which, through a hazy channel, reports to the
Foreign Office, MI5 is directly responsible to the Home Office.

The GCHQ, like our own National Security Agency (NSA), is the code-
breaking element of Her Majesty's intelligence community.

I have described virtually more than I know about this subject. After
many years of dealing with or being exposed to these matters, I have learned
it is better to suspect than to ask.

*   *   *

The autumn of 1954 marked the United States' first tentative steps to replace France as the dominant influence in South Vietnam. In North Vietnam, that role was taken by, if not given to, China. The Soviet Union would, in due course, muscle its way into Hanoi's grace and favor, but Moscow's immediate concerns focused on Europe—East and West. Neither Beijing nor Moscow made much of an issue of the fact that, despite the Geneva accord, elections (free or otherwise) were not held throughout Vietnam.

The leadership in Hanoi claimed then, and would continue to claim over the following decades, that Washington planned to replace Paris as the colonialist master of Indochina. The truth was, however, that the United States had no such designs. Washington's policy was driven by its determination to halt the spread of Communism in Southeast Asia at Vietnam's seventeenth parallel. To accomplish this, Ngo Dien Diem, the president of South Vietnam, was Washington's chosen instrument.

Early in his tenure, Diem surprised and pleased his American supporters. By the late fifties, however, Diem's fecklessness, his brother Nhu's corruption, and his sister-in-law Madame Nhu's machinations had begun to take their toll. The South Vietnamese generals spent their time and energy in conspiring and jockeying for power instead of fighting the growing Communist threat. By the early sixties the two brothers were assassinated in a military coup. (The malicious Madame Nhu had already dashed off to France.) A procession of generals marched into and quickly fled out of the presidential palace. Instability and inertia in Saigon were the hallmarks of the anti-Communist effort.

It was my luck to go off to London at the peak of Diem's success and to return to Washington and back into Vietnam's grasp when Diem and his government lost their mandate. In the late spring of 1955, I was summoned by my boss, Sherman Kent, the assistant director for national intelligence estimates. Kent and his boss, Robert Amory, deputy director for intelligence, were smiling when I entered Kent's office. I was pretty sure I wasn't in trouble.

"How would you like a three-year assignment to London?" Amory asked. "Sherman says you ought to go."

"Sherman is right, as usual. The answer is yes, I would."

In August, Orah, Joan, Susan, and I were comfortably settled in first-class cabins on the USS *United States*. (This was before civil servants traveling overseas were shoehorned into the economy-class sections of jumbo planes.)

Once in London and after much searching, we found a modest, but adequate, mid-nineteenth-century house near Kensington Gardens. A visiting CIA colleague described it as a "vertical rambler." The entrance from the street led into the dining room and kitchen; a tiny den was on the next landing, with a large living room above; then, two more floors contained two bedrooms each. There was one bathroom and a coal cellar (but no coal). We had electric heaters in the dining room and living room, and a portable kerosene heater in an upstairs hall, but no other source of heating (except for blankets and hot-water bottles).

We had deposited our CIA friend in the top-floor bedroom adjoining Susan's. He asked Susan, one afternoon, if she would get him a pencil. "The pencils are in the kitchen," she said. "Come down with me, so the next time you'll need one you'll know where they are." It was that kind of a house.

Orah enrolled Joan and Susan in a Montessori school not far from our home. On the Saturday morning before school opened for its autumn term, I brought the girls to school. Miss Humphrey, the headmistress, wanted to meet them and show them the school before the hubbub of opening day. During the short drive, I explained that they would not find the informal atmosphere and country setting of their school at home. They were not to call their teachers by their first names; they would wear school uniforms, not jeans; and the playground was a city backyard, rather than the country field they were used to. Then came two firm admonitions: "Spit out your gum.

And when I introduce you, I want you to shake hands and say, 'How do you do, Miss Humphrey.'"

"Oh, Daddy," was their response, "we know all that!"

Miss Humphrey, a formidable figure in a cardigan, tweed skirt, and sensible shoes, was waiting for us at the school gate. I introduced myself and then, with unwarranted confidence, said, "This is Joan and this is Susan."

Each of my well-briefed daughters gave a casual wave and then, through big wads of gum, came "Hi!"

A couple of days after school opened, Orah had an errand, and I left the embassy early to pick up the girls. As they filed out in their new, crisp uniforms and jaunty straw boaters, each paused at the gate where Miss Humphrey was again stationed. They curtsied and said (through unencumbered mouths), "Good afternoon, Miss Humphrey."

Miss Humphrey has remained one of our great heroes ever since.

*   *   *

The CIA station in London was divided into two groups under the station chief. One group, the spooks, had its own quarters a block away from the embassy. They worked closely with the British secret intelligence, counter-intelligence, and operations people. Most of the other group, the intelligence analysts, were assigned to work with the Joint Intelligence Board (JIB). The JIB was based in an old, cold, dreary building near Trafalgar Square. (On a visit there one December day, I found our two CIA secretaries gamely typing away in their overcoats and gloves.) The JIB's military specialists, economists, scientists, and geographers—much like their opposite numbers in Langley, Virginia—researched and analyzed the open and classified information flowing to London from British sources around the world. In addition, they had access to selected intelligence that the CIA shared with them. Much of the material produced by the JIB was fed into the Joint Intelligence Staff. The staff, comprised of representatives from various government departments, prepared intelligence assessments for senior Whitehall officials of the Joint Intelligence Committee. Patrick Dean of the Foreign Office, who soon became and remained a close friend, chaired the committee. (A year later, this friendship would stand us and our two countries in good stead when we spent two weeks in hell together.)

My assignment in London was to head the group of CIA analysts and researchers. I was based in the embassy building and carried the somewhat dubious title of political attaché. My office adjoined that of the CIA's chief of station. He was the very model of a modern vice admiral (retired)—tall, erect, proper, demanding, and not overly bright. I was the American representative on the Joint Intelligence Staff; he was the liaison with the Joint Intelligence Committee. As a former admiral, however, he was used to having an aide close by; I accompanied him to the committee sessions, sat behind him, and took notes.

The JIC was established in 1941 by the Chiefs of Staff in response to Churchill's strong interest in and insatiable appetite for good intelligence. The chiefs were worried that absent a JIC, Churchill would establish his own centralized intelligence body.[1]

Neither the admiral nor I participated in every meeting or in the entire proceedings of the JIC and JIS. The British had matters they did not wish to share with Americans, just as we had much information labeled "US Eyes Only." In the normal course of events, this was not awkward or troubling, but a time would soon come when it proved to be extremely awkward and gravely troubling.

The Joint Intelligence Committee met once a week and its staff met twice weekly. The meetings were held in what was then the Ministry of Defense building in the heart of Whitehall, a few steps from the Foreign Office and the Treasury, a few minutes from 10 Downing Street, near the Horse Guards Parade and the Cabinet Office.

I appeared at my first JIS meeting soon after I arrived in London. After waiting in the anteroom for several minutes (while, presumably, "UK Eyes Only" matters were being discussed), I was ushered into a gloomy, crowded, and cluttered conference room dominated by a table covered with a green, tea-stained baize cloth. A dozen or so men were slumped in chairs at the table or were haphazardly seated around the room. When I walked in, however, they all rose. To my horror, several were six inches or so taller than I. They introduced themselves, but I caught only a few names. "Howjedo. Name's ——ery." Gerry? Terry? Perry? Kerry? "Welcome. Chek Cropper, is it? No. Sorry." (Looking at a paper on the table.) "*Chet Cooper.* Anyway, commiserations and all that. Name's ——an." Brian? Ian? Evan? Either they mumbled, or spoke in what seemed to be a foreign tongue. Perhaps, I thought, because of the secret nature of their jobs, they were forbidden to reveal their names.

The subject at issue at the moment was Kenya, still then a British colony, where, I learned, a nasty anti-British insurrection was gathering steam. It quickly became apparent that this was of concern primarily to the army, the Colonial Office, and MI5 (the internal security agency). The owlish-looking man next to me (who mumbled "economist, JIB" when we were introduced) was thoughtfully absorbed in a Greek pentameter he was composing. The navy commander on my other side was dozing. (I discovered later that he commuted every day from Portsmouth.)

My own reverie was interrupted by the Foreign Office man. "Chet—may I call you Chet?—can you tell us what our friends at the agency think about this?" I started to point out that Kenya was low on our list of concerns when the door flew open and someone shouted, "240 for 60!" I heard cheers and groans. The intruder slammed the door behind him.

I barely had a chance to make my profound contribution with regard to Kenya when there was a gentle knock on the door. The navy officer stirred himself, opened the door, and happily announced, "Elevenses!" Tea and biscuits were passed around. And then, once again, the door swung open and the mysterious interloper yelled, "310 for 80!"

"What's all this about?" I whispered to my scholarly neighbor.

"I'm the last person to ask," he murmured. "Probably has to do with cricket. I think there's an important match going on."

I quickly learned that my first impression of this group was completely wrong. Yes, they were laconic. Yes, cricket, elevenses, afternoon tea, and Greek pentameters were nontrivial considerations. Yes, they all spoke a version of English, if not a Bostonian's version. But, as I was soon to discover, they were bright (which was why they had been selected for the staff). They were also serious and hardworking—as I was to learn when matters at hand called for them to work a long day and well into the night. Several of them were to rise to high rank—ambassador, air marshal, colonel, admiral, senior civil servant. Long after my tour in London ended, we kept up our friendships.

*   *   *

Orah and I came to London as confirmed Anglophiles. Nothing we experienced there changed this. We spent many delightful (albeit mostly rainy) weekends in the country. We saw scores of plays and heard dozens of concerts. We collected friends, pubs, and good, inexpensive restaurants. We frequented the open-air silver markets, the auctions, the Derby, football matches, and used-book shops.

Life in London during the midfifties was not, however, all wine and roses. The thick, black fogs encountered by Sherlock Holmes seem romantic in print, but in reality were frightening and deadly. Joan would complain bitterly on Monday nights when she discovered cold, clean sheets on her bed.

The three and a half flights of stairs gave us exercise, but were otherwise a nuisance; we referred to our top floor as Mount Everest. (Once, when Orah had left her gloves in the upper reaches and asked Susan to fetch them, Susan's response was, "Mummy, I'm a person too.") The early winter darkness that enveloped England from three o'clock in the afternoon until nine o'clock the next morning would, if one let it, become depressing. And then, of course, for fifty-two weeks a year, there was the weather. Yet washing with overcoats on, being lost in fog, and our longing for the sun detracted not at all from the pleasures of that first year in London.

Orah was a splendid and wise hostess. She realized that our British friends and colleagues were still struggling with Britain's postwar economic strains and were significantly less well-off than their American opposite numbers. (For example, the salary of the chairman of the Joint Intelligence Committee, a senior Foreign Office official, was comparable to that of my secretary. Although he managed to send his two sons to Rugby, he could not afford a car. When he was knighted, he and his wife arrived at the gates of Buckingham Palace by bus.) We entertained frequently, but modestly and informally; our guests were thus able to be our hosts. Consciously or not, we laid a foundation of mutual trust, affection, and respect that, in the not-too-distant future, would serve both us and US-UK relations well.

The joyous arrival of spring in 1956 was spoiled by dark clouds forming in the Middle East. It became obvious that the congenial days, the pleasant evenings, and the enjoyable weekends were not to last. Gen. Gamal Abdul Nasser in Cairo, Anthony Eden in London, and John Foster Dulles in Washington would see to that. The special relationship between the United States and United Kingdom, between Washington and London, between the US Embassy and Whitehall, and between me and my British colleagues was about to be sorely tested.

*   *   *

In 1869 a waterway across Egypt's Isthmus of Suez was finally completed. The Suez Canal sliced a path from the city of Port Said in the north to the town of Suez in the south, a distance of one hundred miles. Amid a grand international celebration, marked in part by the premiere of Verdi's opera *Aida*, the waters of the Red Sea sloshed into the waters of the Mediterranean. It was not only an engineering triumph for Ferdinand de Lesseps, but also a geopolitical and commercial one for Benjamin Disraeli; it provided a money-saving, time-saving shortcut between the Indian subcontinent and the continents of Europe and North America. A decade earlier I had reason to appreciate this when I was counting every day that stood between me and my arrival home from Asia.

The canal, jointly owned by Britain and France, was leased by the Suez Canal Company from the Egyptian government for ninety-nine years, that is, until 1968. Although every maritime nation in the world had a consequential interest in the safe and dependable operation of the canal, Britain had a special stake; the canal was its commercial and military lifeline to India, the most precious jewel in the imperial crown. Within a year after its dedication, two-thirds of the ships passing through the canal flew the British flag.

To the British, and to the French as well, it was far from a trivial matter when Colonel Nasser, the president of Egypt, nationalized the canal on July 26, 1956. Although trouble had been brewing with Nasser for many months, his announcement came as a surprise to President Eisenhower, Prime Minister Eden,[2] and Premier Mollet.

In the mid-1950s, a tide of nationalism and anticolonialism was beginning to sweep through the so-called third world. The British Union Jack and the French Tricolor were flying from shaky flagpoles in Africa, the Middle East, and Asia. This was when the so-called neutralist nations loosely banded together as the "unaligned states" under the leadership of Tito in Yugoslavia, Nehru in India, and Nasser in the Middle East. The truth was, of course, that, except for the anti-Soviet Tito, they were neither neutral not unaligned. Rather, they were anti-Western and pro-USSR. Yet many of them successfully used the threat of even closer political, military, and economic ties with Moscow as a means of obtaining economic aid from Washington. In 1956 Nasser shoved himself well in the front of this line. (Tito was ahead of Nasser because he had genuinely split with the USSR.)

During this period, Britain's influence over many Middle Eastern states—Sudan, Iraq, Iran, Aden, Yemen, Jordan, Bahrain, and the Emirates—was on the wane. The Union Jack was becoming an increasingly rare sight in the region. Nonetheless, the American and British intelligence services continued to observe the long-established arrangement that MI5 and MI6 were primarily responsible for intelligence collection and operations in the Middle East.

By 1955, however, this arrangement was already unraveling. Secretary Dulles, on his return from the Middle East in the spring of 1953 announced, "The day when the Middle East used to relax under . . . British protection are gone. . . . We must convince the Arab states that the United States operates on a policy of its own."[3] This, despite the fact that the United States had had

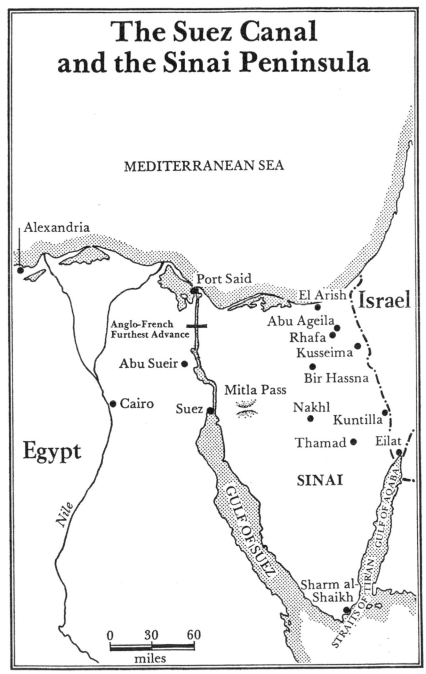

The Suez Canal and the Sinai Peninsula

Source: Selwyn Lloyd, *Suez 1956* (London: Jonathan Cape, 1978), p. xii.

little experience in dealing with Arab countries, except in the case of American oil interests in Saudi Arabia.

As 1956 dawned it was becoming increasingly evident that Dulles's views had prevailed. America's approach toward the Middle East was steadily veering away from Britain's. To some extent this reflected Washington's antipathy concerning the British (and French) attempts to retain some semblance of their colonial past, and some sympathy for nationalist yearnings. In part, too, the divergence was in recognition of Britain's declining international role and America's consciousness of the need to extend its global reach, especially in the face of Soviet attempts to seduce or subvert third world nations. And then, of course, there was the decadelong poisonous relationship between Secretary of State Dulles and Prime Minister Eden, a relationship made even more acrimonious during the Indochina conference in Geneva just a year before.

In an effort to secure some US support for Britain's eroding position in the Middle East, Eden, accompanied by his foreign minister, Selwyn Lloyd, traveled to Washington in early January 1956. He had three principal concerns: American participation in a new Baghdad Pact, organized by the pro-British prime minister of Iraq, Nuri Said; a UK-US guarantee of Israel's borders, which would protect pro-British, militarily weak Jordan from becoming engaged; and a US effort to dissuade Saudi Arabia from funding revolutionary elements in the region.

Perhaps in the light of his past experiences with our secretary of state, Eden expected little to emerge from his Washington trip. Eden actually achieved less than little: He returned to London empty-handed. The good diplomat that he was, however, he put a brave public face on the failed effort.

There was, however, one Middle East matter that both the secretary of state and the prime minister could agree on—charismatic Colonel Nasser was a personage to be reckoned with. He was a principal player on the Middle East's revolutionary stage and a vocal participant in meetings of the unaligned nations. To be sure, the brash and thrusty colonel was hardly the type John Foster Dulles would sponsor for membership in Washington's Metropolitan Club; aside from anything else, Nasser had become much too cozy with the movers and shakers of the USSR and with countries in Eastern Europe. In spite of, or because of, this, Nasser's growing influence among Arab leaders warranted modest, albeit wary, efforts to court him.

Eden, on the other hand, regarded Nasser not as a second-class nuisance worth cautious care and feeding, but as a first-class troublemaker who was undermining the already shaky foundation of Britain's influence in the Middle East.

As for Nasser, he had no illusions and not much concern about how Dulles and Eden felt about him. He had no aspirations to join Dulles's Metropolitan Club, and no desire to have a warm and fuzzy relationship with Eden. What he did have was a high card up his sleeve, and he knew the secretary and the prime minister were aware of it: He had received tempting economic, political and military overtures from the USSR. Indeed, since Nasser had already negotiated an arms deal with Moscow, he would almost certainly be able to consolidate his relationship on the economic front.

If the price was right, however, Nasser appeared willing to hold off playing the Soviet card. His price was Western funding for an enormous dam that would tame the Nile River—mitigate the seasonal floods, irrigate parched agricultural areas, and provide electrical power for Egypt's industrialization. If the Aswan High Dam could be built, it would be the largest civil works project of the century.

Engineering studies had indicated that, from a technical point of view, the project was feasible. What was required now was the funding—estimated at $400 million. (In the end, the dam cost over $1 billion.) Nasser agreed to a financial arrangement in which the World Bank, the United States, and Britain would foot the bill. If Washington and London wouldn't play, he knew Moscow was impatiently waiting. The Eisenhower administration did decide to play for at least a few innings, in an effort to keep Nasser out of Moscow's embrace.

Negotiations with the Egyptians proceeded in fits and starts through much of the spring of 1956. The World Bank was opposed to providing any money unless the United States and Britain agreed to pay for the preliminary engineering work (a total of $70 million—$55 million from the United States, $15 million from the UK) and half the cost of actual construction, a sum estimated at $200 million. (In 1956 these were nontrivial sums.) None of the funders was prepared to give Nasser a blank check; considerable haggling, threats, and counterthreats dogged every phase of the negotiations.

In the meantime, both France and Britain were facing serious problems in the Middle East, in no small part a consequence of vicious attacks over Cairo Radio. The French were engaged in an unpopular, "dirty" war in Algeria; the British were hanging on by a thread in Jordan, one of their last outposts of influence in the region. Secretary Dulles, for his part, had little interest in or sympathy for either the French or the British. He regarded their Middle East difficulties as the last gasp in their pre–World War II colonialist policies and a diversion from their vital responsibilities for the defense of Europe.

In any event, the American negotiators kept plodding along with World Bank officials and Egyptian representatives—until Nasser committed the worst of all crimes in John Foster Dulles's book. In the middle of the negotiations, Egypt recognized Communist China. Dulles abruptly broke off the talks. True to his record, he presented an infuriated Eden with a fait accompli, rather than warning him in advance. If there had been any chance of Washington maintaining a modicum of influence in Cairo, it had now gone down the drain. And, since Nasser blamed the UK as well as the United States for the breakdown in talks, Britain was in an even worse situation with regard to the Egyptians than ever. And, adding a soupçon of poison to the whole affair, Moscow came through with the funding.[4]

*   *   *

In late June, Orah, the girls, and I fled the growing tension in London for a week's holiday at a remote Norwegian fjord. We reveled in the peace and quiet, and enjoyed the water and forests surrounding our small inn. The peace and quiet were short-lived, however. A few days after our arrival, on returning to the inn from a walk, my eye caught a large, black headline on a Bergen newspaper lying on a table. It was in Norwegian, of course, but the meaning was clear: On July 26, Colonel Nasser had nationalized the Suez Canal. A hasty phone call to the duty officer at the US Embassy in London, and our holiday was over. We packed, drove to Bergen, and flew home. The next morning, there was an emergency meeting of the Joint Intelligence Committee. That afternoon, there was a special meeting of its Middle East subcommittee—which, I noted, was without its chairman, an amusing, edgy Foreign Office official. (His wealthy wife expected him home every day for lunch and a nap.) He showed up two weeks later, whining about having to abort his four-week holiday and leave his wife, two children, and nanny behind at their Swiss resort. It came as no surprise that he never became an ambassador.

The Middle East meetings, together with those of the Joint Intelligence Staff, became virtually everyday events over the next few months. Their agendas were consumed almost solely by the Egyptian problem, although, by early September, USSR–Eastern European tensions also headed the JIS trouble list.

*   *   *

Nasser's snatch of the canal was a grave political and economic blow, primarily to Britain, but also to France. Ships were soon safely guided through the canal with Egyptian and Soviet pilots and technicians—much to the astonishment of the British and French, who had expected their departure would soon lead to chaos. Egypt could now dictate the nationality of ships using the canal and collect the tolls. (Israel had long since been prevented from transiting. It was now the turn of Britain, France, and others.)

Nasser was now a hero among the revolutionary Arab governments, the members of the Soviet bloc, and such "unaligned" countries as India and Yugoslavia. Meanwhile, France's tenuous military situation in Algeria and Britain's eroding position throughout the region became further threatened thanks to the increasingly strident and hate-filled messages emanating from Cairo Radio.

To add to Eden's ill humor, and to exacerbate the chronic pain he felt in his gut due to a botched surgery, word of Nasser's act reached him during a ceremonial dinner he was hosting in honor of Nuri Said, Iraq's prime minister. The US secretary of state offered little solace to Britain's prime minister during this time of trouble. According to one senior State Department official, Dulles "saw the Suez as a dying gasp of British (and French) imperialism."[5] Dulles's indifference was especially galling to Eden and French foreign minister Christian Pineau, who were convinced that Nasser's seizure of the canal was a direct result of Washington's reneging on funding for the Aswan Dam.

Dulles made a hasty trip to London soon after July 26 to urge caution, patience, and prudence in the face of the apparent determination of Eden and Pineau to retrieve the canal. After the meeting with Dulles, Pineau recalled, "Eden detested the American Secretary of State. I will not repeat certain harsh remarks made about him, in order not to tarnish Eden's legendary reputation for courteous behavior." Pineau noted, however, that during the talks "Eden grew increasingly angry and Dulles became increasingly colder."[6]

In due course, as days folded into weeks, Eden's anger would turn into fury, and Dulles's coldness would become frigidity. And, for whatever it is worth, I would not remain untouched by either.

*   *   *

The difficulties London and Paris faced during 1956 had consequential implications for their future political and economic influence in the Middle

East. But nationalist yearnings elsewhere in the world were not put on hold while Eden and Pineau tried to sort out their relations with revolutionary Arab leaders. Far from the tensions between Britain and Egypt and between France and Algeria, the leaders of the Soviet Union, Nikolai Bulganin and Nikita Khrushchev, were also confronting rumbles of trouble. In Eastern Europe, particularly in Poland and Hungary, the Communist paradise was not serene and the natives were restless. The Kremlin became all too aware that Marshall Tito of Yugoslavia presented a nettlesome model. In 1948 he had broken the yoke of Soviet control and, afterward, managed to keep his distance from Moscow and to establish a modus vivendi with the Western powers. He demonstrated for all to see that it was possible, and even advantageous, to pursue a truly *national* Communist line.

Ironically, it was Soviet Communist Party secretary Nikita Khrushchev himself who lit the fire in Eastern Europe. His speech at the Twentieth Communist Party Congress, early in 1956, denounced Josef Stalin, a hitherto untouchable personality. Although his speech was addressed to the people within the Soviet Union, it soon kindled long-smoldering passions of anti-Soviet elements within Poland. Factory workers in Poznan went on strike in protest against low wages and high prices, and were quickly joined in a widespread movement throughout Poland opposing Soviet control and Communism generally. It took three days to beat down the bloody riots. Although there were no further outbreaks of violence for many weeks, the Polish Communist Party was seething. In mid-October, a more moderate government under a recent political prisoner, Wlalyslaw Gomulka, took over under the banner of "national Communism" and embarked on a "Polish path to socialism."

Hardly had the situation in Poland been contained when Moscow confronted a more serious outbreak of anti-Soviet, anti-Communist sentiment. Hungary had long been restive under the harsh control of Moscow-appointed officials. On October 20, emboldened by the success of the Polish uprising, a broad cross-section of Hungarian intellectuals and workers confronted the Soviet-controlled government with demands to eliminate the hated secret service, order the departure of occupying Soviet military units, return to power the nationalist political leaders who had been evicted several years before, and conduct a trial of current hard-line Moscow-appointed officials. By October 23 fighting in the streets had reached the point where Soviet troops and tanks pushed their way into Budapest to quell the unrest. Casualties were heavy among both the anti-Soviet, pronationalist Hungarian insurgents and Moscow's military and secret service forces.

After a week of violent fighting, a new Hungarian government, under a popular nationalist prime minister, managed to secure some semblance of order—at least for the moment.

Despite their preoccupation with Nasser and the fate of the canal, developments in Eastern Europe during the summer and autumn of 1956 could not be ignored by Whitehall's military, foreign affairs, and intelligence communities. The hard-pressed JIC, JIS, and JIB now had to devote scarce time and effort to tracking and analyzing the events and eventualities across the English Channel, in addition to those in the Mediterranean region.

*   *   *

For Eisenhower and Dulles, the anti-Soviet activities in Eastern Europe, Moscow's backyard, turned out to be tough competition for Washington's attention. This, after all, was the stuff of the cold war. Neither the president nor the secretary seemed to be experiencing a surge in blood pressure as a consequence of the developments in Egypt and Algeria. (They didn't have to deal with the British intelligence community virtually every day, as I did.) They did, however, enjoy a rush of adrenaline when Bulganin and Khrushchev faced serious uprisings in Poland and Hungary. After all, a rallying cry of Eisenhower's administration, from its early days, was the "liberation of Eastern Europe." And now, in the early autumn of 1956, Eastern Europe seemed ready, anxious, and able to be liberated.

What, one may rightly ask, did the president and his advisers do when push finally came to shove in Eastern Europe? Well—they scolded the Soviets and applauded the Hungarians. Almost five decades later, there are those who still become livid when they recall how the Hungarian freedom fighters confronted Soviet tanks with sticks and stones, waiting in vain for American forces to come to their assistance. (One senior CIA official had a nervous breakdown as a result.) So much for Washington's "liberation of Eastern Europe."

One explanation for Dulles's cautious approach toward Egypt's bellicose behavior and the Polish and Hungarian uprisings was the presidential election scheduled for November 1956. From the onset of that summer, Ike's reelection prospects played an important role in virtually every consequential decision faced by the White House. (Does this remind you of the summer of 2004?) According to the Republicans, it was only under a Democratic administration that America went to war. Thus: World War I under Woodrow Wilson, World War II under Franklin Roosevelt, and Korea under Harry

Truman. The last thing Eisenhower and Dulles wanted was for the United States to be fighting a war in the Middle East or Europe, and certainly not in both, on the eve of Election Day. And so, despite Dulles's calls for stout resistance against "international Communism," he was content during the latter half of 1956 to stand there, rather than do something.

*   *   *

Whether for domestic, political, or loftier concerns, Dulles obsessively urged diplomacy, negotiation, compromise, concession, or delay as the British and French became increasingly anxious to face up, militarily if necessary, to Nasser. Each time London and Paris displayed impatience and frustration about lack of progress in resolving the canal situation, Washington came up with another pale, feckless, time-consuming proposal to resolve the issue by nonmilitary means. Some of Dulles's ideas were dead on arrival; a few seemed promising but turned out to be too little, too late. Nonetheless, Eden, who apparently had lost the energy to fight Dulles off, agreed to give most of the American ideas at least a half-hearted try. Eventually, however, impatience and frustration won the day, and he and Pineau decided to take matters into their own hands.

It was my lot to explain and defend, as best I could, the stream of advice, admonitions, proposals, and cautionary tales emanating from Washington. I did what I could in the face of growing restlessness and skepticism on the part of my associates on the senior-level Joint Intelligence Committee and their staff. In the meantime, my boss, the admiral, had, with an exquisite sense of timing, headed off to Hawaii on an extended vacation. I was left flying solo.

July and August are traditional vacation periods in England, as elsewhere. Except for tourists, London is an empty city during the summer. Nonetheless, it seemed odd to me that the lieutenant commander, lieutenant colonel, and wing commander, together with an economist and a communication intelligence expert on the Joint Intelligence Staff, should have relinquished their places to more junior representatives at such a delicate time. It also seemed strange that, ten days or so later, they all reappeared, remarkably pale and drawn for folk who had been "on holiday." I had a sneaky feeling that, far from lolling in the South of France, my British colleagues had been slaving away in some cloistered building analyzing photographs of airbases, landing beaches, and army depots. It was not altogether improbable that they were also working up invasion scenarios and identifying bombing targets in—guess where. I confided those suspicions to my Washington associates, and, presumably, these morsels became ingredients in the simmering intelligence stewpot.

There were, in fact, several more tangible indications that military action against Egypt was in the offing. Eden informed Parliament, just as the members were leaving for their summer recess, that his government was making military plans "as a precautionary measure." He warned that he would probably soon be calling up the reserves. It was no secret that high-ranking French army and navy officers were bustling back and forth across the channel. On August 8, plans for Operation Musketeer, a joint British-French attack on Egypt, were completed.

The following days were tense and hectic. Dulles and several senior State Department officials flew to London to meet with the British and high officials of those nations (except Egypt) originally involved in the nineteenth-century international convention governing the operation of the Suez Canal. Dulles busily lobbied against robust action. Charles "Chip" Bohlen, a former US ambassador to Moscow, who came to London to meet with the Russian participants, described the secretary's behavior as "too slick—in the manner of a Wall Street lawyer."[7]

The Suez Users Conference adjourned on August 23, having churned up much rhetoric but little that was meaningful. The participants agreed that representatives of five participating countries (including a middle-grade State Department officer) would proceed to Cairo to convince Nasser to hand back the canal—or else. They went. They failed. The enterprise, which had little promise in any case, was not helped when Eisenhower told the press that the United States had no intention of using force to settle the canal issue. In effect, then, there would be no "or else." Eisenhower underlined this with a veiled warning to Eden: "I am afraid, Anthony, that from this point onward, our views on this situation diverge. . . . I must tell you frankly that American public opinion flatly rejects the thought of using force. . . . We must put our faith in the process . . . to bring Nasser peacefully to accept the solution proposed in a resolution following the international meeting in London."[8]

Dulles went off to his retreat on Lake Ontario over Labor Day weekend. He emerged with yet another goofy goody for Eden: a proposal to establish a Suez Canal Users' Association comprising a panoply of maritime nations, including Egypt. A complicated formula involving the frequency and tonnage of national shipping through the canal would determine the toll structure. The revenues would be divided among Egypt, Britain, and France. The acronym for the association, SCUA, was soon transformed to "Screw ya" by my irreverent colleagues in Whitehall.

At the SCUA planning conference in London, I became more familiar with Ethiopian, Iranian, and Danish annual shipments through the canal than I had ever thought or hoped I would be, or wanted to be. The time-consuming, complex exercise was, of course, yet another Dulles ploy to delay British-French military action, at least until after the presidential election in November.

I had begun to look forward with less and less joy to my daily sessions with the British. There was no more informal banter, no more small talk. My attendance at the JIC and JIS consisted solely of their quest for information and my providing inconsequential bits. Since British intelligence sources in the Middle East had been drying up week by week, I tried to squeeze as much useful information out of the CIA, the State Department, and the National Security Council as they were willing to share (which, as September marched on, proved to be less and less).

Since Washington was five hours behind London, and with developments in the Middle East and Eastern Europe heating up, my days and weeks seemed to stretch out to infinity. The JIC met at 10:00 AM (5:00 AM Washington time), and the workday at CIA Headquarters now came to a close at 7:00 or 8:00 PM (12:00 or 1:00 AM in London). Saturdays became much like Wednesdays. Sundays were spent at the embassy reading and sending telegrams.

Duty officers at the CIA and the Department of State seemed anxious to hear my voice virtually every night—that is to say, 8:00 or 9:00 PM in Washington, 1:00 or 2:00 AM in London. A typical exchange between me and the CIA communications officer on the night shift at the embassy went very much like this:

"Mr. Cooper."

Grunt, yawn, cough. "Yes."

"Hate to wake you again, but I've got an urgent top secret message."

"*Really* urgent?"

"It *says* urgent."

"Can it wait for a few hours?"

"Dunno. I can't make that decision. Your call."

Grumble. Curses. "OK. I'll be there in half an hour."

The odds were 3 to 1 that the message could have waited until the morning, but Peter was right; it was my call, not his. I dashed to the embassy, worried that I truly needed to see it at dawn instead of later in the morning. By mid-September, the odds decreased to about 2 to 1; things were getting dicey in Washington, London, Paris, Cairo, and Moscow.

*   *   *

The Middle East situation in itself was enough to keep Eden and much of Whitehall on edge during August and September, but there were also a few other matters that in more normal times would have, alone, warranted considerable attention. In Malaya, an English colony for three-quarters of a century, British troops were waging a difficult "police action" against Communist guerrillas. By the late summer of 1956, several years into the insurgency, thousands of British troops were still hacking through the jungles in pursuit of the elusive Communist-supported enemy.

Meanwhile, on the island of Cyprus, also an English colony of long standing, Greek Cypriots, supported by the government in Athens, were conducting a costly campaign to wrest control of the island from their Turkish neighbors and the British colonial government.

In Malaya the situation was pretty much being dealt with by British civil and military officials in Singapore and Kuala Lumpur. In Cyprus, however, London itself was carrying the burden of the insurgency. Complicating the issue for the Colonial Office, Foreign Office, Defense Ministry, and counter-intelligence folk in MI5 was the energetic, charismatic, and politically astute Archbishop Makarios (aka "Black Mac" within the Joint Intelligence Staff). Makarios was the spiritual and political leader of the Greek Orthodox Church on Cyprus.

Aside from his influence on Cyprus and in Athens, Makarios was an active charter member of the unaligned nations club. Further adding to his qualifications as a member of Whitehall's most-hated list was his influence over the thousands of Greek Cypriots living in England. They were at his beck and call for noisy, crowded anti-British, pro-Cyprus-for-the-Greeks demonstrations in Hyde Park and Trafalgar Square.

In March 1956 Her Majesty's government decided that it had had enough. Makarios was shipped off for an involuntary, open-ended vacation to the remote Seychelle Islands in the Indian Ocean. This, of course, only served to add reinforcements and additional enthusiasm to the almost weekly rough-and-tumble gatherings in the heart of London. It was also an unpopular move in Washington, sensitive to the mood of America's large Greek community. And so it added one more cross to those Anthony Eden would have to bear before his horrific year, 1956, could come to a close.

*   *   *

It was a portentous shake of the dice that brought John Foster Dulles and Anthony Eden onto center stage for two of the most dramatic developments of the 1950s.

The Indochina Conference of 1954, which Eden cochaired (with Soviet apparatchik Molotov) and which Dulles regarded as a spectator sport, shoved France off the world stage and marked the beginning of the United States' dolorous experience in Vietnam. The Suez Canal crisis of 1956, which Eden gamely but fecklessly tried to manage and in which Dulles mischievously meddled, provided proof positive that Britain had become a supporting player and pushed America, willingly or not, into the marathon nightmare of Middle East politics.

Perhaps two other men with two different temperaments could have obtained a less troublesome arrangement in Indochina and a more satisfying settlement of the Suez Canal affair. But perhaps not. Eden was laboring under the shadow of Winston Churchill and his stubborn refusal to give up the prime minister's post; Dulles was, together with Dwight Eisenhower, obsessed with an anti-Communist mindset and, later, with the 1956 election campaign.

But this is idle speculation. The game was played with the cards already dealt. And Eden was Eden and Dulles was Dulles; fate dictated that the two never would or could agree. In the end, it was Eden—not Dulles, or Pineau, or Ben-Gurion, or Nasser—who paid the price of Suez 1956.

Anthony Eden's curriculum vitae was impressive: an ancient, upper-class family; Eton College; the Military Cross (Britain's second-highest decoration for valor) in World War I; a good record at Oxford, and, later, in Parliament. From 1935 to 1938 he served (at the ripe old age of thirty-eight!) as foreign minister, again from 1940 to 1945 in Churchill's War Cabinet (where he worked closely with both Gen. Dwight Eisenhower and, later in the war, with John Foster Dulles), and, then, yet again from 1951 to 1955. He achieved his ultimate ambition, the post of prime minister, when Winston Churchill finally agreed to resign in the early spring of 1955.

Eden's childhood was far from idyllic. His father was an eccentric with little concern for his several children and with a vitriolic temper he both visited on and bequeathed to his son Anthony. His mother was a greedy, albeit generous, woman, with little interest in or awareness of the harsh realities of life.

Eden had hardly passed from childhood to boyhood when, like his peers, he was packed off to preparatory school (where he was unhappy), and, then, when he barely reached his teens, to Eton College (which he found barely tolerable). By the time Eden was ready for university in 1920, his mother had squandered the family fortune.

A hint of the man to come was provided in 1913 by his tutor at Eton, who wrote to Lady Eden that Anthony was "rather volatile in disposition." Several months later, the tutor reported that Anthony "has quite ceased to be petulant and childish . . . a certain heedlessness and lack of restraint . . . seems to be becoming a thing of the past . . . and he has grown out of his tantrums."[9]

When war broke in the summer of 1914, Eden, at seventeen, was too young to join up. In any case, his poor eyesight would have precluded his enlistment. A year later, however, by dint of family connections and fiddling with the eyesight test, Eden became a second lieutenant in the King's Royal Rifle Corps. He had what the British call "a good war," and was mustered out in 1919.

After the war, Eden read Oriental languages at Christ Church, Oxford. The extent to which this prepared him for a life in politics may be a matter for debate, but an Oxford or Cambridge education in almost any field was a necessary, if not sufficient, requirement for election to Parliament on the conservative ticket. Eden did well in Commons and enjoyed politics.

My first exposure to Eden was in the spring of 1954 in Geneva. Even then, he was a legendary figure. I had read about him in the context of his role as Churchill's wartime foreign secretary and his close relationship with Eisenhower. What I was not aware of then, however, was that behind the smooth, impeccably dressed and coiffed surface (Orah once asked me to get the name of his tailor and barber), there was a prima donna and a workaholic; someone with no hobbies except for his art collection; a man unable to make small talk and without a sense of humor.

In Geneva, as I watched him deal with the Communist participants on the one hand and John Foster Dulles on the other, I wondered how he maintained his poise and contained his temper. The answer, I soon realized, was "at high personal cost and with difficulty." The fact was that Anthony Eden was a sick man. Barely a year before the Indochina meeting convened, in April 1953, he had made an emergency trip to Boston where he underwent a complicated and not entirely successful gallbladder operation.[10] The aftermath of this surgery, including the drugs he had to take, was to plague Eden for the rest of his life. Surely the accumulation of stresses—Egypt, Jordan, Malaya, Cyprus—which was becoming thornier and more intense each day during the spring and summer of 1956 contributed to a flare-up of his gallbladder problem. In October, during the peak of the Suez crisis, he was taken ill with a menacingly high fever. Although he was back at Downing Street within a few days, his colleagues and subordinates told me later that they had become increasingly aware of a personality change.

*   *   *

Churchill was a tough act for Eden to follow when he finally moved into 10 Downing Street; Eden lacked Winston's oratorical skills, colorful persona, resilience—and, it would turn out, his strategic insights. Eden himself must have been aware of this, but, nevertheless, regarded Churchill as his mentor and model. Thus, throughout the Suez crisis, Eden delegated little to Foreign Secretary Selwyn Lloyd or to his defense minister, Antony Head; he was a micromanager—even worse, an ill, uncertain, and indecisive micromanager.

In any event, it was into the boiling pot of Eden-Dulles and Eden-Nasser animosity, Eden's failing health, British public distrust, and America's opposition to Britain's Cyprus and Suez policies that Dulles (himself ailing) had added his SCUA brainstorm in early September. For the next four weeks, there was a cascade of meetings; tête-à-têtes; secret and public visits between and among the United Nations, Americans, British, and French; and suggestions, additions, and revisions to the original, hastily prepared SCUA draft. Somehow, however, there was an air of unreality about the whole enterprise—much motion, but little progress. There was considerable suspicion among many Americans, including the US ambassador (Winthrop Aldrich) and the political attaché (me), that, behind the curtain of bustle and rhetoric, the real show—one involving bombs and bullets rather than pens and paper—was in its final rehearsal.

On the evening of Saturday, October 27, Aldrich confronted Foreign Minister Selwyn Lloyd at a Foreign Office cocktail party. Aldrich murmured that he had heard rumors of British military movements. Were the British about to undertake an attack on Egypt? Lloyd assured Aldrich that the British were not about to undertake an attack on Egypt. Lloyd lied.

On the next day, the Coopers had a date with Pat Dean, chairman of the Joint Intelligence Committee, his wife, Patricia, and their two small sons. We were to drive into the country for a walk and a picnic. Since the Deans had no car, we would all pile into our commodious Chevrolet—a feat we had often accomplished. At nine o'clock that morning, just as we were preparing to pick up the Deans, Pat called to say they had to cancel the outing. He had an urgent appointment at 10 o'clock with Foreign Secretary Lloyd. He sounded so agitated that I thought that fighting had broken out in Hungary. I dashed over to the embassy to go over the incoming telegrams. There was nothing especially alarming, just the on-again, off-again stuff I had been reading all week.

Soon after I returned home there was another call from Pat. Could we go for an abbreviated jaunt—to Greenwich, say? We set off about noon. Pat was grim and troubled.

"What's up?" I asked. "The Hungarian situation seems fairly quiet, and Lloyd assured Aldrich last night that Eden wasn't about to go to war."

Pat was silent for a minute. Then he grasped my knee. "Look, the problem isn't with Hungary. But you and I are in for a difficult time. Let's be as straight with each other as we can!" End of conversation.

We had a cheerless afternoon—aside from Dean's mood, it was raining, as usual. As soon as I brought the Deans home and then delivered Orah and the girls, I rushed back to the embassy and sent an urgent telegram to Washington. In effect, it related the events of that morning and afternoon, Dean's sudden meeting with Lloyd, his agitated behavior, and his words of foreboding. I promised to pursue the matter early the next morning.

If I had been smart, I would have added another sentence to this message: "Seems clear British/French military action imminent." But I wasn't smart; I had simply assumed that the implications of my message would be clear. The missing final sentence has haunted me ever since.

I arrived at the embassy early Monday morning. My message apparently had not rung any alarm bells in Washington; there were no middle-of-the-night telephone calls. My telegram must have reached the CIA and the State Department about noon on Sunday. Unless the right person happened to see it, there was nothing in it to warrant special attention on a Sunday.

I called Dean, but he was "at a meeting" and would be tied up all day. So was everyone else on my MI6, JIC, JIS, and Foreign Office phone lists. No one on the embassy staff seemed aware of anything untoward happening. In Hungary, Soviet troops were reported to have withdrawn from Budapest. The Polish Communist Party had declared its support for the Hungarians. Soothing noises were coming out of the Kremlin. Eastern Europe seemed ominously quiet. But dark clouds were gathering elsewhere.

Reports started to come in around noon of Israeli attacks, first against Jordan (which proved to be a feint) and then into Sinai, threatening the Suez Canal. Eisenhower, Dulles, and lesser lights in Washington were furious at the Israelis, in general, and Prime Minister David Ben-Gurion, in particular. A surprise attack against Egypt would have been difficult for them to swallow in the midst of tenuous relations with London and the tension in Hungary. But to launch such attacks one week before the presidential election!

Ike was in Richmond, Virginia, where he was making a campaign speech, but he returned to Washington in a hurry. At a hastily called National Security Council meeting, he could barely contain his anger. "All right,

Foster," he growled to Dulles, "you tell 'em [the Israelis] that, goddamn it, we're going to apply sanctions, we're going to the United Nations, we're going to do everything that there is so we can stop this thing."[11]

The problem, as would soon be evident, was that Eisenhower was threatening the wrong country. The president and the secretary (to say nothing of peons such as I) did not realize that Monday morning that the British and French had, for several days, been conspiring, with Israeli participation, to implement a foolish, threadbare, and, in the end, costly scam.

NOTES

1. David Stafford, *Churchill and Secret Service* (London: John Murray, 1997), p. 190.

2. Anthony Eden, after waiting in the wings for Winston Churchill to resign, had finally made it to 10 Downing Street in the spring of 1955.

3. John Foster Dulles Papers, Princeton University Library, Princeton, New Jersey.

4. For more details on the Aswam Dam debacle, see Chester L. Cooper, *The Lion's Last Roar: Suez 1956* (New York: Harper & Row, 1978), pp. 83–101.

5. Charles E. Bohlen, *Witness to History: 1929–1969* (New York: W. W. Norton, 1973), pp. 504–505.

6. Christian Pineau, *1956/Suez* (Paris: Editions Robert Laffort, 1976), pp. 92, 95.

7. Bohlen, *Witness to History*, p. 430.

8. Dwight D. Eisenhower, *The White House Years: Waging Peace, 1956–61* (Garden City, NY: Doubleday, 1965), pp. 664–65.

9. Robert Rhodes James, *Anthony Eden, A Biography* (New York: McGraw-Hill, 1987), p. 25.

10. Anthony Eden, *Full Circle: The Memoirs of Anthony Eden* (Boston: Houghton Mifflin, 1960), pp. 56–57.

11. Townsend Hoopes, *The Devil and John Foster Dulles* (Boston: Little, Brown, 1973), p. 374.

8

THE JUNGLE OF EDEN

ABOUT THE AMERICAN-BRITISH "SPECIAL RELATIONSHIP"

Much has been said and written about the "special relationship" between the United States and Britain. The truth of the matter is that the relationship goes back to 1776, and it has not always been so "special." By the early nineteenth century, our two countries had been at war with one another on two occasions. And as this chapter reveals, Washington virtually broke relations with London in 1956 over the Suez Canal.

In 1962, US-Anglo relations again became chilly. President Kennedy canceled a costly American ballistic missile system, Skybolt, which was under development and which had been promised to the British. His decision had consequential military and political implications for Her Majesty's government. Relations between Washington and London remained cool for many months.

Four years later President Johnson was barely speaking to Prime Minister Wilson, whose government (perhaps in response to the Suez and Skybolt affairs) refused to lend military support to the US effort in Vietnam.

Despite all this the relationship has remained intact; the bonds between the two countries had become too many and too strong to sever.

My own relationship with my British friends and colleagues has stood the test of personal, professional, and national stress. It has indeed been "special."

*   *   *

T he choreography of Britain's Grab-Back-Suez campaign in the summer and autumn of 1956 was designed to end with Nasser's downfall and Egypt's surrender of the canal. It involved, first, a quick solo turn by Israel and, then, a dazzling pas de deux by Britain and France. The plan was agreed upon in two tense, secret meetings held in obscure surroundings outside of Paris during the week of October 21. The mood music there was somber—cellos, rather than piccolos, carried the theme.[1]

According to Gen. Moshe Dayan, chief of staff of the Israeli Defense Forces, who was present at the definitive first session, the discussion among the three partners in the enterprise was far from cordial: "Britain's Foreign Minister [Selwyn Lloyd] may well have been a friendly man. . . . If so, he showed near genius in concealing those virtues. His manner could not have been more antagonistic. His whole demeanor expressed distaste—for the place, the company, and the topic. His opening remarks suggested the tactics of a customer bargaining with extortionate merchants."[2]

In his own version, Lloyd points out that "a possible explanation of this rather unflattering account is that Dayan had been working at high pressure and very closely with the French. . . . Perhaps he was irritated by what he thought was my pretended ignorance . . . I was not aware that . . . France and Israel were virtually allies in an imminent offensive against Egypt." Lloyd goes on to note that Ben-Gurion, who was also present at the meeting, said "I treated him like a subordinate. No doubt we were both tired."[3]

Patrick Dean, my Foreign Office friend, who had been unaware of the first meeting, was dispatched to Paris together with a midlevel colleague later that week to work out the final arrangements for the Israeli attack and the subsequent events. He later told me that it was a "miserable experience." By all accounts, the two gatherings were hardly fun parties for any of the participants.

*   *   *

The plot that emerged (and it *was* a plot, in both senses of the term) involved, first, an Israeli military feint at Jordan followed by a full-scale attack on Egypt through the Sinai desert. The British and French would immediately express deep shock and righteous anger at Israel's breach of international good behavior, especially since it threatened their already tenuous position with regard to the Suez Canal. To assure the safety of the canal, London and

Paris would order the Egyptians and Israelis to cease fire and, within twelve hours, withdraw ten miles beyond the canal. Failure to comply would result in an attack by British and French forces.

According to the plan, the Israelis would start their assault on Monday, October 29 (which they did); the British-French ultimatum would then be delivered on the thirtieth (which it was) and would expire on the thirty-first (which, in fact, it did not). Since it soon turned out that the Israelis had previously agreed to stop their thrust into Sinai well before they reached the canal, it did not take a genius to conclude that the whole affair was a clumsy, transparent fraud.

The Israeli attack and the devious goings-on in London aside, President Eisenhower and Secretary Dulles were facing several thorny international challenges just days before the presidential election. In Hungary, the streets of Budapest were swarming with crowds calling for the removal of all Russian troops and the ouster of Moscow's puppet government. In Algeria, the situation had come to a boil following the French kidnapping and imprisonment of the rebel leaders. In France, moderates and leftists who had been advocating a conciliatory, rather than a confrontational, approach to the Algerian uprising were demonstrating against the government.

Yet another, and perhaps more influential, factor was in play that autumn: four of the principal players in the Suez affair were ill. Eden's unfortunate surgery gave him constant, severe pain; Ben-Gurion had a chronic case of the flu; Eisenhower had recently recovered from a heart attack and was troubled with ileitis; Dulles was haunted by the specter of cancer. This was hardly a formula for a careful, thoughtful diplomatic resolution to a set of serious, complex problems.

*   *   *

Monday, October 29, 1956, started out quietly enough, but Pat Dean's Sunday warning quickly became a reality. As the hours ticked by, the day became raucous and frenetic. Adlai Stevenson, the Democratic candidate for president, accused his opponent Eisenhower of telling "less than the truth" about the exploding situation in the Middle East. This, of course, made Ike even more furious with the Israelis (and, soon, with the British and French). Meanwhile, Washington ordered the evacuation of Americans from Egypt, Israel, Jordan, and Syria.

In London, Eden summoned his angry cabinet members to inform them of the ultimatum scheme that had been cobbled up during the previous week.

High-ranking civil servants and military officers felt betrayed, since few of them had been told of the transpiring developments. Among those in the know were only a handful among the Joint Intelligence Committee: Pat Dean, of course; the head of MI6; the director of the GCHQ; and one or two others. (I had made it my business to learn all this because, six weeks or so later, I was summoned to Washington to explain why it was that *I* did not know. Of course, I *almost* knew, but that did not count.)

By noon on Monday morning my embassy colleagues and I were desperately and fruitlessly trying to reach anyone we knew in Whitehall. It became clear, however, that the US Embassy had been declared persona non grata. Prime Minister Eden must have decided that conversations with any member of the US Embassy would further roil the already turbulent state of affairs within his own government.

On the next day, Tuesday the thirtieth, the British and French managed to compound Washington's ill will. That morning the UN Security Council convened, but then agreed to postpone its session at the request of the British, French, and Israelis. Meanwhile, American embassy officers in London and Paris were anxiously trying to eke out some clarification of British and French intentions with regard to the UN. Their efforts produced only vague statements about their introducing a resolution accusing Israel as an aggressor.

Ambassador Aldrich met with Foreign Minister Lloyd later that morning. It was a barren session. Lloyd asked Aldrich to return in the afternoon, when, presumably, he would share some useful information. Aldrich did so, but Lloyd was in the House of Commons answering sharp questions from angry members of Parliament. A senior foreign service official handed the ambassador a copy of the ultimatum, which the ambassador had not yet seen.

The ultimatum "requested" Israel to cease "all warlike action on land, sea and air forthwith," and to "withdraw all military forces to a distance ten miles east of the Canal." Egypt was "requested" to cease hostilities and to withdraw its forces from the neighborhood of the canal, and to accept the temporary occupation by Anglo-French forces of key positions along the canal at Port Said, Ismailia, and Suez. Israel and Egypt were given twelve hours to comply. Otherwise, "United Kingdom and French forces will intervene in whatever strength may be necessary to secure compliance."[4]

Later that day, the British chargé d'affaires in Washington (the British ambassador had returned to London to prepare for another assignment) and the French ambassador called on Dulles with messages to Eisenhower from

Prime Minister Eden and Premier Mollet, explaining why the United States had not been consulted, or even informed, in advance. Eden's note was particularly defensive: "My first instinct would have been to ask you to associate yourself and your country with this declaration. But I know the constitutional and other difficulties in which you are placed. . . . It would help . . . very much if you found it possible [to approve of] what we have done, at least in general terms."[5] In his memoirs, Eden notes that Eisenhower's response "expressed his disquiet."[6] In fact, "disquiet" was an extremely mild description of the tone of Ike's message.

Time ran out for Egypt early Wednesday morning. (Israel had, by now, achieved its objectives in Sinai and was already "in compliance.") Egyptian forces were still in position along the canal. By that afternoon, British and French planes started bombing Egyptian airfields. Someone who saw Secretary Dulles on Wednesday evening described him as "almost totally exhausted, ashen-gray, heavy-lidded, shaking his head in glazed disbelief."[7] After all his vigorous, albeit feckless, efforts to avoid war in the Middle East, Dulles must, indeed, have been in anguish. Compounding his emotional reaction was the fact that cancer as well as armed conflict was on the march.

Eisenhower, too, was shaken. "Bombs, by God! . . . Why is he [Eden] doing this to me?" he exclaimed.[8]

Washington revealed its anger not only in words, but also in action. Ambassador Aldrich was unceremoniously summoned home and the London embassy was instructed to cut off contact with Whitehall. In effect, the United States broke its relations with the United Kingdom—the first time since the War of 1812.

On that Wednesday I was summoned by Minister Walworth Barbour. A rotund and hearty veteran foreign service officer, he was second in command at the embassy. The mood in his office was one of gloom and despair. His ample bulk was slumped deep in his chair; he looked grim, depressed, and tired. He waved me to a seat near his desk. The State Department and CIA, he said, had agreed that the US-UK intelligence relationship was too firmly established and too important to jeopardize, especially at a time of crisis in both the Middle East and Eastern Europe. On that account, I was to continue—even increase—my contacts with the British intelligence community. Moreover, I would be the channel to Whitehall for economic and political matters too important and urgent to wait until normal relations between Washington and London were restored.

"Keep in close touch. Let's try to see each other every day. And good luck," he said as we solemnly shook hands.

*   *   *

When I told Pat Dean about my conversation with Barbour, he made it clear that I would be just as welcome at the JIC's formal and informal meetings as I had been before. Meanwhile, he would help me maneuver my way through unfamiliar sections of the Foreign Office if I had to contact anyone in connection with nonintelligence matters.

At the Joint Intelligence Committee meeting the next day, Thursday, I learned that several committee members, all senior officials, had been left in the dark until the announcement of the ultimatum. They were embarrassed by and angry about what had been done, and how it was done. Sir Kenneth Strong, director of the Joint Intelligence Board, was livid. He had been General Eisenhower's intelligence officer during World War II; the sanctity of Anglo-American relations was one of his three high priorities. (The others were his health and his financial portfolio.) Other committee members, those who had been in on the secret as well as those who hadn't, made it clear that my presence (or at least an American presence) would be essential and welcome in the time ahead.

In the days to come, the problems I would have would not be so much with the British in London as with my bosses, colleagues, and subordinates in Washington. There had been a perceptible (perceptible to the British, I was sure, as well as to me) drying-up of valuable intelligence on the Middle East well before October 29. Sharing information on Eastern Europe would continue to be permissible, but there would be precious little I would be able to contribute to the one issue that, to the British, was then the most troubling. Of course, they, too, were under constraints about sharing certain information with the Americans. The time I spent waiting in the anteroom of the JIC conference room until their British-eyes-only business had been discussed grew longer each morning.

One matter that my friends kept to themselves was of keen interest to Washington: When were the British going to move from their airfield bombing campaign (which soon involved blasting every conceivable landing strip throughout Egypt) and move forward with their announced objectives: removing Nasser, destroying Cairo Radio, and taking back the Suez Canal? Although I hadn't yet received confirmation from Washington, I was sure that, despite Dulles's finger-wagging and scolding, and Washington's demand for a cease-fire, there would be great relief if the British quickly accomplished their goals. In moments of frustration and in fits of indiscretion, I made these views known to whoever, American or British, was within earshot.

In the meantime, all was not quiet on other fronts. Eden was faced with a sullen cabinet and a furious and noisy House of Commons. The mass demonstrations outside 10 Downing Street revealed deep divisions among the British public that were said to rival those during the Boer War more than a half century before.

*   *   *

Anti-American sentiment ran high as well during those hectic days. My two daughters professed to have "headaches" and begged not to be sent to school, where they were the only American children. (They went anyway.) Gasoline rationing (I think the equivalent of five gallons per car per week) was introduced. When I went to a gas station, however, I was given only one gallon—"Here's enough to get you home. That's it." Dinner parties with British or American expatriate friends were unpleasant. Nonetheless, my relations with the intelligence community remained amiable and somewhat useful, if guarded.

By Friday, November 2, forty-eight hours after the ultimatum had expired, British air bombing was continuing, but there were reports from Cyprus of troops boarding ships and of landing craft heading toward the Egyptian coast. Warlike noises from the British-French command there implied that landings were imminent. In fact, however, they turned out to be nowhere near imminent. After a Joint Intelligence Staff meeting that Friday, I accosted my lieutenant colonel friend: "Where the hell are the troops?"

He beckoned me to a curtain hanging on the wall. Sweeping it aside, he pointed to a map of the Mediterranean where twenty or so red and blue pins were arranged in a jagged line. "There!" he snorted, "still in the middle of the bloody Med!" What he didn't say, but what another officer did, was that the landing force had not yet been given orders on where and when to land. What neither said, but what I was told later, was that Lord Mountbatten, the head of the Royal Navy, was in strong disagreement with Eden and was in no hurry for the convoys to reach Egypt.

At dawn on Saturday morning, the phone rang and once more I tried to avoid getting out of bed and dashing to Grosvenor Square. But when the man from the communications room said I was to dash to the embassy and call the CIA over a secure phone, there were no arguments. The caller turned out to be an irate Bob Amory. "I saw your cable about the troopships. What in God's name are your pals doing? Tell them to either implement the US-UN call for a cease-fire or go ahead with the goddamn invasion. Either way, we'll back them up. But tell them to do one or the other fast. What we can't stand is their goddamn hesitation waltz while Hungary is burning!"

Finally, I had confirmation of my own, unofficial, unauthorized, and indiscreet just-get-on-with-it admonitions. When I arrived at the Ministry of Defense later that morning, I asked the friendly JIC gatekeeper, a lady with a big smile and big ankles, to inform Chairman Dean that I had something important I'd like to share. Could he squeeze me in as soon as he could?

I grinned (probably my first grin, smile, or chuckle in several days) as I announced, "Gentlemen, you have friends in Washington." I gave them Amory's message, emphasizing the prospect of at least implicit US support if they launched an invasion soon. It was not beneath me to remind them that I had been telling them this for the past two days. I was not sure of the reaction I expected from the JIC members. What I did get were solemn nods and glum silence.

When the meeting adjourned, the lieutenant colonel, who had been taking notes in the back of the room, whispered that landings and parachute drops were not scheduled until Monday, November 5. I asked him if the British planners had realized that November 5 was the day before Election Day in America, and that Britain's old friend Ike would be more furious than ever.

That Saturday afternoon, the British and French rejected the UN's demand for a cease-fire, which had originally been called for by the United States and, in a rare moment of solidarity, was strongly supported by the Soviet Union. Eden, in a nationwide speech, referred to the impending British-French invasion as a "police action" and—a new element in his position—said that "if the United Nations would take over the police action, we would welcome it."9

That evening, Pat Dean explained the JIC's disappointing reaction to Amory's telephone call. They were disheartened and frustrated by the crawling pace of the invasion force, and troubled by the UN's demand for an immediate cease-fire. While they appreciated and understood the import of Amory's message, they realized it would have little or no impact when they transmitted it to 10 Downing Street. Eden seemed unable to make a decision as to whether or not to continue the action against Egypt. Indeed, in the face of the demonstrations in London, the anger in Washington, and bellicose noises coming from Moscow, the prime minister had evidently lost his nerve.

Whether the feeling within the JIC was an accurate reading of Downing Street or not, Eden obviously was feeling isolated, ill, and persecuted. According to his biographer, "[T]he price [of the Suez crisis] in fatigue, self-control and nervous tension was gradually being exacted. . . . The emotional link between Eden's temperament and his eventual physical collapse . . . must have been of considerable significance."[10]

David Cornwell (aka John le Carré) told me several years later that when he was a master at Eton College his bed-sitting-room overlooked the college courtyard leading up to the main entrance. On two or three occasions during this stressful week, he noticed the prime minister emerging from his car around midnight. Eden had come to sit at the feet of his old public school tutor, now retired but still in residence at Eton, to seek his solace and support.

*   *   *

Bob Amory's message was on the mark: While Britain was fiddling, Hungary was burning. I was permitted to share with the British CIA reports that Soviet army units were moving through Poland into East Germany; in Budapest, Soviet tanks were fighting off unarmed groups of desperate protesters; in Romania and Bulgaria, the governments announced their support for Soviet actions in Hungary and beefed up their own internal security arrangements.

In the midst of this horrific period, some State Department officers, living in their own confined world of Foggy Bottom, contacted the embassy about issues they thought should be raised with the Foreign Office and which, in their view, could not wait for a more propitious moment. Barbour put several of these matters on hold, but a few fell through the cracks. It was my lot, according to Barbour's earlier instructions, to deal with them. One had to do with US landing rights at Heathrow Airport, and, in a frosty but polite discussion, Mr. Heathrow Landing Rights and I agreed to postpone a final decision for a month or so. Another was a "démarche" I was told to deliver to the Cyprus desk. An irate midlevel State Department officer demanded to know when the British intended to release Archbishop Makarios from his house arrest in the Seychelles. This involved a less onerous exchange, largely because I had met Mr. Cyprus socially on several occasions. "Tell your chums on the Greek desk at State, Chet," he told me over a cup of coffee, "that we'll have to release the archbishop fairly soon from the Seychelles because we're running out of small boys." The hard part of that errand was to compose a telegram to Washington that would convey the spirit, but not the substance, of our conversation.

While the British and French were shilly-shallying, the Israelis had not been idle. They were close to capturing the Egyptian base that menaced Israeli shipping to and from the port of Eilat. Ben-Gurion made it clear that

Israeli forces would pull out of Sinai only if the Arab countries halted their terrorist attacks (lots of luck!), and if Israel were free to pass through the Suez Canal and the Gulf of Aqaba.

On Sunday, November 4, there was a desperate, poignant plea from Budapest for Western paratroopers to engage attacking Soviet troops: "For the sake of God and Freedom, help Hungary."[11] But the United States, Britain, and France had tuned out the Hungarian uprising; their attention was fixed elsewhere. Whether any of the three would have responded to Hungary's cry for help if Suez had not been the focus of their attention is, in my view, doubtful; with regard to Eastern Europe, each of these countries had been long on rhetoric, but short on action.

Eisenhower and Dulles deserve their share of criticism. There is evidence that the Hungarians had been told that American help would be forthcoming; several CIA officers, who, soon after, became dispirited and distraught, certainly understood that to be the case. But no help came, and, despite John Foster Dulles's blustering and strident calls for "the liberation of Eastern Europe," the door to freedom was slammed shut for another thirty years. It is no small irony that on that tragic day for Hungary, the secretary faced his own crisis: He was rushed to the hospital for cancer surgery.

Hungary was all but forgotten in the fervor of anti-Eden outbursts on that Sunday. Twenty thousand angry, jeering people crowded into Hyde Park. Other protests were being held throughout Britain. I walked from the embassy across Grosvenor Square toward the park to observe a march that was heading toward Downing Street. A much smaller, pro-Eden, pro-Suez demonstration was assembling nearby; masses of policemen were preventing the two groups from physically assaulting each other.

*   *   *

By November 4, Israel's two partners had not yet begun their assault on Egypt, although it was now ninety-six hours after the "twelve-hour" deadline. Israel, having accomplished its objectives, announced its readiness to comply with the UN's call for a cease-fire—much to the chagrin and irritation of its lollygagging allies.

Egypt, determined to deny the canal to every maritime nation, had scuttled several ships at both ends of the canal. Syria did its duty by sabotaging several critical oil pipelines. Europe was now facing an imminent oil shortage with winter on the near horizon.

The USSR, for its part, was now breathing easier. It had shoved the Hungarians back in their cage and had reinstalled its obedient servants in Budapest. Moscow could now turn its attention to the Middle East. Its first step was to brand the British-French closure of ports in the Red and Mediterranean seas an "aggressive act." London and Paris shrugged this off, but Moscow's second step was yet to be taken; this one would be more robust.

I returned to the safe haven of our house late on Sunday afternoon. The past week had been one of unending stressful days and sleepless nights. But here, in our cozy but chilly sitting room, there was quiet, and tranquility, and sanity. Orah made tea and we played Monopoly. (Joan, as usual, won.)

*   *   *

On Monday, November 5, almost five days after the ultimatum expired, the day of attack came. British and French parachuters, about a thousand in all, dropped near Port Said early that morning. The Egyptians put up slight resistance and, later that day, reinforcements secured and expanded the British and French positions. There was considerable confusion as to whether or not the Egyptian general at Port Said had surrendered. If, in fact, he had, he soon changed his mind. (Eden, who certainly did not need any more problems with Parliament, had prematurely announced the surrender in his eagerness to provide cheerful news.) No matter; despite the many weeks of planning, preparations, and marching to and fro in England, Cyprus, and Malta, the invasion turned out to be limited, puny, and almost a week tardy. Meanwhile, Britain was becoming financially more anemic every day. By early November the pound was in peril.

In addition to the financial threat, Eden, together with Mollet and Ben-Gurion, faced another, even more worrisome danger. Bulganin, with the Hungarian crisis behind him, decided it was time for the Soviet Union to barge into the Middle East mess. He wrote to Eisenhower urging joint US-USSR military action against Britain, France, and Israel to "curb aggression" in Egypt. Ike turned down the idea, pointing out that the matter should remain in UN hands. A few hours later (on Monday), Moscow sent a message to the UN Security Council announcing its own ultimatum: If Britain, France, and Israel did not cease all military action within twelve hours and withdraw their forces from Egypt within three days, UN members should provide military assistance to Egypt. The security council rejected the Soviet proposal out of hand.

Later that day, Bulganin followed his salvo at the UN with the heaviest weapon that could be brought to bear—nuclear blackmail. "There are countries," he warned Eden and Mollet, "that are so powerful they need not attack

Britain and France by naval and air power." "Rocket technique" was also available.[12] His message to Ben-Gurion was even more brutal. And, just for kicks, mobs were unleashed to harass and bully the British, French, and Israeli embassies in Moscow.

At just about the time the USSR emerged from the wings, attacks on the Suez Canal had intensified. French and British reinforcements were fanning out along the canal. What their commanders apparently had not yet been told, however, was that on Tuesday morning, November 6—Election Day in the United States—Eden had already informed both his cabinet and Premier Mollet that he had decided to comply with the UN cease-fire order.

I had, by then, received several messages from both the CIA and the State Department reporting the Soviet warning. One CIA message was of particular interest: A special meeting of Washington's experts on the Soviet Union was to be held later that day (Washington time) to assess the credibility of the nuclear threat.

Before leaving the embassy for home on Monday night, I called Bob Amory. I told him I was embarrassed and ashamed to have to sit silently during the JIC meetings of the past several days. There had been valuable information I should have been able to share with the Brits. I then issued my own ultimatum: Unless I could share our Soviet experts' detailed findings on the Soviet threat with the JIC at its meeting the next morning, I would pack up and immediately return to Washington. Amory agreed it was time to stop playing games. In the meantime, "Go home, have a drink with Orah, and keep cool."

At 8:15 on Tuesday morning the critical message was waiting for me: Washington experts were confident that Moscow did not have the delivery capability to warrant concern. In short, Moscow was bluffing. The message concluded with words to the effect: "Tell them."

The word around Whitehall in late 1956 and early 1957 was that, from the moment Bulganin issued his threat, the British had shrugged it off. But that was by no means my impression when I walked into the JIC conference room at 10:30 AM on November 6. The committee's meetings were hardly merry occasions during that summer and early autumn, but on that day, from my seat at the foot of the long table, I saw grim, pale faces, fingers drumming nervously on the green baize cloth, and eyes bloodshot from the lack of sleep. (I could match them on that score.) The room was filled with uncertainty, worry, and, yes, fear.

"We were addressing the Bulganin threat, Chet," Pat Dean said as I walked in. "Do you have any views on that—views you can share?"

This time, I didn't shrivel up, frown, and shake my head. "Yes, Chairman.

I'd like to tell you yesterday's conclusions of our experts on Soviet nuclear capabilities. I can leave a copy with you, if you like." I read the report.

Pat smiled. "Thank you. Our chaps had pretty much come to the same view, but I think you know how important it is for us to have Washington's opinion." Someone sitting next to me (General Strong, I think it was) patted me on the knee. The black fog had lifted.

As I look back on my forty-year relationship with Sir Patrick Dean, I realize it was on that morning in November 1956 that we moved from friendship to brotherhood.

*   *   *

In the course of the next six weeks, the British and French forces, under strong pressure from the UN and Washington, pulled out from their positions along the canal. The Israelis, having secured an outlet to the Mediterranean, if not peaceful overtures from Egypt and its neighbors, moved well back from their advanced position in Sinai. Nasser postured and strutted around Egypt and the Middle East and among the unaligned nations. He was dutifully cheered as a great hero. The United States, together with the International Monetary Fund, rescued the British pound. A serious oil shortage threatened the tottering British economy. Anthony Eden, sick, badgered, and chastened, left for sun and rest in the Caribbean. An ill Secretary of State Dulles was out of action until early December. And, oh yes, Dwight Eisenhower embarked on his second term, having trounced Adlai Stevenson on November 6.

*   *   *

London was a different place in the winter of 1957 than it was when we first arrived in the summer of 1955. Anthony Eden had resigned on January 10 and Harold Macmillan, who had been chancellor of the exchequer, was now prime minister. There were long lines of would-be emigrants waiting outside the entrances of the Australian and Canadian High Commissions. The British economy was struggling against the onslaught of the financial and oil crises. The notion of "Little England" was becoming part of the lexicon, especially among the young. The Suez fiasco and its aftermath had taken an enormous toll.

Well into the winter of 1957 British and Americans conducted official and informal postmortems in Whitehall, in the US Embassy, and in pubs, clubs, and sitting rooms. Suez was high on the list of subjects for review in Wash-

ington as well. I was ordered home in early December to explain to Bob
Amory and Allen Dulles why, with my "good connections," I was unable to
give Allen and John Foster Dulles ample warning of British-French intentions.
It was then that I showed them my list of those who knew in advance and
those who did not. "If General Kenneth Strong didn't know, if the number two
guy in MI6 didn't know, how could I possibly know?" I reminded them that
American's didn't tap British phones, and, in any case, I wouldn't have known
how to do it. I took some relish in pointing out that I had forwarded an account
of my session with Pat Dean on the Sunday before the fateful Monday; if I had
been too dense to draw the appropriate conclusions, so had they. I returned to
London the next day, and heard no more from Washington on this matter (until
I got a medal several years later).

I hesitate to bid the Suez affair "good-bye and good riddance" without
three quick visits: one with Foreign Secretary Selwyn Lloyd and Secretary of
State John Foster Dulles; another with former prime minister Winston
Churchill; the third (this one, a personal visit) with former prime minister
Anthony Eden.

Lloyd was in Washington in mid-November 1956 and, with the recently
arrived Ambassador Harold Caccia, went to see Dulles, who was recuper-
ating from surgery at Walter Reed Hospital. Lloyd reported later that Dulles,
with "a kind of twinkle in his eye," asked, "Why did you stop? Why didn't
you go through with it and get Nasser down?" Lloyd replied, "Well, Foster,
if you had so much as winked at us we might have gone on." Apparently,
Dulles indicated he could not have done that.[13] Lloyd's account was confirmed by Caccia in a conversation he had with John Colville, Churchill's
former private secretary.[14] For the record, I would like to report that I did not
go back to my JIC colleagues and say, once again, "I told you so."

Churchill's view of the manner in which Eden handled the Suez incident
was less than enthusiastic. In November 1956, after the British stand-down,
Colville asked him, "If you had been Prime Minister [at the time], would you
have done this?" Churchill responded, "I never would have dared, and if I
had dared, I never would have dared stop."[15] A few weeks later, according to
Colville, Churchill said "the whole operation was the most ill-conceived and
ill-executed imaginable."[16]

Almost twenty years later, I interviewed Anthony Eden (then Lord Avon)
in connection with a book I was writing on the Suez crisis.[17] Eden, weak and
ailing, had fled England's winter cold and, with his wife, was spending several weeks with Averell Harriman at Hobe Sound, Florida.

I called Harriman and asked if Eden would be willing to talk about Suez with me, just for an hour or so. I would fly down whenever it would be convenient. Harriman gave me short shrift: Didn't I know that Eden had never given an interview on Suez? Didn't I know Eden was on vacation (of course, for years, Eden had been on vacation)? Didn't I know Eden was sick? "I'm surprised you asked, Chet." But, Harriman promised, if I sent him two or three questions, he would show them to Eden. Then, if Eden wished, he could dictate something, and Harriman would mail that back. "But I doubt if he'll bother," Harriman concluded.

A few days later, Harriman called. He tried hard to mask his surprise. Eden was interested in my questions and my Suez experience. Would I come down and talk to him? But only for a morning, Harriman warned; Eden retired at lunchtime and was too weak to engage in conversation after that. In the end, Eden talked to me for three consecutive mornings about his frustrations, about how he had been misunderstood, about the problems he had had with Dulles. As I said good-bye at the end of our third session, he promised that when he returned to London in early May, he would assemble his Suez War Cabinet and have me join a day's discussion of what did and could have happened. Sadly, Eden died at his Caribbean home in March.

*   *   *

In the new year, relations with the British were getting back to normal—more or less. A new ambassador, Jock Whitney, and a new chief of the CIA station, Tracy Barnes (Whitney's cousin and a veteran OSS and CIA officer), arrived at the embassy. Both were considerable improvements over their predecessors.

Despite the end of the Suez war and the resignation of Anthony Eden, Orah and I were aware of a lingering, troubling anti-American feeling. We felt it in the shops and restaurants and on social occasions. I even sensed it in contacts with Her Majesty's government. Lyndon Johnson was to experience the backlash ten years later, when he sought British help in the Vietnam War.

The atmosphere around the CIA enclave at the embassy was lightened in early 1957 by the appearance, seemingly out of nowhere, of Douglas Fairbanks Jr.—aging, but still debonair, disarming, and scandalously (to me, at least) promiscuous. He had, by then, been a longtime London resident and an enthusiastic member of the "smart set." I never discovered whether he was an agency recruit or a privileged friend of Tracy Barnes. (Tracy had many friends in both high and low places.)

Fairbanks was often at loose ends, and, in the absence of more glamorous opportunities, occasionally invited me to lunch. Our lunch typically took place at the posh Connaught Hotel. On each occasion, Fairbanks insisted on stopping in at the Connaught's men's room even when we had just used the embassy's plumbing. When I once mentioned this, Fairbanks confessed that the men's room attendant was the only person in London who addressed him by his honorary title, Sir Douglas. He enjoyed that.

Spring of 1957 came to London overnight. One day it was gray, rainy, cold, and miserable. The next morning, it was sunny under blue skies; the daffodils had burst open and spirits soared. Orah and I decided we deserved a holiday after the difficult, stressful autumn and the dark, dreary winter. As soon as the girls had their spring school break, we set off for Juan les Pins, then a small, modest town on the Riviera (now large, noisy, and crowded). It was there that I had another, albeit brief, encounter with one more Middle East crisis.

Toward the end of our holiday, I took the train to nearby Cannes to confirm our air reservations back to London. Errand accomplished, I went to a bar adjacent to the station for a beer while I waited for the return train. There, I joined several young American men, dressed, as I, in sport shirts and slacks. We had hardly gotten through the "Where do you come from?" stage when the door burst open and four burly American navy shore police moved menacingly toward us. "OK, guys, back to your ships. Liberty boats are at the dock. Move!"

Some of my companions gulped down their drinks and dashed out. A few hesitated, and were pushed out. I calmly continued to eat peanuts and sip beer, remembering that I had heard something on the radio that morning about trouble in Lebanon.

Two of the SPs trundled up to me. "Are you deaf? Move out! Fast!" I started to explain that I wasn't a sailor. I was in the ——. "We've heard that story in every goddamn bar and restaurant in town! Move it!" Each grabbed an arm and marched me across the road toward the harbor, which, I could now see, was bustling with American warships. As we approached the dock, dozens of men were scrambling into a liberty boat. When I had a chance to reach for my wallet, I fished out my embassy ID card. "Look!" I yelled.

"Oh," grinned one of my captors. "Sorry about that. Go back and finish your beer."

And that is how I almost got a free trip to Lebanon.

*   *   *

In December 1957 I was assigned to the American delegation attending the NATO summit meeting in Paris. I was to provide President Eisenhower and Secretary Dulles with early morning briefings and perform whatever other tasks might be roughly in the province of an intelligence officer. And so, each morning at 5:00 AM, I yawned my way along the dark, quiet Rue Rivoli from my hotel to the embassy, begged a cup of coffee from the sleepy CIA communications officer, and read the cable traffic that had come through since I last perused it the previous evening. I would then prepare a ten-minute briefing and be driven to the ambassador's residence, where Eisenhower and Dulles were staying. At about eight o'clock, while Dulles was having breakfast, I provided a rundown on what I considered the most important developments involving NATO and the world at large. I would then go upstairs and, having checked with the Secret Service man outside Eisenhower's bedroom, would brief the president as he breakfasted at a bedside tray.

The first day's session seemed to be problem free. But while I was (finally) having my own breakfast in the embassy cafeteria, I discovered that two or three items I had included in my briefings had already been printed in that morning's *Herald Tribune*. I decided to avoid such embarrassing redundancies in the future.

The next morning, on my way to the car, I pinched somebody's copy of the newspaper from the pile on the receptionist's desk and scanned it on my way to the residence. I made note of a few items, and then my eye caught a column by someone named Art Buchwald, identified as a "Paris correspondent." It described, in hilarious detail, a fictional press conference in which Ike's press secretary, Jim Hagerty, answered a series of reporters' questions about the president's bedtime mood and state of health.[18]

"What did the president say to you before he went to sleep?"

"Good night."

"Did he say this in a tone indicating that he expected to see you the next morning?"

"There was every evidence that he expected to wake up the next morning, and, since I would be sitting by his bedside, of course, he would then see me."

And so it went.

I thought my Dulles briefing warranted at least two cheers. Since he seemed to be in a good mood, I took the plunge: "Mr. Secretary, perhaps this piece I read in the *Herald Tribune* may amuse you on this cold, rainy morning." He took the paper, read the column, and gave forth several honest-to-goodness chuckles.

I repeated the performance when I finished briefing the president. I took out some disaster insurance, however: I said that Secretary Dulles had read it and found it amusing. The president read the column, smiled, put the paper on a chair beside him, and thanked me. I left glowing with my success.

An hour later, the cafeteria cashier beckoned me. There was a telephone call from Jim Hagerty, the president's media maven. This was an enraged Hagerty, an irate Hagerty, a Hagerty on fire. Apparently, he had seen the president shortly after I left, read Buchwald's piece, and, to put it mildly, was not amused.

"Look," I said when I was able to squeeze a word in, "I didn't write it, I just read it. And I'm sure the president thought it was perfectly okay."

"Well, I didn't. I'm going to get that guy. Whatsisname? Booshwold? And I'll get back to *you* later."

Hagerty circulated a note to the press later in the morning. At his afternoon press conference he would make sure that "Booshwold" apologized for his inappropriate piece. The Hôtel Crillon ballroom was chock-a-block full of reporters that afternoon. Hagerty insisted that the offending "Paris correspondent" write a piece for the next morning's *Herald Tribune*, apologizing for and retracting his column. Buchwald did so—in a piece that was even more amusing than the first.

Not long after, Buchwald was transferred to New York. So it was that, at a considerable risk to my own career, I enhanced his. Incidentally, Hagerty never followed through on his promise to "get back" to me.

*   *   *

September 1958. It was time to leave London. My replacement had arrived, and, although we were sorry to go, we were also anxious to return home. The girls' school in Washington would start soon, and we had many chores and obligations, professional and personal, awaiting us.

One of these chores was a long-delayed physical exam. "Were you under stress at any time in London?" the doctor asked.

I told him about the difficult weeks during the autumn of 1956.

"Well, it was then that you probably had a cardiac incident. No tennis, no pushing cars, no snow shoveling." As I was leaving, he shook my hand. "You have the distinction of probably being the only American casualty of the Suez war. Don't do anything foolish until I see you again."

NOTES

1. A more detailed account of the weeks following October 1956 can be found in Chester L. Cooper, *The Lion's Last Roar: Suez 1956* (New York: Harper & Row, 1978).

2. Moshe Dayan, *Story of My Life* (Tel Aviv: Steimatzky's Agency Ltd., 1976), p. 180.

3. Selwyn Lloyd, *Suez 1956* (New York: Mayflower Books, 1978), pp. 182–83.

4. US Department of State, *The Suez Canal Problem, July 26–September 22, 1956: A Documentary Publication* (Washington, DC: US Government Printing Office, 1957), p. 359.

5. Anthony Eden, *Full Circle: The Memoirs of Anthony Eden* (Boston: Houghton Mifflin, 1960), pp. 56–57.

6. Ibid., p. 587.

7. Townsend Hoopes, *The Devil and John Foster Dulles* (Boston: Little, Brown, 1973), p. 377.

8. Terrence Roberts, *Crisis: The Inside Story of the Suez Conspiracy* (London: Hutchinson, 1964), p. 170.

9. Eden, *Full Circle*, p. 611.

10. Robert Rhodes James, *Anthony Eden, A Biography* (New York: McGraw-Hill, 1987), p. 556.

11. Anthony Moncrieff, ed., *Suez Ten Years After* (New York: Pantheon, 1967), p. 16.

12. *New York Times*, November 6, 1956.

13. Lloyd, *Suez 1956*, p. 215.

14. John Colville, *On the Fringes of Power* (New York and London: W. W. Norton, 1985), p. 725.

15. Martin Gilbert, *Churchill: A Life* (New York: Henry Holt, 1999), p. 950.

16. Colville, *On the Fringes of Power*, p. 721.

17. Cooper, *The Lion's Last Roar*.

18. What follows is a paraphrase, so please don't sue me, Mr. Buchwald. Actually, I think my version is more amusing than the genuine original.

9

MUCH ADO ABOUT LAOS

ABOUT LAOS

Laos is a country of fewer than four million people. Six centuries ago, it was the center of a strong kingdom that, by the seventeenth century, controlled parts of China, Thailand, Burma, Vietnam, and Cambodia. By the early nineteenth century Thailand had become the region's dominant power, but later in the century the French established a protectorate over Laos and, soon after, incorporated the country, together with Vietnam and Cambodia, into French Indochina.

The Japanese invaded and occupied Laos and its neighbors early during World War II, but were kicked out in 1945 by Allied forces. The early postwar period was marked by competing Laotian factions under the ineffective rule of the French colonial government. After the 1954 Geneva Conference the local Communists, abetted by North Vietnamese troops, took over approximately half of Laos. By 1960 three separate political movements, each headed by a royal personage and each with its own troops, jockeyed for power. The listless right-wing force, advised and supported by Americans, turned out to be hopeless in both the political and military realms. The Communist group (the Pathet Lao) was supported enthusiastically by the North Vietnamese (and somewhat less enthusiastically by the Chinese and the Soviets). The third group made up for its lack (initially at least) of outside support by the diplomacy and integrity of the energetic, effective Prince Souvanna Phouma.

In 1960 Washington decided that a rightist victory was critical to halting the further spread of Communism in Southeast Asia. In fact, the National Security Council had given serious thought to the deployment of US forces to buttress the rightists.

And this is about where matters stood as I set out once again to Geneva.

*   *   *

It was pleasant and important to be back in Chevy Chase. Our house needed attention after the ravages of careless tenants; our yard, which had once aspired to be a garden, was again just a yard; friends and relatives deserved some time; creditors needed stroking. In addition, Joan and Susan had to adjust to their new schools, Orah's father was ill, and I had a new job.

In my new incarnation as chief of the CIA's estimates staff, I supervised a group of supercharged and overworked experts and generalists. We were called upon day and night, weekdays and weekends, to pronounce on a host of issues ranging from Soviet nuclear capabilities to probable developments in Kashmir. Happily, Allen Dulles and his immediate subordinates, Robert Amory and Sherman Kent, were still in place; I would be in familiar territory.

Life, professionally and personally, continued to be dominated by the cold war. Bomb cellars and air-raid shelters in public buildings, department stores, and hotels were a common sight in downtown Washington.

One did not need an advanced degree in physics to realize that such precautions would be pathetically inadequate if push ever came to shove. Nor did it require an IQ over 100 to conclude, as one crawled through the evening rush hour or maneuvered through clogged streets in an inch or two of snow, that an orderly, expeditious evacuation of Washington, or, indeed, of any large American city, was just a pipe dream.

On the other side of the Atlantic, Harold Macmillan, who had succeeded Anthony Eden as prime minister, was confronting not only cold war problems, but also domestic economic difficulties and popular malaise in the aftermath of Suez. And across the channel, France's premier, Charles de Gaulle, was faced with the debilitating effects of the long, costly, unsavory war in Algeria.

In Vietnam, President Ngo Dinh Diem had succeeded in crushing the religious sects and criminal elements which had been threatening the stability of his fragile new government. In no small part because of American assistance, South Vietnam's economy was now reasonably healthy. What Diem, his political courtiers, his highly placed relatives, and most American officials (but not, I must say, some in the CIA) chose to overlook, or did not realize, however, was that the "Diem miracle" was confined to Saigon and a few other urban centers; the countryside, by now, was being ravaged by Viet Cong guerrilla fighters.

The mild Christian Herter had taken over the State Department in 1959 after the ardent cold warrior John Foster Dulles lost his battle with cancer. President Eisenhower seemed to grow more mellow as retirement beckoned, but exchanges between Washington and Moscow were as shrill as ever. West Berliners continued to live under the shadow of political isolation and economic strangulation. Nikita Khrushchev was threatening to sign a separate peace treaty with East Germany and force the Americans, British, and French out of West Berlin. Adding seasoning to this bubbling pot, on May Day in 1960 a high-flying CIA reconnaissance plane was shot down over the Soviet Union—on the eve of a summit meeting between the Soviets, Americans, British, and French!

Life was lively on the national as well as on the international stage. Vice President Nixon and a few hopeful Democrats were poising themselves and polishing their rhetoric in preparation for the looming 1960 presidential campaign. Among the aspiring Democrats was the former ambassador to London and Moscow, former governor of New York, former many other important things, Averell Harriman. He lost out in the presidential primaries, but would soon be more or less compensated by becoming my boss.

Sen. John Fitzgerald Kennedy defeated former vice president Richard Nixon with a few electoral votes to spare. His running mate was Sen. Lyndon Baines Johnson. I have often wondered if, in the light of what was in store for each of them, each would have rather remained in the Senate.

*   *   *

On the day before Inauguration Day, 1961, about-to-be-former president Eisenhower briefed about-to-be-president Kennedy on those international issues that worried him most. The Soviet Union in general and Moscow's threatening stance toward West Berlin in particular were high on this list. Strangely enough, he did not mention Vietnam. But Laos, where the Communist Pathet Lao was creating chaos throughout the country, was a topic of conversation.

Eisenhower's warning with regard to Laos was prescient. The deteriorating situation there received prominent billing in JFK's first State of the

Union message: "We seek in Laos what we seek . . . in all of the world—freedom for the people and independence for the government. And this nation shall persevere in our pursuit of this objective."[1] Soon after, Kennedy reinvigorated and strengthened the army's special forces, which, soon enough, would be dispatched to both Laos and Vietnam.

Aside from problems many thousands of miles away, Kennedy inherited troubles closer to home from the previous administration. (All new presidents are indebted to their predecessors for many pieces of nasty unfinished business.) One such problem was in the backyard of the Kennedy family's Florida estate.

By January 1961, plans for an invasion of Cuba by a CIA-trained anti-Castro force were well under way. In mid-April the assault on the Bay of Pigs began. It was a fiasco. Not only a fiasco, a *disastrous* fiasco; it haunted the new, once-confident, and ebullient administration, and signaled the end of Allen Dulles's career and those of several other key CIA officials in the covert side of the agency.

The group that had planned and implemented the Bay of Pigs extravaganza kept the plans and progress of the ill-starred enterprise so secret that even the CIA's Latin American and Cuban analysts were not aware of it. They first learned of the invasion from the Associated Press news ticker, which, during the first hour or two, reported considerable success—thanks to the agency's disinformation experts.

*   *   *

In addition to my new responsibilities in the Office of National Estimates, I continued, along with William Bundy, to be Director Allen Dulles's assistant for National Security Council matters. In preparation for the Thursday NSC meetings, we provided Dulles with a preliminary briefing on Tuesday evenings and a final briefing on Wednesdays. The briefings usually started at five or so in the afternoon and concluded whenever Dulles said so. On rare occasions, I was able to join Joan and Susan for a Tuesday or Wednesday dinner. More often, however, I arrived in Chevy Chase at 8:30 or 9:00 PM, when Orah and I dined alone. Much depended on whether the director had a sudden mid-briefing call from some covert agent who had just arrived in town from god knows where. Dulles had an insatiable appetite for spy tales, especially from his own spies. Although these unscheduled interruptions were a source of great pleasure for him, they were annoying for Bundy and me. We would exchange looks of resignation and settle back, impatiently, until we could finally return to the problems of Eastern Europe, the Congo, or Laos.

One Wednesday evening in late January 1961, our session was moving along nicely until Dulles's secretary announced that Prof. Walt Rostow was in the outer office. Rostow wished to "pay his respects" to the director. My heart sank. I had known the bright, articulate, voluble Rostow for several years, and was sure that this would be a ten-o'clocker once Walt entered the room and embarked on his "respects." With relief, I heard Dulles say, "I'm busy. Could Mr. Rostow come back another time?"

The secretary tiptoed out and then back. Professor Rostow would be only a minute or two, she said. He was on his way home, and since he had just come to Washington as part of President Kennedy's White House team, he wanted to make a courtesy call. Dulles shrugged and mumbled, "Okay."

Walt entered cheerily, greeted Dulles, Bundy, and me, and, to my horror, sat down—a sign of a long visit. I was wrong. The discussion was brief.

"Walt," said Dulles, "I've often wondered how you got along with your brother Gene. Gene, after all, is dean of Yale law school, a very prestigious position."

"Well . . . ," Walt hesitated. Then he nodded to Bundy. "Bill, how do you and your brother Mac get along? He's younger than you and already has had a brilliant career as dean of Harvard. Now he's the president's assistant for national security affairs."

Bill, somewhat startled at how the conversation was developing, thought for a minute. "Allen," he said, turning to Dulles, "Chet and I have often wondered about you and John Foster. What was your relationship with him?"

Allen looked at Rostow with something less than affection. "Thanks for coming by, Walt, but you can see I'm getting ready for tomorrow's NSC meeting." He stood up, extended a limp hand, and looked in the direction of the door. The afternoon ended well. I was home by seven.

On another occasion when Bundy and I were discussing the next day's NSC meeting, we were again interrupted by an unexpected visitor. But this was time well spent.

Dulles's secretary came in to say that the head of the Middle East Division was calling. "He says it's urgent." Allen reached for the phone. I crossed my fingers. Bill rolled his eyes.

"Yemen?" Dulles asked. "Who's he? . . . Oh. Is it really important? . . . Well, send him up." And up he came.

He was the agency's (and in the late 1950s, perhaps Washington's) only card-carrying expert on that small, recently relinquished British colony. He stood fidgeting before his boss's boss's boss's boss.

"Well?" Dulles stared at the obviously frightened analyst. "Yemen?" he asked again. "What's the Yemen? . . . A country? . . . Never heard of it. Where is it?"

The expert pointed with a shaking finger to a small speck on the edge of the Red Sea. "There, Mr. Dulles."

"I can't see it. But what's happening there that's so important?"

"It's the imam, sir."

"Imam? Never heard of that either."

"It's a person, sir. A religious person. He's the head of the government—the imam of Yemen."

Dulles's eyes were wandering. He looked first at Bundy, who shrugged. Then at me, who was trying to keep a straight face. Then at his watch. "All right. What about him?"

"He's leaving the country, sir. The first this has ever happened—the imam leaving Yemen. There may be a coup."

"Where's he going? Moscow? Beijing?"

"No, sir. He's going to Switzerland. Zurich."

"Very nice. A holiday?"

"No, Mr. Dulles. He's going to see a doctor. A specialist."

Dulles suddenly became interested. "Oh, why?"

"He has syphilis, sir."

"Well," sighed Dulles, "you've finally told me something that will interest members of the NSC. Thank you. Good night."

*　　*　　*

Reflecting back on the close of the fifties and the dawn of the sixties, I find it surprising that, despite Berlin, Cuba, the Middle East, and the US-Soviet nuclear standoff, I had spent so much scarce time, weeks and months, on Laos, a country few American officials could find on an outline map of Southeast Asia. No matter; the growing strength of the Chinese-supported Communist insurgency against the US-supported right-wing government had become, willy-nilly, high on Eisenhower's, and then Kennedy's, worry list. So much so, in fact, that, in the latter part of Ike's administration, and in the early days of JFK's tenure, serious consideration was given to sending American troops there.

In early 1961 several nations with a stake in a peaceful settlement of the problems in Laos agreed to meet in Geneva in early May. Once again, the proceedings would take place under the cochairmanship of Britain and the Soviet Union. This time, however, unlike 1954, the United States readily agreed to participate. Since I was a veteran of the 1954 conference, Allen Dulles volunteered my services to Ambassador at Large Averell Harriman, who headed the American delegation. Neither he nor I, and, for that matter, no one on any of the delegations, realized then how long the stay in Geneva would be.

Almost seven years had passed since I first walked into the Palais des Nations. I would like to think I was somewhat more worldly, but the art nouveau building on the edge of Lake Leman still gave me a sense of awe. In the years following World War I, if it had not been for a few American senators, the United States might have joined the League of Nations, and the league might have become an effective instrument for peace.

I had barely entered the Palais when an usher beckoned me to his desk in the lobby. *"Votre pipe, monsieur,"* he said, smiling. Where else but in Switzerland could this happen?

Malcolm MacDonald of Britain and G. M. Pushkin of the Soviet Union shared the conference chairmanship. MacDonald, an expert on Southeast Asia, was less high-strung, more low-key, and lower in the Whitehall pecking order than Anthony Eden, the 1954 Indochina Conference cochairman. Pushkin was a retired Communist apparatchik who turned out to be more flexible, but had considerably less clout in the Kremlin, than his predecessor cochairman, Vyacheslav Molotov.

Since 1954 the Chinese had gained more experience and confidence on the international stage. This was also true for the North Vietnamese, who, to the naked eye, seemed to defer less to their Chinese and Soviet allies. None of this is to say, however, that any of the Communist delegations had become more congenial.

Since 1959 I had been a strong supporter of a few young CIA analysts who had been smart enough to detect friction between Beijing and Moscow. This, despite the fact that their views had been scoffed at by senior experts and officials in both the CIA and the State Department. At Geneva in the spring of 1961, however, my junior colleagues were vindicated; the strains between the Chinese and the Soviet delegations became increasingly evident. A mischievous State Department colleague and I did what we could to advance the cause. We took pains to engage in conspicuous, amicable small talk with members of the Soviet delegation whenever we were in sight of the Chinese.

As for the delegates from Hanoi, they became more and more offensive and disruptive when it became evident that, despite their protestations, Viet Minh troops had joined forces with the Pathet Lao against the Laos government in clear violation of the 1954 agreement. (Forty years later, at a lively meeting with former North Vietnamese officials, they admitted that Viet Minh army units had been in Laos not only before and during the Laos talks, but after the settlement as well.)

*   *   *

The formidable Averell Harriman was familiarly known as "Guv" from his term as governor of New York and confidentially known as "the Crocodile," in recognition of his appearing to doze just before he lashed out at someone or something he saw or heard that displeased him. He had come to Washington with the Kennedy administration. His position as assistant secretary of state for the Far East was a downward slide from the more prestigious positions he had earlier held under Presidents Roosevelt and Truman. But the Guv was anxious to serve; status was less important than influence.

At his first staff meeting, it was obvious that Harriman was displeased with the size and composition of the delegation the State Department's hierarchy had selected. There were too many people he regarded as extraneous. There were also several who may not have been extraneous, but to whom he had taken a dislike. And then there were a few senior State Department folk he distrusted (and vice versa). Within a week or so the delegation was slashed to a quarter of its original size. Remaining were a dozen or so Far Eastern and Soviet experts from the State Department, a few military specialists from the Pentagon, me (with a couple of assistants), and a small support and security staff. Harriman was now ready to do business and to do battle.

The Guv was hard of hearing and resorted to a hearing aid, which he turned on or off depending on whether he was interested in the speaker or the subject. (I've gotten pretty good at this myself in recent years.) During an interminable Chinese intervention I leaned forward from my seat behind him to suggest a riposte. Harriman had his hearing aid off, but his microphone on. He grunted, for all to hear, "Take your damn pipe out of your mouth. I can't hear a word you say." My friend in the secretariat told me, I hope in jest, that Harriman's remark was translated into Chinese and had a brief half-life in the record of the day's proceedings.

The first few weeks provided an unappetizing foretaste of the months to follow. Venomous tirades from the Chinese and Vietnamese Communists; harsh interventions from the Soviets when Pushkin was not in the chair and somewhat milder ones when he was; blunt, if not electrifying, remarks from Harriman; tough anti-Communist speeches from the Thais; elegant and knowledgeable contributions from the French (who, after all, knew the territory, and who were less emotional then they were when they were kicked out of the region in 1954); calm, knowledgeable remarks from the British; silence from the Burmese; shrill and angry exchanges from and among the three Lao delegations (rightist, neutralist, and Communist); and flowery and interminable orations from the Indians.

The only surprise was provided by the small South Vietnamese delegation. Although the conference had been convened to address the problems of Laos, the South Vietnamese made sure that Viet Cong attacks against the Saigon government and South Vietnamese villages were not overlooked. Their chilling accounts of murder, mayhem, and kidnapping in the rural areas of South Vietnam may have been somewhat exaggerated, and the South Vietnamese refused to acknowledge the sins of their own government. Still, their intensity, energy, and intelligence made a favorable impression on the Western delegations, especially the Americans. Indeed, Washington's subsequent decision to give major support to the Vietnamese as opposed to the Laotians was, in no small part, due to the activities and comportment of the South Vietnamese delegation.

*   *   *

Just as the conference in Geneva was settling down for what promised to be a long, hot summer (and, as it turned out, a cool autumn, a dreary winter, a wet spring, and a bit of another summer), even more auspicious conversations were taking place a few hundred miles away in Austria.

In early June the president flew to Vienna from Paris. In Paris, thanks in no small part to Mrs. Kennedy's beauty, charm, and fluent French, the sessions with de Gaulle were friendly and constructive. Kennedy was confident that his meetings in Vienna with Chairman Khrushchev would go equally well. They did not.

According to Chip Bohlen, Soviet expert and former US ambassador to Moscow, the initial session started well. There were a few pleasantries and mutual expressions of peaceful intentions. Then, "Kennedy made a mistake. He let himself be drawn into a semi-ideological discussion," which Khrushchev was "a master in handling. . . . Khrushchev sounded like a libertarian, Kennedy a colonialist . . . the results of the discussion were meager." Bohlen reports that Kennedy was "a little depressed" by his exchange. As he left, Kennedy said to Khrushchev, "I see it's going to be a very cold winter."[2]

Harriman, who had flown from Geneva to Vienna to be briefed on the meeting, reported that Kennedy had been chastened and humiliated. In retrospect, he thought, it may have been a mistake for Kennedy to have agreed to see Khrushchev so soon after the Bay of Pigs disaster.

Kennedy returned to Washington all the more determined that the United States must stand firm against Soviet and Chinese encroachments. Berlin and Southeast Asia would, in his view, be early tests of this resolve. While this, in fact, proved to be correct, there was another more dangerous test on the near horizon. It would be a test the new administration would not reckon with until it was almost too late.

Well before he met with Kennedy, Khrushchev had made an important decision. Its implementation may have been advanced by his meeting with Kennedy in Vienna. Shortly after the chairman returned to Moscow, the people of East Berlin were fenced in by barbed wire, and, soon after, by a high concrete wall, monitored by armed police.

Meanwhile, it became apparent that while Kennedy regarded a favorable outcome of the Laos negations as a high priority, Khrushchev, according to Bohlen, "showed little interest" in the Geneva proceedings.[3]

*   *   *

Harriman returned from his overnight stay in Austria convinced that, as head of the American delegation, he was responsible directly to the president, rather than to Secretary Dean Rusk. This may have stemmed from a conversation he had had with Kennedy in Vienna; Harriman was vague on this. Whether Rusk had such an understanding is doubtful, and this led to tension between the two men and between the Geneva delegation and the State Department.

It did not take long before the US delegation's patience with the representatives of the rightist Laotian government ("our" side) was wearing thin. The dapper government delegates were clearly enjoying Geneva's nightlife, and seemed to regard the negotiations, on which their country's future hung, as a boring residual claimant on their time. They apparently felt the need to make hay while some sun still shone. Charles Cross, our liaison with their delegation, had an appointment to meet with them each noon to discuss plans for the afternoon's session at the Palais. More often than not, our staunch Laotian allies were still in their pajamas.

The dolorous situation of Laos's rightist government was confirmed one morning when a Department of Defense representative briefed us on the military situation there. "We have good news today, Governor Harriman." He tried not to grin. "A few days ago, there was an engagement between Laotian government forces and the Pathet Lao. As usual, the government guys ran away, but, this time, they took their weapons with them."

Much to the concern of some State Department officials in Washington, for whom neutralism was a cardinal sin, Harriman began to talk seriously with the delegation of Lao neutralists. Prince Souvanna Phouma, an urbane, French-educated member of the old royal family, was head of the neutralist party. The leader of Souvanna's delegation took the Geneva negotiations more seriously than either his rightist or his Communist counterparts. He was an active, constructive participant.

Harriman was tough and single-minded. Despite backbiting from Washington, he doggedly pursued the neutralist solution. I was in his office one evening when an irate Secretary Rusk called. I did not hear Rusk's side of the heated exchange, but it was evident that he was upset by Harriman's growing relationship with Souvanna Phouma. Finally, Harriman exploded. "I work for the president, and I'm here to do what he wants. I'm not responsible to you." Then, turning toward me, he came close to signing my death warrant: "Chet is here with me and absolutely agrees."

Later that evening, when I was having dinner with Orah (she and the girls had joined me for the summer), I described the conversation. "I certainly admire Harriman's independence."

"With his money he can afford to be," Orah reminded me, "but you've got two children and not much money, so be careful that you don't get fired along with the governor." (Several years later, he was still there, but I had quit.)

The talks went on—and on—and on. Weeks folded into months. Nonetheless, Harriman stayed the course. The American delegation was further pared down, but he made sure there was no slackening off. Lunches with him amounted just to another hour or so of work. Dinners, for anyone unlucky enough to be in sight when Harriman was leaving the delegation offices, involved a discussion of the day's events and plans for the next meeting—matters already discussed that afternoon. These dinners were all work, no fun. Moreover, since the Guv never carried money, his "guest" usually wound up paying for the meal. After several such experiences, I was not above hiding in a stall in the men's room until I was sure he had left.

One day when I had successfully evaded the Guv, I had dinner with Sidney Gruson, a reporter from the *New York Times*. "What's going on?" he asked. "Things seem awfully quiet."

"I'll tell you what's going on. Practically nothing. It's at a point where we've been talking about getting Harriman to buy Laos so we can all go home."

Much to my horror, the next morning's *Herald Tribune* had a story that negotiations in Geneva were at such an impasse that the American delegation was considering . . . Harriman opened the ten o'clock staff meeting that day by looking coldly around the room. "Who saw the *Times*'s Gruson yesterday?"

"I did, sir. I had dinner with him." I tried hard to be brave.

"I wondered where you were. Well, that was a stupid idea of yours. What would I do with Laos?"

I thought I caught a hint of a smile, but maybe it was just a twitch. Anyway, for better or worse, I was not sent home.

Winter in Geneva is damp, dark, and dismal. Sun, snow, and skis are not part of a Geneva January; these delights are for chic mountain cities like Saint Moritz or Gstaad. During most of the gray, dreary winter I was unable to wiggle my way out of Harriman's clutches, but I did manage to get home for a few weeks. I returned to Geneva on the cusp of spring.

Back at the Palais, the speeches were still droning on, with little to show for them except for a few memorable moments. For example, there was one afternoon when the Chinese delegate shouted a serious of accusations and questions in the direction of the Americans. "You did thus and so. Yes or no, Mr. Harriman? The United States did not honor such and such. Yes or no, Mr. Harriman?"

Sitting behind Harriman, I saw him write on his notepad, "When did you stop beating your wife?" I leaned over and whispered that only the Americans, British, and Canadians would understand what he was trying to say. His clever remark could not be easily translated into Chinese, or, for that matter, any other language.

Harriman gave me a blank stare. "I know what I'm doing." And then, out came, "I can only say to the delegate from China, when did you . . . ?"

I looked up at the translation booth and saw consternation on the faces of the English and Chinese translators. I switched on the Chinese channel on my headset. There was only silence. Eventually, there came an outpouring of Chinese lasting three or four minutes. Later, at the break, I asked the English-to-Chinese translator how he managed. "I didn't," he shrugged. "I tried to dig up a Chinese proverb or a children's story, but it didn't work. Why didn't you tell your boss not to use such a stupid expression? Or was that your idea?"

That incident had staying power. In 1998, when I was in Hanoi, one of the Vietnamese participants at our meeting, Mr. Buu van Loi, who had been a member of the Viet Minh delegation in Geneva, approached me during a tea break. "Mr. Cooper, something has been bothering me all these years. During the Laos meeting, what did Mr. Harriman mean by asking the Chinese, 'When did you stop beating your wife?'" I fared no better in trying to explain it to Mr. Buu than the UN translator did in 1962.

*   *   *

In the final week of the Laos conference, several delegations hosted receptions. (The American delegation did not.) Although the Americans and the Chinese had avoided contact throughout the conference, we, together with the other delegations, were invited to the villa where the senior Chinese representatives had been staying. Secretary Rusk (who had come to Geneva for the closing sessions) and Ambassador Harriman decided it would be courteous if one or two Americans (but not they) accepted the invitation. The assignment fell to the State Department's Bill Sullivan (who was to become the American ambassador to Laos) and to me.

When Sullivan and I entered the Chinese villa's crowded reception room, there was an audible gasp of surprise. Most of the guests could not believe we were invited; probably all could not believe we had accepted. The Chinese foreign minister, Chen Yi, who, too, had come for the final ceremonies, immediately elbowed his way toward us. He was accompanied by an interpreter. After we shook hands, Chen Yi ushered us to a quiet corner. We toasted peace over drinks, and the foreign minister, Sullivan, and I exchanged a few pleasantries. Meanwhile, Chinese houseboys were serving hors d'oeuvres. Without thinking, I declined some, accepted some, and thanked them—all in my best Chinese-restaurant Mandarin.

"Do you speak Chinese?" Chen Yi suddenly asked—in Chinese.

"Yes, but not well," I replied in Chinese, dredging up, from the bowels of my long-ago elementary Chinese, an idiom, "mah-mah hoo-hoo," Horse-Horse, Tiger-Tiger—which is to say, comme ci, comme ça, or so-so.

Chen Yi was clearly impressed with my use of the idiomatic expression. He mistook virtual ignorance for becoming modesty. To my horror and to Sullivan's astonishment, the foreign minister dismissed his interpreter and launched into a monologue that went on for several minutes. I caught one word in ten, but nodded and murmured an occasional "yes."

Sullivan and I escaped from the villa soon after. As we entered the hotel dining room for coffee, Rusk and Harriman were having dinner and beckoned us to their table.

"How did it go?" Rusk asked.

"Okay," I replied.

"Okay?" Sullivan exclaimed. "It was fantastic! Chet had a ten-minute private conversation with Chen Yi!"

"My God," Harriman looked at me with sudden avuncular affection. "Why didn't you tell me you spoke Chinese? What did he say? What did he want?"

"Well, you know, the same old stuff." I gave what I like to think was a modest shrug.

"I want to send a telegram about your session to Washington," Rusk said. "Let me have a two-page summary in the morning."

Desperation is the mother of necessity, which is the mother of . . . whatever. I dashed up to my room and found the telephone number of my friend, the UN Chinese translator. Luck was with me; he had just returned from the reception. "What were you and Sullivan doing at the villa? I thought that would be off-limits? And what was all that business with Chen Yi? I didn't know you spoke Chinese."

"There's a lot you don't know. But listen, I need your help. Rusk wants to send a report of that conversation to the department, but I don't want to trust my memory. Strike a blow for diplomacy and democracy. Go to their villa early tomorrow and get word to Chen Yi that I would like his version of what he'd like me to send to Washington. It would be only fair for me to use his words instead of mine. Translate it and let me have it before noon. I'll buy you lunch."

It was a win-win-win deal. According to my friend, the Chinese were pleased at my offer. I know Rusk liked my plagiarized two-pager. I could tell Harriman was proud. My friend enjoyed his lunch. I still had a job. And, oh yes, Chen Yi's message turned out to be "the same old stuff."

*   *   *

Sixteen months after the delegates first convened, Souvanna Phouma was installed as the head of a neutralist government in Vientiane, the Laos capital. Although his situation promised to be fragile, there was hope that, in the light of a "gentleman's agreement" between Harriman and Pushkin, foreign troops, whether American or Communist, would respect the neutrality of Laos. So far as I know, the Harriman-Pushkin agreement was never formally signed, sealed, or delivered, by either Washington or Moscow. Pushkin died soon after, perhaps without ever informing Moscow, Hanoi, or Beijing of his bargain with Harriman. In any case, it did not take long before Souvanna's government was undermined and then removed by the Pathet Lao with the support of the Viet Minh.

A few years later, General de Gaulle proposed a neutralist solution for South Vietnam. In the light of what happened to "neutralist" Laos, neither he nor the Communist government in Hanoi should have been surprised at Washington's cold reception.

The Laos conference adjourned, at last, on July 23, 1962. This was one of two happy events Orah and I celebrated that evening. The other was her birthday.

NOTES

1. *Public Papers of the Presidents of the United States: John F. Kennedy, 1962* (Washington, DC: US Government Printing Office, 1963), p. 23.

2. Charles E. Bohlen, *Witness to History: 1929–1969* (New York: W. W. Norton, 1973), pp. 480–82.

3. Ibid., p. 482.

This is the army, 1943. The author in infantry basic training.
(Author's collection)

Indochina Conference, Geneva, Switzerland, 1954.
(US National Archives)

Delegates to the Indochina Conference, Geneva 1954. From left: Gen. Bedell Smith (United States), Foreign Minister Georges Bidault (France), Lord Rufus Isaac Reading (United Kingdom), Ambassador Jean Chaval (France), Secretary of State John Foster Dulles (United States).
(US National Archives)

Suez crisis 1956. Meeting in Geneva, from left, are: Sir Roger
Makins, British Ambassador to the United States; Foreign
Secretary Anthony Eden; Secretary of State John Foster Dulles;
Winthrop W. Aldrich, US Ambassador to Great Britain.
(US National Archives)

Cuban militia on parade prior to the 1961 Bay of Pigs invasion.
(US National Archives)

MRBM FIELD LAUNCH SITE
Sagua la Grande No. 2
17 OCTOBER 1962

ER 63 LONG

TENT AREA

MISSILE CONTAIN

MOTOR POOL

ERECTORS

JNCH PADS
H ERECTORS

LAUNCH PADS

LA
WIT

An aerial view of a missile site at Sagua, Cuba, taken October 17, 1962, by air force surveillance.
(US Air Force)

Vice President Hubert Humphrey and other US officials arrive in Bangkok, Thailand, in 1966, to explain US policy regarding Vietnam. Chester Cooper is fourth to the left, behind Humphrey, who shakes hands with US officials as he deplanes.
(US Information Agency)

Governor Averell Harriman *(second from left)* and Chester Cooper *(far right)* arriving in Sri Lanka (Ceylon) in 1967, to meet with Buddhist religious leaders regarding Buddhist unrest in Vietnam. *(Author's collection)*

US-Vietnam peace negotiations, Paris 1969. *(US Information Agency)*

Henry Kissinger signing the Vietnam Peace Accord, January 1973. *(US National Archives)*

From left: Robert McNamara, Nicholas Katzenbach, Chester Cooper, and Francis Bator (*standing*) in Hanoi, Vietnam, 1997, to meet with former North Vietnamese officials to review the mindsets and policies during the Vietnam War. *(Monica d. Church © 1997)*

Robert McNamara *(left)* and (North) Vietnamese general Vo Nguyen Giap, Hanoi 1997. *(Monica d. Church © 1997)*

Chester Cooper *(right)* and Luu Doan Huynh (former North Vietnamese soldier and diplomat, presently Senior Research Fellow, Vietnamese Institute for International Relations) in Hanoi in 1998 for continuation of discussions about the Vietnam War. *(Janet Lang)*

Clockwise from right: Robert McNamara, a former Hanoi diplomat, an interpreter, and Chester Cooper at the White Oak Plantation, Florida, 1999, for further discussions about the Vietnam War, primarily the failure of the negotiations effort. *(Monica d. Church © 1999)*

Chester Cooper at US-Vietnam meeting, White Oak Plantation, 1999. *(Monica d. Church © 1999)*

IO

"The Most Dangerous Moment of the Cold War"

ABOUT US-CUBAN RELATIONS

Cuba, discovered in 1492 by Columbus, became a Spanish colony in 1511. It had a checkered, colorful early history marked by piracy, a prosperous slave trade, and internal unrest and revolts. In 1895 a war of independence was soon supported by the United States after the Spanish attack on the USS Maine. The Spanish were defeated and Cuba was declared an independent country in 1898, although the treaty gave the United States the right to meddle in Cuban affairs. During the following years American investments, particularly in sugar production, dominated the Cuban economy.

In 1933 a coup brought Fulgencio Batista Zaldívar, a former army sergeant, control of the country. With US assistance, Batista ruled Cuba with a heavy hand until 1959, when Castro, with the help of the legendary Ernest "Che" Guevara, ousted Batista after a prolonged guerrilla war.

Castro soon turned to the Soviet Union for political and economic support. This was accompanied by virulent anti-American diatribes, expropriation of American property, and harsh internal actions against prodemocratic individuals and institutions.

In 1961 the United States severed relations with Cuba. Thousands of anti-Castro Cubans fled to the United States, especially to Miami and surrounding areas. The refugee Cubans soon became an influential political force and played a principal role in the Bay of Pigs fiasco described in chapter 9.

193

*   *   *

Soon after we arrived home, CIA cables were reporting that Moscow had sharply increased its military shipments to Cuba. On August 1, 1962, an ambivalent national intelligence estimate concluded that Moscow is "deeply committed to preserve and strengthen the Castro government . . . [but] has avoided any commitment to preserve and protect the regime in all contingencies."[1]

At a meeting of the National Security Council on August 10, John McCone, who, after the failed Bay of Pigs invasion, had replaced Allen Dulles as head of the CIA, reported a "burst" of Soviet arms arriving in Cuba. Although the CIA was unable to specify the nature of the shipments, McCone speculated that Moscow might be installing medium-range ballistic missiles. Ten days later, he reported that the CIA had identified surface-to-air missiles in Cuba and, once again, he suggested that ballistic (nuclear) missiles might be next. As the days went on, McCone became increasingly insistent, in the face of skepticism among his colleagues and subordinates, that the placement of a large number of costly defensive weapons on several Cuban sites augured Soviet determination to protect such major strategic weapons as medium-range nuclear missiles.

McCone was right. Most of his CIA analysts and senior colleagues in the Departments of State and Defense were wrong. Subsequent information revealed that, by early August, Soviet engineers were constructing antimissile sites throughout the island and that Soviet armored units had already arrived. Meanwhile, the flow of arms accelerated. By late September intermediate and short-range missile sites were under construction.[2] Although this ominous activity was hidden from American intelligence sources on the ground, high-flying U-2s carrying sophisticated photographic equipment provided excellent pictures of ships loaded with suspicious cargoes and of heavy truck traffic in and around Cuban ports. The CIA warned the president of the buildup of Soviet forces and the installation of nuclear weapons pointing toward the United States.

On October 16, 1962, all doubt about the nature and purpose of Moscow's busy military activity in Cuba was dispelled. At noon that day, the CIA presented its findings to a small senior group of government interagency officials (the Executive Committee of the National Security Council, or "ExComm"). Detailed photographs taken by the U-2s showed the sites where surface-to-air missile launchers were being constructed. This was all the more galling because Soviet ambassador Anatoly Dobrynin had, only a few days before, assured one of the members of ExComm, Robert Kennedy, that Moscow would not install surface-to-air missiles in Cuba.[3]

Information about the Soviet weapons was closely held within the White House and within a small circle of officials and analysts in the national security community. For several days, neither the Cubans nor the Soviets had any hint that the United States knew about their rapidly budding missile capability. In the CIA, only a few analysts, several members of the national intelligence estimates staff, and some photo interpreters held the special clearance, "Psalm," that allowed them access to the relevant intelligence. Indeed, the Psalm clearance was so carefully guarded that I did not know who among my colleagues was also cleared until I attended a Psalm-cleared meeting.

It was a stroke of irony that, on the day after the CIA got its first information about the missile-launching sites (Wednesday, October 17), Andrei Gromyko, the Soviet foreign minister, had a long-standing appointment to see President Kennedy. Kennedy decided not to cancel the appointment lest the Soviets suspect something of consequence was amiss. According to Robert Kennedy, Gromyko assured President Kennedy that the only assistance Moscow had been giving Cuba was for agricultural purposes; Gromyko said that the Soviet Union did not intend to provide Cuba with offensive weapons.[4] The president did not reveal to Gromyko that, while they were talking, American officials were in a nearby room considering an attack on the offensive missile sites.

Early in the ExComm deliberations, the CIA estimated that Cuba's intercontinental ballistic missiles (ICBMs) would, if launched, kill eighty million Americans in cities within a thousand-mile radius of Cuba. By Saturday, October 20 (a crucial day), the CIA reported that Cuba already had a formidable air and coastal defense system. At least twenty-four surface-to-air missile sites covered most of the island. Of these, seventeen appeared to have missiles on launchers. MiG fighter aircraft and coastal defense missile sites were identified. Several launching pads for one-thousand-mile missile sites and several two-thousand-mile ICBM launching pads were under construction, with some nearing completion.[5] So much for Mr. Gromyko's "agricultural assistance."

Kennedy's advisers, in day and night sessions, debated a range of preemptive and retaliatory military options. Ultimately, four actions were under consideration: a blockade, an air strike, an invasion, or some combination of these. By October 20, largely at the urging of Robert Kennedy and Robert McNamara, with US military forces already on the highest alert, the presi-

The Range of Soviet Nuclear Missiles in Cuba, 1962.

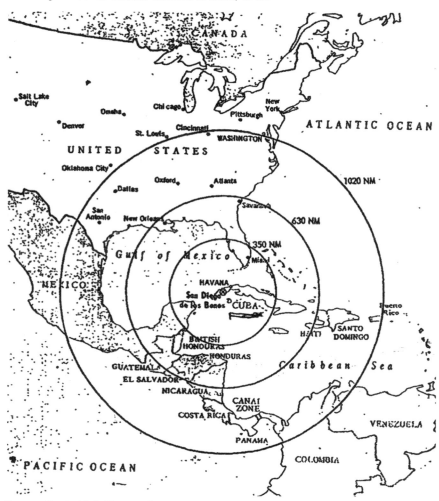

Source: Central Intelligence Agency

dent chose the blockade option. By now, the stress level among the ExComm members and their assistants was so high one could virtually see it, feel it, breathe it.

Soon after the president informed his advisers that he had decided on and would immediately implement a blockade, he scheduled a speech to the nation and the world on the evening of Monday, October 22. He planned to reveal the seriousness of the Cuban/Soviet threat, his determination to remove or destroy the missiles, and his decision to blockade Cuba.

From Saturday afternoon through Monday night, the Oval Office at the White House, Secretary Rusk's office at the State Department, and Secretary McNamara's and the Joint Chiefs' offices at the Pentagon were scenes of frantic, secret activity. The cabinet and selected members of Congress had to be informed, the navy had to assemble the blockade force, and America's allies as well as the UN had to be warned and their support attained.

I was called to Secretary Rusk's office late that Saturday afternoon. There I found former secretary of state Dean Acheson, presidential assistant Mac Bundy, CIA colleagues Jack Smith and Sherman Kent, and Art Lundahl, the CIA's chief of photographic interpretation. The meeting was short. We were told that cars were waiting to take Acheson, Kent, Smith, and me home. We were to pack a few clothes and return immediately to the State Department. There we would each be given a packet of the U-2 photographs, a special passport, and a few hundred dollars. A military plane would be waiting at Andrews Air Force Base to fly us to Europe—me to London, Acheson and Kent to Paris, and Smith to Bonn. An armed guard would meet each of us at remote airports in England, France, and Germany. Prime Minister Macmillan, President de Gaulle, and Chancellor Konrad Adenauer would be expecting us on Sunday morning, when we would brief our assigned allied leader on the nature and significance of the incriminatory photographs. We were forcefully instructed to emphasize how important it was for President Kennedy to have their full support over the next dangerous days and weeks.

The problem, or at least my personal problem, with Secretary Rusk's choreography was one awaiting me at home. As author Arthur Schlesinger has pointed out, a group of intelligence analysts from Britain, Canada, Australia, and New Zealand had been meeting with their CIA counterparts all that week. "Suspicions had been aroused early in the week when the meeting drew a diminishing American representation or were called off altogether . . . by Saturday night the team was alive with speculation and anticipation."[6]

That Saturday night, Orah and I had planned a good-bye reception and dinner at our home for a dozen or so of our allied colleagues. As the State Department car sped up Connecticut Avenue toward Chevy Chase, it occurred to me that I would be arriving home at about the same time as our guests. Luckily, I beat the first arrival by a few minutes, gave Orah a hasty, guarded rundown, threw some clothes in a suitcase, and dashed out the back door. Orah, an unflappable and always gracious hostess, got through the evening alone with a few lame excuses and more or less without incident. Several days later, in reviewing that evening, Orah and I were sure that my mysterious absence was made known later that night to whomever our guests reported.

While this may seem amusing in retrospect, it was deadly serious at the time. I realized then that the situation could change quickly from a blockade to an exchange of fire, to sunken ships and heavy casualties, to an American air assault on Cuba followed by invasion, and, then, a full-scale US-Soviet war with the launching of nuclear missiles from either Cuba or the Soviet Union. My good-bye kisses to Orah and the girls carried a special, unspoken meaning.

Many years later, Robert McNamara, in an interview with a CIA historian, reported on conversations he had had about the missile crisis with his Soviet counterpart. We were "very, very close to nuclear war."[7] Schlesinger, who was then on President Kennedy's staff, recounted his impressions of that time at a Kennedy Library meeting forty years after the crisis: "The . . . crisis was the most dangerous moment of the Cold War. It can be argued further that it was the most dangerous moment in human history. . . . We were lucky to have survived it."[8]

*   *   *

There was little small talk on Air Force One (Junior Grade) as we flew across the Atlantic. Acheson had the foresight to bring a bottle of whiskey, and somehow, we got an hour or so of sleep. It was dawn when we landed at a remote corner of a military air base north of London. Although it was dark and foggy as we taxied toward the far edge of the airfield, I could discern a tall man standing beside a large car. As I climbed down the steps onto the tarmac, the man waved. He was US ambassador David Bruce, one of America's ambassadorial greats. Dean Acheson took Bruce aside for a brief, solemn talk. Then Bruce turned to me. "Let's head back to London. You've got a long, hard day ahead."

Acheson gave me a firm handshake. He whispered, "Good luck," and waved to Bruce. "Keep in touch, David."

I was surprised that the ambassador himself had driven to the airfield at that hour from London, and even more surprised that, despite Secretary Rusk's promise, there was no armed guard accompanying us. I mentioned this to Bruce. "You have an armed escort," he grinned, and pulled his overcoat open. I saw a pistol in a holster. "I'm your escort." I was soon to learn that Bruce was on the US revolver team in the 1924 Olympics.

I had a few hours' sleep, a shave, a shower, and breakfast at the embassy residence. The ambassador and I then went off to 10 Downing Street for our Sunday morning appointment with Prime Minister Harold Macmillan.

The prime minister, with his private secretary, was expecting us in his private office, which, to my astonishment, was small and simple. Indeed, the living quarters of 10 Downing Street, to the extent I could see them, were less grand than those of some of my well-off CIA colleagues.

After introducing me, Ambassador Bruce indicated that he, himself, had not yet seen the photographs of the missiles and that I would, as a result, be briefing both him and the prime minister. I unwrapped the pictures and pointed out the ICBM sites under various stages of construction. Macmillan and Bruce were clearly amazed at the details and clarity of the photographs. They shook their heads in disbelief at the risks the missile sites presented and at the Soviets' gall and chicanery.

Macmillan's first words, which he addressed more to himself than to Bruce or me, were to the effect that the British people, who had been in the shadow of Soviet nuclear annihilation for the past many years, had somehow been able to live more or less normal lives. He felt that the Americans, now confronted with a similar situation, would, after the initial shock, make a similar adjustment. "Life goes on somehow."

The prime minister, aware that his remarks might be misinterpreted, explained that they were more of a philosophical commentary on human nature than an indication that he was unsympathetic with the US situation. He went on to say that if the president was convinced that the missiles presented a meaningful offensive capability, "that is good enough for me." He thought, however, that a blockade would be difficult to enforce and that the United States would have problems getting solid UN support. He wondered whether it would not have been better to have confronted Khrushchev directly and given him a private ultimatum.[9]

As we were leaving, Macmillan urged me to brief the Labour opposition so as to dispel any doubt in their minds as to the reality and seriousness of the threat. This was especially important because of the vocal, leftist "Ban the Bomb" demonstrations[10] then occurring all over Britain. (Indeed, as Ambassador Bruce knew all too well, the demonstrators were a noisy and frequent presence in Grosvenor Square fronting the American embassy.) One of his aides, Macmillan said, would notify Hugh Gaitskill, the leader of the Labour Party, that the American ambassador and someone from Washington wanted to meet with him urgently on an important matter.

Ambassador Bruce arranged for the meeting to be held that evening at the home of Archie Roosevelt, the CIA's chief of station. Either Bruce deemed it unwise to meet with members of Her Majesty's opposition party, or he had another, more important engagement. In any event, he suggested I go alone.

Early that afternoon, I informed CIA of the forthcoming session, took a long walk, and returned to the embassy to discover that, sure enough, a large "Ban the Bomb" crowd was once again gathering in Grosvenor Square. I made my way up the steps leading to the embassy entrance with the help of a few policemen and to the sound of jeers and shouts.

I removed the photographs from the CIA's vault and, accompanied to the rear entrance of the embassy by a marine guard, was driven to Roosevelt's house. Hugh Gaitskill (then head of the Labour Party), George Brown (shadow defense minister), and Dennis Healey (shadow foreign secretary) were already there. After my briefing, Brown and Healey, whom I had known well since my London embassy years, immediately promised their support. Gaitskill, however, was somewhat skeptical; since the locations of the sites were taped over (I'm not sure why), he wanted assurance that the missile sites I had shown him were actually in Cuba, not, say, in Russia.

Luckily, in one photo one could discern a grove of palm trees. Another had a good shot of a coastal stretch bordering a farm where another missile launch pad was being constructed. I had a detailed map of Cuba with me, and Gaitskill and I compared the coastal outlines. Gaitskill was satisfied and promised to back Macmillan in Parliament and to support an American blockade.

I called the embassy at about ten o'clock to say I was ready to return and asked for the car. Although Roosevelt's house was not far from Grosvenor Square, a half hour passed and there was no sign of the car. Eventually, a marine guard called. The crowd around the embassy was so large and so aggressive, he said, that it would be unwise to leave the building until the demonstration was over. Could I stay the night with Mr. Roosevelt?

George Brown, overhearing the conversation, was irate. "The buggers! I'll take you back. Don't worry, they all know me."

I wrapped up the pictures, hid them under an old blanket in George's Mini-Minor, and off we went. The marine was right: The embassy was surrounded by a milling, shrieking mob. George was not daunted. We crawled up Brooke Street with Brown leaning out the car window, shouting, "Get the bloody hell out of the way! I'm George Brown. I'm one of you buggers! Move!"[11]

He inched the car into Grosvenor Square and as near as he could to the embassy steps. We then signaled to the police to hustle me inside the building.

In the years to come, when he was foreign secretary and, later, when he was in the House of Lords, Brown gave me many difficult moments, but nothing he said or did was enough to cancel out his gallantry and help that night.

It had been a long, jet-lagged, food-deprived, frenetic day. I got back to the embassy residence well after midnight. A bottle of whiskey and some ice were on the table beside my bed. I slept well, which, considering what was awaiting me the next night, was a Good Thing.

*   *   *

When foreign service officers, both those still on active duty and those long retired, get together, a favorite subject of conversation (and complaint) is how presidents and secretaries of state reserve the best US embassies abroad for well-heeled friends, or generous campaign contributors, or the socially ambitious in-laws of a wife's cousin. Those are the ones who wind up as excellencies in Paris, London, Rome, Tokyo, and the Bahamas. Addis Ababa, Vientiane, Damascus, and Lagos are handed out to professionals who have slogged their way up the foreign service ladder.

Diplomacy, especially in times of trouble, requires different skills, experience, and temperament than one acquires in merchant banks, Wall Street brokerages, Palm Beach salons, Chicago law offices, or San Francisco dot-com enterprises. No wonder, then, that at the end of the day, many noncareer ambassadors turn out to be duds or ciphers. But Ambassador David Bruce, friend and supporter of Jack Kennedy, was neither a dud nor a cipher. He was at least as knowledgeable, effective, unflappable, energetic, and skilled as any professional foreign service officer. One reason, I should admit, for my long-time enthusiasm and admiration for Ambassador Bruce is that he stood up for me when I needed him. As, for instance, on Monday night, October 22, 1962. And as he did, again, a few years later. David Bruce was a first-class diplomat, a splendid boss, and a good friend.

My problems on Monday started with a phone call to Ambassador Bruce early that morning from 10 Downing Street. Would Chet Cooper hold a press conference for British defense correspondents with regard to the missiles in Cuba? Macmillan's press aide suggested it would be best if I could brief the London-based press just prior to the president's speech, scheduled around midnight London time. He assured me that only accredited defense correspondents of British papers would be invited. The time difference would ensure that no stories would be available in the United States until the next morning. (He was wrong about that.) Macmillan's press adviser went on to say that the British press, much of it anti-American (Ban the Bomb, the Suez aftermath, and all that), would be highly skeptical of Kennedy's revelations unless they could actually see the photographs themselves.

Bruce agreed to the press briefing and arranged for it to be held in the embassy's conference room. Despite the ambassador's approval, I found the notion of a press conference troubling. I worried that the British press would know about the missile sites before the American media, since London was five hours ahead of Washington. Moreover, as far as I knew, the photographs were still considered top secret by both the Pentagon and the White House. Finally, large press conferences were not my best subject; I was much more comfortable, and likely to be more circumspect, on a one-on-one basis with reporters.

All things considered, I felt it would be prudent (realizing that prudence was also not my best subject) to seek Washington's advance approval. It was already Monday afternoon; there was little time to squander. I sent an urgent telegram to Ray Cline (who had recently replaced Bob Amory as deputy director, and was my immediate boss). I related the story of the somewhat chaotic state of play in London, of Bruce's approval of a press conference, and of my own uncertainty. I realized, I said, that he and others in Washington would be preoccupied, but I needed a yes or a no by eleven o'clock that night London time (six o'clock Washington time). If I did not get a reply by my deadline, I would assume silence meant consent and would go ahead with my briefing.

Eleven o'clock came and went. No reply. A score of impatient reporters, including, to my consternation, two from the BBC who were gathering material for a forthcoming Cuba special, were waiting outside Bruce's office. We decided to go ahead. We adjourned about 11:45, so that the reporters could listen to Kennedy. Bruce felt the session went well. I got back to my hotel nearby, where I had moved that morning, in time to hear all but the first minute or two of the president's speech.

Exhausted, I then went to bed. At about three in the morning, the phone rang. It was Ray Cline. Ray could be a world-class whiner, and he whined through the next several minutes. What did I think I was doing? Who gave me permission? I was in trouble. He was in trouble. The CIA was in trouble. We had better have a talk as soon as I got back. I couldn't wait.

I had hardly hung up when Kennedy's press secretary, Pierre Salinger, called. He didn't whine. He exploded. Several of the London papers had wired their New York offices with a summary of my briefing, including the pictures (which they had gotten from the BBC film). He was in a hell of a jam with the American press. They were bitching that the Brits saw the photos before the Americans. "As for you, Cooper, you are *really* in a mess." I was to check in (check out?) with him when I got back to Washington. I couldn't wait for my session with him either.

Then came Arthur Sylvester, the Pentagon's press man. He didn't explode. He went ballistic, perhaps in no small part because he had been trying to reach me on the phone. "Who the hell have you been talking to at this hour of the night?" And then, "What made you think . . . ? Why didn't you ask . . . ? You really goofed." He didn't invite me over, however.

I tried to tell my friendly callers that I had asked for a green light and gave them a deadline. They had some explaining to do, not I. But they weren't listening.

Sleep was impossible. I left the hotel soon after seven on Tuesday morning, hunting for copies of the *Times*, *Guardian*, *Telegraph*, *Mirror*—any paper. After all, my fate was now in the hands of reporters. I needn't have worried. Virtually every correspondent, even the snotty questioners from the *Guardian*, even the self-important ones from the *Times*, had reported straightforward accounts of the previous night's session. More important, they had written approvingly of Kennedy's speech. The ambassador was delighted. As soon as Washington was awake, he called Cline, Salinger, Sylvester, and a few others to say what a great job I had done; congratulations, not carping, were in order. Later in the day we heard from 10 Downing Street. The prime minister was most pleased, and, as of that moment, was giving a speech in Parliament giving Kennedy his full support.

I returned to Washington a few days later. I heard no more from Salinger or Sylvester, although Cline continued to whine. I was a wiser man, however, than I had been only a week or so before. I now realized that silence could mean not only consent, but also silence.

*   *   *

Back at the CIA I rejoined my colleagues on the National Intelligence Board in waiting and watching for Moscow's reaction to the US Navy blockade. There had been no indications of a Soviet stand-down in Cuba on the day following Kennedy's speech. Quite the contrary. Construction on several missile sites was continuing. A CIA memorandum sent to selected national security officials on October 24 reported that "[s]urveillance . . . indicates continued rapid progress in completion of IRBM and MRBM sites. No new sites had been discovered. Buildings believed to afford nuclear storage are being assembled with great rapidity."[12] On October 25, the CIA reported that "no change has been noted in the scope or pace of the construction at the IRBM and MRBM missile sites." The CIA also reported that as of dawn on October 25 "at least 14 of the 22 Soviet ships . . . en route to Cuba had turned back."[13]

Nevertheless, on October 26, construction on the missile sites was apparently still proceeding.

President Kennedy was growing increasingly impatient and had activated twenty-four troop-carrier squadrons of the air force reserve in the event of a decision to invade Cuba.[14] On October 26, however, Khrushchev sent a letter to Kennedy, the first of a few exchanges, which, in the end, resulted in a satisfactory conclusion—for the Americans, if not for the Soviets and the Cubans. On Sunday, October 28, Khrushchev ordered the dismantling of the missile sites and the removal of the missiles. The denouement came not a day too soon. An invasion of Cuba was highly likely if the standoff had lasted much longer. There was a sigh of relief audible from Portland, Oregon, to Portland, Maine.

According to two American scholars of the missile crisis and its aftermath in Cuba, "The shock to the Cubans [of Moscow's agreement to remove the missiles] can hardly be overemphasized. . . . [T]he Cubans would never fully trust the Soviets again for the security of their island. . . . Having dreamed of a Soviet umbrella of protection . . . they suddenly, on Oct. 28, 1962, found . . . they were shockingly and absolutely *alone*."[15]

*   *   *

A by-product of the crisis was a decision by President Kennedy and his special assistant for national security affairs, McGeorge Bundy, that the White House needed a closer relationship with the CIA's intelligence analysts. Despite the early morning shouting matches between Washington and London on October 23, I was promoted to assistant deputy director of intelligence and designated the CIA's point man with the National Security Council staff. This confirmed my long-held conviction that it is easier to get forgiveness than permission.

NOTES

1. Central Intelligence Agency, "The Situation and Prospects in Cuba," National Intelligence Estimate 85-2-62, August 1, 1962. From Mary S. McAuliffe, ed., *Cuban Missile Crisis, 1962* (CIA history staff, October 1962).

2. McAuliffe, *Cuban Missile Crisis*, pp. 13–16.

3. Robert Kennedy, *Thirteen Days* (New York: W. W. Norton, 1969), p. 24.

4. Ibid., p. 52.

5. Central Intelligence Agency, "Soviet Military Buildup in Cuba," briefing

notes for heads of government, October 21, 1962. From McAuliffe, *Cuban Missile Crisis*, pp. 248–58.

6. Arthur M. Schlesinger Jr., *A Thousand Days* (Boston: Houghton Mifflin, 1965), p. 809.

7. Robert McNamara, interview, Central Intelligence Agency, June 1998.

8. *Washington Post*, October 21, 2002, p. A7.

9. This account of the meeting with Prime Minister Macmillan on October 22, 1962, is taken virtually verbatim from a top-secret memorandum for the record that I prepared for CIA Director John McCone on October 29, 1962. It has since been declassified, and excerpts from the memorandum, including the material cited here, appeared in a declassified article by Sherman Kent in *Studies in Intelligence*, Spring 1972.

10. These demonstrations were directed at the American Strategic Air Command bases located in a few airfields around Britain.

11. This, obviously, is based on my memory, although in this case I was able to refresh my recollection during an alcohol-fueled evening with Brown a few years later.

12. McAuliffe, *Cuban Missile Crisis*, p. 296.

13. Ibid., p. 304.

14. Kennedy, *Thirteen Days*, p. 109.

15. James G. Blight and Philip Brenner, *Sad and Luminous Days* (London: Rowman Littlefield, 2002), p. 71.

11

LBJ's "Gray Book"

ABOUT THE PRESIDENT AND THE PRESS

Other than a terrorist attack, there is probably nothing that captures a president's attention as much as a leak. Even when the leak can be traced back to the president himself (as it often can), the Great Man's reaction can make even the strongest staffer cower. Some presidents will go to inordinate lengths to preempt, neuter, or end-run leaked confidential information. Note, for example, the incident described below with regard to appointing an ambassador to Japan.

The relations of a president to a particular correspondent or to the press in general vary depending on the mindset and personality of the president and how he interprets the time-honored dictum about the public's "right to know."

President Kennedy got along with the press in general and, indeed, had close relations with several reporters—Joe Alsop of the Washington Post, *Scotty Reston of the* New York Times, *Henry Brandon of the* London Sunday Times. *In part because of this (and probably because the standards of the '60s were less intrusive than those of the '90s) Kennedy got away with his sexual foibles.*

Lyndon Johnson, I know all too well, not only distrusted the press, but also distrusted anyone on his staff who had even trivial contacts with the press. If he could, Johnson would have been his own public affairs officer. He

had three television sets in his office, each tuned into one of the major sta-
tions. (Back in Texas, the Johnson family owned a group of TV stations.)

Richard Nixon's relationship with the press was secretive, distrustful,
even hostile. The media, for its part, returned the ill will. At his final press
conference, just before he left Washington in disgrace midway through his
second term, he told the press, bitterly, that they would not have him to kick
around anymore.

In the cases of Johnson and Nixon (and during the last year or so of
Kennedy) the issue of the "credibility gap" with regard to Vietnam did much
to poison White House–media relations.

President Clinton's press tended to be dominated by his ill-concealed
and apparently uncontrolled sexual appetite. Even serious-minded corre-
spondents became diverted from writing about Clinton's acknowledged
accomplishments by the daily salacious tidbits. (Jack Kennedy was lucky.)

As for President Bush the Younger, he has tried mightily to conduct the
White House's activities in a carefully monitored, leak-proof container. Except
for occasional moments of banter and banal exchanges, his direct contact
with the media has been limited to a handful of press conferences and one or
two one-on-one interviews. It will be several years before we know what really
went on behind the closed doors of the White House Cabinet Room.

*   *   *

My White House connection started early in 1963. As the CIA's assistant deputy director of intelligence (long title!), I was to provide a bridge between the agency's estimators, analysts, and researchers and
the National Security Council staff. On the one hand, I would ensure that
issues of current concern to the NSC received whatever intelligence support
the agency could provide. On the other hand, I would alert the NSC staff to
the CIA's assessment of security problems on the horizon. This was a new
arrangement put in train after the Cuban Missile Crisis.

I spent mornings in the White House Situation Room, where McGeorge
Bundy held his staff meetings. At midday, I drove to the CIA, informed the
director and his deputies of the NSC's concerns, and, on the following
morning, provided the council's staff with spot information, intelligence estimates, and longer-term analyses. The knowledge that their work was directly
relevant to the NSC agenda motivated the CIA's analysts, and their intelligence was relevant and timely—a win-win situation.

This arrangement was tested early in my new incarnation. It was a time when the long-simmering war between China and India was coming to a boil. Chinese troops were massing on India's mountainous northeast border. If they broke through Indian defenses, they would have an easy descent into the plains and be in position to threaten New Delhi itself. One of Bundy's morning staff meetings was almost entirely devoted to whether the Chinese or the Indians were better trained, equipped, and acclimated to fight in high altitudes. Since none of the former academics or current professional civil servants on his staff had ever been within hundreds of miles of the area in question (or, for most of them, including Bundy, in either China or India— or, for that matter, anywhere in Asia), I was astonished at their readiness to deal seriously with such an arcane matter.

I have since learned that White House staff members, particularly those with little previous practical experience in public policymaking, have a high specific gravity of hubris. It takes a long time before they come to know that they do not know. Indeed, some of them never have such an epiphany.

One staffer out-hubrised them all—on any subject. On this occasion, he delivered a facile exegesis about the high winds in the mountain passes. He professed to know whether the winds from the east or west, north or south would favor the attackers or defenders.

For my first few staff meetings, I quite uncharacteristically held my tongue. I was a new boy and wasn't sure of the ground rules. It soon turned out there were no ground rules; it was a matter of "do not speak while I am interrupting." The discourse on January winds in the high Himalayas, however, triggered my indignation and prompted my maiden speech. I was surprised, I said, that the staff was prepared to waste its time on a subject its members obviously knew nothing about. I promised to have some reasonably solid information soon.

On the following morning, the CIA's Office of Geographic Research and its Office of Current Intelligence had the answers waiting when I arrived at the White House Situation Room. They provided a detailed map, comparative assessments of Chinese and Indian cold-weather equipment, training and clothing, and an order-of-battle table. The frosting on the cake was their judgment that the winter winds in the mountain passes at issue would almost certainly be at the backs of the Indian defenders. Kudos to the CIA!

One person who would have been entitled to an opinion on this subject was former Harvard professor, and then ambassador to India, John Kenneth Galbraith. Prior to leaving for his embassy in New Delhi in early 1961, he was briefed at CIA by an eager young newly minted PhD specialist. Despite

Galbraith's impressive reputation and my own seniority, the briefing was pedestrian, pedantic, and condescending. I was becoming increasingly embarrassed and Galbraith increasingly restless. When the analyst unveiled a map of northeast India and, in painful detail, began to describe the area of conflict, Galbraith's patience snapped.

"Don't bother any further, young man. I know the area well. It's where I was trekking when I was bitten in the testicles by a mad dog. Thank you. I have another appointment."

Many months later, during the Laos Conference, Galbraith passed through Geneva on his way to Washington. In a taxi on our way to dinner I asked him if his dog story was true. He unzipped his trousers and asked, "Do you want to see?" I took his word for it.

An enterprise far less successful than the winds-in-the-Himalayas caper had to do with Premier Khrushchev's visit to Washington after the Cuban missile crisis had been laid to rest. In preparation for the visit, Bundy reminded his staff that Khrushchev was not interested in the usual sight-seeing tour. He wanted to visit places and groups in Washington relevant to his concerns about raising living standards in the Soviet Union.

I had, a few years before, volunteered to be a guinea pig for an experimental drug at the National Institutes of Health (NIH). This involved an initial stay of two weeks at the NIH hospital and monthly checkups for a few years thereafter. I had been impressed, not only with the NIH staff and facilities, but also with the fact that the medical personnel as well as the patients, black and white, had long been integrated. I suggested that Khrushchev be given a tour of the NIH facilities. Bundy was enthusiastic and asked me to work out the arrangements. The folk at the NIH were pleased, as well. All was ready on the day of the visit. At the last minute, however, Khrushchev insisted on visiting, instead, the National Institute of Dry Cleaning, where hard-to-clean garments were dealt with. So much for that great idea.

*   *   *

If Cuba was no longer among the most urgent issues on the NSC agenda, Vietnam, the proverbial "tar baby," would not go away. By early 1963 the situation in Vietnam was getting worse, week by week. In January the South Vietnamese army was badly beaten in the battle of Ap Bac. There were heavy casualties, including three American military advisers.

By early spring, there were twelve thousand US Army advisers in Vietnam. Although a Pentagon spokesman claimed that "the corner has definitely turned towards victory," CIA Director John McCone was dubious. He sent me to Vietnam to assess whether we could "win with Diem," or whether Diem should be deposed.

I spent a week or so in Saigon and a few days in the field. In Saigon, I met with President Diem for five hours, during which he lectured to me in a combination of French and English through a haze of cigarette smoke. I drank at least a dozen cups of tea without any plumbing in sight.

I came to the conclusion that Diem was living in an isolated fantasy world. He was told only what his courtiers thought he wanted to hear—which had little to do with the actual situation. On the following afternoon, I spent three hours with Diem's brother Nhu, who, together with his manipulative wife, the "Dragon Lady," provided the power behind the scenes.

On my return, I reported to McCone, members of the State and Defense departments, and the NSC staff. Diem, in my opinion, may have been mentally ill. He talked incessantly and repetitively, he was nervous, blindly confident, a chain-smoker, and tea drinker. He may not have been committable, I said, "but if I were his mother, I'd be worried about him." Nonetheless, I thought it would be prudent to continue the United States' present relationship with him until an effective alternative was in sight. (The CIA was not very good at kingmaking.) It would not be long before tensions between the Buddhists and the predominantly Catholic Diem government escalated into riots, the self-immolation of monks, and, soon, martial law.

It was during this period that I resigned from the CIA to accept a senior position on Bundy's staff. My responsibilities would include the Far East, Australia, New Zealand, and Canada—a fair amount of real estate, much of it in sorely troubled Asia. Unlike subsequent bloated NSC staffs, Bundy's was lean, if not emaciated. I would be allocated two assistants and a secretary.

This was not an easy move; I had been at the CIA since early 1947. (Some suspicious souls never quite believed that I wasn't still employed there.) The NSC staff quarters were in the Old Executive Office Building adjoining the White House on Pennsylvania Avenue. The building dated back to the nineteenth century and, until the 1930s, housed the Departments of State, Army, and Navy. My vast, old-fashioned office had a fireplace, a floor-to-ceiling Victorian mirror, a balcony, an ancient, mammoth desk, and too many heavy armchairs. I also had inherited an impressive desk chair that, reportedly, once graced the vice president's office a floor below. (Several years later, just as I was leaving the White House, I saw an NSC colleague, a Harvard economics professor who was jealous of his perks and envious of others', wheeling the chair into his own office.)

I settled into my new role not a moment too soon. On November first, President Ngo Dinh Diem was murdered in a military coup. Within days, for all practical purposes, my Far East portfolio narrowed from Asia to Vietnam. I presented the rest of Asia to my two assistants, but kept Canada, Australia, and New Zealand; their ambassadors had become good friends of mine during my CIA days.

*   *   *

Three weeks after Diem's death, President Kennedy was assassinated and, in due course, his New Frontier evolved into Lyndon Johnson's Great Society. On the morning after the tragedy, I happened to be outside Bundy's office in the White House basement commiserating with his secretary. A grim John McCone walked in, soon followed by an ashen, haggard Lyndon Johnson. Johnson nodded to me, shook McCone's hand, and disappeared into Bundy's room. In a moment, Mac came out and beckoned McCone to join them. McCone pointed to me. Bundy waved me in.

For the next hour and a half, McCone gave the new president a rundown on the global problems he would be facing—Berlin, Vietnam, southern Africa, China, the USSR. It was an impressive performance. Bundy added his views now and then. I answered a question or two and took notes. At noon, the president left for a meeting with J. Edgar Hoover. Johnson had not yet moved out of the Old Executive Office Building, having decided to give Kennedy's staff time to remove the late president's personal possessions and papers from the Oval Office. I was going back to my office and followed President Johnson to the White House exit. It was pouring—an appropriately dismal day—and I held an umbrella over Johnson as we crossed West Executive Avenue. The media were out in force and the nightly news broadcasts gave the impression to my friends, relatives, colleagues, and distant acquaintances that I had been snatched from the ranks to become Johnson's executive assistant, or at least his umbrella carrier. (They soon were put right.)

When I eventually arrived home that night, I found a worried thirteen-year-old waiting up for me. Susan had a tearful confession. A few weeks before, she had lent Lucy Johnson, her older schoolmate, fifty cents. Now she was afraid to ask for her money, lest President Johnson fire me. I told Susan that Lucy's father had just gotten a raise and that she was to ask for her fifty cents the next day. I recounted this to Lucy in Austin thirty-five years later, and she assured me that she had repaid Susan the fifty cents.

*   *   *

Soon after Johnson took over, I was summoned to the Oval Office, and, after cooling my heels for a half hour or so, was ushered in. I was relieved to discover a steward just leaving; it was about 1:45 and I hadn't eaten since an early breakfast. I welcomed the prospect of lunch. Johnson had some questions about Vietnam and the discussion went well. We were interrupted by the steward. There was only one lunch on his tray. I spent the remainder of the session trying to focus on Vietnam while watching the president enjoy his meal.

In the end, my performance, however well it may have gone, was overshadowed by my subsequent linguistic ignorance. As I rose to leave, the president pointed vaguely at the table beside my chair.

"Mash that button, Chet, will you?"

What the hell did that mean? What button? How to mash it? Johnson, realizing that I was one of the unschooled New Englanders left over from Kennedy, waved me out and, presumably, he mashed the button, because his secretary went in as I left.

*   *   *

On his first full day as president, Johnson informed the NSC staff that, unlike his predecessor, he intended to hold regular meetings of the National Security Council so that key members of his administration would be kept closely informed. This, I'm sure, reflected his own frustration at having been frequently kept out of JFK's deliberations on national security. President Johnson was as good as his word—for a few weeks.

The president's first NSC meeting was held within a week or so of his taking office. Just as the meeting was starting, someone realized that the Speaker of the House of Representatives, John McCormick, who would assume the presidency in the event that Johnson died or was incapacitated, had not been asked to attend. A hurried call went out to the Hill and, twenty minutes later, a breathless McCormick showed up at the guard's desk outside the Cabinet Room. A new problem then arose: the congressman was not cleared for the issues on the council's agenda. Clearance forms were looked for, found, and signed. Then someone found a Bible, had the Speaker take the oath and sign a copy. A bewildered Speaker joined the waiting council and the meeting, at last, began.

Johnson soon discovered, as had Kennedy, that attendance at NSC meetings included several people who, more often than not, were extraneous to the matters at issue—the head of the Office of Emergency Management, the director of the Information Agency, and, in Johnson's case, the Speaker of the House. There were others who were relevant, but not officially members of the council—the director of the CIA, the chairman of the Joint Chiefs, and, in Kennedy's case, the attorney general. It was not long before Johnson, like Kennedy, assembled the council only for ceremonies, photo ops and formal approval of decisions already taken. Instead, he relied on a few, more knowledgeable people from State, Defense, and the CIA. Aside from its other advantages, a leaner, more select group was less likely to spawn leaks to the press—and leaks made Johnson very unhappy indeed.

By late winter 1964, many of Kennedy's New Yorkers and New Englanders had melted away, and the president's personal staff became dominated by people who knew how to mash buttons. By and large, however, the national security group under Mac Bundy remained intact. The people who had been closely involved with Vietnam—Secretary McNamara, Secretary Rusk, Mac and Bill Bundy, and me—stayed on, for better or worse.

An important change was the departure of John McCone, who felt himself increasingly closed out of policy discussions. McCone was succeeded by Richard Helms, a former OSSer and a longtime CIA career officer, who had stood aloof from the Bay of Pigs disaster and survived the purge.

During the remaining months of his accidental presidency, Johnson was anxious to demonstrate by word, if not entirely by deed, that his approach to the delicate and increasingly thorny Vietnam situation was basically a continuation of Kennedy's policy. This was becoming increasingly difficult; both the political and military situations in Vietnam were deteriorating. Nonetheless, Johnson wanted to keep Vietnam on hold until he could acquire some measure of intellectual control over the manifold problems that he suddenly and unexpectedly had to confront. In his first State of the Union message, he barely mentioned Vietnam.

*   *   *

Unfortunately, events in Vietnam had an ill-starred life of their own, and did not lend themselves to being put on hold. A succession of Vietnamese generals, some feckless, some corrupt, some feckless as well as corrupt, succeeded each other in Saigon's Presidential Palace. Fighting the Vietcong turned out to be less attractive and less remunerative to them than being president or playing courtier. The course of the war showed the effects of this.

The American press, led by several smart young reporters in Vietnam, was becoming more and more skeptical of American claims emanating from the military headquarters in Saigon and from the Pentagon that all was swell; the "credibility gap," first identified during the Kennedy period, was growing wider and deeper.

Officials in Washington seemed unable to sort out, in a credible way, US objectives with regard to the fighting in Vietnam. Different variations were provided by different spokesmen on different days: preserving democracy, assisting an ally in need, complying with the terms of the Southeast Asia Treaty Organization, making a stand against the Sino-Soviet bloc, concern lest the "dominoes" fall.

A white paper, which was originally prepared to show that the Vietcong were supplied and supported by the Communists, came up with a ludicrously frail case (although a stronger case could have been made if highly classified intelligence could have been used). When it was finally published, its findings were ridiculed even by the sympathetic press.

Another problem faced by administration spokesmen was that too many US agencies, civilian and military, in Vietnam were reporting too much junk to too many people in Washington. Secretary McNamara sent me to Vietnam to streamline and simplify the reporting system. Of course, he did not help matters with his penchant for measuring military progress through quantitative techniques, which he had learned at Harvard Business School and used at the Ford Motor Company.

Robert McNamara was not the only senior American official becoming obsessed with Vietnam by late 1963. Despite Lyndon Johnson's early attempts to focus on domestic problems, he found himself, willy-nilly, focusing on Southeast Asia rather than Southwest or Northeast America. After his victory in the 1964 presidential election, he was a legitimate, rather than a replacement, inhabitant of the Oval Office, and, now, Vietnam, like Hamlet's ghost, was hovering over him day and night. The secretaries of State and Defense and the director of the CIA also had Vietnam high on their worry lists. Indeed, McNamara and Rusk soon became their departments' virtual Vietnam desk officers; much of the rest of the world became a residual claimant for their time and attention.

*   *   *

Meanwhile, America was being polarized between the so-called hawks and doves. Where was I? First, a "hawk"; then, a "hawve"; finally, a "dove"—or, anyway, dovish. During much of the Kennedy administration, I was a target of many of our liberal friends. One dinner guest accused me of favoring US policy only because we had two daughters and no sons, and then sulked through the rest of the evening. Orah soon forbade any discussion of Vietnam at our dinner table—the weather, politics, religion, sex, but not Vietnam. By mid-1964, however, I came to be regarded as the White House's closet dove. For my sins, I became the liaison with various peace groups—the Student Nonviolent Coordinating Committee, the Women's Strike for Peace, SANE, and the university teach-in movement. For the record, SANE was the only group with which I could sensibly discuss the issue. As for the rest, shouting was the usual mode of discourse. Indeed, in the case of the university teach-ins, physical as well as oral violence was often the case—until I cut off contact with them altogether.

Joan and Susan were then at the National Cathedral School, hardly a hotbed of agitation. Nonetheless, it was not easy for them to live with the fact that I was "Mr. Vietnam" at the White House and their mother was at the CIA. (She was an economist, not a spook.) Later, when both were at university, the going was rougher. Somehow, the four of us worked it out. Orah and I stayed in constant communication with Joan and Susan on the phone and through letters, and encouraged frequent trips home. Perhaps because of this, Joan became active with regard to the civil rights issue rather than with Vietnam. During her summer vacation in 1964, when the civil rights advocates were picketing the White House, I dropped Joan off on the picket line in the morning and picked her up in the evening. But after Johnson sent his bill to Congress, I refused to do this, and Joan understood.

My twinges of doubt and concern about our Vietnam policy began in mid-1964 when the likelihood of a stable government in Saigon seemed increasingly remote. Whom were we binding ourselves to? A procession of unimpressive generals? Without the American crutch, would any one of them have the backing of their own people? The 1963 coup that resulted in the murder of Diem and his brother Nhu simply replaced one ineffectual regime with a series of others. The Buddhist uprisings and the growing strength and bravado of the Vietcong augured ill. The twenty-three thousand American troops already in Vietnam were too many to pass off as an unengaged advisory team and too few to influence the course of the military situation. As our commitment of economic aid, military manpower, and political prestige grew, so did my concerns and doubts.

Having said this, I, no less than most of my personal and professional associates, felt that the dolorous Vietnam situation, warts and all, was part of the cold war. With the costly, indecisive Korean War and the Cuban Missile Crisis fresh in my memory, and with the bellicose threats coming out of Beijing and Moscow, Vietnam seemed to be a place to put down our marker. (If this sounds like a condition of anguished uncertainty, that is precisely the case.)

As for the president, he was altogether frustrated. On April 20, he told Robert McNamara, "Let's get more of something [in Vietnam]. . . . I'm not doing much about fighting [this war]. I'm not doing much about winning it. Let's get somebody that wants to do something besides drop bombs. . . . We're losing. So we need something new."[1]

*   *   *

An event soon occurred that would change Washington's view of the fighting in Vietnam from a "hostility" to a war—or as close to a war as Lyndon Johnson would permit himself or the country to acknowledge. In early August 1964 an American destroyer in the Gulf of Tonkin, which Washington and the US Pacific Command in Honolulu judged to be international waters, was shot at by a North Vietnamese torpedo boat. The president ordered all US naval vessels to move a few miles farther away from the coast of North Vietnam and delivered a comparatively mild warning to Hanoi. On the next day, however, the destroyer reported suspicious activity by North Vietnam patrols and, later in the day, that it was fired on again.

An attack on American ships on the "high seas" was so brazen, so fraught with dangerous political and military implications, that it seemed to Washington that it could not have been undertaken without direct orders, or at least approval, from Hanoi's highest officials. This, of course, added to the apparent audacity of the attack.

I dashed across West Executive Avenue to the White House Situation Room as soon as the message about the first attack came across my desk, and I was actually in the Situation Room the next day when the report of the second attack came through. This time, unlike the day before, the report was by no means definite; the mood in the Pentagon and in the White House Situation Room was one of confusion and uncertainty. The incident (if there had actually been an incident) occurred at night, the seas were rough, and the sonar technician on watch was young, inexperienced, and jittery. Johnson, however, was seeking answers, not guesses. But McNamara was not sure. Neither was I, and I told Bundy we needed another day or so to verify. Admiral Grant Sharp, commander of the Pacific Fleet, had no doubts. The president ordered retaliatory strikes.[2]

Sixty-four bombing sorties were launched against the torpedo base and support buildings. On the following day, August 5, the president asked Congress to approve a resolution "to promote the maintenance of international peace and security in Southeast Asia" and to pledge Congress's full support for American troops in Indochina. Two days later, the resolution passed both houses. The vote in the House of Representatives was unanimous. The vote in the Senate passed with only two nays. The president signed the Gulf of Tonkin Resolution into law on August 11. (Although uncertainty about the second attack persisted for many years, there was ultimate agreement that an attack had not actually occurred.)

The initial congressional support for Johnson's Vietnam policy was soon marked by misgivings on the Hill, in the press, and among the academic community. Suspicions were rife that the joint resolution was not a direct response to the incidents in the Gulf of Tonkin. More likely, many felt, the wording had been prepared several weeks before and was lying close at hand waiting for the first excuse to use it. This was, of course, denied by the administration, although there was some truth to the allegation. As the number of American troops in Vietnam increased and the level of fighting escalated, congressmen, editorial writers, and political pundits accused the administration of sending Americans into battle without a declaration of war. This, too, was denied; the joint resolution was, according to LBJ, the equivalent of a congressional declaration of war.

What was undeniable was that the American presence in Vietnam was entering a new phase; our military advisers were becoming combatants, and the "hostilities" were becoming outright war, with or without a declaration.

*   *   *

In Saigon, meanwhile, the political situation was kaleidoscopic and the security situation chaotic. Between August 1, 1964, and February 1, 1965, there were several changes in government through coups or more amicable arrangements. Street riots by Buddhists and students (almost certainly egged on by Vietcong agents) were common occurrences.

During the autumn of 1964 and early winter of 1965, the CIA's views of the political situation in Saigon both mirrored and influenced my own. In early September, a national intelligence estimate concluded that "[at] present the odds are against the emergence of a stable government capable of prosecuting the war in South Vietnam."[3]

Three weeks later, the CIA reported that "the situation has continued to deteriorate . . . the conditions favor a further decay of . . . will and effectiveness. A coup . . . could occur at any time."[4] And so it could. And so it did. On January 27, 1965, Gen. Nguyen Khanh led a coup against the civilian government, the seventh change in government since early 1964. Many of these had been instigated by Khanh, who, himself, had been tossed out the previous summer. Two days later, the CIA concluded that Khanh's coup had "given South Vietnam one more, perhaps fleeting, opportunity to . . . prosecute the war effort more effectively." However, the agency added, "We believe the odds weigh heavily against success."[5]

The CIA's judgment of the odds proved correct. Matters continued to get worse instead of better. On Christmas Eve, an American officers' quarters was bombed. Two Americans died and more than fifty were wounded. There was no American retaliation; Johnson appeared to be holding back until after his inauguration. Nonetheless, Washington's Vietnam-policy community was anxious to start bombing North Vietnam. In a note to Bundy, I disagreed. Bombing the north, I said, would not force Hanoi to stop its support of the Vietcong or to become more amenable to negotiations. Our actions would be more productive if we focused on improving the performance of the South Vietnamese army.[6]

Soon after Lyndon Johnson was sworn in as president in his own right, he would no longer need to claim that he was simply following the course of his predecessor; for better or worse, Vietnam was now his problem.

So it was that, in mid-January 1965, President Johnson posed three options, which Mac Bundy referred to as confronting "a fork in the road." It was time to decide whether to escalate US military action, to continue on the present course, to dampen down American participation and seek a way out.

There was little support, except from Secretary Rusk, for the second option; neither the political or military outlook held promise. McNamara and Bundy favored the first course; I, together with some others, advocated the third course; a few within McNamara's office advocated "losing more slowly" in the hope that, in the meantime, the Saigon government would pull up its socks.

At this point, the president appeared to keep his own counsel. In his State of the Union speech, however, he told the American people, "To ignore aggression now would only increase the danger of a much larger war. . . . What is at stake is the cause of freedom, and in that cause America will never be found wanting."[7] As matters turned out, we did not "ignore aggression," but we were soon confronted with the much larger war.

*   *   *

In early February, just at the start of the Vietnamese New Year, Mac Bundy and a half dozen others, including myself, set off for Vietnam. Our assessment would pretty much determine which path—escalation or mitigation— would be taken.

When I got off the plane in Saigon and was walking along the tarmac, the CIA chief of station grabbed my arm. He whispered that a senior official of our economic assistance (AID) mission had been kidnapped by the Vietcong just an hour before. His name was Gustave Hertz. I would know a great deal about Hertz, his family, and his capture before long.

Once in Saigon, I arranged for Bundy to meet with some Buddhist priests and dissident students. It was Mac's first trip to Vietnam—in fact, his first to Asia. I wanted him to have a firsthand sense of the public opposition to the Saigon government. I had hoped, in each case, that a productive dialogue would emerge. I was wrong. With his sharp, acerbic approach, Bundy was unable to address or understand the fuzzy, unfocused views of the Vietnamese. Beyond their plea for "social justice," there was little we carried away from two hours of conversation.

Our unproductive explorations of social justice were soon overshadowed by a more tangible development. During the night, an American barracks at Pleiku, in the Vietnamese highlands, had been attacked. Eight GIs were killed, more than one hundred were wounded. That such an attack had been launched during the Vietnamese New Year's de facto cease-fire was outrageous enough. But the fact that it took place during the visit of a senior White House official could not have been a coincidence; the attack had to have been ordered, or at least approved, by Hanoi's high command. (Shades of the Gulf of Tonkin.)

Any chance of proceeding along the deescalation-and-then-get-out road had now diminished to zero; on this day, the war reached a new, ominous milestone.

The bombing of North Vietnam started on February 7, 1965. It would continue, with a few brief interruptions, for almost seven years. During this period, US planes dropped more explosive tonnage on Vietnam than had been dropped on Germany during World War II—this, despite North Vietnam's few consequential targets.

Almost thirty years later, at meetings in Hanoi, the Vietnamese colonel who had been in command of the area in and around Pleiku in February 1965 told a group of Americans that he personally ordered the attack on the American barracks. Hanoi was informed of the attack only after it had occurred. According to the colonel, he, as other local commanders, was given a great deal of independence and was authorized to attack the enemy anywhere at any time. He pointed out what we should have known: He did not have communications equipment capable of sending and receiving instantaneous messages to and from Hanoi. Moreover, the command structure in Hanoi was in no position to micromanage tactics in the field. The colonel said, sheepishly, he had never heard of Mr. Bundy and did not know that a senior White House official was in Saigon. In any case, it would have made no difference; he would have ordered the attack even if he had known.[8]

It also would have made no difference with respect to Washington's reaction if we had known in February 1965 what we were told in February 1999. It was naive of me to think the deescalation course was a viable option. The odds were high that, whatever Bundy learned in Vietnam, and even if there had been no attack in Pleiku, option one had already been chosen.

The bombing of North Vietnam increased in volume and frequency as spring approached. So did the antiwar demonstrations. Families and long friendships became bitterly divided. I was spending long, difficult hours in conversations and confrontations with antiwar delegations. My colleagues and my various bosses (yes, and I, too) were becoming increasingly edgy.

*   *   *

President Johnson, concerned that American and world opinion would now regard US policy as solely focused on the destruction of North Vietnam, launched a "two track" approach. In a speech at Johns Hopkins University in early April 1965, he offered a billion-dollar aid package to Southeast Asia, and said he would go "anywhere, anytime" to discuss peace with representatives of the Hanoi government.

Johnson's offer was a serious one. Soon after his Baltimore speech, I had lunch with one of his personal aides, who sounded me out on the prospect of a face-to-face meeting with Ho Chi Minh. We talked about having such a tête-à-tête on a ship off the coast of Vietnam. Jack Valenti, the president's special assistant during this period, recalls Johnson saying, "If I could just get into a room with Ho Chi Minh, we could just settle this thing."[9]

Of course the president wanted to "settle this thing." The "thing" was eating away at his domestic and international support and making his primary goal, the Great Society, increasingly difficult to achieve. However, despite Valenti's claim that "unconditional surrender" was not Johnson's objective, the US terms were, through most of Johnson's tenure, beyond what Hanoi would be likely to accept.

Within a week of the president's Johns Hopkins speech, Hanoi rejected Johnson's proposals and came up with its own terms. The Viet Minh would start the peace process provided that Washington agreed to accept four conditions as the basis of negotiations:

1. The United States must withdraw militarily from South Vietnam and cease acts of war against North Vietnam.
2. Pending unification, no foreign troops should be stationed in either North or South Vietnam.
3. The internal affairs of South Vietnam must be settled in accordance with the programs of the National Liberation Front (i.e., the Vietcong).
4. The reunification of North and South Vietnam must be settled without outside interference.

Three points—numbers 1, 2, and 4—could probably have been negotiated in talks leading to a peace agreement. Point 3, and Hanoi's apparent insistence that the package be *the* basis for negotiations rather than *a* basis, seemed to me, as well as to my colleagues, unacceptable.

Hanoi's four points continued to be presented on a take-it-or-leave-it basis until January 1967, when Phan Van Dong, premier of North Vietnam, changed the formulation, perhaps inadvertently, from "*the* basis" to "*a* basis." This was the first sign, witting or unwitting, that Hanoi might be ready to begin to start to commence the process of negotiation. Of course, there was still the bombing issue; without an unconditional bombing halt, Hanoi would not consider discussing peace.

Meanwhile, LBJ was anxious to recruit other nations into the fight against the South Vietnamese Liberation Front and the North Vietnamese. He did not want only the United States and its South Vietnamese ally to bear the onus and the burden. Although the SEATO pact was often cited as one (of many) justifications for US intervention, only Thailand and the Philippines among the SEATO members answered the call: the Thais with troops, the Filipinos with nurses. In addition, Australia, New Zealand, and South Korea deployed military units. But, when all was said, we couldn't honestly count the Thais, Filipinos, and South Koreans in the "More Flags" program, since we literally bought and paid for their participation.

On my trips to London during this period, I tried to convince the British to send troops, or at least medical personnel, to Vietnam; I was pointedly reminded, however, of America's unhelpful behavior during the Suez crisis a decade before. France, for its part, was a nonstarter; they had been there and done that. Forty years later, President Johnson could have given President George W. Bush some advice about "going it alone."

*   *   *

By March 1965 life on Pennsylvania Avenue was on fast-forward. LBJ had become increasingly absorbed in the Vietnam problem, which meant that Special Assistant Bundy had become increasingly absorbed—which meant that I, already heavily absorbed, was spending more and more scarce time putting out fires emanating from Johnson's Oval Office and Bundy's office in the West Basement. Then, of course, with the bombing of North Vietnam, antiwar groups were constantly banging on my door. It was against this background that I was given yet an additional assignment: work with a State Department colleague to find and free Gustave Hertz, the kidnapped American AID officer.

For several weeks following Hertz's disappearance in early February, busy American officials in Saigon and Washington paid little attention to his plight. After many weeks of inaction, Hertz's wife and brother solicited Robert Kennedy's assistance. In a matter of a few days the White House was contacted, and I added "Find Hertz" to my to-do list.

For the next few years Gus Hertz was my close, if invisible, companion. His family took pains to make him so. Nellie Hertz, his wife, and Burke Hertz, his brother, called or visited me periodically to discuss progress or, more usually, the lack of progress, and to think about new approaches. With Abba Schwartz, a State Department officer, I spent many days in Geneva working out a plan for the intervention of the International Red Cross. Through them we were able to get wisps of rumor or information, the gist of which was that Hertz was in a Vietcong prison camp in the jungle somewhere on the Cambodian border. We also learned that his health was deteriorating. We explored a channel to the Vietcong through the Algerian embassy and with the Aga Khan (who had connections to the Vietcong through the International Red Cross). Neither of these proved useful. There were two heartbreaking false leads. Ransom money was offered, accepted, and then absconded with by a shadowy middleman. The family pleaded with American officials to swap the Vietcong terrorist who had bombed our Saigon embassy and caused many American and Vietnamese casualties. This was discussed, but, in the end, was quite properly rejected by Washington.

In 1968 I learned that Gus Hertz died of malaria in a prison on the Vietnam/Cambodia border. The memorial service in Washington was, at least for me, a pro forma exercise; I had been mourning Hertz for more than a year. It was only a small satisfaction to read in *Life* magazine that I was "conspicuously exempt from the Hertz family's general bitterness towards the US government."[10] The story in *Life* had "legs"; a few years later, it got me involved in another search, one more bizarre, but with the same sad ending.

*   *   *

In the spring of 1965 the White House felt like a besieged fortress. Pennsylvania Avenue was crowded and noisy with picketers day and night. Lafayette Park, across the avenue from the White House, had become a virtual campground for taunting protesters. Lucy Johnson, the president's daughter, has been unable to forget the "lullaby" that kept her awake night after night: "LBJ, LBJ, how many boys did you kill today?"[11]

The atmosphere within the White House was dark and forbidding. One had to be careful about expressing doubt about either the prospects of victory or the wisdom of our Vietnam policy. I found myself resorting to handwritten notes that I handed directly to Bundy, lest my skepticism about the effectiveness of our bombing and my pessimism about the political prospects of one or another government in Saigon fall into unfriendly hands.

Meanwhile, the president's view of the press was becoming more hostile, and vice versa. He was paranoid about leaks; White House staffers had to account for any contacts they may have had with the media. Indeed, it was a session with Max Frankel of the *New York Times* that made me one of the usual suspects whenever there was leakage—even in those cases when Johnson himself was the source.

Bundy asked me one day in late February to meet with Frankel. Mac wanted to provide him with some background information on North Vietnamese military support to the Vietcong. A white paper on the subject was scheduled to be published. I spent an hour or two with Max and showed him some of the material, which was still in draft form. I thought, as presumably Bundy also did, that when our white paper was released, Frankel would prepare an informed and, hopefully, constructive story. I emphasized that the draft I let him read was still a background document. I thought he understood.

Much to my horror, Frankel's story was on page one of the *Times* the following morning. I was livid. I called him and accused him of jeopardizing my job in exchange for his headline. He mumbled something of an apology, but we haven't spoken to each other since. Thirty-five years later, in his autobiography, he pleaded guilty. "Without asking permission of my informants, I turned their 'background' briefing into a screaming front-page article. . . . I think I got Cooper into some difficulty."[12] He was right. He did.

The president's anger at being preempted by the press was legendary. Perhaps one of the most dramatic examples of his ire was when he chose Undersecretary of State Alexis Johnson to fill the empty ambassadorial post in Tokyo. Before the White House could announce the appointment, the *Washington Post* revealed the choice. LBJ exploded. As the NSC staffer in charge of Asia, and in light of the Frankel episode, my name was high on Johnson's list of suspects. I was treated to an irate cross-examination:

Why did I do it? (I didn't.)
Who did you talk to? (No one.)
How did they find out? (I don't know.)
Would Alex have said anything? (I doubt it.)
Well, see that *you* don't. (I won't.)

A week or so later, the mystery was solved, the villain was found: A reporter in the *Post*'s Tokyo bureau was at a cocktail party at the embassy residence when he saw Mrs. Alexis Johnson in another room, measuring the windows for new curtains.

The president had his revenge on both the *Post* and Mrs. Johnson. He refused to announce Alex's appointment for several months. In the meantime, the United States was without an ambassador to an important country.

*   *   *

In July, Henry Cabot Lodge went back to Saigon for a second stint as US ambassador. Prior to his return, Ambassador Lodge and I spent many hours discussing the problems he was likely to encounter, preparing lists of Americans and Vietnamese he thought would be useful, and reading reports and telegrams. He urged me to join him in Saigon as his special assistant. I had mixed feelings about this. On the one hand, I felt a sense of obligation and responsibility to participate firsthand. On the other hand, I had doubts about how I could perform with an enterprise with which I was becoming increasingly disenchanted. In the end, the matter was resolved by neither Lodge nor me. After examining my medical records and then me, the White House medics found that my Suez souvenir, the cardiac problem, made me too high a risk in the face of the stress of that job in that place.

Lodge was more successful in his recruitment of his "Special Group," which he ordered to report to him outside the bureaucratic and diplomatic constraints of the embassy. I met with the group shortly after they were assembled. They were a motley crew of guerrilla fighters, psychological and economic warriors, and unfriendly looking adventurers, all led by Gen. Edward Lansdale, of Filipino antiguerrilla fame. (*Edward Lansdale, The Unquiet American*[13] is his biography.) I had known a few of them, from past encounters. There was a cheerful Filipino whom I remembered "riding shotgun" for Lansdale in Manila; Lou Conein, a colorful, not-so-secret secret agent who had, or professed to have had, wondrous experiences including a stretch in the Foreign Legion; Mike Deutch, a Belgian-born engineer, friend of Nelson Rockefeller, father of a CIA director-to-be, and a talented name-dropper; and Dan Ellsberg, a former RAND Institute analyst who became a darling of the antiwar movement after he swiped secret documents (known as the Pentagon Papers) from the Department of Defense.

Once in Saigon, the group seemed to accomplish little to the naked eye. Perhaps Lodge found them useful, although I suspect they became more a liability than an asset. One member swaggered around with two pistols on his belt. He was said to be heavily armed, not to protect himself against a possible confrontation with the enemy, but rather to ward off an attack by a jealous husband (who was an allied ambassador). Mike Deutch made economic intelligence his personal specialty. He took me to a Saigon dock before dawn one morning to demonstrate what was widely suspected; the Vietcong were stealing vast amounts of newly arrived US military equipment.

*   *   *

Soon after Lodge's appointment was announced, McNamara, Lodge, and a few others, great and small, were off (yet again) to Saigon. This time I left Washington before McNamara. Traveling with the secretary, I had learned, was hardly a matter of "getting there is half the fun." Rather, it was all work and no sleep. His plane (not one of the Air Force One fleet, but a converted, steerage-class, windowless tanker) left Andrews Air Force Base on a Sunday precisely in time to taxi up to the Saigon airport tarmac at eight o'clock on a Monday morning. A convoy of cars, with its police escort, would screech up to the gate of the US military headquarters in time to permit a hasty washup. Then, jet lag or no jet lag, sleep or no sleep, we would be subjected to a series of briefings until noon. The rest of the week would involve discussions in Saigon with American and Vietnamese officials, and inspection trips around the country. We would leave Saigon on Saturday morning in time to arrive at Andrews and brief the president at nine o'clock the next morning.

After several such relaxing experiences, I was finally blessed with an inspiration: I would take a Pan Am flight (first-class) to Honolulu, visit with the Pacific Command staff at Pearl Harbor, get a decent night's sleep, and arrive in Saigon, reasonably fresh, a day before McNamara and his bedraggled fellow passengers. Once in Saigon, I would tidy up McNamara's schedule and deal with some of the logistical problems that tended to plague every visit. Then I would remain in Saigon for a day or so after McNamara left to clean up the garbage, and fly back to Washington in style on Pan Am. I was a slow learner, but faster than those of my colleagues who continued to remain clueless and sleepless on the windowless tanker.

The object of the July trip was to assess (yet again) the political and military situation prior to high-level decisions regarding the deployment of additional combat troops. Before departing, McNamara hinted at what might be in store. If large numbers of additional soldiers were to be sent to Vietnam, he warned, "it will be necessary to consider calling up the reserves, extending tours, and increasing the draft."[14] In the end, Johnson refused to do the first two, but did increase the draft.

In Saigon, McNamara had his first contact with Gen. Nguyen Van Thieu, the new chief of state of South Vietnam, and Gen. Nguyen Cao Ky, the new premier. Thieu, an army general, was reported to be a good soldier, somewhat reserved and shy. Ky, the head of the air force, was neither shy nor reserved. Rather, he was flamboyant and outgoing. At the first introductory dinner, Ky walked into the ambassador's residence clad in a skintight white jacket and pointy shoes. He sported a thin moustache and moussed hair. I saw McNamara stiffen and grimace. Whatever else Ky was, he was not the secretary's idea of the leader of an allied country in trouble. The secretary's opinion was not altered after an hour or two of discussion.

*   *   *

McNamara and his far-from-merry men returned to Washington on July 21. It was a foregone conclusion that thousands of additional American troops would be sent to Vietnam. The open questions had to do with numbers, timing, and dispositions. Despite Undersecretary of State George Ball's (lonely) cautionary views, the president decided, after a series of solemn meetings with his advisers, to increase US troops in Vietnam immediately from 75,000 to 125,0000. He also increased the draft quotas from 17,000 to

35,000 a month. If Gen. William Westmoreland requested additional troops, Johnson promised to provide them.

In an effort to soften the impact of these decisions, Johnson once again said he was ready to reach a peace agreement. He invited the UN to sponsor negotiations among all the interested parties (excluding the Vietcong). The proposal had a brief half-life; Moscow refused to participate, and Hanoi, remembering its experience during the 1954 Indochina conference, displayed no interest.

Johnson's call for a political settlement was largely, but not wholly, a public relations gambit. He was ready to negotiate, but only if the terms would provide the United States and its South Vietnamese allies with, in effect, a clear-cut victory. In due course, this would change, but in the summer of 1965, neither Johnson nor his close, hawkish advisers were ready to compromise.

As summer turned into autumn, Congress was asked to provide more funding for the Pentagon, additional American troops were deployed (by October 150,000 were in Vietnam and more were on the way), and Arlington National Cemetery was the site of more and more military funerals. I became increasingly engaged in searching for signs that Hanoi was ready to negotiate and in dealing with the accelerated tempo of the peace movement.

Whether his meetings, briefings, and inspection trips that summer triggered McNamara's change in mood and tone about an early victory, I'm not sure. Yet it was sometime in the autumn of 1965 that people close to him began to sense a shift from confidence to doubt.

In mid-October, there were mass demonstrations in cities across America. Young men burned their draft cards, and many fled to Canada. In early November, one pacifist set fire to himself within eyeshot of McNamara's Pentagon office. Another burned himself to death in front of the UN building in New York. Meanwhile, Orah and I were worried about Joan and Susan, who were bravely trying to keep afloat in the sea of student uprisings.

In meetings with the sponsors of a peace march on Washington scheduled for November 29, I reminded them that peace was a two-way street; Ho as well as Johnson had to come forward. If Ho did, I promised, the United States would be ready to talk. Dr. Benjamin Spock (the famous pediatrician) and Sanford Gottlieb (director of the antinuclear organization SANE) agreed to contact both the Viet Minh and the Vietcong. Spock sent a message saying, "An indication of your willingness to participate in a ceasefire and in negotiations . . . would be welcomed by us in our efforts and by many Americans."

Gottlieb's telegram was more direct: "Again urge you respond favorably to immediate peace talks . . ."

Ho responded a few weeks later. He reiterated Hanoi's four points as the sole basis for a peace settlement.

On the morning of the peace march, I met with Norman Thomas, Mrs. Martin Luther King Jr., Dr. Spock, and Sanford Gottlieb. They urged a bombing pause over Christmas as a token of the administration's interest in peace. A pause had already been planned, but I was unable to tell them so. In the event, bombing stopped on Christmas Day. By a combination of factors including some decisions by design and some by default, the pause lasted almost six weeks. A plethora of officials were dispatched on hasty missions to a plethora of countries. Each of them was armed with a peace proposal prepared by Secretary Rusk. (Three decades later, I quoted Rusk's proposal to the North Vietnamese participants at a meeting in Hanoi. Although they had been personally involved and seemed to be steeped in the history of this period, they were unaware of and taken aback by the concessions inherent in the secretary's proposal.) Nothing came of all this—in part because it turned out to be a noisy, ill-planned enterprise.

A month into the new year (on January 31) bombing resumed. It came as no surprise that Hanoi used the respite to augment its forces in South Vietnam. Johnson later referred to the bombing pause as a "big mistake."

*   *   *

Within a few days of the renewed bombing, Bundy asked me to stop by his office. He seemed more than usually cordial. I expected trouble in the offing. I was prescient. The president had decided that morning to have a "summit" meeting with Generals Thieu and Ky to review Vietnam's political and military situation. The meeting was to be held in Honolulu on the weekend of February 6. I was to make the necessary arrangements by the end of the day.

"Mac," I said in what I hoped was not a whining tone (Bundy didn't like whiners), "February sixth is the day after tomorrow."

Mac nodded, trying not to smile.

"Mac," I said in what I am now sure *was* a whine, "we are talking about taking over two luxury hotels on a busy weekend, in the height of Hawaii's tourist season. And on forty-eight hours' notice."

Mac nodded, and pointedly looked at his watch.

Within minutes, the White House operator, efficient and insistent as always, reached the managers of the Royal Hawaiian and Sheraton hotels. I explained the situation. They told me what I already knew. They whimpered. I sympathized. They whined. I told them that the White House did not like whiners. This was a national imperative; I was not asking them to clear out their overbooked hotels, I was telling them to—please.

On February 6, the presidents and their entourages assembled in the ballroom of the Royal Hawaiian Hotel for the first session of the summit meeting. On the plane, a few colleagues and I prepared a draft of what was later to be called the Declaration of Honolulu. It focused on economic development, reconstruction, and social policy instead of the usual military themes. General Ky, now imbued with a sense of gravitas and in conservative dress, gave an impressive speech, very much along the lines of our declaration. It had been drafted on the plane from Saigon. Johnson and McNamara were suitably impressed.

The meeting was planned and implemented in such great haste—very much the way LBJ tended to operate—that it didn't occur to me until the morning of our departure that neither I nor anyone from the State Department had thought of inviting South Vietnam's ambassador to the United States, Vu Van Thai, to attend the meeting. Luckily, we found him at home. We sent a car for him and I brought an emergency kit of toiletries from my desk. He arrived at Andrews Air Force Base, bewildered and harried, just in time to make the plane.

Three decades after this helter-skelter conference, Orah and I were staying at the Royal Hawaiian on our way back from Hanoi. I asked one of the assistant managers if he had heard about the 1966 meeting. "Oh, that," he laughed. "The old manager used to regale us with, 'Well, let me tell you about the time when . . .'"

*　　*　　*

The resumption of bombing and the transparent public relations nature of the so-called search for peace during the halt were troubling. By early 1966 the White House was deluding itself and the American people that the war was noble and that victory was close at hand. It was time for me to go.

I had no job in sight, but Orah agreed that, for our own peace of mind, I should resign on March first. It turned out that, perhaps for reasons very similar to my own, Mac Bundy had also decided to leave in March. He asked me to stay on at least until his replacement was found. I agreed.

Among the many who were optimistic and hawkish—and therefore found favor with the president—was Walt Rostow, head of the policy planning staff at the State Department. So anxious was he to attract the president's attention that he had been sending starry-eyed memoranda directly to the president, bypassing both Secretary Rusk and Mac Bundy.

After Bundy left Washington to assume the presidency of the Ford Foundation, I called Rostow and suggested we meet. I wanted to tell him that his back-channel messages to the president were unhelpful to both the hard-pressed secretary and the NSC staff. Furthermore, he was giving the president a distorted view of the situation in Vietnam. We were having lunch in a small dining room in the secretary's suite at the State Department when our discussion was interrupted by a phone call. Rostow returned smilingly to the table five minutes later and we talked for another few minutes. When I returned to my office, I was greeted with the news that Rostow had just been appointed to succeed Bundy. That did it. I resigned from the White House a few days later.

I was packing my books when one of Johnson's personal assistants came by to wish me well. "I think you should know," he said as if he were performing a benediction, "that you're not in the president's black book. But of course, you're not in his white book either. I guess that means you're listed in his gray book."

Gray book or not, I had a tremendous sense of relief when I handed in my badge and beeper and headed out Connecticut Avenue toward Chevy Chase and home. I noticed that the sun was shining.

NOTES

1. Michael R. Beschloss, *Taking Charge: The White House Tapes, 1963–1964* (New York: Simon & Schuster, 1997), p. 338.

2. A detailed description of the Gulf of Tonkin incident and resolution is provided by A. J. Langguth in *Our Vietnam: The War 1954–1975* (New York: Simon & Schuster, 2000), pp. 299–307.

3. Central Intelligence Agency, "Chances for a Stable Government in South Vietnam," Special National Intelligence Estimate 53-64, September 8, 1964, p. 1. Available from the National Security Archives, George Washington University, Washington, DC.

4. Central Intelligence Agency, "The Situation in Vietnam," Special National Intelligence Estimate 53-2-64, October 1, 1964, p. 1.

5. Central Intelligence Agency, "Short-term Prospects in South Vietnam," Special National Intelligence Estimate 53-65, January 29, 1965, p. 1.

6. Chester L. Cooper, *The Lost Crusade* (New York: Dodd Mead, 1970), pp. 258, 259.

7. *Public Papers of the Presidents of the United States: Lyndon B. Johnson, 1963–1964* (Washington, DC: US Government Printing Office, 1965), bk. 1, p. 116.

8. "Missed Opportunities," conference sponsored by Brown University and Vassar College, Institute for International Affairs, Ministry of Foreign Affairs, Hanoi, Vietnam, June 1997.

9. *Washington Post*, November 28, 2001, p. A35.

10. "Secret Struggle to Free Gus Hertz from the Viet Cong," *Life*, July 21, 1967, pp. 24–29.

11. According to Lucy's remarks at a meeting at the Johnson Library in Austin, Texas, in 1992.

12. Max Frankel, *Times of My Life* (New York: Dell, 2000), pp. 280–81.

13. Cecil B. Currey, *Edward Lansdale, The Unquiet American* (Boston: Houghton Mifflin, 1988).

14. *New York Times*, July 15, 1965.

12

THE ILL-STARRED QUEST

A "CLASSICAL GREEK TRAGEDY"

ABOUT THE BOMBING

As described in the previous chapter, the American bombing of North Vietnam started within hours after a North Vietnamese army unit attacked a US army barracks in South Vietnam's highland region north of Saigon. Although, to the naked eye, the bombing appeared to be in retaliation for the Pleiku attack, the bombers had been waiting for a credible excuse to attack North Vietnam. Pleiku provided this.

The bombing continued with few interruptions throughout the Vietnam War.

Because of the risk of inducing Beijing and Moscow to join Hanoi in its war with the United States, the weekly schedule of bombing targets was subjected to close scrutiny in the Pentagon, the State Department, and the White House. Areas close to China's borders, Haiphong Harbor with its traffic of Soviet ships, and the Red River dikes were off-limits to US bombers. But these constraints aside, rural North Vietnam offered few inviting targets, and the bombing did little of consequence to stem the flow of North Vietnamese personnel and equipment into South Vietnam.

In the end, the US bombing effort may well have done more to delay the achievement of a negotiated settlement than it did to expedite it. This chapter tells why.

*   *   *

H ardly had I driven out of my White House parking place and headed toward Chevy Chase, when I felt relieved, relaxed, unleashed, unencumbered, free from dawn phone calls, insistent beeper rings, Sunday crises. There was now time for a proper lunch, time to read, time with my family.

Orah and I put aside concerns about my finding another job in favor of taking advantage of the girls' summer vacation. We decided to celebrate our twenty-fifth anniversary, Joan's high school graduation, Susan's confirmation, the Fourth of July, and Halloween. We took off for Greece. There would be many more family trips, but this would be the last as a family of four. We traveled through Greece and a bit of Turkey for six weeks by car, bus, and ferry. It was during this period when I decided that a book about my Vietnam years would be a catharsis, one that would free me to move on to new and less traumatic challenges. That was thirty-five years ago, but the albatross hasn't yet released me.[1]

On my return to Washington, I went to New York to see Mac Bundy, who, after leaving the White House, had become president of the Ford Foundation. I described the book I planned to write—part history, part memoir, part cautionary tale. I sensed he was somewhat uneasy (this was well before the flood of books probing America's Vietnam experience), but, nonetheless, he provided a grant that would start me off on the venture. The Institute of Defense Analyses, the think tank for the Joint Chiefs of Staff and the secretary of defense, awarded me an appointment as a visiting scholar, a post that was pleasant and fruitful, but turned out to be all too brief.

In September 1966 President Johnson charged Averell Harriman to seek a negotiated settlement of the Vietnam War. Harriman, who privately, at least, was becoming more and more dubious about the wisdom and cost of pursuing the war, welcomed the assignment. He urged me to join him at the Department of State as his deputy. I agreed, providing that we would be engaged in a genuine, not a cosmetic, effort to end the war. The Guv assured me that he had carte blanche to find a way out. I had reservations that Walt Rostow and Lyndon Johnson would give Harriman the authority and flexibility his new responsibility required. Nevertheless, I signed on. In retrospect, my concerns were well-founded.

*   *   *

I first met former ambassador to the United Kingdom, former ambassador to the Soviet Union, former special assistant to President Truman, former secretary of commerce, former governor of New York, former candidate for president, former assistant secretary of state, former undersecretary of state, and ambassador at large Averell Harriman in Geneva in 1961. He was seventy years old then, but still energetic, physically fit (although becoming hard of hearing), and the equal in mental alertness to any of his much younger staff.

Harriman's father was one of the "robber barons" of his time. He built and owned the Union Pacific Railroad, and possessed many other goodies as well. Averell, aka "Ave," "Guv," and "the Crocodile," was rich—not Gates rich, or even Rockefeller rich, but rich enough that he never needed to think about or carry money. His everyday needs were met without having to resort to the use of squalid cash or bothersome credit cards. There was always at hand someone who "took care of" his meals, taxis, and tips. For several days in the early stages of the 1961 Laos Conference, that someone turned out to be me—until I discovered that Hildy, his wonderful longtime secretary, was equipped and authorized to repay me. She, in turn, resorted to a mysterious person named Mr. Rich (honestly!), of Brown Brothers Harriman, in New York for reimbursement.

The Guv, unlike most of his neighbors and acquaintances on New York's East Side, or Hobe Sound in Florida, or Sands Point on Long Island, or Georgetown in Washington, was a loyal Democrat—indeed, a loyal *liberal* Democrat. He was either courted by, or he himself courted, every Democratic president since Franklin Roosevelt. He and (especially later) his third wife, Pamela Harriman, contributed and raised significant sums of money for Democratic campaigns. During the Nixon administration in the 1970s, when the Guv was out of the government, he invited me to a Democratic strategy meeting. After he berated Nixon for Vietnam, I pointed out that Kennedy and Johnson should be given their share of the blame. He scolded me, "You can be for the Democrats or for God, Chet. If you choose God, you better leave the meeting." I left.

Harriman was a fair target for many charitable causes. But, at least during my time, he was, to put it kindly, a careful donor. He demonstrated this caution on one occasion in the 1960s, when I was asked to take on a few modest fundraising chores for Washington's new Kennedy Center. Harriman's seventy-fifth birthday was approaching, and I thought I could kill two birds with the proverbial one stone. I planned to ask Harriman's former assistants to contribute to buying a seat in the new Opera House in the Guv's honor, and then to seduce him to buy the adjoining chair in honor of Marie Harriman (the second Mrs.). I succeeded in the first endeavor, but failed in the second. It seemed the Guv didn't like opera. Someplace in the Opera House there is a single lonely Harriman seat.

Several years later, I had an hour or two to spare between meetings in New York, and walked into Central Park. As I approached the Children's Zoo, I saw a score of smartly dressed moms, nannies, and children petting and cuddling the animals. It was a charming scene and, yet, lacking in something that I only then vaguely sensed. On the way back to Washington, I realized what was missing—not-so-smartly dressed moms and kids.

The next morning I told Harriman about my zoo problem. The kids I saw all looked as if they came from Fifth Avenue or the East Sixties and Seventies, kids who probably spent their holidays and summers in the Hamptons, or on Martha's Vineyard, or in Maine. They knew a pony or a duck when they saw one. The kids who really needed a petting zoo within walking distance or a short bus ride didn't have one. So, Guv, I said, why don't we establish five or six zoos in less affluent parts of the city? They could be the Averell (or Marie) Harriman Children's Zoos.

He listened, nodded, and suggested I pull together some details. I spent a few evenings spelling out the idea, made a few calls, and came up with some preliminary information and ballpark cost estimates. I discovered that New York City owned scores of lots in every borough that were occupied by abandoned buildings or were completely vacant. Many were large enough and were near bus or subway stops. Barns and sheds to house a cow, a few ponies, sheep, goats, chickens, and rabbits would be inexpensive to construct and maintain. The Parks Department could provide a custodian or two. The cost of, say, five such zoos would, with the city's help, not be much more than a million dollars, about 1 percent of what I guessed the Guv was worth. "And think of the pleasure you'd get watching poor kids play with animals they might otherwise not get to see!"

Harriman took my notes home, which I thought was an encouraging sign. Two days later, he called me into his office. "Sorry," he said, "it wouldn't work."

"Why not?" I demanded.

"Because the places where you want me to put those things are just where people will come at night, steal the animals, and eat or sell them the next day. That's why not." I decided that I couldn't win them all, and called off my campaign.

I often wondered whether the Guv, with all his money, was truly a happy man. I'm sure that Marie and Pamela, the two wives I had gotten to know, gave him joy, but as I look back he seemed to be a driven man. I don't remember hearing him laugh. There was an occasional wry smile, or a broader, but fake, photo-op smile. As for a genuine grin, or chuckle, or hoot, never—or "hardly ever."

In the two decades I knew him, I don't think he ever attended the theater or a concert. (Of course, the fact that he was hard of hearing may have explained this.) He read voraciously, but his reading was confined to the *New York Times* and State Department telegrams. His social life, to the extent I was aware of it, was confined to people involved or interested in politics and foreign affairs. Sitting next to him at dinner, according to Orah, was heavy going. Lunchtime discussions with him were dominated by a *Times* article he had read that morning, or his seeking information, or his guest seeking a favor.

After Marie died, the Guv was lonely and depressed. I called him one morning and asked if I could come over for lunch. We talked about how Nixon was ruining the world and, then, over dessert, he asked, "What would you like?"

I must have looked puzzled. "Isn't there something you want?" he asked again.

"I don't want anything. I just came over to see you."

"That's really nice." He reached over and patted my arm.

During the long months of the Laos Conference, the haughty and insulated members of Genevoise society were anxious to entertain the internationally famous and socially acceptable Averell Harriman. After two or three "boring" evenings, however, he confined himself to small working dinners with members of his staff or with the heads of other delegations.

He truly enjoyed traveling abroad on official missions, in part, I think, because he flourished when he was thousands of miles away from the bureaucratic constraints of Washington. I was in his office one afternoon when Johnson called and asked him to pop off to Europe the next day. "My bag is always packed," he said. And off we went (although, unlike the Guv's, my bag had yet to be packed).

An important compensation for the Guv's penchant for travel was that we flew on a comfortable, official plane[2] with bunks, stewards, expedited arrival and departure arrangements, and VIP lounges. A favorite destination was Moscow. Because of his experience there, dating back to the early post–World War I years and his World War II tenure as ambassador and expeditor of economic and military aid, Harriman had many acquaintances among the Soviet leadership and was treated with respect and courtesy, if not affection. He was fond of regaling Soviet officials with stories of his meetings with Lenin and Stalin—two figures known to them only through legends and history books.

The Guv was a demanding, sometimes maddening, always interesting boss. As time went by, I came to regard him almost as a favorite uncle; there were alternating periods of affection, anger, pride, and frustration. His prodigious memory for faces, places, dates, and incidents posed a constant challenge. "Chet, what day was it, a few years ago, when we had lunch with Krishna Menon?" Then, as I desperately tried to recall our various sessions with the Indian foreign minister, he would say, "Oh yes, it was in early February, two years ago, in Lausanne."

Sunday and holiday mornings must have been particularly lonely for Harriman—at least until he married Pamela. It was on those days that Harriman chose to telephone his staff. Orah and I soon became targets. She often recounted the Sundays when the phone would ring at dawn and the Voice would ask, "Is Chet there? Asleep? Well, what do *you* think of that article on page 18 of the *Times*?"

The wife of a New York congressman told us how she finally put a stop to the calls. The congressman was then an aide to Governor Harriman. "Is Jack there? In bed? What's he doing in bed at this hour?"

"Well, Governor, until you called, he was making love."

The last time I saw Averell Harriman was on a cold, dreary day in March 1986. He was ill and confined to his bedroom in the house Pamela had bought in Middleburg, Virginia. We chatted for a few minutes, but he was tired and it soon became evident that I should leave. As I walked toward the bedroom door, I felt a sneeze coming on and fished in my trouser pockets for some tissue. I heard a weak but scolding voice: "How many times do I have to ask you to take your hands out of your pockets!" Those were his final words to me, his admiring, faithful servant. He died not long after.[3]

*   *   *

By the time I left the White House in June 1966, there had been no dearth of peace proposals from foreign governments and private individuals (some, no doubt, with an eye to a Nobel Peace Prize). Even though virtually all of their proposals provided for an unconditional halt to the bombing of North Vietnam, Hanoi rejected or ignored all of them. Washington, for its part, refused to consider stopping the bombing unless it was clear, in advance, that

Hanoi would stop the flow of soldiers and materiel across the seventeenth parallel and into South Vietnam. Since neither side would yield, Harriman's peace quest started with little promise.

In the face of the barren landscape we confronted, any prospect for engaging Hanoi seemed worth following up. So, not long after I arrived at the State Department, I was ordered to dash off to Oslo. The timing was personally inconvenient. Joan was starting college at Washington University in St. Louis. Orah and I had planned to drive her there, but Joan had a medical examination that delayed our departure. I decided to fly to St. Louis with her, fly back the next morning, and leave for Oslo the following day. So off Joan and I went with all her possessions, including a dozen of her many stuffed animals, which she couldn't squeeze into a suitcase. I found myself holding a large teddy bear, while Joan was practically buried under rabbits, frogs, dogs, and cats. I'm afraid I was not my usual charming, mellow self. Joan was treated to many complaints about college-bound young women who still required the company of a menagerie of stuffed animals.

The Oslo trip was as hastily arranged as the flight to St. Louis. According to our embassy in Oslo, the Norwegian ambassador to Hanoi had come home for a medical checkup. He would be in Oslo for just a few days. We quickly contacted our embassy to arrange a meeting. The Norwegian foreign minister agreed, providing we kept the meeting secret and that we had some new, forthcoming message to pass on. Under these conditions, their ambassador would seek an appointment with Ho Chi Minh as soon as he returned to Hanoi.

I had been brooding about the no-bombing, no-reinforcement deal and had scribbled out a possible formula well before the Oslo opportunity had come to light. Upon being assured privately by Hanoi, directly or through a reliable third party, that, within, say, two weeks after we initiated a bombing pause, there would be an observable halt to the flow of North Vietnamese forces into South Vietnam, we would then engage in what Hanoi could claim was an "unconditional" halt. Such an arrangement might satisfy both Hanoi and Washington and start the process toward a negotiated settlement. Harriman and Rusk (and, I was told, Rostow) thought the idea had merit and agreed that I should pass it along to the Norwegian ambassador as our "new message."

Ambassador Margaret Tibbets, then one of a handful of female American diplomats, met me at the Oslo airport on a brisk, bright afternoon. On the way to her residence she told me that I would be meeting with Norway's foreign minister and its ambassador to North Vietnam on the following afternoon.

She (rightly) assumed she would not attend. After I unpacked, she invited me to her bedroom for tea. There were a few comfortable chairs and a table in one corner of the room, but I hardly noticed them. What caught my eye was her bed. It was covered with stuffed animals. After dinner, I wrote Joan an apology: If an ambassador can travel around with a load of teddy bears, puppies, and kittens, you can, too.

My meeting at the foreign ministry went well. The ambassador to Hanoi felt the no-bombing, no-reinforcement arrangement was worth a try. He would make the effort, but only if we stopped bombing Hanoi from the day of his arrival until after his meeting with Ho. That sounded reasonable. Indeed, I thought that I had such a guarantee from Secretary Rusk before I left Washington.

I asked the ambassador to let us know of his Hanoi arrival date and requested the foreign minister send us a report on the meeting with Ho. During this period, I assured both of them, we would not bomb Hanoi.

I then went to the American embassy, told Ms. Tibbets that she did a swell job by arranging the meeting, and sent a message to Washington describing the session at the ministry. I felt I deserved some quiet time, and set off for a long walk. When I returned to the embassy, I found a nasty State Department telegram waiting. An assistant secretary demanded to know who gave me permission to make a no-bombing commitment. I had gotten way out of line. Et cetera.

My return message was blunt: It was not my impression that I had to answer to assistant secretaries. Even if that was the case, however, I was not about to ask an important foreign official to deliver an important message to another important foreign person in the middle of an American bombing raid. Et cetera. I left the next day for Paris, where I would be meeting with embassy and CIA staffers. When I arrived, I was handed another telegram from the assistant secretary: "Apologies. Misinformed. Sorry. Great job. Regards." So far, so good. Nevertheless, I decided, when back in Washington, to make sure he understood that I was responsible only to Harriman and to Rusk. Period.

In Washington, however, I discovered that matters were clearly not "so far, so good." The department's executive secretary warned me that the moratorium I had agreed to on bombing Hanoi had by no means been worked out with the Pentagon. In fact, the air force was scheduled not only to bomb Hanoi but, even worse, to bomb a truck park adjoining the airport on the day that the Norwegian ambassador was due to arrive. It was the same old problem: My meeting in Oslo and the arrangement we had agreed upon were so secret that the air force knew nothing about them.

I told Harriman of the imminent bombing raid and pleaded that he get it canceled or at least postponed. Harriman reminded me that only the White House could change the timing or the target at such a late stage. "Well, call Rostow and remind him of the deal we made with Oslo," I urged. He shook his head; he didn't want to erode his "political capital." Since, as we both knew, I had little, if any, political capital to lose, he suggested that I try to persuade Rostow to call off the raid.

An hour later I was in Rostow's office and put the case. Walt listened, or appeared to listen, and then sallied forth to explain his concept of counter-insurgency. Shaken, I returned to the relative sanity of my office.

The day of the Norwegian ambassador's arrival and the scheduled truck park raid came. God was on my side. The weather turned too unfavorable for bombing sorties, but just good enough for the ambassador's flight to land. In the end, it made no difference: Yes, the ambassador was granted an appointment with Ho and his aides; yes, he presented our proposition; but Ho and company turned it down. End of the Oslo initiative.

*   *   *

Late that summer of 1966, President Ferdinand Marcos of the Philippines proposed a summit conference of the chiefs of those governments participating in the war against North Vietnam—South Korea, South Vietnam, the Philippines, Australia, New Zealand, Thailand, and the United States. By then, there were more than three hundred thousand American troops in South Vietnam. Johnson, McNamara, and Rusk felt it was high time for the allied countries to compare notes and agree to next steps. It took many weeks to sort out an agenda and coordinate schedules, but, in late October, the participants convened in Manila.

For Harriman and me, the conference had a special significance. A major item on the agenda was the matter of encouraging the South Vietnamese government to develop a peace plan of its own. After all, as Washington occasionally reminded itself, it was *their* war, not ours. Well, their war or our war, I was handed the task. As the plane flew westward, I composed a peace initiative to be put forward by the Saigon delegation. My draft stressed that "[w]e, the Government of South Vietnam, would be prepared to" proceed with a program of national reconciliation, subscribe to the terms of the 1954 Geneva Conference on Indochina, and recognize that US forces would be withdrawn from Vietnam in the relatively near future.

In Manila, before the conference started, the Saigon delegation accepted the first point (reconciliation) and rejected the second (terms of the 1954 conference). The third point (near-term withdrawal of US forces) was discussed at some length with my State Department colleagues on the plane. Well before we landed, we had prepared a careful, forthcoming wording to submit to the Vietnamese. But we hadn't reckoned on Johnson's personal entourage.

Jack Valenti, LBJ's former assistant, who had left the White House earlier that summer to head the Motion Picture Association of America, had been invited to come with the president to Manila. In a previous incarnation, Valenti had been in the public relations business. It still showed. At the reception on the evening just before the conference started, he cornered me. The withdrawal point should be "shorter and snappier." I told him it would be dangerous to regard the withdrawal commitment as a public relations ploy. Particularly if the South Vietnamese were to incorporate it as their initiative, we had to be especially careful about the wording.

Valenti won. No surprise. During the reception, the American worker bees were summoned into a back room. Johnson wanted us to work up a statement to the effect that all US troops would be withdrawn within six months after the North Vietnamese forces left South Vietnam. A quick withdrawal would be no easy task, in no small part because of the sheer logistical problem of accomplishing an orderly removal of three or four hundred thousand troops and their equipment. But we were told that the six-month commitment would "get the headlines." So six months it was.

The final communiqué was, to be sure, front-page news. The withdrawal formula, however, thanks to the midnight efforts of stressed-out, jet-lagged, food-deprived American authors, was neither "short" nor "snappy." Nor, unfortunately, was it crystal clear. In effect, it promised that the United States and other third-country troop contributors would withdraw from South Vietnam "as the other side withdraws its forces to the north, ceases infiltration and the level of violence thus subsides . . . as soon as possible and not later than six months" after Hanoi disengaged.

Aside from that awkward sentence, there was the word "thus" to be reckoned with. How it crept in and why it stayed in successive drafts remains a mystery. No matter; it caused much confusion. What did "thus" mean here? Did it have some special, arcane significance? How could "thus" be properly translated into Vietnamese, or Thai, or Korean?

When push came to shove, the results of the Manila meeting notwithstanding, the media hype concerning American withdrawal had a short shelf life. Worse than that, the withdrawal issue, however it was phrased, stirred up a great deal of suspicion about US motives among the Vietnamese, Thais, and Filipinos.

*   *   *

As soon as the meeting adjourned, President Johnson announced his intent to visit US troops in Vietnam and then several countries in the Pacific region. Harriman and I were also sent off. Our destinations excluded countries on Johnson's itinerary, but otherwise the itinerary and timetable were left up to Harriman. Our mission was vague—explain the withdrawal formula and put some beef into the discussions that had just been held in Manila. In the event, he, his secretary Hildy Shishkin, a veteran public affairs officer, and I managed to engage in more or less useful conversations in eleven countries during the course of seventeen days. It was on this journey that I experienced the longest single day of my life: dawn takeoff from Sri Lanka, breakfast with India's prime minister in New Delhi; flight to Peshawar to change planes for Rawalpindi where we had lunch with Pakistan's prime minister; back to Peshawar on our own plane; tea with the shah in Iran; arrival at Rome's airport at 3:00 AM (goodness knows what time it was in Sri Lanka). Nonetheless, despite the hour, Harriman, all smiles, gave an interview to the waiting Italian press. He was at the Vatican bright and early on the following morning for an audience with the pope.

It was in Rome, following the Vatican session, where we had the most important meeting of our trip. The foreign ministry had arranged a splendid lunch at the elegant Villa Madama on the outskirts of Rome. Harriman was seated on the right of the foreign minister, Amintore Fanfani; I was on the right of Giovanni D'Orlandi, Italy's ambassador to South Vietnam. D'Orlandi was dean of Saigon's diplomatic corps and a friend of both Ambassador Lodge and Janusz Lewandowski, Poland's representative on the International Control Commission. Lewandowski's responsibilities involved frequent trips between Saigon and Hanoi. D'Orlandi, Lodge, and Lewandowski often met informally to discuss prospects for ending the conflict.

D'Orlandi told me that he would be returning to Saigon on November 9. He knew Lewandowski was scheduled to go to Hanoi on November 11. Would it be possible, he asked, for Washington to conjure up some new initiative to replace the tired existing ones? He would give this to Lewandowski, who, in turn, would present it to the leadership in Hanoi.

I told D'Orlandi that Harriman and I would not be back in Washington until the ninth. In the meantime, I would report our conversation to Secretary Rusk, and we would do some serious thinking about what we could forward for D'Orlandi to pass on to his Polish colleague.

From Rome we stopped in London and met with Prime Minister Harold

Wilson and George Brown, who was now foreign minister. Brown was planning a trip to Moscow late in November and hoped to have a new US negotiations initiative to bring to the Kremlin. It was at this lunch that Brown, spurred on by a generous amount of gin, made a maudlin comment on Harriman's wisdom in choosing me as his deputy. After the Guv put both of us in our respective places, we promised to send Brown a new proposition he could discuss with his Soviet hosts. We did not mention our meeting with D'Orlandi, but the Guv and I later agreed that if we could develop an innovative approach for the Italians, we would send it to the British as well.

The plan developed for both D'Orlandi and Brown in the few days we had available was a more embellished and carefully worded statement of the Phase A–Phase B notion than I had earlier passed on to the Norwegian ambassador (and also, later, to UN Ambassador Arthur Goldberg for UN Secretary General U Thant). In essence, the United States would halt the bombing of North Vietnam, ostensibly without conditions. Within a few weeks, Hanoi would stop the infiltration of North Vietnam troops and supplies across the seventeenth parallel into South Vietnam. This mutual act of restraint, we hoped, would produce informal, secret discussions which, in turn, would lead to serious peace negotiations. In addition to the burnished A-B formula, we provided D'Orlandi with a version of the material prepared for the Manila Conference, including the withdrawal proposition (minus "thus").

When Foreign Secretary Brown subsequently discovered that he was not the exclusive bearer of the newish US negotiations proposal, he was outraged. (It took another trip to London to pacify him.) In the event, neither D'Orlandi nor Brown was able to elicit a positive reaction from the North Vietnamese. Indeed, it was not clear whether either of them had been able to get the message through to the leadership in Hanoi or Moscow. Nonetheless, Phase A–Phase B became the core of several Washington negotiating initiatives during late 1966 and much of 1967.

*   *   *

For much of this period Harriman and I labored hard and traveled far to uncover, develop, or follow up every hint that Hanoi would favorably consider one or another of the United States' negotiating initiatives, or was ready to advance one of its own. Our efforts were supported by a few midlevel State and Defense Department officers, but Secretary Rusk was either openly skeptical or mildly acquiescent. In a poignant moment, however, sensing my frustration, he took me aside. When we, in fact, achieved a peace agreement, he said, he "would beat me to the exit."

Secretary McNamara gave us private encouragement and support, but, until the late winter of 1967, seemed anxious to avoid isolating himself from a grudging president and a hard-line White House staff. Walt Rostow was especially unhelpful. He not only denigrated Harriman's mission in general but, I became quite certain, undermined many of our efforts. As one observer noted, "Let a group of Democratic Congressmen propose a peace conference, and Rostow lectured them about the folly of pressing for talks and a cease-fire."[4]

To the hawks in and out of the government, any US proposal that appeared to offer genuine rather than cosmetic concessions or compromises was anathema. So long as we simply went through the motions, the White House and many of the president's advisers would ignore or tolerate our activity. But once there seemed to be a prospect of attracting Hanoi's interest, we would discover some booby traps along the way.

In part, our problems were not simply a consequence of official indifference, but were inherent in the secrecy of our quest. Knowledge of a particular effort tended to be confined to no more than a score of people at State, Defense, and the White House; the peace hunters and the warriors were reading different texts. In part, too, the Guv and I were the victims of the absentmindedness or myopia of officials whose sign-off was needed, but who had forgotten, if, indeed, they ever bothered to focus on, initiatives approved and already in train; bombing targets were their high priority.

The Oslo effort is a good example of the muddled policy process. The bombing raid scheduled near Hanoi's airport for the day the Norwegian ambassador was to arrive was planned by air force officers unaware of our attempt to get a message to the leadership in Hanoi. The assistant secretary's irate message to me in Oslo reflected the fact that he hadn't paid sufficient attention to, or had forgotten, the terms of the agreement with the Norwegians. Rostow's insouciance with regard to the ill-timed raid illustrated his indifference to the Oslo initiative. In most efforts to bring Hanoi to negotiations, the right hand was not only unaware of what the left hand was doing, but one right hand was also often unaware of what the other right hand was doing. The assistant secretary of state for the Far East was fond of pointing out the need to "fine-tune" State Department–Defense Department policy. But the instruments employed were not violins, flutes, and harps, but rather bass drums, tubas, and tympani. Instead of fine tunes, there was cacophony.

Washington's ignorance and ideological mindset about Vietnam and the Vietnamese, and fear of "falling dominoes," contributed to the problems we had. For their part, Hanoi's leaders and officials were not only ignorant about the policies and decision makers in Washington, but also blinded by their own ideological prejudices. Whether President Johnson knew it or not, or even cared, he had given Harriman an almost impossible task—which, of course, did not deter the Guv.

*   *   *

Of the various alarums and excursions that kept those in quest of a Vietnam settlement on edge during the autumn of 1966 and much of 1967, three seemed to hold some promise: a proposed meeting in Warsaw between representatives of the United States and North Vietnam; an attempt to recruit a French intermediary; and a joint US-UK initiative. In the end, each came to a bizarre, unfruitful conclusion.

The first effort was spawned at the lunch in Rome in October 1966, when D'Orlandi, Italy's ambassador to Saigon, suggested that his Polish colleague might be willing to deliver a "new" US proposal to Hanoi. Two weeks later Ambassador Lewandowski received our proposal. He took it on himself to reword some of it and then presented his edited version to the North Vietnamese foreign minister. On his return to Saigon, he reported that Hanoi had expressed some interest. Although we were annoyed about the changes Lewandowski had made, none of them was so serious as to warrant withdrawing from the enterprise, especially in the light of Hanoi's reportedly positive reaction.

There were months of clandestine meetings between Lewandowski and US ambassador Lodge. These were followed by several secret meetings between Lewandowski and the North Vietnamese foreign minister, additional sessions between Lewandowski and Lodge, all accompanied by closed meetings at the State Department and the White House. Finally, it was agreed that an American emissary would meet in Warsaw with a North Vietnamese representative to discuss a process for engaging in substantive talks. Neither Washington nor Hanoi wanted to reveal that such a meeting would be occurring; arrangements were made known only to Ambassador Lodge and a handful of people in Washington. The proposed meeting was probably at least as closely held in Hanoi.

To preserve secrecy, it was decided that neither Harriman nor I, nor indeed any recognizable Washington official, should go to Warsaw to meet with the North Vietnamese representative. Rather, we would rely on the US ambassador to Poland, John Gronouski, the former postmaster general. Hanoi, in turn, would send its ambassador to Scandinavia, Nguyen Dinh Phuong.

Gronouski, until this point, knew virtually nothing about American–

North Vietnamese relations and probably could not find Vietnam on a map of Asia. He was brought to Washington and carefully briefed.

The Warsaw choreography involved, first, a session between Gronouski and Polish foreign ministry officials. When a few substantive matters (including some rewording of Lewandowski's version of the US position) and some procedural points were sorted out, the Vietnamese representative, who would be waiting in the wings, would be invited to join the Polish intermediary and Gronouski. In due course, the Pole would bow out and the American and Vietnamese would get down to business.

The meetings were scheduled to start on December 5, 1967. On December 3 and 4, after two weeks of bad weather which precluded any bombing, bombs once more fell on Hanoi. The Vietnamese interpreted this as a signal that Washington was calling off the Warsaw rendezvous. Yet again, the Warsaw meeting was so secret that the Pentagon was unaware of the consequences that would follow the resumption of bombing.

But worse was yet to come. On December 13 Gronouski met with Polish foreign minister Adam Rapacki. According to Rapacki, Hanoi had decided to postpone the discussions indefinitely as a result of the renewed attacks. During their meeting, fierce bombing raids were unleashed on Hanoi. There was much damage to Hanoi's diplomatic quarter.

The timing, the context, and the consequences of the December 13 attack finally caught the attention of senior officials in Washington, who came to realize that they could not regard US bombing as a spectator sport; attention must be paid to the "peace track." On December 21 Gronouski was summoned home to brief the Great Men on the state of play in Warsaw. Gronouski returned to Poland with Washington's commitment not to bomb within a ten-mile radius of Hanoi. Despite this concession (referred to as a "Christmas present" by some of my colleagues), Rapacki informed Gronouski that there would be no further US-Vietnam talks. So ended many weeks of intensive effort and high hopes.

In the various postmortems that took place on Pennsylvania Avenue and in Foggy Bottom and the Pentagon, there was agreement that Hanoi had, from the outset, no intention of meeting an American representative, and that the bombing on December 13 provided a convenient cover for reneging on Hanoi's agreement with Lewandowski. But we were wrong.

Thirty years later, in Hanoi, I met with Ambassador Phuong, a gentle, scholarly diplomat. He told me he had waited for two weeks in Warsaw expecting any day to meet with Gronouski, but to no avail. It turned out that Gronouski had the impression that Poland had the task of organizing the meeting—probably at a Polish government meeting place. US ambassador Lodge said later, however, that Lyndon Johnson himself told Ambassador Gronouski that he was to meet Phuong at the Vietnamese embassy.[5] If this sounds confusing to the reader, think how Phuong and Gronouski must have felt.

The Poles may have fumbled the ball; Gronouski may have been too passive or mistaken about his rendezvous; the Vietnamese ambassador may have been out of touch with his Foreign Office; or the prospects for the meeting were favorable until the bombing raid on December 13. Anyway, it was easy come, easy go.

*   *   *

England is the setting for the next chapter in "The Quest," a dark tale of Washington's shambolic, feckless pursuit of peace during 1966 and 1967.

In late December 1966, the Poles leaked news of the aborted secret Warsaw meeting to U Thant. He, in turn, spilled the beans throughout the UN. I learned of this when the normally placid Australian ambassador stormed into my office shortly after New Year's Day. "What's all this about Warsaw? Why didn't you inform us, your closest ally in Vietnam?"

I heard from Foreign Secretary George Brown the next day. His fury made Ambassador Bob Furlonger's anger seem mild. Not only had the Warsaw meeting been planned without London's knowledge, Brown howled, but we had provided Lewandowski with the Phase A–Phase B formula, which he and Prime Minister Wilson had assumed had been given exclusively to him for his discussions in Moscow. In a subsequent call to Secretary Rusk, he charged that we had pulled the rug out from under him; we had made him look like an idiot. The rage emanating from Whitehall required soothing. I was the designated soother.

As Brown recalls, "When the Americans heard how angry I was . . . they sent an official to London to calm us down. . . . [W]e were in daily, sometimes hourly contact. He breakfasted with me several times. He knew of the differences of nuance, of sentiment, between the Prime Minister and me, and he understood the similarity of view on many matters between Secretary Rusk and me."[6]

Brown's description of our relationship was something of an exaggeration. Still, I had known him since I first arrived at our London embassy in the midfifties. He was then the Labour Party's shadow defense minister. I had followed his career since then, and we became personally as well as professionally close over the years. I knew the brand of bourbon he preferred. I had gotten to know and admire his wife, Sophie. I helped smooth over his stormy relations with several members of his own British embassy in Washington. I opened the safe in his office at the House of Parliament for him late one night when he was too unsteady to deal with the combination lock. He could yell at me. I could yell back. We were friends. (At a British embassy reception for him one evening, he spied Orah and me across the ballroom. He skidded across the floor, embraced her, and kissed me. Rusk and McNamara were standing nearby. "I must admit," Rusk said, "I've never been kissed by a foreign minister—not even by Golda Meier.")

Friends or not, the temperature inside 10 Downing Street when I arrived early in January was as chilly as it was in Saint James Park outside. Wilson was less apoplectic than Brown, and professed to understand why planning for the Warsaw meeting should have been kept secret. Nonetheless, he felt strongly that he and Brown should not have had to rely afterwards on outside sources to learn about the ill-fated event.

Wilson felt particularly aggrieved because he was having a difficult time with his colleagues and his constituents. His support of American policy in Vietnam was more difficult than Lyndon Johnson was ready to acknowledge. A senior cabinet minister wrote in his diary at the start of 1967, "There's a lot of trouble ahead if we don't watch out. Our back-benchers not only detest our support of the Americans in Vietnam—they also resent the weight of the defense burden."[7] Wilson faced the complicated problem of continuing Britain's close relationship with the United States while warding off attacks from within his own party. His balancing act would be put to a stern test in the next two weeks.

In his book about his tenure as prime minister, Harold Wilson relates that he asked President Johnson "to send a representative in whom he had confidence to put me fully in the picture before Mr. Kosygin [the Soviet Premier] arrived. . . . [H]e sent Mr. Chester Cooper. . . . When Mr. Cooper arrived, he told me that he had instructions to give me the whole picture. He emphasized the almost total secrecy of what he was telling me."[8]

As part of my stroking exercise I was told to reveal to Wilson and Brown all recent, current, and future diplomatic developments with respect to Vietnam. I was authorized, for example, to describe the details of a carefully developed planning paper prepared in the aftermath of the meeting Harriman and I had in Rome. It was referred to as the "negotiate first, settle later" document, and we hoped it would serve as the basis of the settlement with Hanoi. It included our views on a cease-fire, prisoner exchanges, and such thorny political issues as the participation of the Vietcong and eventual unification. (Although Rostow complained that the paper was "too soft" and Rusk barely gave it the time of day, it had been sent to our ambassador in Moscow for the Russians to pass along to Hanoi.)

I then told Wilson, and later Brown, that shortly after my arrival in London, we had started a direct discussion with the North Vietnamese. John Guthrie, a senior member of our embassy in Moscow, had met with his counterpart in Hanoi's embassy and provided him with a list of issues (based on the settle first, negotiate later proposal) we would be prepared to discuss. The Vietnamese diplomat agreed to send the list to Hanoi and notify our Moscow embassy when he had a reply. At last, I told the British, conversations might begin. (But this was just another vain hope. A week passed before Hanoi's representative contacted Guthrie. He treated Guthrie to a vitriolic, insulting attack. Our offer was not even mentioned in Hanoi's diatribe.)

Finally, I told Wilson privately about a letter being prepared for Johnson to send to Ho and gave him the gist of the draft I had seen as I was leaving for London. I warned him that only a few people in Washington were aware of this initiative. He was not to mention it during Soviet premier Aleksey Kosygin's forthcoming visit. I left London feeling confident that Wilson and Brown could deal with Vietnam, if and when Kosygin raised the matter.

My next stop was Paris where, several weeks before, the Guv had met with Jean Sainteny, an aristocratic associate of President de Gaulle and a man highly regarded by the North Vietnamese leaders. Sainteny had been in Hanoi during the previous summer and felt certain that the Viet Minh would make an "important gesture" in response to the cessation of American bombing. He was also confident that Hanoi would accede to reconvening the Geneva Conference of 1954. Although Sainteny was noncommittal about his becoming a bridge between Hanoi and Washington, Harriman felt it would be worth a try. My present chore in Paris was to convince Sainteny to go to Hanoi and establish such a working relationship. I was not authorized to tell Sainteny of our previous unsuccessful efforts or to reveal any specific proposals we had in mind. I did tell him, however, that we had given careful thought to a final settlement and would like to discuss the terms with representatives of Hanoi's government.

Sainteny said he knew we were serious about negotiations and that the peacemaking enterprise was important. Despite his personal reluctance to make the journey in the light of his failing health, he would be willing to undertake the task. He would, however, require de Gaulle's permission, since even though his visit to Hanoi would be a personal one, it would still be interpreted as an official French initiative. We met again a few days later. De Gaulle had said no. I returned to Washington convinced that my life was being dominated by Mars rather than Venus.

* * *

Wilson hoped that Kosygin's visit would provide an opportunity to discuss Vietnam and, perhaps, a way to bring about a negotiated settlement. Although Kosygin had not included Vietnam on the list of matters he wished to raise, Wilson was confident that it would inevitably come up. In anticipation of this, he asked LBJ to send me back to London. Wilson was prescient; Vietnam turned out to be a principal subject for discussion: "I knew that a great deal could happen in a week, so I asked the President to send Chet Cooper . . . for a last briefing before the Russians, and to stay here for a day or two of consultation. . . . I hoped he might stay longer."[9] Back to London I went.

Harold Wilson, George Brown, Aleksey Kosygin, and Walt Rostow were the principal characters in this act of "The Quest." My role—indeed, my very presence in London—during Kosygin's stay would be concealed, invisible to the Russians and to the press.

Kosygin's visit, perhaps coincidentally but probably purposefully, occurred during Tet, the Vietnamese New Year. In deference to both the premier and to Tet, Washington had decreed a bombing halt to prevail during the few days of Wilson-Kosygin talks. This is not to say that Rostow, Rusk, and McNamara were enthusiastic about Wilson's pushing his role as a Vietnam intermediary. Quite the contrary: they were concerned that the prime minister would make commitments Washington would be unable or unwilling to fulfill.

I met with Wilson and Brown briefly after their initial session with Kosygin. (I had been hustled into 10 Downing Street through the rear garden gate.) They were overflowing with confidence; Kosygin was ready to discuss Vietnam. Indeed, on the second day of the meeting the focus was almost entirely on Vietnam. Kosygin had been much impressed by a recent conversation that an Australian Communist journalist, Wilfred Burchett, had had with Hanoi's foreign minister, Nguyen Duy Trinh.

According to Burchett, Trinh had said that talks could start if the United States unconditionally stopped bombing. Up to this point, Hanoi had used the phrase "unconditional and final." The omission of "final" was regarded by Burchett and others as a significant concession. But however earnestly those of us in Washington were looking for a breakthrough, Burchett's interpretation of this change in Hanoi's demand did not appear to be one.

Kosygin urged Wilson to call Johnson with the news that he (Kosygin) took Trinh's remark as a positive step. Wilson rightly pointed out that Johnson would give this short shrift and urged Kosygin to consider reconvening the 1954 Geneva Conference. (This was attractive to the British since they, together with the Russians, had chaired the 1954 conference. Reconvening it would give both countries an influential role in a settlement.) Kosygin was noncommittal. Wilson then put forward the Phase A–Phase B approach. Although George Brown had taken this to Moscow only six weeks before, Kosygin apparently regarded it as a fresh, new idea. He asked to see the proposal in writing. Wilson agreed to have a copy available before Kosygin left for an overnight visit to Scotland. (The premier was a Robert Burns buff.)

I reported all this to Washington that evening. There was a telephone call early the next morning instructing me to urge Wilson and Brown to avoid getting involved with Trinh's statement and to steer clear of the 1954 Geneva Conference notion. Instead, Wilson should promote the Phase A–Phase B formula as a starting point for US-North Vietnam negotiations. My write-up of the formula for Wilson to give to Kosygin should elaborate Phase B. Thus: Phase A involved a halt to US bombing. Phase B would now include not only a halt to the infiltration of North Vietnamese troops, but also a halt to the augmentation of US forces in South Vietnam.

Prospects seemed bright, but a telegram I received later that day promised trouble. It reported a significant increase in the number of North Vietnamese troops entering South Vietnam, an increase that came on the heels of the US bombing halt.

Together with US ambassador David Bruce and Brown's senior staffers, I drafted a paper reflecting Washington's new version of Phase A–Phase B and sent the draft off to Washington early that afternoon for approval. I waited several hours for a reply, but there was none. Once again, I assumed silence meant approval (I'm a slow learner). I looked forward to my first free evening in London and accepted an invitation to attend *Fiddler on the Roof* from a friend who had a leading role. Fortunately, I told the embassy duty officer where I was going—and I warned the usher that I might be getting an urgent call.

The call came in the middle of the first act. I was taken to a phone backstage. Above the sounds of the orchestra and the singing, I could barely hear Rostow. But I could tell he was angry. Very angry. "Where are you?" I told him. He was not amused. "Get back to the embassy damn fast and call me!" I did. He had chilling news. There was now an entirely different version of the message for Wilson to give Kosygin. It would soon be on its way. Wilson and Brown were waiting for me at Downing Street. I was to get there (run, don't walk!) immediately.

I was terror stricken. The odds were high that Kosygin had already been given the version of Phase A–Phase B that had come to me overnight. A tense group was waiting for me in the cabinet room at Number 10. There were Wilson and Brown, Burke Trend (the cool and competent cabinet secretary), a few staff members, and—thank goodness—wise Ambassador Bruce.

Wilson suggested I call the White House. Over the wide expanse of the Atlantic Ocean I could sense Rostow's vitriolic mood. His message, he said, had just been sent.

In the light of the telephone conversation earlier that day, the new communication was hard to believe. What was once Phase B was now Phase A: If Hanoi stopped its infiltration, we would stop bombing, and then talks could begin. Whether Rostow and company realized it or not, Hanoi had rejected this formula a dozen times. I called Rostow again to make sure that his message was accurate. His secretary said that he was in a meeting with the secretaries of Defense and State. I told her to get him on the phone anyway. Yes, said Rostow, it meant exactly what it said. "This is what the President wants. Period. Good night."

Wilson and Brown exploded. "We were staggered, all of us. . . . I was furious. I hope I can say icily so, though as the evening went on the language in which I expressed myself was less and less parliamentary. The Americans [i.e., Ambassador Bruce and I] were equally angry."[10]

Anger and frustration were justified, but had to be put aside, if not squelched; the first task now was to compose a new letter to Kosygin and get it to him before his train left for Scotland. This was done with only minutes to spare. The next task was to send a message to Johnson from Wilson. "Before sending it I gave myself time to cool down," Wilson later recalled. The message was "dictated by me after consultation with the bewildered Ambassador and the outraged Chet Cooper."[11]

The message to Johnson read, in part: "You will realize what a hell of a situation I am in for my last day of talks with Kosygin. . . . I have to reestablish trust because not only will he have doubts about my credibility, but he will have lost credibility in Hanoi. . . ."[12]

Foreign Minister George Brown, whose dealings with Wilson had long since become tense and wary, stood somewhat aloof from the heated discussions around the table. But in Brown's memoir he reveals his own frustrations with Washington:

Every time we were getting something squared away . . . , some sinister figure from the [White House] basement would get the ear of the President, or just *say* that he had the ear of the President, and everything would get changed. . . . [T]here came a moment when we seemed on the very brink of achieving something. Through the American official [i.e., me] we finally cleared with Washington just what we were to say to the Russians. . . . And then, at the last minute, a correction came from Washington. . . . I suspect we looked about as foolish as intermediaries as anyone could look. So the whole thing petered out.[13]

As for me, I was sure that the already fragile relationship between Johnson and Wilson, and indeed the relationship between the Foreign Office and the State Department, would now be sorely strained. I had an uncomfortable feeling of déjà vu; a decade ago I had witnessed a sharp deterioration in American-British relations over Suez. Was this a repeat performance? It was David Bruce who restored some measure of calm and perspective.

We spent a final hour discussing the next session, to be held on Sunday, when Kosygin and several British officials would be meeting at Chequers, the official sixteenth-century country residence of the prime minister. I was to arrive there an hour before Kosygin and would be installed in the attic room that had served, in 1565, as the prison for Lady Jane Grey. A direct telephone to both the White House and the State Department had been installed, as well as a bottle of premium Scotch and an ample array of delicacies. I was to fare better than poor Lady Jane Grey, who, at the age of fifteen, was queen of England for little more than a tumultuous week before she, too, was deposited in the attic.

When I came to the embassy early Sunday, the worse for a sleepless night, a telegram from Rostow was waiting. Walt may have thought his message would take some of the sting out of Saturday night's unpleasantness, but it served only to make me angrier. According to the telegram, Johnson had sent his personal letter to Ho on Thursday. It was because of the increased infiltration of North Vietnamese that the order of Phase A–Phase B had been reversed. The new point about no further augmentation of US forces, Rostow maintained, should soften the effect of the change. But why hadn't the Great Men in Washington let me know of the change in enough time to work out an appropriate letter from Wilson to Kosygin? (I discovered why much later when I accosted McNamara. "Geez," he said, "we just forgot.")

A Foreign Office car sped me to Chequers early that dreary, drizzly Sunday afternoon. Wilson, Brown, and Burke Trend had already had lunch there. Wilson seemed fairly relaxed. He had played golf that morning and, just before I arrived, had had a "good" talk with the president. Trend, a friend dating back several years, showed me my hideaway. He would be my "minder" during the course of the afternoon and evening.

I checked out the phone connections to Washington. The group that had been meeting in Rostow's office the previous afternoon (Washington time) would reconvene in time for me to deal with them during the Wilson-Kosygin discussions. Brown and Trend helped themselves to my whiskey, and I then had a thirty-minute snooze on what may well have been Lady Jane's hard, lumpy bed. I was awakened by the sound of Kosygin's motorcycle escort pulling into the courtyard below my window.

During the course of the afternoon, Wilson's aide made several ascents to the attic to report on progress below. It seemed that Kosygin enjoyed his brief stay in Scotland, was in good spirits and had not mentioned, at least thus far, the abrupt change in the American position. We went over the British draft of the final communiqué on Vietnam—anodyne and lofty prose that made no mention of either reconvening the Geneva Conference or the Trinh interview.

Later that afternoon, Trend trudged upstairs for a chat and a drink. We probed how Wilson might yet salvage something from the Russian visit. We kicked around the notion that Hanoi might stop further infiltration in exchange for an extension of the Tet bombing pause. The respite might provide breathing room for more consequential tension-reducing measures leading up to talks. Trend went downstairs to test the idea with Wilson and came back with Wilson's endorsement. Before I broached the matter with the group sitting in the White House conference room, however, I decided to try it out with a less edgy colleague in the State Department.

It was Sunday, and there were few people in the department. Luckily, however, Ben Read, the cool, competent executive secretary (who had been kept in close touch with the London venture) was on duty. He thought our new idea made good sense, but in the light of the events of the past few days urged that we get Rostow's clearance before Wilson went ahead. Ben said he would forward it to Rostow, since Walt might now say "no" to me automatically. I should hear back from Rostow within the hour.

Meanwhile, business downstairs was coming to a close. Throwing caution to the winds, I made two calls to the White House. Walt assured me the president was considering the deal. The meter was ticking, but no return call from Washington. Trend dashed in to say that Wilson was stalling over the good-byes, but couldn't keep Kosygin there much longer.

Outside my window I heard the premier's police escort revving up. I called Rostow again and dangled the phone out the open window so he could hear the roar of the cycles. "Walt, " I shouted, "yes or no? Kosygin is about to leave for London and will be going back to Moscow early in the morning." Rostow finally got it; the president (or Rostow) would have a reply by midnight London time. Wilson should tell Kosygin to expect a new proposition to take back to Moscow and forward to Hanoi. I should call Ambassador Bruce and have him join me at Downing Street to await the word. At last, the skies had cleared. Wilson, Brown, and Trend joined me and the ghost of Lady Jane for a celebratory drink.

At Downing Street two hours later, the word from Washington arrived. It was yes, but qualified by an impossible caveat. If Hanoi stood fast north of the seventeenth parallel, the current bombing pause, now scheduled to be over as soon as Kosygin left London, would be extended until 10:00 AM London time. It was now past midnight. This would hardly be enough time to allow Kosygin to arrive in Moscow, let alone contact Hanoi, permit the North Vietnamese to discuss the proposal and send him their reply, and to contact Wilson, who would then contact Washington. Several days, rather than several hours, would be needed to complete that process.

Once again I called Rostow. Realizing that the White House, in its present mood, would not even listen to a plea for an extension of several days, I begged for forty-eight hours. Rostow said he'd try to get more time, but any extension would amount to hours, not days. Wilson called the White House. It was not clear to me whether he was talking to Rostow or Johnson, but he squeezed out two more hours, until noon, about eleven hours hence. Whoever he was talking to suggested that Wilson and Kosygin "work fast."

It was now one o'clock on Monday morning. Wilson, Brown, and two senior staff members dashed off to Claridge's Hotel and awakened Kosygin. According to the notes taken by Wilson's assistant, Wilson read the key sentence from the message received from Johnson an hour before: "I agree . . . you should go forward [with] further balanced measures of de-escalation [i.e., the notion Burke Trend and I had earlier forwarded to the White House from Chequers]." If there was agreement on this, Johnson went on, "the Americans were ready to go to a neutral spot and engage in unconditional talks in order to achieve peace."

Kosygin replied that he saw "nothing new in the proposal," and since there was a very short deadline for Hanoi's response, the proposal was actually an "ultimatum." Nonetheless, Kosygin agreed to send the proposal to Hanoi. He doubted, however, that Hanoi would accept it; much more time was needed for Hanoi to discuss it.

Both Prime Minister Wilson and Foreign Minister Brown told Kosygin that "peace was now available and within their grasp." They urged Kosygin to give the American proposal his "full backing in communicating with Hanoi."

Kosygin promised to transmit the message (many years later, we learned that he did), but, once again, doubted that Hanoi would accept it: ". . . the whole of the South [i.e., South Vietnam] would say that [Hanoi] were traitors if movements of troops and supplies were stopped."[14]

Bruce and I returned to the embassy after we heard Wilson's report. It was about 2:00 AM London time, 9:00 PM in Washington. Bruce called Secretary Rusk, who was still at his desk. He told Rusk that the deadline was absurd and urged him to get the president to extend it by several days. Rusk icily responded that the British had already gotten all they were going to get. End of conversation.

Early the next morning (Monday), I arranged with Wilson's staff that if the prime minister received a response from Moscow or Hanoi, they were to call Rusk or Rostow directly and then get back to me. I stationed myself at a desk outside Bruce's office. Within easy reach were a pot of coffee, a telephone, and a clock. Ten o'clock ticked by. No call. Wilson's aide told me that Kosygin's plane was now scheduled to take off from England at noon. This was the moment Washington's deadline would end. I called my phone pal Rostow. (By now, our conversations had the tone of an irate, recently divorced couple.) Walt agreed to give the London-Moscow-Hanoi-Moscow-London arrangement a few more hours. At 3:30 I learned that Hanoi had broadcast a letter to the pope with a blistering demand that the United States order an immediate, unconditional cessation of bombing. At four o'clock, Washington called. Bombing had resumed.

*   *   *

Several days later, back in Washington, Ben Read described the events in Washington during that traumatic London weekend. No one with authority in Washington had taken the London talks seriously. They regarded Wilson's discussions as of little consequence when compared to what might emerge from Johnson's letter to Ho. My message to Washington with a draft of the letter Wilson wanted to pass on to Kosygin had received scant attention. When Johnson finally saw it, more than a day later, however, he was furious. He assembled his small group of advisers—Rostow, McNamara, and company. None of them registered on the fact that Phase A–Phase B had, by now, become the core of several proposals, which, wittingly or not, they had approved. My message seemed to have been regarded as a new, quick-and-dirty deal that I had prepared in haste and without their knowledge for Wilson's use. (I suspect that I had now graduated from Johnson's Gray Book to his Black Book.)

Many years later, a former official in Hanoi's foreign ministry told me that the last-minute initiative cooked up in Lady Jane's attic cell had, in fact, reached Hanoi. The hour or so they had available to consider it was regarded as an insulting ultimatum. Ho's letter to the Vatican was their reply.

According to a deeply disappointed Harold Wilson, "A historic opportunity had been missed. The Washington decision . . . was decisive and disastrous. . . . I have never been able to get away from an impression of a classical Greek tragedy."[15]

*   *   *

It took a week or so before I could regard the London effort objectively. I knew from the outset that Wilson was being overly optimistic and that he, like many others, had a vision of receiving the Nobel Peace Prize. I also knew from bitter experience that a bombing pause would be exploited by Hanoi to expedite the flow of troops into South Vietnam. And I knew Hanoi's actions would decrease the chances that hawkish Washington officials would offer concessions that might lead to a peaceful settlement. Most of all, I knew that Harriman, and especially I, had become suspect characters in a White House where Walt Rostow wielded influence. I began to wonder whether I was doing more harm than good to the cause of a negotiated settlement.

NOTES

1. The book, *The Lost Crusade*, was published by Dodd Mead in 1970.

2. Unlike Robert McNamara, who used a converted windowless air force tanker.

3. For a biography of Harriman, see Rudy Abramson's *Spanning the Century* (New York: William Morrow, 1992).

4. A. J. Langguth, *Our Vietnam: The War 1954–1975* (New York: Simon & Schuster, 2000), p. 432.

5. "Missed Opportunities," conference sponsored by Brown University and Vassar College, Institute for International Affairs, Ministry of Foreign Affairs, Hanoi, Vietnam, June 1997.

6. George Brown, *In My Way* (London: Victor Gollancz, 1971), p. 144.

7. Richard Crossman, *The Diaries of a Cabinet Minister*, vol. 2 (New York: Holt, Rinehart and Winston, 1997), p. 183.

8. Harold Wilson, *The Labour Government 1964–1970* (London: Weidenfeld and Nicholson; Michael Joseph, 1971), p. 346.

9. Ibid.

10. Ibid., p. 357.

11. Ibid., p. 358.

12. Ibid., p. 359.

13. Brown, *In My Way*, p. 146.

14. An unabridged copy of the Claridge's meeting notes is available from the British National Archives, Ref. PREM 13/1718.

15. Wilson, *The Labour Government*, pp. 365, 366.

13
ON THE STREET

ABOUT LYNDON JOHNSON

President Johnson cannot possibly be given justice in a few paragraphs. All I can do here is sketch out the man as I observed him during the period of his presidency, from November 1963 until December 1968. Moreover, I cannot claim to be objective. Perhaps no one can honestly claim to be; LBJ was much too complicated, much too flamboyant, much too fulsome to permit cold, unbiased opinions.

Among Kennedy's legacies was his White House staff—largely northeastern Ivy Leaguers who came to Washington directly out of university or from prestigious law firms. Some knew Kennedy from his prepresidential years; some knew somebody who knew Kennedy. On the National Security Council staff there were a couple of men (the staff had no women other than the secretaries) who had served under Eisenhower, a few who had been seduced from the State Department, and me, who was recruited from the CIA.

Johnson's initial attitude toward the people he inherited from Kennedy was a mix of distrust and deference. The distrust lingered; the deference eroded. In any case, several from the Kennedy period soon drifted off, and those who remained established a modus vivendi with or became ardent admirers of Johnson and the Texas coterie. (I was in the former group—more or less.)

One of the great unanswered questions about this period is what would

Lyndon Johnson's administration have been like if it had not been immured in Vietnam? But, as this chapter relates, LBJ in effect became a prisoner and his Great Society became a casualty of the Vietnam War. But give him this: his civil rights program was a class act.

*   *   *

I wish I could say that on my return to Washington in mid-February 1967, I brushed off the ashes from the ruins of the London effort and set out with zest for another bold try. If I did say anything close to this, however, I would be lying. The fact was that I spent an angry several days trying to piece together what had actually happened in Washington and Hanoi during the critical days, February 10, 11, and 12.

Much of the blame rested with the leaders in Hanoi, of course. They used the bombing pause during Kosygin's visit to London to increase the infiltration of troops and weapons into South Vietnam. If Ho and his advisers had halted the southward flow during this period, or at least kept it to its pre-Tet levels, perhaps Johnson and his advisers would not have reversed the order of Phase A and Phase B. The Wilson-Kosygin meeting might then have served as a catalyst for starting peace negotiations.

Perhaps. But perhaps not. My personal postmortem convinced me that the senior American officials involved had refused to focus seriously on the London effort. They, Johnson especially, took a dim view of Harold Wilson thrusting himself onto Washington's sacred turf—negotiations about negotiations. Wilson should not have been unaware of this. After all, LBJ had earlier scolded him about his meddling in Vietnam: "I won't tell you how to run [the insurgency in] Malaya, and you don't tell us how to run Vietnam."[1] Nonetheless, Wilson seemed sure that this time around, he could deliver the goods to the White House, and perhaps win a Nobel Peace Prize. What he didn't reckon on (nor did I) was that the president and his advisers either had never focused on the A-B formula or had forgotten all about it. In any case, when they—especially Johnson and Rostow—finally woke up to it, they regarded the formula as a new, cheeky, unauthorized, Cooper-invented initiative.

Secretary Rusk himself was obviously troubled by what had transpired at Downing Street, Chequers, and the White House in February. In his memoir, written a few years later, he confessed, "I don't know why we delayed responding to Cooper's cable [requesting approval of the draft of the letter Wilson would give to Kosygin]. Perhaps we were unable to get to the President. But Cooper had a right to think that the message he drafted for Kosygin was consistent with his original instructions. . . . Johnson was upset when he heard Cooper's draft had already been sent to Kosygin because he felt he hadn't had a chance to review the text." Rusk went on to say that "this was perhaps as close as we came to setting up talks before 1968 (when talks actually started). . . . I cannot assign fault for the mix-up. . . . It was an unfortunate slip of communication."[2]

I'm convinced that it was not just an "unfortunate slip"; it was an earnest of Johnson's and Rostow's indifference to the efforts Wilson was expending to contact Hanoi. So it was that the urgent, high-priority cables I had sent to Washington during Kosygin's London visit were shuffled around the White House with all deliberate speed, and then put aside. The message I had sent with the draft of the letter for Kosygin had rested undisturbed on someone's desk for forty-eight precious hours.

The sorry ending to Wilson's attempt had a chilling effect on further third-party initiatives. Moreover, Ho's angry response to Johnson's letter (written, to be sure, after bombing resumed) provided little encouragement to would-be peace seekers in both the United States and abroad. For that matter, neither Harriman nor I could summon much enthusiasm to continue our efforts to capture the elusive peace dove throughout the rest of that winter and the following spring. On May 1, Secretary Rusk, frustrated with Hanoi's refusal to talk, or even listen, listed twenty-eight proposals made by the United States and other countries that had been rejected by Ho Chi Minh. Ho, Rusk said, did not want peace.

*   *   *

By early 1967 one could virtually smell and touch the miasma that hung low over Washington's players in and spectators of the Vietnam drama. More than a half million American servicemen and women were engaged in the war, including four hundred thousand soldiers and marines on the ground. Funerals had long since become a fixture of the Arlington National Cemetery's landscape; traffic over Memorial Bridge was constantly slowed by corteges on their way to the burial ground. Scores of college campuses and many cities were rocked by noisy, frequently violent demonstrations. Members of Congress were increasingly asking unfriendly questions. Bobby Kennedy, setting the stage for the 1968 presidential primaries, was attracting media attention and large audiences with his antiwar speeches.

Among the millions of Americans who had become unhappy campers were Robert McNamara, Averell Harriman, and Dean Rusk. I suspected Lyndon Johnson was as well. And this I knew beyond a shadow of doubt: so was I. The promised "light at the end of the tunnel" was very dim, if not invisible.

The political situation in Saigon continued to be fragile, thanks to the restive Buddhists and jockeying generals. The ground war had become increasingly bloody for North and South Vietnamese military and civilians, as well as for the Americans, Australians, New Zealanders, and South Koreans. And there were no definitive signs of early, or even eventual, victory. The air war, despite its intensity, showed no signs of staunching the flow of North Vietnamese troops and equipment into South Vietnam.

A respected *New York Times* correspondent, Harrison Salisbury, managed to get to Hanoi in late December 1966. He reported having seen large numbers of missed or mistaken targets and a great deal more "collateral damage" than the air force had acknowledged. Nevertheless, his firsthand assessment was that the North Vietnamese war effort was less damaged by the war than most Washington officials were claiming. Robert McNamara, however, had become more realistic. He warned in early 1967 that the war could not be won solely by bombing North Vietnam; the ground war in the south was where the war would be won or lost. (This is what I told Mac Bundy a year before.)

Rosy reports of military progress and political accomplishments were still touted by senior American civilian officials and military officers in Saigon (but not by their less starry-eyed subordinates) and by their counterparts in the State Department, the Pentagon, and the White House (but not from the CIA). Some of Dr. Pangloss's clones were incurable optimists, some were fawning courtiers, and some were just old-fashioned "team players." In Saigon, the conductor of the hallelujah chorus was General Westmoreland, commander of US forces. In Washington, Walt Rostow had begun to regard his job as involving purveying only good news and shortchanging the bad.

In late April, Westmoreland traveled to Washington to brief Congress, the president, and his advisers on the situation in Vietnam. He assured Congress that the United States would prevail. He was careful, however, to avoid predicting when and at what price, but did ask the president to increase the US military force level in Vietnam to 600,000 (there were then 440,000 American and 50,000 foreign troops), and to send reinforcements as soon as possible.

However Westmoreland truly felt, and whatever he claimed about the progress of the war, it would be astonishing if he had not begun to sense, by early 1967, that he was losing the battle of credibility at home.

*   *   *

The mounting loss of lives and substance was not the only burden the United States had to bear as a consequence of its role in Vietnam. There was another, wider toll, one that could not be quantitatively measured, but was nonetheless costly. The war was diverting Washington's attention from developments beyond Indochina, developments that also had important international policy implications. Worrisome events and trends in the rest of the world did not remain on hold until the Vietnam problem was resolved. Yet, *perforce*, they remained residual claimants on the time and attention of the president and his key national security advisers.

Meanwhile, the advisers were becoming slaves to the clock and the calendar. Careful analysis, thoughtful planning, and prudent implementation were put aside in the urgency of today's bombing schedule and tomorrow's inspection trip. This frenetic activity, conducted during sixteen-hour days, did not come cost free; it had a worrisome effect on the physical and emotional well-being of senior officials and their subordinates. Robert McNamara and goodness knows how many on his staff were taking sleeping pills.[3] In the spring of 1967 Dean Rusk, concerned about his health and that of his colleagues, told the president that changing key officials "to meet the charge that Washington's tired and stale" should not be ruled out.[4] He confessed to being "bone tired. . . . Eight years is just far too long for this job."[5]

Averell Harriman would have disagreed with both McNamara and Rusk. He would have liked nothing more than to keep going well after his eight-year stint. When I first met him in early 1961, he was seventy years old, older by a decade than both McNamara and Rusk. In those days, he was tough, energetic, and single-minded. Ten years later, he walked more slowly and showed up at the State Department a bit later in the morning, but he was still tough, energetic, and single-minded.

Admittedly, my responsibilities did not compare in weight to those of my various bosses, but I do not look back on that period as a joyous romp in the garden. I was blessed, however, with a caring, understanding family. No matter how late I returned in the evening, and no matter if I planned to dash back to the office, Orah always provided a drink and a proper dinner, complete with candles and music, when I finally got home. Joan and Susan (then in their teens) and I often discussed Vietnam, but our conversations never became confrontational. Orah continued to prohibit discussion of Vietnam among our dinner guests.

Aside from an understanding family, I had an escape hatch. In 1961, when I no longer had time to sculpt, I embarked on the construction of a massive, scale-model, three-ring circus—tents, audience, animals, performers, wagons, even the sawdust. It became a substitute for a sleeping pill. Before going to bed, I would spend a profitable hour sculpting an elephant or a clown on stilts. Great therapy! (I eventually finished the project and presented it to the children's ward at the National Institutes of Health.)

*   *   *

Almost from my first days at the State Department, I sensed that Johnson never fully trusted Harriman; when the chips were down, LBJ regarded the Guv as a "Kennedy man." Harriman was rarely invited to attend meetings with Johnson and his other senior advisers, even when the subject involved negotiations with Hanoi. He was not included in the White House Cabinet Room sessions during the Wilson-Kosygin meetings, and I'm sure he wasn't told what had transpired there until I told him on my return from London.

My suspicions that LBJ had given him the search-for-peace mission in September 1966 to keep him busy but out of the policy mainstream was validated in late June 1967 when Johnson and Kosygin held a "summit" meeting at a small college in New Jersey. Two days before the participants were to convene, my friend in Secretary Rusk's office showed me the still-secret list of invited US participants. I noticed with disbelief that Harriman's name was not on the list. (Neither was McNamara's.) This would probably have been the only occasion since Kennedy's inauguration (except during the Cuban Missile Crisis) that the Guv was excluded from high-level US-USSR discussions. This was an ineffable discourtesy to the only historic figure and one of the few true statesmen in LBJ's administration. Moreover, the Guv was still an expert on US-Soviet relations. Aside from the sheer stupidity of the omission, this would have been a serious blow to Harriman's morale and self-esteem, and would have further cooled his relations with Johnson, Rusk, and Rostow.

Together with the department's executive secretary, Ben Read, I urged Rusk to amend the delegation list to include Harriman. Rusk agreed, providing Rostow approved. Astonishingly enough, in the light of the events of the past several months, Rostow still accepted my calls. I squeezed out a grudging "all right," and the deal was done.

Harriman was perceptive enough to realize that he had become an outsider in the Johnson administration. Nevertheless, until the eve of Richard Nixon's inauguration, he would become furious whenever his declining influence was hinted at in the media, or by a rash colleague or subordinate.

Johnson's meeting with Kosygin in Glassboro, New Jersey, concluded on an even less promising note than Wilson's session six months before. In a news conference following his talks with the Americans, Kosygin demanded an immediate withdrawal of US forces from Vietnam and the unconditional cessation of the bombing.

*   *   *

In June 1967, a few weeks after the unfruitful Johnson-Kosygin summit, prospects for talks with Hanoi once more showed signs of life. On stage this time were three interesting characters, none of whom had yet made an appearance in Vietnam's long-running melodrama. One of these was a familiar personality on the Washington scene, Harvard professor Henry Kissinger. The other two were Frenchmen no one in Washington's Vietnam community had met, except for Kissinger and me—and, except for the two of us, would ever lay eyes on.

At an international meeting in Paris late that spring, Kissinger ran into an old French friend. Herbert Markovich told Kissinger about a person he knew, Raymond Aubrac, who, after World War II, shared his Paris home with Ho Chi Minh. Not long after, Ho became godfather to Monsieur Aubrac's son. The Ho-Aubrac relationship had remained close through the postwar years. Markovich asked Kissinger if Washington would have any interest in having Aubrac use his influence to try to arrange a dialogue between the Vietnamese and the Americans.

Kissinger promptly flew to Washington and met with Rusk, Harriman, and one or two others. It was agreed the venture would be worth a try, but Rusk specified three conditions: Kissinger was not to represent himself as an official US intermediary; the two Frenchmen (it was decided that both should go) should understand that they were on a personal, unofficial journey; and the whole enterprise should be treated with great secrecy. (Yet again, we have the makings of the right hand–left hand problem.) It was clear that Rusk was wary of the two Frenchmen, and that he had developed a strong distaste for unofficial, would-be peacemakers—including Prof. Henry Kissinger.

It came as no surprise that Kissinger was more than willing to assume sole responsibility; Vietnam was the most important foreign policy game in town, and Henry was anxious to get involved. This would be an opportunity for him to run with the ball. Even better, he would have the field all to himself.

The two Frenchmen—Markovich, an earnest and naive scholar, and Aubrac, a shrewd and hardened former resistance fighter—flew to Hanoi in July and met with several Vietnamese officials, including Ho Chi Minh and Premier Pham Van Dong. On their return to France they sent a James Bond-esque signal to Kissinger. He dashed off to Paris to meet with them. They had positive news. In his message to Harriman in Washington, Kissinger reported:

- Hanoi would agree to start negotiations soon after a bombing cessation.
- Hanoi would be prepared to negotiate with the United States on matters affecting North Vietnam without the presence of the NLF.
- Hanoi recognized that "some US forces" would have to remain in the South until after a political settlement.
- According to Hanoi, the NLF envisaged a "broad coalition government" that would include members of the present Saigon government.[6]

Washington's Vietnam "A" team was encouraged by this report. We decided that Aubrac and Markovich should now be provided with a forthcoming new proposal that they could deliver to Hanoi. It was also time to convince the Frenchmen that Kissinger had, in fact, official US bona fides. I was ordered to accompany Henry to his next meeting with Aubrac and Markovich and to sprinkle holy water over the enterprise.

Except for a few people in the State Department, McNamara, Rostow, and, of course, LBJ, my overnight trip to France was kept a dark secret. Orah, of course, knew I would be away for a brief time, but didn't know where I was going. But the best laid plans . . . Henry and I were just walking into the Hotel Pont Royal when I heard a familiar—*very* familiar—voice. "Hey, Chet, you didn't tell us you were going to Paris!" It was Mitch and Renee, my brother and sister-in-law. I gave them what Damon Runyon used to refer to as a "small hello" and made it clear, sotto voce, that I hadn't seen them, they hadn't seen me, and they should stay away from me and have a good time. I took some comfort in knowing that, by now, nothing would surprise them about my comings and goings, and they would swear to anyone who asked: "Chet? Paris? Not that we know of, and he certainly would have told us."

Markovich and Aubrac met us at lunch. I explained who I was, and that, in this instance, key Washington officials were ready to have Professor

Kissinger act as their intermediary. I also presented the new US proposition: The United States would stop bombing in exchange for Hanoi's agreement to negotiate. This was the first time a swap was stated in such bold, unconditional terms. (A few weeks later, President Johnson would make the same offer in a speech in San Antonio.)

The meeting in Paris was convened in an air of optimism, but once again, the justifiable secrecy of the enterprise poisoned the atmosphere. One of the heaviest bombing assaults of the war had started just as I arrived in Paris with our new message. Markovich and Aubrac rightly wondered how they could successfully deal with Ho and other high-level Vietnamese officials under the circumstances. They felt that the bombing should be sharply reduced as a signal of America's genuine interest before they set off for Hanoi once again. But it was the same old problem: LBJ, McNamara, and Rusk felt unable to explain to the Pentagon brass and bureaucrats (or, for that matter, the press) why they had ordered a sudden, sharp reduction of the bombing, short of revealing the highly delicate attempts to contact the Vietnamese leadership. This is not to say, of course, that if LBJ or McNamara had really wanted to, it was beyond the mind of man to have found a way. After all, what is the use of being a commander in chief or a secretary of defense if you can't give unpopular, unquestioned orders?

The Aubrac-Markovich trip to Hanoi was canceled by officials in Hanoi on the (perhaps legitimate) grounds that, because of the bombing, the city was now too dangerous for foreign visitors. Instead, the two emissaries were told to deliver the message they had received from Washington to the North Vietnamese representative in Paris. He, in turn, would inform them when he had Hanoi's reply. Weeks folded into months. We in Washington concluded that, despite this venture's early promise, our initial optimism was ill-founded and that Aubrac's influence in Hanoi was much exaggerated. But, finally, in December, Hanoi responded. The message was short, abrupt, and angry: no visit, no talks. That seemed to be the end of the Aubrac-Markovich story.

But it wasn't. Thirty years later, when Robert McNamara and I were in Hanoi reviewing the events of that period with several former Vietnamese diplomats and generals, we spent many hours discussing this and other US peace overtures. According to two former senior foreign ministry officials, the message prepared in Washington for Hanoi was regarded as the most serious US proposition they had received thus far. The proposed trade-off between stopping the bombs and starting the talks was discussed at length in both the prime minister's office and the foreign ministry.

Apparently, by October 1967, the odds were high that Hanoi's foreign minister would send a reply to Aubrac encouraging further exchanges. But the North Vietnamese leadership also had a case of left hand–right hand confusion. While the civilian officials were discussing a possible negotiations scenario, however, the military were starting a major mobilization and training program for young Vietcong recruits who would play the major role in the heavy attacks scheduled for Tet on January 30 and 31, 1968. General Giap, Hanoi's senior military commander, did not want peace talks with Americans while he and his generals were launching what they expected to be a devastating blow against South Vietnamese, American, and allied forces. Giap insisted that the Frenchmen's initiative be stopped in its tracks. It was.

Sitting around the table in the dreary, small room in February 1998, a dozen American and Vietnamese scholars and veterans could only think about what might have been if . . .

*   *   *

In late August, appearing before a Senate committee, Robert McNamara had doubted the usefulness of continuing the bombing of North Vietnam. President Johnson did not take kindly to in-house disagreement. He was forced to deny to the press and to the world in general that there was a deep division within his administration on the bombing issue. There was probably another reason for Johnson's break with his secretary of defense: McNamara's continuing close relationship with Bobby Kennedy had become increasingly irksome to the president.

In late November 1967 McNamara resigned as secretary of defense. This was quickly followed by Johnson's announcement that he had appointed him president of the World Bank. McNamara's departure was not unexpected. He had become increasingly vocal in his discomfort with the administration's policies regarding developments in and prospects for Vietnam.

"I do not know to this day," McNamara wrote many years later, "whether I quit or I was fired. Perhaps both."[7] Either way, he sensed that his day of reckoning was approaching: "I had come to the conclusion, and had told him [i.e., the president], point-blank, that we could not achieve our objective in Vietnam through any reasonable military means and we therefore should seek a lesser political objective through negotiations. President Johnson was not ready to accept this. It was coming clear to both of us that I would not change my judgment, nor would he change his. Something had to give."[8]

Early in the new year, Johnson announced McNamara's replacement,

Clark Clifford. The new secretary of defense was a longtime Washington fixture, a member of Johnson's kitchen cabinet, and a Vietnam hawk—until he moved from the spectator stand onto the field.

McNamara's departure left Harriman as the only voice in the higher reaches of the administration strongly advocating an early negotiated settlement. The Guv was a weak reed, however. If he needed a hint as to where he stood in the hierarchy, he was given one during the dark autumn of 1967: Johnson asked him to head a low-level delegation to witness the opening of a dam in Pakistan. (Harriman accepted, of course, and then used the journey as an excuse to proceed to Rumania to discuss a possible contact with Hanoi.)

In late February 1968 LBJ, at Mac Bundy's suggestion, assembled a group of former government officials and eminent outsiders, dubbed the "Wise Men," to review the Vietnam situation and recommend a course of action. Several current officials and military leaders were invited to participate. Harriman, the highest-ranking civilian working full-time on Vietnam, was not included.

The Guv tried hard to guard whatever political capital he still had at the White House. His candid personal views of the Vietnam situation were reserved for trusted colleagues, sympathetic acquaintances, and friendly members of the media community. He did not wish to follow in McNamara's footsteps. But I did.

*   *   *

Soon after the collapse of Kissinger's initiative, I realized that my efforts, if they ever had been useful, had pretty much run their course. I saw no point in hanging around the State Department waiting, like Mr. Micawber, "for something to turn up." I wanted, now, to return to my aborted writing project. This time, I knew, the task would not be interrupted by anyone from the administration asking for my services. I took extended leave without pay and returned to the Institute for Defense Analyses, where the hospitality of the house was once again extended.

I was now fifty years old, with two daughters still in university. I had no idea what I would do once the book was finished. I decided to continue writing and let events unfold. I was, after all, still a civil servant and thus, at least theoretically, eligible to go back to the State Department. In any case, I suspected the CIA would be ready to have me on board once again.

My new incarnation was stimulating and pleasant. I discovered, once again, that there is a life outside the halls of officialdom. I was satisfied to rely on the *Washington Post* and the *New York Times* for information on Vietnam. It was from this remote vantage point that I learned of the bullish predictions General Westmoreland made during his visit to Washington in December 1967. In his comments to the Congress and the press the general was overflowing with optimism.

Meanwhile, as a few of us were told in Hanoi three decades later, the feverish mobilization of raw Vietcong troops taking place under Westmoreland's nose strangled what may well have been the most favorable chance for peace since 1963. On January 30, the first day of Tet, 1968, the Communists unleashed attacks throughout South Vietnam. Virtually every large town became a battleground. Enemy troops even scaled the walls of the US Embassy in Saigon.

Over the next few weeks, American and South Vietnamese casualties were high, but Communist losses, especially among the young Vietcong recruits, were horrendous. North Vietnam's General Giap's expectations of a general uprising throughout South Vietnam came to naught. A good case could be made—and the Pentagon and Westmoreland's headquarters made it—that the Communists had suffered a major military defeat. But, in part because of Westmoreland's optimistic predictions just a month before, political considerations at last had taken over. Tet 1968 was not "the beginning of a great defeat for the enemy," but of an acknowledgment in Washington that victory was beyond reach at any cost Americans would deem acceptable. Not long after the Tet attacks, Westmoreland, ignoring obvious political reality, asked Johnson to commit more than 200,000 additional troops. As a sign of things to come, the president agreed to a reinforcement of only 10,500.

Once installed at the Pentagon, Clark Clifford had an opportunity to grasp the true nature of the military and political outlook for American success in Vietnam. The highly classified cable traffic from Saigon and the briefings from Pentagon and CIA experts were eye-openers. Within weeks, instead of advocating the hawkish views the president, Walt Rostow, and Dean Rusk had expected from him, he became an even more outspoken advocate than McNamara for a negotiated settlement.

Complicating Johnson's already complicated life was the approach of the presidential primaries. Eugene McCarthy, an ardent antiwar, prosettlement senator, won 40 percent of the vote in New Hampshire in early March. Then Bobby Kennedy decided that he, too, would enter the race on a peace platform; on March 16 he announced his candidacy.

On March 18 Johnson made clear that, notwithstanding the recent Communist military offensives and McCarthy's and Kennedy's views, he would not change his policy on Vietnam. But within a few days, he revealed that the US position was under comprehensive review. On March 31, in a dramatic televised speech, LBJ announced a major military concession, and an earth-shaking political statement: He said that all bombing outside the area around the Demilitarized Zone between North and South Vietnam would cease, and asked Hanoi to respond by agreeing to peace talks. He concluded the speech with an announcement which astonished even his closest advisers: he would not seek or accept the nomination for another presidential term. Within seventy-two hours, Hanoi agreed to meet with US representatives and discuss Johnson's offer to stop the bombing.

*   *   *

I felt a twinge of restlessness after hearing Johnson's speech—much like an old fire horse at the sound of a bell. Yet the sensation soon passed. I still found stimulation and satisfaction in writing, and considerable pleasure in gardening, antiquing, and reading. I had no appetite for more government cables and reports. I saw the Guv occasionally at dinner and my former colleagues frequently at lunch. Nonetheless, I kept the alarums and excursions about Vietnam at a safe distance—for several weeks. My respite was temporarily interrupted in mid-January when Hildy, Harriman's assistant, called. The Guv wanted to see me. It was important. And it was urgent. I agreed to meet with him late that afternoon.

Harriman lost no time in pleasantries. He wanted to write (which was to say, he wanted me to draft) a note to the president. It should be ready for delivery to the White House the next morning. He told me to close his office door and take careful notes of what he wanted to say.

For the next hour or so the Guv gave vent to all his pent-up feelings about the folly of US policy in Vietnam. Much of this I had heard before—in his discussions with McNamara, or when he shared his private thoughts with me. This would be the first time, however, that the president would be made aware of Harriman's views on the need to move from bombing to negotiating, and to offer Hanoi terms that had promise of being accepted. The Guv may have been influenced by McNamara's departure, or by Johnson's speech the previous spring, or perhaps he had decided, come hell or high water, it was time for Johnson to hear his true voice.

I called Orah to say that I wouldn't be home for dinner, found an empty office, arranged for a secretary to come in at 6:30 the next morning, and

started to transform Harriman's ruminations, expostulations, and proposi-
tions into a coherent memorandum. I wanted to convey a sense of sweet
reason without losing the emotional force that had come through in his discussion. There had also been more than a hint of his readiness to resign—a
threat I wanted to preserve but not emphasize.

I finished a first draft by about 7:30. I read it to myself aloud. It sounded
too much like me, not enough like Harriman. I rewrote it, trying to capture
his (somewhat wooden) style. I did a word count. It was too long. I performed major surgery. It was now about six hundred words—the standard
two pages. I rewrote it as legibly as my awful handwriting permitted. It was
after ten o'clock. I was hungry and tired, and went home.

The next morning, the secretary and I arrived about the same time. I gave
her the draft and asked for a double-spaced copy. By the time I returned from
the cafeteria with a couple of cups of coffee and some Danish pastry, the draft
had been typed. I reread it in the fresh light of day, made a few corrections,
and asked for a clean copy, single-spaced. It turned out to be a bit short of
two pages and seemed to convey what, according to my notes and my
memory, Harriman had said. There was nothing more to do except wait. The
Guv came in at 9:30. I gave him the draft and reminded him that if he wanted
to have it available for Johnson's night reading, the memorandum would
have to be in Rostow's hands by noon.

Harriman read the piece. Then reread it. He handed it back to me and I
could tell, from long experience, that he did not like it. "I can't say this!" he
shouted angrily. "And I *won't* say this!"

"But you *did* say that. Look at my verbatim notes of what you said."

"I can't say that. Don't you realize this would burn my bridges? *You* can
say that. You *would* say that. You probably *did* say that. And that's why
you're on the street, but I'm still here."

I'm not sure what my response to that was. I would like to think I said
something like, "Well, I'm going back to the street. You can write your own
thing." In truth, I probably was too annoyed to say anything. I do know that
I walked out—to the street.

The aftermath of all this was that Harriman never sent that note, or any
other. He did, however, send me a case of elegant Bordeaux wine. I didn't
contact him for about two weeks, but after a couple of soothing calls from
Hildy, I agreed to have lunch with him. The fact of the matter is that I was so
fond of the Guv, warts and all, that I would have eventually telephoned him,
even without Hildy's coaxing.

*   *   *

American and North Vietnamese political representatives were in tenuous contact through most of April 1968. At around this time, General Westmoreland, perhaps by coincidence, issued another ebullient prediction: "[T]he spirit of the offensive is now prevalent throughout Vietnam . . . militarily we have never been in a better relative position." Nonetheless, President Johnson announced on May 3 that the United States and Hanoi had agreed to meet in Paris to talk about talking.

Averell Harriman, together with Cyrus Vance, a distinguished lawyer, a former deputy secretary of defense under Robert McNamara, and a future secretary of state under Jimmy Carter, would head the small US negotiations team. Vance's appointment was just another indication that Johnson, Rostow, and even Rusk did not entirely trust Harriman; during the Laos negotiations, the Guv had shown too much independence to suit the Washington officialdom.

According to Dean Rusk, "President Johnson had enormous confidence in Vance. . . . Johnson was more comfortable with a Harriman-Vance team than if State [by which Rusk clearly meant Harriman] alone had been represented."[9] But even Vance's participation apparently did not provide Rostow with sufficient insurance. William Jorden, a member of Rostow's staff and a hard-liner, was dispatched to monitor the proceedings and provide the White House with confidential, back-channel reports.

The talks in Paris soon became bogged down in protocol and procedural matters, but events were moving along briskly elsewhere. Bobby Kennedy was assassinated in early June. Hubert Humphrey, with the grudging endorsement of Lyndon Johnson, announced his candidacy for president. Clark Clifford, now a convinced peace seeker, was in open disagreement with Johnson, Rostow, and Rusk. The North Vietnamese, as if to mock Westmoreland's optimistic predictions, had stepped up their military activity. The administration turned down all suggestions (including Clifford's) for a complete bombing halt.

In Saigon, the government of South Vietnam warned the US negotiators that, in case they had any thoughts to the contrary, it would "never cede an inch of land to the northern Communists, would never set up a coalition government and would never recognize the National Liberation Front" (i.e., the NLF, aka the Vietcong).[10]

The NLF, for its part, made clear that it could not "be absent from the settlement of any problem in South Vietnam."[11]

Meanwhile, the political campaigns were heating up. Richard Nixon and his foreign affairs adviser, Henry Kissinger, were keeping a careful watch on the negotiations in Paris and making it known that they had a "secret plan" to end the hostilities with honor. (The details of this plan were apparently so secret that they could not be revealed before the election, after the election, or during the Nixon presidency.)

Hubert Humphrey was desperately trying to free himself from Johnson's Vietnam policy. He was walking on eggs in this regard, lest he so anger LBJ as to completely lose the president's support—support which, in any case, was being doled out in spoonfuls. Meanwhile, Humphrey's friends were concerned that Johnson was providing Nixon with more and better information on foreign affairs in general and the Vietnam talks in particular than he was sharing with Vice President Humphrey, who was his party's likely candidate for president.

My status with the State Department during the period after I left for "the street" was in a twilight zone. I was on extended leave, but had a vague consultancy relationship with Governor Harriman. Until early July, my services were neither sought nor offered. But suddenly, Harriman and Vance asked me to spend a couple of weeks with them in Paris. The peace talks were then hung up on a new, more generous twist to the Phase A–Phase B formula. Perhaps I could join the delegation's deliberations about getting the talks going in earnest.

A few days before I left, Robert Nathan, an old friend and a campaign adviser to the vice president, asked for an "important and confidential" favor. Humphrey had prepared a major speech he hoped to deliver in late July, before the Democratic platform drafting committee met. Although the president had been insisting that the platform endorse his own Vietnam stance, in the proposed speech Humphrey would press for a bombing halt and a cease-fire in Vietnam. This would be his definitive break with Johnson on Vietnam, freeing him from the shackles of the administration's Vietnam policy.

Nathan gave me a draft of the speech and asked me to show it to Harriman and Vance, both of whom were Humphrey's friends and political allies. My task was twofold: make sure that the bombing halt and cease-fire Humphrey was advocating would not damage the US negotiating position in Paris, and persuade Vance and Harriman to make public their assurances to this effect after Humphrey's speech.

I found Nathan's request congenial on several counts. I felt Humphrey was getting short shrift from Johnson and company. I did not trust Nixon and wanted to see him defeated. I was in favor of a bombing halt and a cease-fire.

And so I agreed to do what I could to get the Guv and Vance to focus on Humphrey's proposal.

Harriman was ill with the flu when I arrived in Paris, and I spent the first several days with Vance and other members of the delegation. Vance was sympathetic to Humphrey's desire to put some distance between himself and Johnson. Moreover, he, too, was in favor of a complete bombing halt and a cease-fire; he regarded these steps as the only way to move the negotiations forward. On the other hand—and this hand proved the stronger of the two—he was anxious not to embarrass LBJ with a public endorsement of Humphrey's stance on Vietnam. He also felt there was some hope of Johnson accepting the notion of a bombing halt, but that this hope might be dashed if Humphrey advocated it. (This is hard to believe, but relations between the two men had become that poisonous.)

Harriman, looking pale and feeble, wandered into the delegation office in due course, and I went over the same ground with him. He agreed with Vance.

Later that afternoon, we persuaded the Guv to take advantage of the warm, sunny day and stroll over to the Musée Orangerie, where there was an exhibition of Bonnard paintings—a half dozen or so were on loan from Harriman's personal collection. He returned in less than an hour, looking even worse than when he left. He reported that when he went to the entrance of the exhibit, "an old lady in a black dress and with a moustache" demanded a ticket. He did not, of course, have a ticket. Nor, of course, did he have the necessary two francs to buy a ticket. Dejected, he decided to take a walk in the Tuileries, the park behind the museum. He walked a bit and then sat down on a chair to rest. Another lady in "a black dress and a moustache" demanded a few centimes. Harriman was bereft of centimes; he was, as usual, bereft of any money in any currency. He was a sad sight on his return to the embassy.

Bob Nathan was out of town when I returned to Washington. I met with another of Humphrey's advisers, Larry O'Brien, a onetime JFK companion and senior member of JFK's White House staff. He told me that the platform committee was sharply divided on the bombing issue. Humphrey's speech, if he gave it, would establish that he was no longer Johnson's acolyte. Our discussion was long and agitated, but we both knew what the outcome would be. Harriman and Vance, despite their friendship for Humphrey, felt the speech would be unhelpful to the negotiations. O'Brien nodded. Regardless of the implications this might have for Humphrey's campaign, the Paris talks were too important to be jeopardized. Humphrey, to his everlasting credit, agreed. The speech was shelved. (Three cheers for Hubert H. Humphrey!)

One of the most ardent and the most influential advocate of a complete and immediate bombing halt was the ex-hawk Secretary of Defense Clark Clifford. But Johnson was so opposed to a bombing halt and so angered by any member of the administration who favored a halt that, in mid-September, Clifford's name was removed from the distribution list of sensitive telegrams relating to the negotiations.

Meanwhile, Harriman and Vance were confronting not only the hostile mood and angry politics going on in Washington, but also opposition in Saigon. The South Vietnamese government resisted participating in talks at which the South Vietnamese Communists (the NLF) had any semblance of equality. For their part, both the Hanoi government and the NLF insisted that the Saigon government, a "puppet" of the United States, should not be given *any* role in the negotiations. This thorny issue was resolved when agreement was reached to divide the four parties into two sides. One "side" would consist of the United States and whomever it selected as its partner. The same arrangement would apply to North Vietnam. With this Solomon-like solution, it appeared that serious talks could begin. But not so. Two difficult issues still remained—the bombing of the North and the participation of the South Vietnamese government in Saigon.

The bombing issue was finally publicly addressed by Mac Bundy. In October, at De Pauw University, Bundy strongly urged a bombing halt and the reduction of US forces. He declared that a negotiated end of hostilities in Vietnam was the only available prudent course. On October 31, perhaps in response to Bundy's speech and Clifford's urging, Johnson announced that the bombing of North Vietnam would cease on November 1. For the hard-pressed negotiators in Paris, this was one more obstacle removed.

There still remained the refusal of the South Vietnamese to attend the meetings. According to Clifford (who, by now, was once again permitted to read telegrams to and from Paris), the Saigon government had apparently decided that the Republicans, not the Democrats, would win the imminent election. If, Clifford's reasoning went, the discussions were started in earnest, even on the eve of the election, Humphrey's chances would be significantly improved. In Clifford's view, Nixon's campaigners would try to convince the Saigon government that a Republican administration would give them a better deal at Paris than the Democrats. The Republicans would, therefore, do all they could to induce the Saigon government to boycott the peace talks until after the election on November 6.

However squalid such a tactic would be, the notion was taken seriously by many in Johnson's administration. After all, Clark Clifford was no political naïf. He had been close to presidential politics since his days as an adviser to Harry Truman. Moreover, there was credible gossip around the White House West Wing and the State Department's seventh floor that Madame Claire Chenault, the wealthy widow of General Chenault of World War II Flying Tigers fame and a Republican activist, had already been promoting this idea with South Vietnam's President Nguyen Van Thieu. Despite denials by Henry Kissinger, Nixon's special assistant, at the time and later, I believe this is what, in fact, happened. (Nothing would surprise me about the behavior of politicians at presidential election time, and Richard Nixon and his entourage were certainly not above such a tactic.)

Nixon's victory meant that Harriman and Vance, no less than Johnson, had become lame ducks. Their task now was, somehow, to keep the Paris talks limping along, until, for them, the exit light flashed.

*   *   *

A week or so into the new year, 1969, I met with a personnel officer at the State Department. With a new administration taking over in a couple of weeks, I wanted to check my status. I was still a civil servant on official leave, and presumably couldn't be summarily fired. On the other hand, I was uneasy about continuing my government career under Nixon, or even Kissinger.

My concern was well founded. Despite the fact that I was not a political appointee, it turned out that someone in my position was now extremely vulnerable. After all, I had spent the past several years working for President Johnson and then Secretary Rusk and Averell Harriman. From all I had thus far seen and heard about the ideologues on the transition team, I would be regarded suspiciously by President Nixon and his key appointees. The personnel officer, a wise lady, pointed out my options: I could spend the next four, possibly even eight years "walking the corridors," or she could arrange early retirement. Actually, I had no choice. I retired from the United States government on January 20, 1969.

The day before Nixon's inauguration was cold and gloomy. Johnson and most of his cabinet had already left town for home or for well-deserved vacations. Harriman and Vance were scheduled to arrive from Paris at Andrews Air Force Base that evening, and Secretary Rusk was giving them a small reception there. A group of fifty or so State Department officials and staffers cheered the two negotiators as they got off the plane. Rusk escorted them to a VIP lounge and gave a heartfelt, emotional toast.

I had a chance to say a few words to Vance and the Guv, but couldn't get close to Rusk, who was surrounded by well-wishers. The next morning I wrote a farewell note to the secretary, a man whom I much admired, despite our differences on Vietnam. Two days later, there was a note from him, replete with typos and obviously typed by himself. It was warm, gracious, and complimentary. The most striking aspect of it all, however, was that he, alone, among his high-ranking colleagues, had remained in town to answer his mail and wish his former staff farewell. Dean Rusk was a fourteen-carat gent.

With my farewell notes to Rusk and a few other fellow Vietnam War veterans, I went back on the street. There was a difference now, however. This time I had plenty of company, including my mentor and tormentor, the Guv.

NOTES

1. Harold Wilson, "How the U.S. Muffed a Chance to End the Vietnam War," *Life*, May 21, 1971, p. 51.

2. Dean Rusk, *As I Saw It* (New York and London: W. W. North, 1990), p. 470.

3. Robert McNamara, *In Retrospect* (New York: Times Books, 1995), p. 260.

4. Ibid., p. 260.

5. Rusk, *As I Saw It*, p. 535.

6. Chester L. Cooper, "Visit to Hanoi by Two Unofficial French Representatives," declassified Department of State memorandum, August 2, 1967, p. 2 (National Security Archives, Washington, DC).

7. McNamara, *In Retrospect*, p. 311.

8. Ibid., p. 313.

9. Rusk, *As I Saw It*, p. 485.

10. *New York Times*, May 10, 1968.

11. *New York Times*, April 29, 1968.

14

LOOKING BACK

WHAT IF . . . ?

ABOUT THE US–NORTH VIETNAM MEETINGS

In 1997, 1998, and 1999, several meetings took place—two in Hanoi, one in Italy, and one in Florida—between American scholars, former civilian officials, and military officers and their opposite numbers from North Vietnam. The Americans were historians of the Vietnam War or veterans (civilian or military) of the war. For their part, the Vietnamese participants were Hanoi diplomats, senior officials, or military veterans (or, at one time or another, all three).

The sessions were sponsored by Brown University's Wilson Institute, the Rockefeller Foundation, and Hanoi's Institute for International Affairs. Prof. Jim Blight and former secretary of defense Robert McNamara were instrumental in organizing the sessions.

The first of these meetings, in June 1997, started with misunderstandings, mutual suspicion, even acrimony. There was much about it that reminded me of the shouting matches between the two sides in Geneva in 1954 and 1962. But, as this chapter relates, organizational and behavioral changes resulted in subsequent harmony and useful, friendly exchanges.

* * *

I have long been afflicted with a possessive, demanding demon: America's experience in Vietnam. In more recent years, perhaps in belated recognition that my time remaining was too precious to squander on frequent emotional revisits to the sixties, I have managed to elude its grasp. Yet there are still moments when its shadow reappears, thanks to a series of encounters with former senior North Vietnamese officials and military officers.

Until a few years ago, virtually every written and oral account of the Vietnam War available to Americans has relied on the memoirs and the research of Western and South Vietnamese participants and scholars, who wrote from the perspective of Washington or Saigon. The war as experienced from the vantage point of Hanoi has, even now, hardly been touched on—not necessarily because it was consciously ignored, but rather because the North Vietnamese story has been available only to the few Americans able to access and read official North Vietnamese documents. Even for those who are fluent in Vietnamese, however, there is probably a treasure trove of government documents that officials in Hanoi still regard as state secrets.

The first set of meetings between North Vietnamese scholars and wartime participants and a like group of Americans was held in Hanoi in late June 1997. The American team included Robert McNamara, a former undersecretary of state, two retired generals, a former White House staffer, six historians, and me. A roughly comparable group comprised the Vietnamese side. The initial discussions boded ill for any future sessions. Not surprisingly, McNamara's presence aroused so much publicity and curiosity that attention was diverted from the serious business at hand. And the two hundred or so "observers," including apparatchiks from Vietnam's Communist Party and Hanoi's thought police, dampened, if not destroyed, any possible spontaneity on the part of the North Vietnamese participants.

My exasperation with the North Vietnamese participants showed through on the afternoon of the first day: "I am just not going to accept that we Americans had a 'mindset' [i.e., a rigid, biased view of the North Vietnamese] and you, the Vietnamese . . . saw everything accurately and objectively, even things about the United States about which, you have admitted, you were woefully ignorant."[1]

On my return to Washington from Hanoi I wrote a piece for the *Washington Post*: "It was evident from the outset that all of the formal Vietnamese presentations must have been cleared, perhaps even composed well in advance by the leadership. Even their informal interventions . . . reflected concern and caution lest they digress from the (party) line. . . . None of those presentations gave evidence that remarks by the Americans were even taken into consideration. . . . [T]he conference was less than a success . . . the sermons and the polemics reminded me of agonizing days in Geneva," many years before.[2]

The Vietnamese and American organizers of this meeting learned some useful lessons. At the next session in Hanoi in February 1998, and in the ones that followed at White Oak Plantation in Florida and Bellagio in Italy, attendance was limited to participants and interpreters—no press, no watchdogs, no groupies. As a consequence, the discussions were more free-flowing, frank, and spontaneous. Moreover, by then, our early hostility and suspicion had given way to friendly, less stilted relations. Sterile arguments were transformed into constructive exchanges. Each side learned much about the other.

My frustration, even anger in the 1960s about Hanoi's egregious dismissal of even the most forthcoming US negotiating proposals became more muted when I learned, firsthand, about the difficulties endured by Hanoi's wartime leadership: its inadequate communication system, the military and civilian differences, Chinese-Soviet rivalry for influence in Hanoi, an understaffed yet stifling bureaucracy, the physical exhaustion of senior officials, the interruptions to daily life and governance as a result of the bombing attacks, and the utter ignorance of the North Vietnamese about Americans (and vice versa).

*   *   *

The Vietnam War was the longest in America's rough-and-tumble history. Its cost—human, emotional, economic, and social—has not, even now, been fully reckoned by the Vietnamese, or by us. What is known is, as in the case of all wars, that the length, intensity, and perhaps even the decision to wage war hung to a fearful extent on snap judgments, zealous ideologies, misinformation, ignorance, and individual and national arrogance. This should come as no surprise to Vietnam (or Iraq) policymakers, veterans, historians, and the informed public. If I was left with any doubt on this score, it would have been dispelled after the face-to-face meetings between Americans and North Vietnamese in 1997 and 1998.

In the wake of these discussions I have wondered about how and whether the course of the war, the number of casualties, the physical destruction would have been changed if only . . . As I reflect on the 1950s, 1960s, and 1970s, my thoughts are full of what-ifs and suppose-thats. Could the war have been avoided or the cost in life and treasure been mitigated, if only . . . ?

Or did the war have such momentum and inevitability that, regardless of different decisions made at critical turning points and moments of opportunity, the outcome would not have been different?

A few considerations, in particular, have been gnawing. First, there is the matter of Ho Chi Minh's unanswered appeal to President Truman for help and friendship, sent through an OSS Thailand group in September 1945. Hanoi's leaders still claim that Truman's lack of response demonstrates that the United States, from the outset of the post–World War II period, had colonialist designs on Vietnam. In Hanoi in June 1997 and in February 1998, this charge was made by virtually every Vietnamese participant at our meeting, later in a private session with the foreign minister, and yet again by General Giap, the former commander of the North Vietnamese army.

In several (and increasingly exasperated) interventions I stressed that the odds were overwhelming that neither President Truman nor any member of his senior staff ever saw Ho's letter. Indeed, it is unlikely that anyone of influence in Washington at that time ever saw it. In the first place, the OSS, under whose auspices the letter had been sent, was disbanded before Ho's letter could have reached Washington. By early autumn 1945, the Strategic Services Unit, a temporary caretaker/successor to the OSS, had more, and more consequential, problems. The hard-pressed officials of that ephemeral body were focusing on the very survival of some form of a central intelligence organization. They had little time to deal with a letter to the president from an unknown anti-Japanese guerrilla leader from a far-flung and then-unfamiliar part of the world. Even if, by some minor miracle, the letter had reached the desk of a staffer in the West Wing of 1600 Pennsylvania Avenue, it would have been given short shrift. Compared to the occupation of Germany and Japan, the provision of postwar assistance to our allies, and the conversion of the American economy from war to peace, Ho Chi Minh's nationalist concerns about French intentions were understandably low on the president's priority list.

But what if the letter had reached the desk of a Truman staffer in an idle moment of a quiet day. And suppose the staffer was inclined to send a reply on behalf of the president. What could she have said that would have satisfied Ho Chi Minh? To be sure, FDR had visualized some form of UN trusteeship for Indochina and India, but he did not reveal this aspiration to Truman or virtually anyone else before he died. The Soviet threat to Western Europe had introduced a thorny new factor into America's postwar policy with regard to French and British colonies in Asia, and by October 1945 Truman's options had already narrowed. America had strong, historic bonds with

France and England. Neither country had shown any disposition to give up its prewar influence in its rich colonies. There was little that was meaningful that America could then do to reverse their policies.

The American position with respect to the French was especially complicated. Truman's highest foreign policy priority was the establishment of a stable, non-Communist Western Europe, not only for its own sake, but also as a bulwark against Soviet westward expansion. French readiness to participate in the European Defense Community was largely dependent on whether America would assist the nation in its struggle to regain its prewar position in Indochina. Washington paid this price until almost the bitter end for what turned out to be a strong NATO.

In Hanoi, however, the hard-pressed Ho Chi Minh judged the United States by the company it kept. And, despite its lofty rhetoric, the United States must have seemed to him to be hardly a model of anticolonialism in that early postwar time, and certainly during the years to follow.

*   *   *

On January 31, 1964, three months after the coup that toppled South Vietnam's President Ngo Dinh Diem, Gen. Charles de Gaulle announced a French plan for a neutral South Vietnam. The general's timing was shrewd. The political situation in Saigon was chaotic; several ambitious, greedy generals were then plotting with and against each other to seize the presidency of the government of Vietnam. This, together with the military failures of the South Vietnamese army, must have given de Gaulle and his advisers confidence that Washington might welcome an opportunity to jettison the mess in Saigon under the cover of neutralization. From the vantage point of the Elysée, if America's departure was accompanied by increased French influence in Vietnam, so much the better.

In June 1997 one of the Vietnamese participants at our Hanoi meeting berated the United States on this score. The Laos Conference in 1961–62, he said, created a "neutral Laos. . . . neutrality . . . of the kind worked out for Laos . . . might have been a possible solution to the situation in South Vietnam."[3] Laos, in fact, might have been a model for a neutral Vietnam, one that Washington might have been ready to adopt. After all, President Johnson had been in the White House only a few months. His agenda was dominated by domestic rather than international concerns, and the situation in Vietnam threatened to shove aside LBJ's visions of a Great Society. But there was one nasty problem—a problem de Gaulle chose to ignore: The Communist Pathet

Lao Party and the leadership in Hanoi could not tolerate a genuinely neutral Laos. In violation of the 1962 Laos accords, Hanoi did not remove its troops, and, as a result, Laos became a North Vietnamese satellite rather than an independent, neutral country. And so, de Gaulle's notion may have had merit in theory, but history had shown it to be tragically wrong.

My reaction to the Vietnamese contention was, I now realize, more heated than polite diplomatic discourse would have warranted. "[I]f Souvanna Phouma's government could have established itself as genuinely neutral . . . then Washington's receptivity to the idea of a neutral South Vietnam would have been very different. . . . But you [i.e., the North Vietnamese] couldn't resist mucking around in Laos and that . . . ruined an opportunity to head off the war."[4]

Of all the what-ifs, this, to me, is one of the most intriguing. Our commitment had been to the murdered Ngo Dinh Diem, not to a bunch of corrupt and incompetent generals who had little public support. The fewer than twenty thousand American troops already present in South Vietnam on President Johnson's accession to the presidency could have been removed quickly and without a public outcry in the United States. A genuinely neutral Vietnam could have been a palatable solution to what was already looming as a nasty, unpopular war. *Suppose Hanoi had respected the Laos accord. Would we have agreed to a neutralized Vietnam?* In the light of the cold war rhetoric and mindset of the time, my answer must be a thin maybe.

* * *

In April 1964, North Vietnamese torpedo boats attacked an American destroyer in the Gulf of Tonkin. The destroyer was supporting a secret operation against North Vietnam. No damage was done, and the US response was relatively restrained. Washington warned Hanoi, however, that if there were another such instance, the Americans would launch a robust counterattack. A day or so later, a second US destroyer, dispatched to reinforce the first, was reported to have been the target of a North Vietnamese torpedo.

The American bombing of the torpedo base was of minor importance compared to the political reaction. Washington officials hastily concluded that an attack on two US warships (barely) in international waters was so brazen ("Remember the *Maine!*") that it could have only been authorized by North Vietnam's leadership. A virtual US declaration of war, the Gulf of Tonkin Resolution, passed Congress with only two dissenting votes. From this point forward, President Johnson maintained he had carte blanche for any military or political measure he chose to take in Vietnam.

It has since been established that there was a great deal of confusion, but no second attack. In addition to other evidence, we learned in Hanoi that it was the local commander at the torpedo base, rather than the Hanoi high command, who had ordered the first and only attack.

Suppose in August 1964 it had been definitely determined that reports of a second attack were mistaken. And suppose we in Washington had the wit to realize that the local torpedo boat base commander did not have the communications ability to get an immediate turnaround on a request to attack the American ships. And suppose we knew that, even if he had such a capability, the various leadership factions in Hanoi would be unable to come to an immediate decision on such a sensitive matter. Would Johnson have then gone to Congress for a blanket advance approval of US actions with regard to Vietnam? Answer: maybe not then, but soon.

I was in the White House Situation Room when LBJ called shortly after the report of the second attack. Was there or wasn't there an attack, he wanted to know; and he wanted to know *then*. Not soon. Not later. I had already been in touch with the Pentagon and the naval command at Pearl Harbor. People on McNamara's staff weren't sure. People at the navy's Pacific headquarters thought there probably was another attack. Uncertainty on this score was rampant not only in Pearl Harbor and Washington, but also on both destroyers; I suggested to the president that we would need more information before making a firm judgment. Johnson mumbled something I did not quite catch and hung up. Within a day or two, however, the general assumption in Washington, Pearl Harbor, and Saigon was that the second attack had actually occurred.

No matter. The resolution had been in draft form for a few weeks and its authors were waiting for their cue to polish it up and put it into play. Thirty years later, we learned in Hanoi that the first and only attack was ordered by a local, low-ranking officer, not by Hanoi's high command. That, however, would have had little practical effect. Knowing that the high command in Hanoi was not involved, we might not have launched the August bombing raid on the torpedo boat base. Nonetheless, the resolution, under a different name, would have been sent to Congress soon anyway, and the president would have had his virtual declaration of war.

*   *   *

An attack on the American barracks in the highlands of South Vietnam in February 1965, causing heavy American casualties, changed the nature and course of the war. The assault occurred during the de facto New Year (Tet) cease-fire. This would have stirred up violent outrage in Washington, in any case. But American policymakers and intelligence officials (including those who happened to be in Vietnam at the time) were convinced that Hanoi's leaders had ordered the attack in a show of muscle for the benefit of Chairman Kosygin, who was then in Hanoi, and McGeorge Bundy, who was then in Saigon. In retaliation, US bombers were unleashed over North Vietnam and, with few interruptions, the "Rolling Thunder" continued for years to come.

At one of our Hanoi sessions in 1997, we learned that Washington's conviction that the Pleiku attack had been ordered by North Vietnam's high command had been mistaken. As in the case of the torpedo boats in the Gulf of Tonkin, the local Viet Minh commander of the region around Pleiku, learning of the juicy target nearby, was solely responsible. According to the former North Vietnamese colonel, he had only a few hours available to achieve surprise. His primitive communications capability did not permit him to seek and receive Hanoi's permission in time. And, again, as in the case of the Gulf of Tonkin, he knew the decision process in Hanoi was too cumbersome to permit a fast turnaround on a request of this kind. As for Kosygin, the colonel had no way of knowing that the chairman was in Hanoi. As for Mac Bundy, he had never heard of him.

What if Washington had been aware that the Pleiku attack was a field rather than a headquarters decision? Would the bombing campaign have been launched? I am almost sure it would have. The American casualties— eight dead, more than one hundred wounded—called for a dramatic and consequential response—a response that had already been prepared and was being held ready for just such a provocation. Within a matter of hours, the war was brought close to home for Hanoi's leadership and for the people throughout North Vietnam.

*   *   *

American efforts to engage the North Vietnamese in discussions about a negotiated settlement, let alone in actual negotiations, were fruitless until late 1968. Washington and Hanoi were trapped by the catch-22 characteristics of a bombing halt: Hanoi would not talk until there was an unconditional halt to bombing; Washington would not halt the bombing until there was assurance in advance that talks would follow. On the face of it, the gap seems trivial in circumstances in which so much was at stake. But, in fact, the issue was enormously complicated.

Because of the perceived, even genuine, need for secrecy in every attempt to engage Hanoi, American overtures were shrouded, indirect, deniable, and closely held. In some instances, only a handful of officials were kept informed. (This was also true in the case of Hanoi.) As a result, virtually all Washington policymakers, especially the Pentagon officers implementing the bombing campaign, were ignorant of the efforts to jump-start negotiations; it seemed impossible to order sudden, unexplained bombing halts without destroying the confidentiality of negotiation initiatives.

A heartbreaking example of this was the aborted fact-to-face meeting between American and North Vietnamese representatives in Warsaw in December 1966. The meeting had been arranged after months of quiet effort among Americans, Italians, and Poles. Because both Hanoi and Washington were anxious to keep such a meeting secret, the American ambassador to Poland and the North Vietnamese ambassador to nearby Nordic countries were designated as the conferees. The American had just two days to prepare; the Vietnamese, perhaps less.

The clumsy choreography, arranged by the Polish prime minister and the foreign minister, involved, first, a session between the American ambassador and the Polish foreign minister, then a session with the American, the Pole, and the Vietnamese and, finally, a meeting with only the two ambassadors. The arrangement soon went awry. The Poles were incapable or unwilling to bring Ambassador Gronouski and Ambassador Huong together on the scheduled day. Gronouski and we few Americans in Washington who were monitoring the meeting were convinced that Hanoi had suddenly decided not to send their representative to Warsaw. And so, bombing, which had been halted for a couple of days by presidential order, and then for a few more days by bad weather, was resumed with increased intensity. Meanwhile, Huong, who had been cooling his heels in some obscure corner of Warsaw, decided that the Americans had no interest in meeting with him. As luck would have it, the skies cleared over Hanoi and bombs once more rained down soon after the day he had expected to meet with Gronouski. Huong packed his bag and returned to his embassy in Scandinavia.

Suppose that the constellations in early December 1966 had all been in propitious formation and the two ambassadors had actually met. What if they had accomplished their mission and reached an agreement about a subsequent meeting at which more senior and more knowledgeable Americans and Vietnamese would discuss the terms of a settlement? Could the war have ended years earlier? And would Hubert Humphrey, rather than Richard Nixon, have won the election in November 1968? Perhaps—but the outcome was in the lap of the gods. They would have had to arrange that the weather over Hanoi in mid-December 1966 remain too cloudy for the resumption of bombing.

*   *   *

The path to a negotiated settlement of the hostilities was tortured, winding, and rocky. As evident by now, my own trek was marked by more than a fair share of false starts, unpleasant surprises, and unfruitful confrontations with wannabe Nobel laureates. If truth be told, however, many of the problems I encountered were spawned not only by officials and bureaucrats in Hanoi, but also by my colleagues in Washington. A prime example involved the British prime minister and the Soviet premier in February 1967, when Kosygin was in London and held high-level, secret discussions about Vietnam.

According to Prime Minister Harold Wilson, the "press and public knew nothing . . . of how near we had been to success . . . a historic opportunity had been missed."[5]

Well, maybe. And, then again, maybe not.

As a member of Wilson's cabinet later concluded, Wilson and Brown "obviously used the opportunity [of Kosygin's visit to London] for a British attempt to get in on the peace negotiations in Vietnam."[6] In his eagerness, Wilson did not take account of Johnson's almost manic determination to control Vietnam policy, to regard the war as his personal turf. Even leaders of those countries—Korea, Thailand, Australia, New Zealand, and the Philippines—that had contributed troops or medical personnel to the US effort in Vietnam had little or no voice and certainly no influence on US policy there. Britain, for its part, had stayed aloof from the fighting (largely, I believe, because of left-wing Labour Party insistence) and, as a result, was regarded in Washington more as a meddler than a helpful participant in the quest for negotiations.

Aside from this, there was a personal factor of nontrivial importance. Lyndon Johnson did not like Harold Wilson and almost certainly did not trust him—despite Wilson's report to the cabinet in the sad aftermath of his meeting with Kosygin that he had "the absolute confidence of LBJ."[7]

LBJ's lack of trust may have stemmed in part from the unwarranted and vicious suspicions contrived and circulated by a few counterintelligence officials in MI5, Britain's internal intelligence department. According to them, Harold Wilson had close relations with, and, in their view, may, indeed, have been a member of, the Communist Party. None of this was actually true.

Nonetheless, James Angleton, the CIA's infamous counterintelligence chief, found such tidbits appetizing and made sure that senior officials in Washington were aware of the story.[8] Incidentally, I was queried by a top British intelligence official in the late 1960s as to whether I had any reason to give credence to the story. My answer was a vigorous no.

I had gotten to know Roger Hollis, director general of MI5, during my London embassy days and found him engaging and pleasant. Ironically enough, while he apparently acquiesced to MI5's anti-Wilson campaign, he, himself, was later charged by his colleagues with being a Soviet "mole." Whitehall was a malevolent and suspicious place in those years. Lurking in the back of my mind since my embassy days in the mid-1950s there has long been a conviction that my home telephone had been tampered with; our housekeeper had discovered a man hastily descending from a rarely opened window of my tiny library when she happened to walk in. The telephone was at the edge of the desk instead of its proper place. Nothing else had been disturbed. KGB? MI5? CIA? No matter; paranoia was rampant. We were careful about our phone conversations for the remainder of our time in London.

*   *   *

Wilson, of course, was naive in thinking that much of consequence could be achieved in the couple of days he had with Kosygin. Such a complex issue had to be first worked out between the Americans and the British, then between the British and the Russians, then between the Russians and the North Vietnamese, and back to Go. Nonetheless, as the more realistic Foreign Secretary George Brown and the somewhat cynical fly on the wall Chet Cooper both agreed, it would be worth a good try.

Even under the most benign circumstances, Wilson's efforts might have come to naught. But the circumstances were far from benign. In the first place, Hanoi chose the respite of the Tet bombing halt to pour more troops and equipment into South Vietnam, thereby raising both the temperature and the negotiations threshold of LBJ and his senior advisers.

Second, from the outset the White House (especially Lyndon Johnson and Walt Rostow) did not put much stock in Wilson or his discussions with Kosygin. I later learned that my messages to them, which I had sent "Urgent. Eyes Only," had rested unread and untouched in someone's inbox for two days. When the telegrams were finally noticed, Rostow shared them with the president, McNamara, and Rusk. Then, when it was too late to address them, all hell broke loose.

But suppose that my urgent message requesting approval for Wilson to provide Kosygin with the Phase A–Phase B formula had been dealt with in a timely manner instead of surfacing at the last minute during the frenetic deliberations taking place in the Cabinet Room of Number 10 Downing Street. Would it have made any difference in the outcome? Apparently not.

According to one ex post facto, contrite participant in that session, the Great Men present during that discussion had either forgotten, or had never really focused on, Phase A–Phase B (they probably had been too preoccupied with bombing targets). They regarded the critical A-B message as Cooper's gratuitous, irresponsible, new, personal proposal. It was only later, back in Washington, that I had an occasion to remind some of them that Phase A–Phase B was not a mad scheme I had hastily dreamt up in the middle of a wild London night. Rather, the formula had long been a part of US negotiating proposals. Unlike several other instances of left hand–right hand mix-ups that plagued America's Vietnam policy, this one was simply a case of absentmindedness.

The Phase A–Phase B schemozzle was not the only melancholy aspect of the London-Washington exchange during those chaotic few days in early February 1967. It will be recalled that Rostow, McNamara, and Rusk had grudgingly accepted the Trend-Cooper proposal that the United States halt the bombing of North Vietnam in exchange for a stand-down of North Vietnamese infiltration of South Vietnam and an agreement to start peace talks. The catch was that Washington insisted that Hanoi had to respond to this offer within ten hours.

The deadline was ludicrous; it would have expired just as Kosygin's plane landed in Moscow and before he had an opportunity to transmit the proposal to Hanoi. Yet Washington expected Kosygin to send the proposition to Hanoi, to have it considered by the North Vietnamese leadership, to have Hanoi's officials prepare a reply and send it to Kosygin, to have Kosygin send their reply to Wilson in London, and to have the British forward the reply to me at the US Embassy in London and/or to Rostow in Washington— all within just half a day.

It took a fair amount of pleading, and some shouting by Ambassador Bruce and by me over the telephone, to get an extension of the bombing pause. In the end, Washington was magnanimous: the pause was extended by another four hours. The situation was hopeless. In London, before he left for home, Kosygin described Washington's time limit as an "ultimatum." And at Hanoi in 1998, the Vietnamese, too, described the American deadline as an "ultimatum" rather than a negotiating proposal.

Suppose Washington had given Kosygin seventy-two, or even forty-eight hours. Would Harold Wilson have been able to put peace negotiations on track? Probably not, if for no other reason than the decision process in Hanoi, from what we have learned, was too cumbersome to have met even a seventy-two-hour deadline. Clearly, Washington was in no mood to accommodate Hanoi's political establishment or to give Wilson a shot at a diplomatic victory.

At the end of the day, when all is said, when push came to shove, it is fair to conclude that Harold Wilson's efforts, sincere and strenuous as they had been, were just another case of love's labor lost.

*   *   *

Finally, in the summer of 1967, there was the initially promising and subsequently disappointing minuet involving Messrs. Kissinger, Aubrac, and Markovich, and Ho Chi Minh. This was, so far as I know, the only third-party effort that actually engaged Ho himself.

According to our interlocutors in Hanoi, the two Frenchmen, armed with a generalized version of the Phase A–Phase B approach, had stirred up the interest of Ho and his advisers. They returned to Paris and reported this to Kissinger, who, in turn, reported it to Washington; a rare glimmer of hope brightened the mood of those slogging through the thickets in a quest for peace. The Frenchmen were then given additional enticing proposals, which they passed to Hanoi through the North Vietnamese representative in Paris.

To add hope to optimism, the US bombing was significantly scaled down—one of the times the administration showed any readiness to coordinate its diplomatic and military activities. Many weeks later, Hanoi's forwarded its response. The answer was, yet again, a sharp rebuff. Negotiations could not—would not—be discussed until the bombing was completely and unconditionally stopped.

But, once again, the full story was not revealed until February 1998 in Hanoi and, later, in Bellagio, where the Aubrac-Markovich affair was a focal point of discussion. According to the Vietnamese participants, the proposals delivered by the French emissaries were given careful and sympathetic attention in Hanoi. Indeed, for the first time, according to the former Hanoi officials, the prospect of peace talks had been taken seriously. But a nontrivial problem of timing complicated and then killed the initiative.

By September 1967, preparations were underway for the Viet Minh's Tet offensive four months hence. The North Vietnamese leadership hoped this operation, involving Vietcong and Viet Minh attacks on cities throughout South Vietnam, would break the spirit of Saigon and Washington; the memory of France's defeat at Dien Bien Phu in the spring of 1954 was still fresh. The senior generals in Hanoi were concerned that the interest civilian officials were showing in the American proposals would jeopardize their mobilization plans. After all, a major military assault throughout South Vietnam could hardly be mounted if peace negotiations were then going on. In the end, the military prevailed. Markovich and Aubrac joined the long list of earnest, disappointed would-be peacemakers.

Obviously, Hanoi's plans for Tet 1968 could not be revealed to the Americans in order to explain Hanoi's shift from positive interest to stonewalling, and then to outright rejection. So the bombing issue was put back on Hanoi's front burner—despite the fact that it had become an issue on which Washington had become flexible.

Suppose Washington had wiped the slate clean of the bombing matter following Hanoi's initial promising reaction to Washington's initiative. In short, what if bombing became, at that point, a nonissue. Would Hanoi's civilian leadership have been able to overrule the generals? After all, the mobilization and training of young Vietcong recruits (who would soon become cannon fodder) had barely begun. Would the autumn of 1967 have gone down in history as the time when peace talks began? Would LBJ, instead of announcing in March 1968 that he would not run again, have been able to bask in the triumph of a long-sought political settlement and have been able to win reelection?

Once again the negotiation effort was mortally wounded by the secrecy surrounding it. How, in September 1967, could LBJ and his close advisers explain the reason for an indefinitely extended cessation of the bombing? On the other hand, Hanoi's secrecy surrounding its plans for the Tet assault might have made it easier for Hanoi to have engaged in negotiations and to have canceled what promised to be a costly offensive. But Hanoi's civilian officials apparently could not have won the day in any case. They were caught up in what Hanoi's leadership frequently referred to as a "complex" situation. But the history of the US experience in Vietnam is full of what-ifs, and this episode, perhaps more than most, provides much room for speculation.

*   *   *

My professional preoccupation with Vietnam ended in December 1968 when I formally and finally retired from the Department of State and government service. I was to discover, however, that my personal, emotional involvement was not as easily shed. In any case, it was high time to seek higher ground and less tempestuous days. I was sure there must be a life beyond Vietnam. There turned out to be such a life, although Vietnam would not—apparently cannot—fade away.

NOTES

1. *Missed Opportunities: Revisiting the Decisions of the Vietnam War, 1961–1968*, transcript of conference sponsored by Brown University and Vassar College, Institute for International Affairs, Ministry of Foreign Affairs, Hanoi, Vietnam, June 1997, p. 54.

2. Chester L. Cooper, "Pilgrimage to Hanoi," *Washington Post*, June 29, 1997, pp. C1, C2.

3. *Missed Opportunities*, p. 28.

4. Ibid.

5. Harold Wilson, "How the U.S. Muffed a Chance to End the Vietnam War," *Life*, May 21, 1971, p. 59.

6. Richard Crossman, *The Diaries of a Cabinet Minister*, vol. 2 (New York: Holt, Rinehart and Winston, 1977), p. 237.

7. Ibid., p. 237.

8. David Leigh, *The Wilson Plot* (New York: Pantheon, 1988), pp. 61, 69, 76, 91.

15

BEYOND VIETNAM

ABOUT THINK TANKS

Since the end of World War II and, in a few cases, even before, America's policymaking community has been blessed with scores of research establishments, large and small, liberal and conservative, well endowed and existing hand-to-mouth. Most are nonprofit, which provides them with tax benefits, but which also constrains them in their choice of clients and in the way they conduct their business. Most of these are nongovernmental organizations (NGOs), which give them access to international meetings and other benefits.

The Institute of Defense Analyses (IDA), where I spent several years, was funded by the Joint Chiefs of Staff and the Office of the Secretary of Defense. Virtually all its assignments were related to the military's concerns, including its interest in international economic and political matters.

The Woodrow Wilson International Center for Scholars (WWICS), the memorial to President Wilson, was, during my tenure, located in the Smithsonian "castle" on Washington's National Mall. Its mission was (and pretty much still is) to provide study and research facilities for selected American and foreign scholars concerned with issues linking scholarly investigation and policy formulation. Approximately thirty men and women are selected each year to spend about eleven months at the center in Washington, where they conduct research, give and attend seminars, and provide an intellectual

feast not only for their fellow Fellows, but also for many scholars and prac-
titioners in the wider Washington community.

This chapter provides a taste of my experience at the Institute for
Defense Analyses and the Woodrow Wilson Center—a rich experience
indeed.

*   *   *

Leaving government service marked a sea change in my workaday life; dealing with researchers rather than policymakers and practitioners became the focus of my concern. For the next three decades and more, my activities, with few exceptions, were far removed from national security crises.

Aside from my new professional life, my departure from the State Department was followed by profound changes at home. Orah's father died in Washington after a long, heartbreaking struggle with Alzheimer's disease. My father died suddenly in Boston from a heart attack. My mother, who moved to Washington after my father's death, died peacefully at our house shortly after her ninetieth birthday. Orah's mother, who had been sickly on and off since I first met her, outlived them all.

There was sadness, but there was much joy as well. Joan earned a bachelor's degree in sociology and soon married her classmate Ron Gould. Susan and her new husband, Tom Duesterberg, were awarded their PhDs in history at the same university on the same day. We were now six instead of four.

Meanwhile, our family expanded through several other acquisitions. Tony Suazo, our housekeeper's son and my godson-to-be, joined us when he was a few days old. Willy Walker, Bernadine Healy, and Greg Bulkley, all young medical doctors, became, over the course of a few years, "adopted" children. So did Manfred and Renate Pollak, who we first met in Vienna early in the 1980s. And, several years later, Orah and I were graced with two granddaughters, Elizabeth and Annah, and a grandson, James. So it was that the family tide ebbed and flowed.

*   *   *

An urgent piece of unfinished or, more accurately, barely started business confronted me as I bade farewell to the State Department. This was the matter of the book. The Institute of Defense Analyses, a think tank for the Joint Chiefs of Staff and secretary of defense, once again accorded me its hospitality—an office and access to its seminars and symposia. Over the next several weeks I developed an outline and planned the scope of the opus-to-be. I also found a publisher (Dodd Mead, a long-established firm now a victim of some mortal commercial blow) and was lucky enough to attract the attention of its brilliant chief editor, Tom Lipscomb. Oh yes, I was also given a modest advance.

What Harriman had derisively called life "on the street" seemed perfectly fine. There were only two problems: money—not enough—and time—too much. I had turned over most of my Ford Foundation grant to the IDA in exchange for editorial and research help. The publisher's advance was barely enough to cover a few months' worth of personal expenses.

As for time . . . my creative juices flow well for four or five hours a day, and then dry up. I can read for only two or three hours. I detest golf. In short, I needed some rewarding activity for the remainder of the day. I needed a job.

I was rescued by Gen. Maxwell Taylor, who had recently retired from the army and had become president of the IDA. Taylor was a trim, punctilious army general, tidy in dress, manner, and work habits. I had gotten to know him when he was President Kennedy's military adviser and, later, when he was ambassador to Vietnam. He was a favorite and a fan of the Kennedys. (One of Bobby Kennedy's sons was named Maxwell Taylor Kennedy.) His office and desk betrayed nothing of a personal nature—no photographs or souvenirs, not even stray bits of note paper, only three or four sharpened pencils and a calendar. I once remarked that he seemed ready to evacuate his office at a moment's notice. He said he was prepared to do just that.

When Taylor decided to replace the director of the IDA's International Division, he offered me the job. He agreed that I could spend a reasonable amount of the IDA's time working on the book. Thus, early 1969 marked my venture into serious writing as well as the start of a new, but, as I was to discover, short-lived career.

The IDA's International Division was a micro-think tank. There were approximately two dozen country specialists, military analysts, and national security experts. Among them were a few army and marine generals and colonels as well as several historians, economists, and political scientists with considerable knowledge of the Soviet Union and Eastern Europe. (One of these was a stuffy young Hungarian count.)

The division's activities were largely a reflection of the current concerns of the Joint Chiefs of Staff and the Office of the Secretary of Defense. We had some latitude, however, to generate our own studies. Since the late 1960s and early 1970s were replete with persistent tensions and sudden crises triggered by Moscow, Beijing, Hanoi, and, yes, Washington, too, many of the division's concerns related to one aspect or another of the cold war in Europe and the Middle East, and its hot manifestation in Indochina.

*   *   *

Not long after I had settled in at IDA I found myself back in Vietnam. What lessons, the Pentagon wanted to know, should be drawn from America's experience there? By then, the peace negotiations in Paris were proceeding, albeit tortuously, and President Nixon had already started a gradual withdrawal of American troops. The Pentagon was obviously preparing for a postmortem.

Accompanied by a pair of IDA colleagues, I had several long, fairly informative sessions with American and South Vietnamese military and civilian officials in Saigon, and more revealing discussions with junior officers and civilians in the provinces.

I am sure we garnered useful information in our interviews at the American embassy and at our army headquarters and from our firsthand exposure to the realities outside the capital. But much of what I was told then has gone through my memory's sieve. What remains is my sense that life in Saigon was even bleaker, tackier, and physically and emotionally more oppressive than I had observed during my many previous visits.

Saigon's daytime sky was darkened and my lungs and eardrums were assaulted by the fumes and sounds of an endless stream of rumbling trucks and roaring motorbikes. At night, the neon lights from bars, massage parlors, and souvenir shops competed for attention with military searchlights and flashing red lights from screeching emergency vehicles. The terrasse of the Continental Hotel on Saigon's main street, once a peaceful oasis, was now a gathering place for whores, black marketeers, drug dealers, horribly deformed beggars, porn peddlers, and skinny, wild-eyed street kids—too many with blond or kinky black hair.

More than anything or anyone else, it is the street kids who have been hard to erase from my mind. They were young in age, but ravaged by time. Ragged and long unwashed, they were accomplished in the arts of begging, stealing, and selling their own or each other's frail bodies. Many were products of Vietnamese women (or girls) and foreign soldiers (white or black American, or leftover French), military contractors, or castaways.

I often wonder what happened to them over the years. How were they affected by the hasty departure of the Americans? Had they ever been restored to health? Do they or can they now lead relatively normal lives, or were they left to rot by a harsh, vindictive Communist government? Did many—did any—escape to better lives in Asia or America? Were the criminal gangs of young Vietnamese that appeared in some American cities soon after the war populated with some of these kids? For a while I had been contributing to a fund to salvage Saigon's street children. After a few years, however, I stopped hearing from the sponsoring organization. Perhaps the task was taken over by CARE or UNICEF. I hope so.

It was on the morning of the day of my appointment with Ambassador Ellsworth Bunker that everything in my pockets—cash, traveler's checks, photos, passport, driver's license, and United Airlines frequent flyer card— was liberated. I was ambushed by four or five scrawny eight-year-olds (perhaps those hanging around the Continental Hotel) on a busy street in broad daylight; their quick, busy hands reduced me to temporary pauperhood. Within seconds after they had finished with me, they disappeared in the crowd. After a young smart-ass American clerk in the American Express office chided me for my "unpardonable carelessness," I spent several hot hours in the local police station and finally in the US Consulate. Was I able to retrieve my treasured possessions? Of course not.

At my meeting later that afternoon with Ambassador Bunker, I asked about our mission's progress in establishing law and order in Saigon. "Chet," he said, "I feel safer here than I do on the streets of Washington." He made this comforting remark to the wrong person on the wrong day, and I told him so.

Our report was duly written, critically read, and meticulously commented on by General Taylor (who, because of his previous post in Vietnam, as well as being our boss, had more than an ordinary interest in our findings). It was then submitted to the Pentagon's assistant secretary for international security affairs. I have forgotten, if I ever knew, what he did with it. Not much, I suspect. Our exercise, like most such exercises, was probably shrugged off or filed away.

In Washington, I had long since observed, "lessons learned" about almost everything were doomed to wind up in oblivion. After all, lessons involve both a pitcher and a catcher, a writer and a reader, a teacher and a student. But here, in our nation's capital, there is a dearth of catchers, readers, and students. Each new administration comes to town accompanied by an eager band of hubris-swollen officials-to-be who scorn everyone, every policy, every experience, every "lesson" associated with the outgoing incumbent. History starts from the moment the starry-eyed, breathless presidential assistant or assistant secretary first walks into his office. There is a dearth of institutional memory. Certainly as far as Vietnam is concerned, a vast forest has been destroyed to provide the paper consumed in reviewing lessons learned. All to little avail.

*   *   *

A more interesting IDA project was one somewhat off the beaten track, but it was well received in spite (or, perhaps, because) of that.

The idea stemmed from a controversy in the early 1960s among White House science advisers over whether the United States should embark on the development of an antiballistic missile (ABM) system. The president's Science Advisory Council, a group of influential American scientists, put forward one or another of four contending positions. The United States:

- could develop such a missile, but, fortunately, didn't need it;
- could, fortunately, develop the missile, and did need it;
- could not develop it, but, fortunately, didn't need it; or
- could not develop it, but, unfortunately, did need it.

In the end, the argument became moot. Both the United States and the USSR could and did develop the missile. Its deployment was limited, however, by a treaty signed by both countries in 1972; deployment was further limited in 1974. (These treaties have since been scrapped by the second Bush administration.)

The ABM discussions were a dramatic example of Washington's decision-making process when highly technical issues are involved. How does a president go about making an informed decision on such issues when his education, background, and experience is usually in the law or politics or, in one case, motion pictures? Once again, I went to see McGeorge Bundy, president of the Ford Foundation. I proposed a case study that might shed some light on this.

Bundy, no stranger to the decision-making process at the White House level, was intrigued. He suggested that I avoid dealing with such sensitive current issues as the ABM. Rather, he thought, it would be wiser to select a matter already in the public domain—Kennedy's decision to go to the moon, for example. I agreed.

Between my managerial responsibilities at the IDA and my own book project, I had little disposable time for the lunar landing project. I recruited a colleague, Howard Margolis, to be the principal researcher. It was an inspired choice. Margolis had been a *Washington Post* reporter who had focused on national issues, especially matters involving science policy. (He later went on to MIT and then became a professor at the University of Chicago.)

We decided not to waste much time on Kennedy's rationale or on his decision to send a man to the moon. That had been simply a matter of national politics and prestige; it was designed to rival, even outdo, Moscow's impressive achievements in space. In our view, the truly interesting issue was the process of deciding *how* to go to the moon.

As with the ABM issue, scientists were not of one accord. There were two strong opinions regarding the best way to accomplish a moon landing. Virtually all of Kennedy's science advisory team advocated a direct ride from earth to moon—an express trip, so to speak—rather than a launch into orbit followed by a transfer to another, smaller landing vehicle. These advisers argued that it was more efficient, and probably safer, to fly from, say, Washington to New York without transferring to another plane in Philadelphia.

The direct journey seemed clear-cut and logical. But why, then, did NASA wind up with the two-stage approach? This was the question that Margolis wanted to address. In the process, he uncovered a fascinating story of human foibles, sheer accident, and good science.

The story—the unvarnished version, not the think-tankish, politically correct one which we ultimately submitted—starts with a political meeting President Kennedy attended in Birmingham, Alabama, on a crisp autumn weekend in 1962. A member of Kennedy's staff on the trip suggested to Kennedy that since no White House meetings were scheduled for that Saturday, they spend that afternoon at the Georgia-Alabama football game. "And why not?" the president's military aide asked rhetorically, when we discussed the trip several years later. Why not, indeed? After all, Kennedy liked football, and, according to a staffer, would enjoy "gazing at cheerleaders' thighs."

During halftime, the aide suggested that on their way back to Washington, they stop off at the Redstone Arsenal in Anniston, Alabama, where space scientist Wernher von Braun had his laboratory. Braun was a vocal and persistent critic of the one-stage lunar landing scheme. Instead, he had been advocating an approach utilizing a small golf cart–like vehicle that would be launched from the mother capsule. The capsule would remain in orbit awaiting the moon lander's return. A brief visit to Braun and a bit of "stroking," Kennedy's group agreed, would soothe Braun's ego and get him out of the president's hair.

Neither a brief visit nor stroking was in the cards. Braun held a willing and fascinated Kennedy hostage for several hours. The president returned to

Washington convinced that Braun was right. He ordered his advisory committee back to their drawing board. From that moment on, astronauts have, in effect, "changed planes in Philadelphia."

Our case history went into considerable technical detail about each of the landing modes, incorporated summaries of interviews with experts and principals, and put forward several well-informed conclusions. Except in a closely held set of notes, however, there was no mention of the role of the football game and the cheerleaders' thighs.

*   *   *

In the meantime, the book was moving along, thanks to a few hours snatched during the work week and many more in the evenings and weekends. Orah, Joan, and Susan were justifiably elated when *The Lost Crusade* was published in the autumn of 1970; I had not been especially sociable during its gestation.

I think I can say that I am as modest as most. Or, anyway, almost as modest as some. In all modesty, however, I feel bound to point out that *The Lost Crusade* had a good send-off. In a front-page review in the *New York Times*, the critic Ronald Steel was laudatory; in a blurb, the philosopher Mortimer Adler called the book a "masterpiece"; and my old boss, Averell Harriman, who originally took a dim view of the enterprise, said in the preface that it was "most distinguished and important." *The Lost Crusade* became the monthly choice of several book clubs and was an alternate selection of the Book-of-the-Month Club. (I don't want to belabor all this. I just thought the reader might be anxious to know.) The only sad aspect of my publication party was that my father had died the year before. He would have been proud.

Anyway, it was back to full-time work. Perhaps it was an author's variant of postpartum depression. Perhaps the work was actually dull. Perhaps, after a few years at the IDA, I was becoming restless. Perhaps the departure of Max Taylor (who may also have become restless) and the appearance of a new, less consequential director set me thinking about the need for a new challenge.

*   *   *

It was at lunch one day during this period of doldrums when I was shoved into action. My companion nodded in the direction of a nearby table where a mutual friend was being seated. "He's a smart guy," my companion said, but then added deprecatingly, "Too bad he turned out to be a one-book man."

The phrase haunted me for several days. I became determined to avoid such a fate. I applied for, and in February 1972 was awarded, a fellowship at the Woodrow Wilson International Center for Scholars. My project? A revisit to the Suez crisis of 1956.

Thirty or so center Fellows were housed in the original Smithsonian building, a replica of a mid-nineteenth-century Italian castle.[1] My fellow Fellows, from a dozen countries and representing several disciplines, had been selected on the basis of their track record in the arts, the social or physical sciences, or public service, and the project they planned to pursue during the standard ten-month tenure. It was my hope to have a viable history-cum-memoir of the Suez crisis when my time there was up. I would put the finishing touches on the manuscript back at the IDA. (Pardon my innocence.)

A burst of unaccustomed prudence led me to take a leave of absence from the IDA, rather than resign. Ten months, after all, was hardly secure employment. My OSS buddy Joe Yager, who had recently retired from the State Department, was now assistant director of the IDA's International Division. I felt comfortable with Joe in loco parentis.

On the first morning of my temporary life among international scholars, I paid my respects to Ben Read, now the director of the center. After a few minutes of small talk and reminiscences about our time together at the State Department, lightning struck. The remainder of my professional life, three decades' worth, was changed in the next five minutes.

It all started under a cloudless sky:

"Chet, you're a social scientist, aren't you?"

"Well, sort of. I used to be. But I'm not sure what I am now. Why?"

"That's close enough. Anyway, weren't you in the auditorium a week or so ago when the Smithsonian and the center hosted the debut of the Club of Rome's study on *Limits to Growth*?"

The clouds were gathering.

"I was there only because one of the speakers invited me. It was interesting, but . . ."

"Well, if Woodrow Wilson could communicate with us, he would almost certainly say that explosive economic and population expansion are critical, urgent global issues, ones that his center should focus on. Wouldn't you agree?"

Dark clouds. Heavy thunder.

"I suppose. So . . . ?"

Now came the lightning bolt.

"So, will you put your Suez book in the oven for a while and organize a center program to address issues of economic and population growth?"

It soon became evident that the Suez book, *The Lion's Last Roar*, was destined to wind up on ice rather than in the oven. Much of my time at the center, which, in the event, amounted to thirty months rather than ten, was spent in developing and editing *Growth in America*, a book published in 1976. By accident, I was embarked on a new career: I resigned from the IDA and became an environmental policy wonk.

In the summer of 1973, the center experienced both a change in directors and a change in style. Ben Read left to assume the presidency of a new foundation, the German Marshall Fund. He was succeeded by James Billington, a professor of Russian history at Princeton.[2] Read had been my colleague at the State Department; Billington had spent his army stint during the Korean War at the CIA, where he was my junior colleague in the Office of National Estimates. (If you hang around Washington long enough, you will have been everyone's boss, or colleague, or subordinate, or all of the above.) Read viewed the center as a bridge between scholars and practitioners, with principal emphasis on the community of public policy practitioners (people like himself and myself). Billington's principal interest, not surprisingly, concerned the world of academe (people like himself).

The center was stimulating and thoroughly agreeable; it was like a university, but one without students. I reveled in my pipe, tweed jacket, morning coffee, lunch in the Smithsonian Commons, afternoon tea or sherry, seminars, lectures, symposia, a wonderful library. All this with a reasonable stipend and in the company of bright, congenial fellow Fellows: a French jurist, a Mexican novelist, an Indian government official, an American historian, and a widely published Catholic priest. The frosting on the cake was an office in the castle tower overlooking the National Mall and the most precious of all perks, a parking space.

I had been at the center for almost two years when Orah delivered a mild ultimatum: Leave the center fairly soon for a "real job" or arrange for a lifetime appointment. A few more months' fellowship on the Mall, she opined, and I would become so spoiled that I "wouldn't be good for anything else."

To be honest, I had begun to feel that way myself. I should somehow contrive to stay there indefinitely, or plan to leave soon. I decided in the summer of 1974 to finish writing and editing *Growth in America*, tidy up some loose ends, and move on. However, my days at the center were so full of intellectual, social, and physical diversions that if the book was ever to be completed, I needed an extended leave somewhere where I would not be distracted. Hearing of my plight, a friend offered me his cabin in the woods of West Virginia, five miles from the nearest town. Soon after Labor Day, I packed my notes and papers, a few paperbacks, and a change of clothes and drove off.

The cabin turned out to be comfortable and well equipped, with adequate plumbing and the necessary kitchen appliances. There were also a stereo, well-stocked bookcases, a fireplace, and a fly fishing rod. Now that summer was almost over, the cabin was well removed from the sight and sound of other people. Indeed, the only other folk I encountered were those I saw on an occasional trip to town for a newspaper, milk, pipe tobacco, and bass fishing flies. I set to work knowing I now had no excuse for failing to finish *Growth in America*.

Orah came to the nearest railway station, Harpers Ferry, each Friday afternoon bearing a container of carefully wrapped and labeled meals—Breakfast #1, Lunch #1, Dinner #1, etc.—each with detailed instructions for preparation. (She and Elsa, our housekeeper, had, with reason, little confidence in my culinary skills.) We spent the weekends, weather permitting, wandering through the town or the woods, going to a movie and picnicking at the nearby pond.

On my first morning I decided not to make the bed, not to shave, not to bother to tuck my shirt inside my trousers. After all, who was there to see? By noon, I reverted to type. I made the bed, shaved, and tucked in my shirt-tails. Why? Ask my mother. Ask Orah. It was apparently too late in my life to shake off these habits.

By the second day, I had settled into a routine: make bed, wash, shave, breakfast #2, write until noon, lunch #2, walk to the pond, chop wood, write, edit. Then another walk to the pond, fish, warm dinner #2, turn on the stereo, make a fire, have a couple of whiskeys, read, eat dinner #2, read, bed. The only variant would be if I caught a fish actually big enough to keep and eat. (This didn't happen often enough to warrant much mention here.)

I returned to Chevy Chase shortly before Thanksgiving. My time in the woods proved to be both productive and instructive. I had practically finished my editing and writing chores, and I also learned that Chester L. Cooper was a creature of habit and routine, but, nonetheless, reasonably good company.

By early 1975, aside from Orah's admonition and the fact that *Growth in America*[3] was now completed, I realized that my contributions to the center, and vice versa, were beginning to thin out. Besides, Nixon's Watergate case was coming to a climax. Virtually all the Fellows, American as well as foreign, were spending a great deal of time watching the Senate hearings on television. Little else was going on.

Late that spring, I once again confronted the question: What next? I was pushing sixty, too young to retire, even if I chose to. I thought seriously of writing full-time. I started working at home on the aborted Suez book and wrote several newspaper articles. But, once again, my muse deserted me each day after four or five hours. For better or worse, I was cut out for a real, full-time, demanding job. And I needed to get into town, to be among interesting young colleagues and, yes, to draw a paycheck.

*   *   *

Hovering unseen above my head, there must be a fairy godmother. I have been too lucky to have survived without one. This time she appeared in the guise of a remarkable, elfin nuclear physicist named Alvin Weinberg. Alvin had recently retired after a long and brilliant career as director of the Oak Ridge National Laboratory. Our tenures had overlapped for almost a year at the Woodrow Wilson Center. Upon leaving the center he established an energy-environment think tank under the institutional umbrella of the Oak Ridge Associated Universities (ORAU). Would I join the Institute of Energy Analysis (IEA) as his deputy director in charge of the institute's Washington office? It was an easy decision: Yes. (Often a deputy, never a bride!)

Alvin ranks high, stratospherically high, among my regiment of bosses over the years. He is a few years older than I, more even-tempered, more scholarly, and more talented. He is a man of many parts—part eminent scientist, part wise philosopher, part accomplished concert pianist, part avid tennis player. Altogether, he is a most remarkable man. If this sounds as if I have admiration, respect, and profound affection for Alvin Weinberg, I have made my point.

I spent seven exciting years at the institute. Energy problems were coming to the fore in the midseventies, not only because of the supply crisis spawned by the Middle East producers, but also because of the growing concern about environmental problems associated with electric power and transportation fuels, and the safety of nuclear reactors. Indeed, soon after I joined the institute, the Department of Energy (DOE), a new US government cabinet entity, was created to address these issues.

In my admittedly biased view, the DOE has ranked low among Washington's official establishments. Perhaps the Bureau of Indian Affairs has ranked lower, but the DOE has not been far above it. With few exceptions, the secretary of the DOE has been a nonentity with little or none of the background and experience required to deal with the department's three major missions—energy, national defense, and environment. At least two secretaries—political hacks—regarded abolishing the department as their highest priority.

Under Alvin Weinberg's leadership, the IEA became a pioneer in the research and analysis of global climate change. In 1975, well before the issue was recognized beyond a small group of American and foreign scientists, the institute had started serious work on this problem. Weinberg was almost certainly a catalyst in stimulating the government to sponsor and fund climate change research.

A few weeks after Jimmy Carter's inauguration in January 1977, his new science adviser, Frank Press, asked his friend Alvin to identify the scientific issues that, in his view, would require the president's attention over the following four years. Alvin asked me to join him in his meeting with Press. He was well prepared for the session. In fact, he was *always* well prepared.

"What should I and what should the president be worried about?" Frank Press asked.

"Carbon dioxide accumulations in the atmosphere, their implications for global climate change, and the impacts of climate change should be given top priority," Alvin said.

Press demurred. He wasn't concerned, at least in his present capacity, with problems on the long-term horizon. What about potent new cases of the flu or new outbreaks of smallpox—problems that might require urgent White House attention during the next four years?

Alvin insisted that research on greenhouse gases and climate change was urgent and critical. Research on this set of problems should be undertaken immediately.

Press asked for a memorandum elaborating Alvin's concerns. The institute had the paper on Press's desk in forty-eight hours. A few months later, the Department of Energy was given responsibility for funding and monitoring work on climate change. Research on the subject started soon after. It still goes on.

*   *   *

The climate change issue is a thorny one for politicians and bodes trouble for corporations relying on fossil fuels, which are a principal source of CO_2. It is, of course, a gold mine for special interest lobbyists and for researchers in a host of fields. Obviously, the problem does not lend itself to quick or simple solutions. Action taken tomorrow will show no perceptible results in the short term, or, indeed, during the next few decades. Furthermore, US efforts involving substantial political and economic costs may, in the end, prove of little value; the problem is global in its causes, its solutions, and its impact. Unless major developing countries—India, China, Brazil, Indonesia, Mexico—pursue economic development without relying heavily on coal, petroleum, and natural gas (especially coal), there is little that the United

States (or any other country) can do on its own to stave off the problem. And yet the United States, indeed no country, can regard climate change as a spectator sport without forsaking its responsibilities to future generations. We must engage in, and promote, both a national and global effort to reduce our consumption of coal and oil, or our grandchildren will pay a heavy cost.

Since that visit in 1977 with Frank Press, I have spent a great deal of time focusing on one or another aspect of global climate change—how to mitigate it, how to adapt to it, how to develop a global approach, how to negotiate an international climate change treaty. Much of my effort at Weinberg's institute, however, involved bickering and quarreling with the DOE official responsible for climate change research. The fact that the institute depended on him for a significant amount of its funding, and that I was a supplicant and he the grantor, made these encounters less miserable for him than for me.

Our relationship was not blessed with love at first sight, or even in hindsight. He was blustering, egotistical, and arrogant. I don't think he thought much of me, either. My purely objective view was that he was too often too positive and very often very wrong. On the other hand, I'm sure his highly prejudiced opinion of me was that I was constantly trying to diminish his wannabe stature and deprecate his deprecatable opinions. I suspect we were both right. Our relationship, in short, was not a marriage made in heaven but out of necessity. In the end, however, he acknowledged that Alvin's institute, despite my view of him and his of me, was worthy of ample funding. I'll give him that. Anyway, we now greet each other warmly.

*   *   *

In the evenings and on weekends during this period, I returned to my account of the Suez crisis. In the autumn of 1978, I ceased being a "one-book man." Modesty must yield to truth: *The Lion's Last Roar*[4] was a good book. Not only my mother and Orah thought so. The critics did, too. The *New Republic* reviewer said it was a "masterly retelling of the Suez affair."[5] The *Foreign Service Journal* said, "Over and above its historical merit [*The Lion's Last Roar*] is impeccably written and enriched with striking pen portraits of the principal protagonists."[6] The *Washington Post* said it was "fascinating."[7]

Despite its many admiring critics in other forums, the book's sales (and my royalties) suffered because of the prolonged strike at the *New York Times*, which prevented both a review and an advertisement. To add to all the bad timing of *The Lion*'s publication date, I was cursed with a galloping case of pneumonia when my book tour was scheduled. In the end, I had to settle for thin gruel: my publisher's consoled me with a note saying the book was a "critical success."

*   *   *

My contribution to America's culture and creative arts was not confined to the literary scene. In 1981 I spent a glamorous ten days (and nights) as a groupie doing one-night gigs with Bob Greene and the World of Jelly Roll Morton.

Bob Greene was a protégé of Edward R. Murrow, the fabled World War II foreign radio correspondent and, later, a celebrated television news analyst. Murrow was summoned to Washington by President Kennedy in 1962 to head the US Information Agency. He brought Greene with him. During the 1964 presidential campaign, Greene was sent to the White House and assigned to my small special speech-writing team. Our principal responsibility was to vet LBJ's speeches for foreign policy errors, inconsistencies, and unnecessary hyperbole. Bob was a better writer than a foreign affairs expert and was soon assigned to write speeches for Lady Bird.

Aside from his many other talents, Greene was a self-taught but accomplished Dixieland pianist. (I'm not sure he could even read music.) Whenever I needed him and he was not within sound or sight, I knew where to find him—jiving at a Georgetown jazz club.

After the election, Greene had a brief stint at the Pentagon as a speechwriter for Secretary McNamara. Within a couple of months, however, he disappeared. Some time later, there were occasional newspaper references to his Jelly Roll Morton retrospective at the Newport and Stockholm jazz festivals and at Carnegie Hall in New York. Nevertheless, it took another decade before I was able to catch up with him.

In the winter of 1982, I was attending a meeting in New Orleans. Having done my penance by sitting through several hours of boring lectures, I thought I deserved time off. I made my way to the French Quarter and Preservation Hall, the rickety old home of New Orleans jazz. Three dollars permitted me to sit on a wooden bench and listen to one set. I asked the lady collecting the admission fee if Bob Greene ever showed up there. "Yes," she said, "whenever he's in New Orleans." I gave her my card with a note to Bob, asking him to call me whenever he happened by.

The band that afternoon—several old-timers including Sweet Emma, an elderly woman pianist without the use of either one leg or one arm (I forget which was missing)—was foot-tapping, finger-snapping, head-nodding wonderful. Hardly had they finished the set when I was grabbed from behind with a crushing bear hug. It was Bob. He was in New Orleans auditioning trumpet players for a road tour of The World of Jelly Roll. We had drinks and then dinner. He and his band would soon be traveling from Portland, Oregon, to Portland, Maine. Couldn't I join him? It would involve "only six weeks." He promised a comfortable bus, good music, good talk, and rotten food.

Since the cost of such a tempting but extended and foolhardy venture would almost certainly include the loss of both Orah and my job, I turned him down, albeit with copious tears and a heavy heart; still, deep in my psyche was the Chet Cooper of the Melodians fame. As solace for both our disappointments, Bob promised to mail me his itinerary; perhaps I could catch up with him somewhere on the East Coast.

Several weeks later the itinerary arrived. By a stroke of luck, the group would be giving a show in Knoxville, Tennessee, about thirty miles from the IEA office in Oak Ridge. I would be at a meeting in Oak Ridge only a few days before. I faxed Bob to ask if the groupie offer was still on. It was. Orah and Alvin Weinberg, each bemused, agreed that two or three days of long bus rides, late nights, and cheap motels would get the foolishness out of my system. Off I went.

There were seven musicians, including Bob at the piano. Three were white, four black. Three of the black players—the saxophonist/clarinetist, the drummer, and the bass player—were in their seventies and had played with Jelly at one time or another. The young trumpet player (the one who won Bob's audition in New Orleans) spent much of his salary on evening phone calls to his wife and young child. The temperamental, grouchy banjo player had brought along his long-legged, pouty blonde girlfriend. She was the only other groupie, but, since she slept most of the time both on the bus and during the performances, I didn't get to know her very well.

The drummer, Tommy, was my favorite. A nimble, gentle, smiling man, he was the one who had had the longest personal relationship with Jelly. On the long bus rides, he would regale me with bittersweet tales about life on the road in the old days. The logistics involved in planning a trip around restaurants and hotels that would then accept blacks must have been maddening, but, nonetheless, Tommy could laugh at some of their misadventures.

I must confess to having a recurring Walter Mitty–like fantasy about my heroically taking over the drums when Tommy fell off the bus. While no Tommy, I was still a triumph, and the applause for my solo breaks was deafening. There was only one redeeming aspect about my grand vision; it made me feel so guilty that I always helped Tommy on and off the bus.

Bob's one-night stands were usually in small cities and were a popular item in a subscription series of music and dance. Audiences for the Jelly show were typically large and appreciative. The enthusiasm was contagious and I managed to squeeze ten days out of my three-day furlough. But all good things, I'm told, come to an end. And so, on the tenth day, in Manassas, Virginia, the axe fell.

I was selling programs at the entrance to the concert hall and was just about to take my position at the rear of the hall to lead the applause (in the old tradition of an opera star's claque) when, to my dismay, I saw Orah and Susan arrive. They were giggling as they approached. "Honey," Orah said, trying hard to regain her composure, "time is up." "Dad," Susan, still giggling, said, "it's time to come home." They were both right. After the concert I bade farewell to Bob, my friends in the band, and my fellow groupie. Thus ended my career in show business, unless . . .

*   *   *

Not long after my brief interlude with Bob and Jelly, I became again immersed in the thicket of international suspicions and machinations. With Ronald Reagan's election in 1980, Washington became the destination for an influx of conservative officeholders and ardent cold warriors. One of the institutions that soon came under their special scrutiny was an East-West think tank located in the countryside not far from Vienna, Austria. It was burdened with a cumbersome name—the International Institute for Applied Systems Analysis (IIASA).

IIASA had been the brainchild of President Johnson. Why, he asked in 1966, couldn't the United States and the Soviet Union pool their talent and address such nonsensitive global issues as environmental pollution, forestry, agriculture, and demography? Why not, he wondered, employ analytical techniques that exploited the relatively new computer tools? Why were relations between the two nations confined to stealing each other's secrets, ballet dancers, and musicians?

In fairly short order, Chairman Leonid Brezhnev indicated his willingness to cooperate with the United States in researching issues outside the military and political realms. President Nixon agreed with the idea soon after his inauguration. McGeorge Bundy set aside initial funding from the Ford Foundation, and the Austrian government agreed to repair and then to donate Maria Theresa's eighteenth-century hunting lodge in the village of Laxenburg. IIASA was soon a reality.

The original composition of the institute consisted of capitalist, Communist, and neutral countries: the United States, Britain, France, Italy, West Germany, Canada, and Japan; the USSR, Poland, Hungary, East Germany, Bulgaria, and Czechoslovakia; Finland, Sweden, and Austria. The United States and the Soviet Union, the principal funders of the institute, would hold the senior operating and policy positions. Thus, an American would be the institute director and a Soviet would chair the IIASA Council (made up of representatives from each member country). There would be two deputy directors, one American and one Soviet. Each member country, and a few nonmember countries, would be entitled to nominate candidates for scholar-places. The tenure of the scholars would normally be two years, and their stipends would reflect their pre-IIASA salaries and positions as well as their scholarly achievements.

The first director, Howard Raiffa, was a distinguished Harvard professor. He remained at IIASA for three years, and was succeeded by Roger Levien, from the Rand Corporation. Levien served six years, two full terms. The chairman of the IIASA Council, Jermyn Gvishiani, a Georgian (a *Soviet* Georgian), was head of the USSR's Institute for Applied Systems Analysis in Moscow. Gvishiani, who knew a good thing when he saw it, held on to his chairmanship for the better part of two decades.

During this period—from the early 1970s until 1981—I was aware of only the barest details of IIASA, although I knew something of Johnson's early thoughts about establishing the institute. In 1980, when a new director was appointed, my innocence came to an end. I was soon increasingly immersed in virtually every aspect, from lofty to squalid, of the organization. But, as my Soviet colleagues at IIASA used to say, "That story will take another bottle."

NOTES

1. The center is now based in the Ronald Reagan Building on Washington's 14th Street.

2. Billington has been Librarian of Congress for many years.

3. Chester L. Cooper, ed., *Growth in America* (Westport, CT: Greenwood Press, 1976).

4. Chester L. Cooper, *The Lion's Last Roar: Suez 1956* (New York: Harper & Row, 1978).

5. *New Republic*, January 27, 1979, pp. 35–36.

6. *Foreign Service Journal*, February 1979, p. 35.

7. *Washington Post Book World*, February 4, 1979, p. 1.

16

The Other Bottle

ABOUT THE INTERNATIONAL INSTITUTE FOR APPLIED SYSTEMS ANALYSIS (IIASA)

IIASA was one of the bits of blue sky among the clouds of the cold war. It was Lyndon Johnson's idea at a moment in 1966 when he could put aside the demands of Vietnam and his civil rights program. Even so, it had to wait until Richard Nixon set the wheels in motion. By 1972 the hunting palace of the Hapsburg empress Maria Theresa was restored after the ravages of its use by Soviet troops during World War II. Soon after, the Austrian government gave the palace, Schloss Laxenburg, and some of its grounds to IIASA for its use as offices and a conference center.

When I arrived at IIASA, it was to take on my duties as one of two deputy directors. The other, by the original charter, was a Soviet (always a Russian). There were seventeen member national organizations (America's was usually the National Academy of Science). It was the only international organization I know where scholars from both East and West Germany could conduct their research over an extended period.

IIASA's name is somewhat misleading; systems analysis is only one of the institute's several fields of study. The founders chose the name because it seemed to be bereft of any political connotation. The shadow of the cold war made the American and Soviet organizers exceedingly wary of stirring up the political ideologues. Despite their care, however, IIASA was never far from the realities that existed outside, and even within, the boundaries of the idyllic world of Laxenburg.

*   *   *

The Institute for Applied Systems Analysis evolved from a speech in October 1966 in which President Johnson elaborated on the need for USSR-US cooperation in addressing worrisome, nonpolitical international issues. After the speech, however, the president had little time to implement steps to realize his lofty aspirations. The next several years saw little progress, but by early 1973 the new organization was in business. Its acronym, IIASA, was even clumsier than its name, especially when spoken rather than written—"Yassa" or "Eye-assa," depending on one's personal preference.

IIASA lives in the Schloss Laxenburg, Maria Theresa's eighteenth-century hunting lodge. The schloss is located in a bucolic village (Laxenburg) about twelve miles from Vienna. It may be a "lodge" when compared to other Hapsburg residences (the vast "country" palace nearby at Schönbrunn, for example), but it is, nonetheless, elegant and palatial.

Laxenburg's center is an eighteenth-century square bordered by the schloss, a baroque church, a convent, the town hall with adjoining shops and living quarters above, a bierkeller, and a café. The buildings are all still painted in Maria Theresa's favorite shade of yellow. To the Europeans at IIASA, this may be just another old square, another baroque church, another pretty palace. To those of us from North America, however, the village was the stuff of Old World romance and childhood fairy tales. If the ubiquitous automobiles were exchanged for horses and carriages, the square would be an ideal setting for a Franz Lehar operetta. A chorus of girls in dirndls and boys in lederhosen would seem very much in place.

During the early post–World War II years, when Austria was divided into four political-administrative sectors (American, French, British, and Soviet), Laxenburg was in the Soviet zone. The schloss became a barracks for Soviet troops and a stable for their horses. By the end of the occupation, Maria Theresa's beautiful little country residence and its lovely park had become a horrific mess, a veritable garbage pit.

When IIASA moved in in 1972, the palace and the grounds had been lovingly restored by the Austrian government. Many of its rooms, large and small, were handsomely decorated and furnished in their original style. They were lit by large crystal chandeliers and graced (but no longer heated) by beautifully crafted white-and-gilt porcelain stoves. The park had groves of healthy trees, tidy paths, a clear blue lake, and a restored play house originally built for Maria Theresa's children.

In late 1973, scholars from the Soviet Union and Eastern Europe, North America, Japan, Western Europe, and several "neutral" countries had settled into the schloss. Collaborative research began.

All went well during the tenures of the first two directors. IIASA was one of the few institutions where scientists from capitalist and Communist nations could work together on global problems over an extended period. It provided an early hint of spring during the ice-cold war years. Indeed, it was one of the very few international institutions at which scholars from East and West Germany had more than transitory, fragile professional associations.

While the quality of research at IIASA did not rival that done in the best universities of Western Europe or North America, the work was eminently respectable and surprisingly free of ideological bias. In a letter to a senior State Department official, the president of the American Academy of Arts and Sciences described IIASA as "a unique institution because it attempts to bring science to bear on policy, which means that it must perform integrative studies that blend the physical sciences with the social and management sciences."[1] The letter was written in 1984 as part of an effort to persuade the Reagan administration to restore the funding that its ideologues had cut off in 1981. The letter had no effect. IIASA's salad days were over. The coldest of the cold warriors had won the day. Since then, IIASA has had to fight a difficult struggle for survival.

*   *   *

Early in the negotiations concerning the organization and governance of the institute, it was agreed that IIASA's director should be an American, and the chairman of the IIASA Council should be a Soviet. The first two directors met this criterion. In 1980, however, the US Committee for IIASA (the non-government body that represented the American scientific community) was unable to unearth a suitable US replacement for Director Roger Levien, who had already served two terms. G. Crawford "Buzz" Holling, a Canadian, was regarded as a splendid alternative. Holling, an internationally respected professor of ecology from the University of British Columbia, had been at IIASA a few years before as head of its environmental program. He was a gangling, long-jawed, attractive, carelessly attired, uneven-tempered gent about fifteen years younger than I. He spoke in full sentences and delivered noisy hoots of laughter when he saw or heard something amusing. During his earlier tenure at IIASA he married a staff member, an attractive Austrian woman. Her bright humor was a great asset when, shortly after Buzz's arrival, the atmosphere in the schloss turned from mostly sunny to mostly cloudy.

Buzz had endearing traits and many talents, but suffering fools and managing a modest-sized institution were not among them. He was overly tolerant or insufficiently intolerant of the occasional freeloaders, prima donnas, and former flower children who basked in the relaxed supervision at IIASA and the delights of Vienna. (I am hardly a strict taskmaster, but compared to Buzz, I was regarded as the bad cop during my own tenure at IIASA.)

I knew something, but not much, about Johnson's original interest in creating a USSR-US research center. I had heard his speech in the autumn of 1966, and some hallway gossip about the notion before and after McGeorge Bundy left the White House for the Ford Foundation. When Holling called me from Laxenburg in the spring of 1981 and asked me to represent him in Washington, I drew a blank. I did not know Holling and I had forgotten about the prenatal discussions that had evolved into IIASA. Nonetheless, I agreed to meet with Buzz during his forthcoming visit to Washington. I wasn't sure what he wanted from me, but I was impressed with him just on the basis of our phone conversation. This gave him leverage with respect to whatever it was that he had in mind. I soon found out what that was.

He put forward his proposal directly: no overture, no mood music. He had heard nasty rumors that the Reagan White House regarded IIASA as a "nest of Communist spies." He had learned that the National Science Foundation (NSF) had been told to cut off its annual dues payment of $2 million— a paltry bit of a trivial amount of an inconsequential proportion of the NSF's budget. This was hardly the best way for him to embark on his directorship. Didn't I agree? If I did, would I keep him informed of developments affecting IIASA on Capitol Hill and Pennsylvania Avenue? Perhaps this would help him ward off trouble, or at least minimize the damage. He pointed out that this, of course, would be a pro bono arrangement. (I could not have accepted any money, in any case.) So long as he did not expect me to do any lobbying, I agreed to help him.

*　　*　　*

It became immediately clear that I needed a refresher course in IIASA 101. I took a week's leave from the Institute of Energy Analysis (Alvin Weinberg was sympathetic to Holling's plight) and flew off to Vienna.

Vienna was much the same as it had been when, during the late fifties, I had visited there to interrogate Soviet defectors. Actually, much of the inner city had changed little from its overall appearance more than two hundred years before; substitute horses and carriages for the automobiles and one would have been back in Mozart's time.

While there were few obvious physical changes, the Viennese themselves, and their quality of life, had changed considerably since my last trip. They no longer looked shabby, the restaurants were crowded, the shops were bustling, the prices were high. Vienna, at least that part of it within the Ring (the center of the city), was no longer poor. As for World War II, Hitler, and the Nazis, Austria had been a "victim," not an accomplice. The Holocaust? What and when was that? The first indication Orah and I had that this subject was open for discussion was an Austrian television program that aired in 1984. It told a story of a young Jewish intellectual's experiences just prior to the triumphant (and welcomed) invasion of Nazi troops.

*   *   *

In early 1983 Holling's American deputy returned to Washington, six months before his three-year tenure expired. Several officials in the Reagan administration (despite their distaste for IIASA) and the US Committee for IIASA were anxious to maintain an American managerial presence in Laxenburg. I was asked to fill the deputy director gap until the search, then underway, for a suitable American director to replace the Canadian Holling bore fruit. (It strikes me that I have spent the better part of my adult life as some director's deputy director.) I squeezed out a six-month leave of absence from the Institute of Energy Analysis; we locked up our house and rented an apartment in Vienna. Our accommodations were barely satisfactory, but we had planned only a short stay. On the initial night there, Orah was seized by the first of many asthma attacks that would plague her for the next two decades.

When I reported for duty in Laxenburg, Holling gave me the choice of a large, imposing room, complete with crystal chandelier, massive porcelain stove, and royal decor, or its smaller, less imposing anteroom. The opulent chamber was hardly my style, and I offered it to IIASA's French secretary (who was comfortable where he was), a Russian colleague (who haughtily turned it down), and a newly arrived English parvenu. The Englishman (about whom more in due course) happily took it. I had made a wise choice; the anteroom was warmer in winter and cooler in summer than Maria Theresa's bedchamber.

Within a few weeks Orah was recruited by an Austrian economic research group housed in one of the old buildings facing the square. Its congenial staff was headed by a courtly professor associated with both the University of Vienna and the Austrian Chamber of Commerce. Her German and the professor's English were adequate enough to permit a happy professional and social relationship, and he soon came to regard Orah with equal parts of respect and affection.

*   *   *

It was not long before I discovered that IIASA's lovely setting and handsome building masked some ugly problems; the institute's beauty, to abuse the cliché, was, to some extent, skin deep. In the winter of 1983, the cold war and the anti-Communist mood of Washington officials had come into full bloom. An overeager and inept Russian member of IIASA's administrative staff could not have picked a worse time to try his hand at spookery. It was thanks in part to him that the cold war gladiators in Washington came to regard the institute with great suspicion.

Several months prior to my arrival, this bungler (without a shadow of doubt, a KGB operative) was caught with his hand—or at least a few fingers—in the cookie jar. Using his association with IIASA as a surrogate for trench coat and dark glasses, he traveled (on "official business") to Scandinavia. There, in the interest of his "scientific research at IIASA," he attempted to acquire confidential information about North Sea natural gas, by then a serious competitor with Russia's gas fields. He was apprehended by the Norwegians, summarily dismissed from IIASA, and sent home. His Soviet colleagues were, of course, "shocked, simply shocked" that a colleague would betray IIASA's trust. More to the point, one of his KGB cohorts in Laxenburg, and a genial lunch partner, doubled up with laughter when, after several beers, he indiscreetly described the clumsy tradecraft his comrade had used.

I took this occasion to put our council chairman Minister Gvishiani on notice that IIASA's future would be at hazard if there were another such incident. As it was, "Operation Natural Gas" provided an opportunity for the institute's critics in Washington to withdraw American financial and intellectual support; the National Science Foundation, IIASA's umbilical cord to the US government, was induced (or ordered) to set the institute adrift. After a few harrowing months of ad hoc, jerry-built efforts in Washington to maintain an American presence in Laxenburg, the prestigious, Cambridge-based

American Academy of Arts and Sciences took over the role of the US Committee for IIASA. Since then it has gallantly kept its thumb in the leaky dike.

*   *   *

Aside from IIASA's financial and political problems, personnel issues occupied an inordinate amount of my time. For openers, there was the employees' association, which convened once a month, or more often if someone had a special gripe. IIASA's salaries and honoraria, especially in the case of non-Americans, were competitive with those offered by other European research institutions; its workweek and holiday schedule were at least as relaxed and generous as most Austrian public and private companies (which is saying a great deal). Its restaurant was subsidized. Everyone at the institute had shopping privileges at the UN commissary in Vienna, where prices were substantially lower than in Austria's private sector. (Scotch whiskey was a few dollars a bottle, French perfume less than half price.) Neither Austrian nationals nor virtually any of the nationals from other countries, especially the Communist countries, probably ever had, or would ever again, have it so good. Nonetheless, the employees' association meetings always had a full agenda. Since Director Holling was blessed with a short temper and a limited supply of patience, Deputy Director Cooper (whose temper also had a short fuse and whose patience was also quickly exhausted) was designated to deal with the union. I came to regard a session with its representatives as being comparable to a long appointment with a periodontist.

What I never understood was why and how men and women on the IIASA staff with whom I had cordial, even friendly professional and social relations every working day of the month turned into snarling, bitter, and uncompromising adversaries between one and three o'clock every fourth Wednesday afternoon. Perhaps my worst experiences in this regard occurred during the time a young English chap, an editor, took over the chairmanship of the union. He seemed to view his tenure as a training ground for a career in the extreme left wing of the Labour Party. Normally genial and mild, he assumed a hostile, confrontational guise whenever he dealt with "management," namely, Holling (who took pains to avoid him) and me.

Actually, the staff at IIASA, from the highest level to the lowest, had little to fear from management. Austrian law and IIASA's traditions assured that the cards were stacked against their ever being penalized, let alone sacked.

John Everett (not quite his real name) taught me more than I wanted to know on this score. He fudged his expense account. He diddled his research budget so that, at IIASA's expense and in its ignorance, he lived in a first-class hotel instead of in the modest establishment IIASA's records showed. He treated himself to expensive cigars and extravagant meals, presumably having entertained world-class scholars or international statesmen. He lied about his having had a lofty former position in Her Majesty's government and about his golden contacts in the world of British politics and academe.

On his arrival, he insisted that his responsibilities warranted a freshly painted, two-chandelier office (the one I could have had, if I chose) and newly upholstered furniture. His crowning success was avoidance of any activity that fell under the heading of research, analysis, or just plain work. In short, Mr. Everett was a first-class, low-class con artist. But could we fire him? Eventually we did, but "eventually" involved employing an independent auditor, retaining a lawyer in addition to IIASA's own counsel, a few months of paperwork, and exchanges of insults: "You must know, Cooper, that I heartily dislike you and I will take steps to ruin your reputation." "You must know, Everett, your lack of affection is a matter of supreme indifference to me. And you, we both know, have no reputation left to ruin."

Everett left us for bigger and worse mischief. He was soon sent to jail in Vienna for cooking the books of a new magazine he was promoting. Not long ago, I heard he was in Scandinavia. Too bad. The Norwegians and Swedes deserve better.

*   *   *

With l'affaire Everett out of the way, I could turn my attention to the Soviet and Eastern European presence in the schloss. This was a matter that was sorely troubling the Reagan White House and threatening the very existence of the institute. At this point, the United States government had only its little toe remaining in IIASA. Thank goodness, the US representative on the IIASA Council was the wise and experienced member of the American Academy of Arts and Sciences and Harvard professor Harvey Brooks. Despite the prestige and the efforts of its new sponsor, the withdrawal of the National Science Foundation funding left IIASA barely able to make ends meet. I decided to do what I could to reassure Washington that IIASA was a trustworthy establishment.

Early after my arrival in Vienna, I had a frank session with Jermen Gvishiani, the chairman of the IIASA Council, and a few members of IIASA's Soviet staff. I reminded them that the American, British, Japanese, and other non-Communist researchers and support staff at the institute regarded Holling, and, to a lesser extent, me, as their boss. On the other hand, it was clear that the Soviets and Eastern Europeans in Laxenburg were expected to be responsible to the political and intelligence officers in their respective embassies, as well as to Gvishiani and the Soviet officers on the IIASA staff. I pointed out that this was not quite what IIASA's American founders had had in mind. In the light of this and the recent spying episode, the Americans, and not just those in the Reagan administration, had become suspicious and wary of how the Communist staff members and scholars conducted themselves. They should know, beyond any doubt, that if there were any other spying episodes, I would urge the Americans to pull out of the institute altogether. I reminded them that my own background in intelligence had given me a sensitive nose for monkey business.

Gvishiani took all of this in good humor. So far as I know there were no further incidents, at least during the eighteen months while I was there. This is not to suggest that the KGB had neither a presence nor a mission in Laxenburg; its principal role was to keep its own countrymen in line.

Communist security in this regard was ill-disguised. To constrain any attacks of wanderlust, all employees and scholars from Communist countries had to surrender their passports to the careful custody of their embassies. Most of IIASA's Soviet staff and scholars lived in the Soviet embassy compound, where rent was cheaper but surveillance was easier. The Communist complement at IIASA met privately, on a periodic basis, to discuss who knows what. (I once accidentally barged into a room in a far corner of the schloss where the group was meeting. Amusement on my part, embarrassment on theirs.) One summer afternoon, when I went to the café for lunch and brought back some ice cream for our two receptionists, an Austrian and a Russian, the KGB member of IIASA's secretariat bounded from his office nearby to snatch Katrina's ice cream for fear that I had poisoned it.

I once discussed with Holling how we could find out in confidence whether his office was bugged. We couldn't work out a way of doing it, however, without the knowledge of the IIASA staff. Thus, whenever we (or, indeed, other IIASA folk) wanted to discuss anything in private, we went for a little "walk in the park."

IIASA's computers were of particular concern to several officials in the White House and the Pentagon. There was talk of the Soviets using the institute's computers to break into or crash sensitive American military data. Since my own computer expertise then (and now) would not have earned me a passing grade at any nursery school, I decided to summon a computer security expert from Washington. The one I chose was a consultant for the FBI. After his inspection, he pronounced that IIASA's computers were less sophisticated than those in most American high schools. His only recommendation was to restrict the freedom the children of IIASA's employees and scholars had on weekends to play with the equipment. (We quickly put a ban on that.)

*   *   *

None of the Communist activity seemed to warrant the "nest of spies" worry. Nonetheless, I wanted to demonstrate, beyond doubt, that Holling and I were sensitive to Washington's nagging concerns. I decided to take a definitive move to reassure the nervous cold warriors that we were on the ball.

I telephoned the American embassy in Vienna and asked for the ambassador. She was out of the city, but the second-ranking official, Minister Felix Bloch, was there. I introduced myself and requested an appointment to discuss a sensitive matter. We agreed to meet in his office on the following day.

The minister was cordial and expressed his interest in IIASA. I invited him to Laxenburg and told him that I was anxious to dispel the remaining concerns of the State Department, the Pentagon, and the White House about Holling's and my determination to keep IIASA free from suspicion. I suggested that he ask the CIA's chief of station (whom I did not know) to join us. Bloch said that the CIA's representative was in Germany, but in any case, whatever I had to say would be more effective if I discussed it with him. After all, he had direct and personal contacts with the appropriate people in the State Department. Moreover, in his view, the chief of station was not top-drawer. (He turned out to be right about that!) In the event, we agreed to meet every two weeks or so; I would report on what I knew of the KGB activities at the schloss. I emphasized, primarily for Washington's benefit, that these seemed to be exclusively focused on keeping Soviet personnel from being polluted. After all, their easy and informal access to Westerners, their freedom to read Western journals, their access to computers and Xerox machines, and the temptations of sparkling, capitalistic Vienna must have made the KGB uneasy.

We had several meetings, principally during lunch. (Bloch seemed to know all the best Viennese restaurants.) He was interested in my snippets of information about the IIASA's Soviet staff, scientists, and visitors. He agreed to visit IIASA, and when he did, several of our scholars gave him presentations on their work. Bloch assured me that our show-and-tell contacts with the American embassy were being sympathetically reported to appropriate officials in the Pentagon, the State Department, and the CIA.

My relationship with Minister Bloch was cut off abruptly after a few months. Much to the apparent surprise of our ambassador to Austria, the CIA chief of station, the State Department, and the Austrian foreign ministry, to say nothing of the genuine surprise of IIASA's deputy director, Bloch was suddenly plucked out of the embassy and escorted to Washington under the suspicion of being a Soviet spy. He was fired, interrogated, and shadowed for a year or more. But, for some reason, he was never tried. The last I heard he was packing groceries at a Safeway grocery store in Virginia. I decided that, in the future, if I had anything worth saying on the subject of East-West relations, I would deal directly with Washington. It would not be too long before I did have something to say.

*   *   *

I was never sure about the reach of the KGB at IIASA. Were the men I identified—the personnel officer, the member of the secretariat, and at least one of the economists—responsible for the correct behavior only of the Soviet people in Laxenburg? Or were they also minding the East Germans, Poles, Hungarians, Czechs, and Bulgarians? If the former, who among the East Europeans in the schloss had this responsibility? If the latter, their vigilance left something to be desired.

A nightmare that both Holling and I shared was that there would be a defection by one or more of the Communist country nationals within IIASA's building or grounds. Such an incident would be bound to mark the end of cooperative research on urgent global problems. Our nightmare turned into a reality on two occasions soon after Buzz unexpectedly left for Vancouver and I became acting director.

One evening I got a telephone call at home from the wife of a Bulgarian economist whose tenure at IIASA was coming to a close. "I need to talk to you." Her voice was strained and urgent. This was not the first such message I had gotten from a worried wife. The air in Laxenburg lent itself to domestic hanky-panky.

"What's the matter?" I asked, trying to recall any extramarital reason why she should be so upset. "And where are you?"

"At a telephone kiosk on the street. And I can't tell you now. When can I meet you? In front of the opera house tomorrow evening?"

Clearly, this was something more serious than her Peter just fooling around with another woman. (My years at the CIA had not been altogether wasted.) We met as agreed. The conversation was hurried and to the point.

"Peter's time at IIASA is almost up," she said.

"I know."

"He—we—don't want to, won't, go home. We want you to help us. The Bulgarian embassy took our passports when we arrived. Will your embassy help us?"

"Look, I don't want Peter to defect while he's still at IIASA. It's only a few more weeks until his tenure is up. Even then it would be a difficult matter. But you are Jewish, aren't you?"

"Peter is. I'm not."

"No matter. As soon as you can, go to the Israeli embassy. Without your passports, Israel is the one place where you can go without a big hassle and some risk. But don't tell anyone we've talked. And don't tell me anything more about your plans."

I got a postcard a few months later: "Good news. Peter has received an appointment as an assistant professor at the Hebrew University. All is fine. Thanks."

The other near miss was one involving a Pole, one of our best systems analysts. His time at IIASA was also running out. He, too, did not want to return home. He assured me, during a long walk in the park and away from any overhearing people or devices, that he was not a member of the Polish Communist Party, "one of the few Easterners in the schloss who is not."

Once again, I emphasized that it would be a serious problem for IIASA if a defection happened there. But after his appointment expired, I told him, he was free to contact the French, British, or American embassies. He promised to wait. I never heard anything further, and for all I know, he is now a high official in the post-Communist Polish government. Life at IIASA during the cold war being what it was, I'm sure word of both these incidents reached Washington, Moscow, Sofia, and Warsaw.

*   *   *

In the late summer of 1983, Orah and I were in London for a holiday, after which I was scheduled to fly to Moscow to discuss some IIASA projects still in the planning stage. Orah planned to stay on in London with our daughter, son-in-law, and granddaughter. She would meet me in Vienna on my return there from Russia. Two days before I left for Moscow, a South Korean jumbo jet strayed into North Korean airspace and was shot down. All aboard—280 people—died. Acrimonious charges and countercharges, threats of retaliation, and vitriolic political rhetoric were exchanged. Seoul and Washington claimed that the airspace involved was trivial, the pilot made an honest error, and the North Koreans had overreacted (all more or less true). Pyongyang and Moscow claimed that the South Korean pilot had purposely flown across the border to engage in photo intelligence on behalf of the United States, an act that had become all too frequent (conceivably true).

Washington halted all flights to the Soviet Union. Moscow suspended all takeoffs and landings of NATO-country airlines. Thousands of Americans and Europeans were stranded in the Soviet Union. Question: Should I proceed to Moscow as planned? Orah was opposed. Pat Dean, my Foreign Office friend, advised against going.

I decided to go. IIASA, after all, was an international nongovernmental institution. The Russians had not, as yet, canceled their invitation. Although I could not now fly directly to Moscow from London, I could fly to Vienna and take an Austrian Airlines flight from there. I told the US Embassy in London of my plans and they, in turn, informed our embassy in Moscow. Pat Dean sent a telegram to the British Embassy. The chief pilot of Austrian Airlines, Manfred Pollak, was my secretary's husband and a good friend. He alerted his Vienna and Moscow offices to hold a seat for me on the Moscow-bound and Vienna-bound flights, despite overbookings.

I survived the torturous procedures at Moscow's airport—the usual hostile stares, long waits, inspections, examinations, interrogations, and checking and double-checking. Finally, on the sunny side of the barriers, I was met by a chubby young man I recognized as having recently attended IIASA's summer student program. I thought then, and am sure now, that he was a KGB trainee—the cut of his clothes, his excellent English, and the deference paid to him by our driver were good clues. Later, I discovered that he had attended one of Moscow's elite private schools, was a good tennis player, and had access to special, no-peasants-allowed shops. Proof positive.

We had hardly left the airport when Sacha called someone, somewhere, on a portable phone, a procedure he followed almost every half hour during the four days he "escorted" me. The hotel was, of course, for foreigners only, although my companion and other Russians with similar connections could get as far as the lobby and the dining hall, providing they were with foreign guests. To make sure that nothing would occur to threaten the security of the USSR or the purity of the Communist Party, a lady of wide girth, advanced age, and perpetual frown was stationed on each floor of the hotel to keep track of guests' comings and goings.

There were no other Americans, or, as far as I could tell, Westerners in the hotel—perhaps because of the sanctions imposed, or perhaps because someone decided I needed careful, isolated handling. Anyway, in the dining room and bar I was neck-deep in Cubans, Albanians, Libyans, Iranians, and citizens of other "Death-to-America!" countries. I did very little table-hopping.

At dinner that evening, Sacha proudly pointed to the old-fashioned chandeliers and the well-carved paneling. He said that the hotel dated back to the prerevolution years. "You see, we regard you as a special visitor." I think he was serious. But "special" or not, I was not permitted to have any meal outside that dining room during the time I was in Moscow.

Much to my surprise, despite the Korean airliner crisis, I did not encounter the slightest hostility on the street or within the various institutes I visited. Quite the reverse: all my discussions turned out to be informative, candid, and cordial. The atmosphere in the hotel, however, was different. I don't think any of the guests liked me.

On my third day, the director of the Soviet Academy of Sciences and I drew up a memorandum of understanding that laid out the terms of Soviet participation in a series of IIASA projects. It was then that I came up against another reality of life in Moscow for a "special" visitor. Sacha's ubiquitous presence was one, my floor watchdog was another. The problem of getting a document copied was the third. (A fourth was yet to come.)

After we were satisfied with the wording of the memorandum, the director (a former IIASA colleague), Sacha, and I trooped down to a lower floor where, in a large, dingy room, two dozen or so women were banging away on ancient typewriters. In due course, we received two typed copies, one in Russian, one in English. We went back to the director's office, I to proofread the English translation, they the Russian.

This done, I requested four copies: one for my colleagues in Washington, another for the academy in Cambridge, and two to keep in Laxenburg. Could I get them copied before I left for dinner? (Escorted by Sacha, naturally. In the hotel, naturally.) Silence. Sacha stared at the floor and then looked, nervously, at the director. The director gazed out the window. Finally, he shook his head. "I'm sorry, Dr. Cooper. The machine is broken."

In the end, I settled for three copies, which Sacha and I laboriously copied by hand from the typed draft. By then, it was almost seven o'clock. "I have pleasant surprise for you," Sacha said once we were in the car. "You have free night. There are no meetings. I also have free night and supper at home."

"You mean I can walk around town after dinner? Wherever I want to go?"

"Of course, Dr. Cooper. This is free country for you. Go where you wish. We meet tomorrow, 8:30. After breakfast. In the hotel."

I had dinner surrounded by my muttering, frowning, nudging, leering companions. My waiter, however, seemed unusually solicitous and was generous with helpings of both liquids and solids.

It was a brisk, starlit night. I was confident, after a few backward glances, that I was not being followed. Reveling in my solitary freedom, I strolled leisurely toward Red Square. But within minutes, I had a desperate and sudden urge to go to the toilet. There were no public lavatories in sight. I virtually ran back to my hotel and reached my room in the nick of time. By then I was exhausted, enervated, and dehydrated. Moreover, I was concerned about another attack. I went straight to bed. So much for "going where you wish." Thanks to my friend Sacha, the solicitous waiter, and possibly the cook, my Russian hosts had no need to be concerned about leaving me to my own devices. And thanks to the efficient people at Austrian Airlines, I had a seat the next day on the crowded plane out of Moscow and back to Vienna.

*   *   *

IIASA, despite its financial and cold war troubles, attracted many competent scientists, and a few brilliant ones. Their work on acid rain, climate change, systems theory, and demography has been highly regarded by outside experts. At least as important, considering the tensions of the period, its research has been pretty much free from ideology, ours or theirs. This was not the case, however, when the IIASA Council (comprised of the chairmen of the national member organizations) met to review IIASA's annual research program. Two projects at issue involved several IIASA member countries, and, in my view, they were relevant and (I thought) free of politics.

I proposed an investigation of the economic, social, and demographic problems of immigrant foreign workers in the relatively homogenous societies of host countries—Algerians in France, Turks in Germany and Sweden, Pakistanis in the United Kingdom, people from the Asian and Muslim Soviet Republics in Mother Russia, and Koreans and Filipinos in Japan. For good measure, I included Latinos in the United States. My Soviet colleagues pointed out that if we wanted to study the problems of America or France, of course, that would be worthwhile. But the Soviet Union had no such problems, despite what was obvious to the naked eye in Moscow or (then) Leningrad. The idea was dropped.

My other project proposal was a study on the causes and possible alleviation of problems presented by the Danube River—pollution, water supply and distribution, hydroelectric power, navigation, and recreation. The

Danube (more brown than blue, it must be said) flows almost eighteen hundred miles through many countries in central and eastern Europe. The study would have been useful to the economic, agricultural, and transportation policymakers in the IIASA community. The notion enjoyed a good reception among virtually all of the member countries, except Hungary and Czechoslovakia. "Don't push that idea, Chet," a Czech colleague urged. "If you think Washington and Moscow have tough exchanges on some issues, you haven't heard the Czechs and Hungarians argue about the Danube. I promise you, this study will lead to much trouble. If you want to sleep at night, forget the idea." And that took care of that.

*   *   *

I had come to IIASA on the understanding that after Holling's replacement had been selected and had taken over the reins, I could return home. Orah and I assumed that the process would involve six months or so. In the event, it took eighteen; the IIASA Committee found it hard to persuade a first-class candidate to take the post in the face of the US member's financial problems.

Our final months in Laxenburg were anxious ones. We missed our family. Our house in Chevy Chase had been vacant for a year longer than we had expected. Our run-down nineteenth-century apartment in Vienna had pretense but no central heating. Moreover, it was too small, the kitchen was grossly inadequate, and the electrical system was old and unreliable. And there was a long steep climb of four flights to our quarters; one tenant used the ancient elevator as a storage closet for skis, wine, and old magazines.

None of these considerations was critical, but together they were a source of worry. Another problem—a truly serious one—added to our anxiety. During my stay in Austria, there had been several consequential changes at the Oak Ridge Associated Universities, the parent organization of my direct employer, the Institute of Energy Analysis. ORAU had a new president, Alvin Weinberg had retired, and the institute had been decimated. More to the point, I was ordered to return to the institute immediately or consider myself redundant.

Clearly, there were good personal and professional reasons to pack up and return home. Yet I felt an obligation to honor my original commitment— to hold the fort until a new director was on board. So there I was—a lame duck in Laxenburg, unemployed at home. And yet, why was I so concerned? I was sixty-five years old, eligible for Social Security. Orah had retired a few years earlier. Both daughters were happily married and financially independent. Once home, I could retire in peace and comfort. Why didn't I? Answer: I couldn't face up to it. I would have to look for some interesting work as soon as I got home.

*   *   *

Meanwhile, and throughout most of our Austrian stay, life was, by and large, full of pleasant surprises and experiences. While our apartment was less than comfortable, its location was most convenient—across the road from the Belvedere gardens and museum, close to the bus and trolley stops, within walking distance of the opera and downtown shops, near a few modest cafés and cozy coffeehouses.

Most of our weekends during the summer and autumn were spent exploring the mountains, lakes, and river towns of Austria; visiting the museums and parks of Vienna; and going to one of many concerts offered every evening. The fact that I rarely, if ever, heard the word "Vietnam" mentioned added to the sense I had that Vienna, and especially Laxenburg, seemed to occupy another planet.

One drawback to the whole experience was Orah's only modest ability and my almost total inability to speak, to understand, or to read German. Within the Ring, this was not a serious problem; many Viennese, especially the younger ones, could speak English. Outside the city center, and particularly in the countryside, however, communication was a struggle. Luckily Renate, my secretary (in due course, to become my "European daughter"), and her husband, Manfred, accompanied us on many of our expeditions.

*   *   *

In the autumn of 1984 the new director was selected, and he arrived at IIASA soon after. We remained in Vienna until the end of the year to provide some overlap and to take care of some unfinished business. At virtually the last minute, my dolorous professional prospects suddenly took a turn for much the better. Resources for the Future (RFF), a prestigious environmental research establishment in Washington, offered me the post of not deputy director, but consultant in residence—a title I never heard of until then. My duties were not well defined. I accepted anyway, and showed up ready, willing, and able shortly after the first of the year.

NOTE

1. Herman Feshbach, president of the American Academy of Arts and Sciences, and Harvey Brooks, chairman, Committee for IIASA, letter to the Hon. Keith W. Dam, deputy secretary, Department of State, February 6, 1984.

17
WINDING DOWN

ABOUT THE NATIONAL LABORATORIES

Aside from the research and analysis performed in the many (perhaps hundreds) of quasi-public nonprofit establishments discussed above, there are scores of national laboratories responsible directly to one or another government department—the Environmental Protection Agency, the Department of Interior, the Department of Energy, and the armed services. The laboratory I refer to in this chapter is the Pacific Northwest National Laboratory (PNNL), a Department of Energy laboratory in Richland, Washington. PNNL, like its dozen sister laboratories under the Department of Energy, is closely monitored by a DOE contractor, in this case the Battelle Memorial Institute.

Many of the DOE laboratories were established not long after Pearl Harbor to undertake highly secret research and the development of a nuclear weapons program. All of these labs were located in remote areas of America. For all practical purposes, they did not exist other than having a nondescript postal address. In every case, they were regarded and operated as secret outposts of the US Army. One of those establishments was Hanford, a plutonium-processing plant east of the Cascade Mountains in the desert of the state of Washington. Plutonium is an extremely dangerous poison that is used as a fuel for nuclear reactors. The waste from the plutonium production is highly radioactive and long lasting.

The PNNL was established in 1965 as an environmental (as opposed to a "weapons") laboratory with its original mission to develop technologies to clean up Hanford's nuclear waste—a gigantic challenge far from being overcome even decades later.

While continuing its work on nuclear waste, the PNNL has broadened its mission and is now one of the world's premier global environmental research laboratories.

*   *   *

Orah and I returned to Chevy Chase in December 1985, just before the Christmas holidays. Our Vienna stay had been an agreeable experience for both of us, even as it was a challenging one for me. Now, in our familiar, centrally heated house with our own furniture, and with some of our children and many friends nearby, we were, once again, "home" rather than "away."

I started my new job at Resources for the Future (RFF) soon after New Year's Day. RFF was founded in 1952 to undertake policy research on environmental, energy, and resource issues. In the early postwar years such matters were of little concern to either policymakers or scholars; RFF was a pioneer in its field.

RFF's focus was primarily on American resource and environmental issues; by the mid-1980s there was growing interest in these problems confronted by both foreign countries and the world at large. In this regard, I worked closely with Bob Fri, RFF's new president.

While my international experience and contacts turned out to be useful to Fri and some of my RFF colleagues, it would be fair to say that RFF and I were an odd match. With a few exceptions, most of my colleagues there were cerebral loners, long on economic research talents, short on social skills. The history and culture of the establishment and the inclinations of the staff tended to produce impeccably objective but colorless research and analyses dealing primarily with domestic rather than international issues. What emerged in report and book form was admirable and useful to specialists and experts, but hardly the stuff for popular consumption.

For better or worse, I have been blessed or cursed with a heavy specific gravity of activism and passion. It must be apparent by now that I have often been impulsive and impatient, and, I suspect, all too ready to proffer my opinions, biases, and prejudices generously, even gratuitously. Moreover, my public policy concerns were more broadly focused and fiercely held than those of most of RFF's staff. If truth be told, I was probably, and with reason, regarded by my colleagues as an ugly duckling among the swans. Or, to put it more charitably (after all, charity begins at home), I soon had the feeling that I was a brainstormer among brooders.

A foretaste of what was in store occurred early in my RFF incarnation. During my time in Austria, I had occasion to make several trips to Eastern Europe—Hungary, Poland, Czechoslovakia. Air pollution in virtually every city and town in each of these countries was horrific. Serious respiratory problems were rampant among the young, the old, and the frail. Because of the political and institutional sensitivities of several of its member countries, IIASA was not then comfortable dealing with that problem, but RFF was under no such constraints. Moreover, RFF had several experts on economic and public policy aspects of air pollution mitigation. In the light of all this, I proposed that they develop a demonstration air cleanup project for one or another afflicted city in Eastern Europe. The findings of this effort could then be adapted to and implemented elsewhere in the region.

The foul emissions from the badly designed and poorly maintained Soviet and Eastern European cars, which were ubiquitous in Eastern Europe, together with their archaic urban traffic systems were major sources of air pollution there. At a staff meeting, I suggested that a useful and inexpensive point of departure for such an effort would be to recruit retired American automobile mechanics and traffic analysts into the Peace Corps. Together with local workers, they could implement a robust campaign of free but mandatory automobile, bus, and truck tune-ups and develop more efficient traffic patterns. The notion aroused some interest, until one young economist fresh from academe asked, "Okay, but is there a book in it?" End of discussion. End of proposal. (Some years later, however, RFF did embark on a research project on Eastern European environmental problems.)

The fact that a Junior Fellow could so easily dispose of what I thought was a promising idea was troubling and said much about how RFF was run. Unlike other places at which I had worked, RFF was characterized by shared power; the director was a facilitator rather than a boss. This, I'm sure, is an agreeable management approach in an institution inhabited by Fellows rather than by staffers or employees. My experience over the previous half century, however, involved taking orders or giving orders. Discussion was expected, but, in the last analysis, the director, ambassador, secretary, or general made the decision. And that was that.

With Bob Fri's encouragement, I was able to broaden the geographic scope of RFF's research menu, even in situations where there was little prospect of adding to a researcher's bibliography. To paraphrase Averell Harriman's remark two decades before, the world had more need for RFF's expertise than it had for another academic book.

I remained at RFF for several years. Looking back, I learned much and met interesting people. I worked closely with the US Council for Environmental Quality and received a commendation for my contribution to a special environmental task force. But I cannot say that I made any lasting contributions either to the organization or to the nation. I was seriously thinking of retiring on the eve of my seventy-fifth birthday. I was saved from such a fate; one of America's great national laboratories made me an offer I could not refuse.

*   *   *

Late in December 1991 I had a call out of the blue from a former colleague at the Institute of Energy Analysis, who was then a senior economist in the Washington, DC, office of the Pacific Northwest National Laboratory. The director of the lab, William Wiley, had arrived in town that day from the headquarters in Richland, Washington, and had asked to see me. I had not heard of either the PNNL or William Wiley, and couldn't understand the reason for the meeting. Nonetheless, I agreed to meet with him the following day.

Wiley was affable, energetic, and bright. Although I didn't know it then, he was a highly regarded biologist. During our first few minutes of small talk, it became clear that he knew a fair amount about my background. I soon realized that he had arranged this meeting with the intent to recruit me. "You can help us make a difference," he said. He invited me to visit the PNNL establishment in Richland and to give a seminar (an audition) there. It sounded interesting. As I got up to leave, Wiley smiled, "You know, I quickly decided you're my kind of guy. I've gotten pretty good at facial expressions and body language, and I watched you carefully when you came into the room. There was absolutely no sign that you were surprised, or even noticed, that I was black."

"Well," I said, "I couldn't care less about that. I was curious what your reaction would be when you found yourself recruiting someone who was pushing his seventy-fifth birthday." We grinned and performed a high-five. Bill Wiley remained a close friend until his death several years later.

Early in 1992 I became (what else?) deputy director of the lab's Global

Change Division. Most of the people in the division were based in Washington (*my* Washington, not the state).

*   *   *

The Pacific Northwest National Laboratory was established in 1965 by the Battelle Memorial Institute at the request of the US Department of Energy. The laboratory is primarily an environmental research establishment and is one of the younger labs in the DOE system; several of the DOE labs (the weapons labs) date back to the early 1940s. This was the time when America was developing its nuclear weapons program.

During World War II, and for many years afterward, personnel at the weapons labs either did not realize the environmental impacts of their activities or were under pressure to produce more and more nuclear weapons. Concerns about nuclear waste were residual claimants on their time and attention. In any case, little was done to mitigate or even to address the vicious environmental hazards that accompanied the program. By the early 1970s, however, the storage, management, and disposal of radioactive waste at various sites throughout the country became high among America's environmental priorities.

At the dawn of America's nuclear weapons program, the village of Hanford, in the desert of eastern Washington, was deemed an ideal place to locate a plutonium-processing plant. It was remote from population centers, but close enough to the cheap and abundant hydroelectric power generated by the great dams of the Pacific Northwest. To be sure, Hanford was (and still is) well within native tribal lands, but that counted little in Washington, DC, when stacked up against the requirements of the war effort. So it was that, by 1943, the Hanford area and the nearby farming centers of Richland, Pasco, and Kennicott were transformed into a virtual US Army reservation. During the 1940s and for many years later, the Hanford plutonium processing plant directly or indirectly employed many thousands of military personnel and civilians—scientists, engineers, technicians, carpenters, dentists, pipefitters, security guards, cooks, barbers, waitresses, and schoolteachers.

The PNNL's assigned mission was an ambitious and urgent one: to develop scientific measures and technologies for cleaning up the mess of radioactive waste at Hanford and the nuclear weapons labs in Oak Ridge, Los Alamos, Sandia, and many other such sites where the storage arrangements for nuclear waste were in worrisome condition and the dangers of radioactive leaks all too real.

When the US Army took over the Hanford site for the plutonium-processing facility, it promised the Native American tribes that, once the plant was no longer needed, it would be destroyed and the area would be restored to its original, "pristine" condition.

It is now more than fifty years later. The tribes are still waiting, with declining patience, for the government in Washington, DC, to deliver on its promise. They will have a long wait. Indeed, the odds are miniscule that any tribal member alive today will live long enough to see this happen. Although cleanup work is proceeding, the government's highest-priority environmental concern in the area is not to restore the safe, prepolluted condition of the five hundred affected square miles of the Hanford reservation (a project that would cost many hundreds of billions of dollars), but, rather, to ensure that the Columbia River, flowing nearby, and the neighboring farmlands and orchards do not become tragically contaminated.

Several years ago, the tribes had a modicum of revenge. In the mid-1990s, officials from the Department of Energy joined the director and staff of the lab and the local press in a groundbreaking party to initiate a new building on the PNNL campus. A young archaeologist on the lab's staff had repeatedly warned that the site chosen for the proposed building was atop holy relics—a Native American burial ground. But what did she know? And so, in a solemn ceremony, a dozen lab and DOE officials plunged their gilded and inscribed spades into the earth. Surprise: Bones! Human bones.

Several months later the ground was again broken—elsewhere on the lab's campus, quietly, and with little ceremony.

*   *   *

My colleagues in Washington, DC, were young, smart, and stimulating. Their academic backgrounds and skills were diverse—several economists, physicists and engineers, a meteorologist, a sociologist, an anthropologist, a few political scientists, and a foreign affairs specialist. Such an array of expertise was well suited to explore the myriad technical, political, and social issues characterizing the global climate change challenge.

This is not altogether the case at the PNNL's headquarters in Richland, nor at its mothership, the Battelle Memorial Institute in Columbus, Ohio. Richland's complement of nearly four thousand is comprised almost entirely of scientists, engineers, and technical support staffers. Most of them have been born and bred on the West Coast, and a surprising number have been employed at the lab for most, if not all, of their working lives. Indeed, many are the children of the workers who had come to Richland and Hanford during World War II. At Battelle's headquarters in Columbus, scientists and engineers also dominate the workforce. And, until recently, Battelle's president and several vice presidents had worked only for Battelle since they had left their universities.

Since the laboratories at both Richland and Columbus employ but a handful of social scientists, their research concentrates on the technological and scientific aspects of the challenging issues on their research agendas. Further narrowing their approach is the fact that few researchers and managers, at both Battelle and the PNNL, have had experience outside academe or the think tank community.

The PNNL and Battelle are not alone in their technological rather than holistic concern. Virtually every laboratory in the Department of Energy's constellation is also dominated by engineers and hard scientists. This is unfortunate, because many of the national and global problems we face call not only for the talents of engineers, but also for contributions from anthropologists, economists, and historians. The lack of concern for the social sciences constrains the broad interdisciplinary approach demanded by the enormous challenges and "problematiques" that beset us. These grand challenges call for heroic measures, Renaissance problem solvers, and fearless politicians. As I peer through the mist, I discern few of them.

*   *   *

Gordon Battelle, an engineer, died without heirs soon after World War I. He requested that his estate be used to found a research and development institute that would employ technology "for the benefit of mankind." Several years later, his mother left her own not-inconsiderable fortune to what became the Battelle Memorial Institute. The institute's activities were originally confined to Columbus, Ohio, but in due course, there were Battelle Research and Development outposts throughout the United States and in several countries abroad.

Like many grand visions, Gordon Battelle's was vague as well as lofty. "Technology," "benefit," and "mankind" are concepts subject to broad interpretation. Thus, the Battelle Institute spawned the photocopying process and has made consequential technical contributions in the field of medicine. But it has also developed seat warmers for the benefit of those members of mankind who may be spectators at late-autumn Ohio State football games.

"Do good while doing well," an old Quaker admonition, remains in Battelle's mission statement, but during the time of my employment there I often wondered if the "well" hasn't wound up being cast in large capital letters, and the "good" in fine print. An aggressive approach toward developing intellectual property and spin-off companies has dominated much of the attention of managers at the lab and the institute.

Survival, naturally, is the highest priority for every worthwhile establishment, private or nonprofit. But organizations that are almost entirely publicly funded, such as those in the DOE's national laboratory system, are, or should be, obligated to think beyond the corporate bottom line: Is this project truly necessary? Has it been done already by another group? Could another group do a better job? Is the project socially desirable? Will it divert the efforts of the best researchers from other, less grandiose but more useful, projects? Finally, who are our most important clients—the US Department of Energy, or the next generation of Americans? (For that matter, who *are* the DOE's most important clients?)

Not long after I arrived at the PNNL, a senior manager asked me to share my thoughts with regard to the ethical considerations that should govern research in the national laboratory community. I prepared a paper, "Beyond Excellence," arguing that first-class technological research was necessary, but not sufficient. In a section headed "Who Speaks for Annah?" (Annah is my youngest grandchild), I argued that she, rather than, say, some obscure official in the government's bureaucracy, was the ultimate customer for the work done in most publicly supported research laboratories. This should be particularly the case for research focusing on long-term environmental, energy, and economic issues. If that be so, I pointed out, social, political, ethical, equity, and stewardship considerations that were typically overlooked, or consciously avoided, by division directors and assistant secretaries at the DOE should play a nontrivial part in the PNNL's research, analysis, and findings. My recommendations met with satisfying praise, but were soon put aside in the face of budgetary and personnel problems.

*   *   *

I retired from Battelle/PNNL with emeritus status in the spring of 2001, nine years after my appointment (and nine months short of my eighty-fifth birthday). During my tenure I had gotten to know only a few dozen of the scientists, engineers, and managers among the four thousand folk in Richland and the three thousand in Columbus. Even with these colleagues, my contacts were intermittent and brief. It was among the group in Washington, DC, with whom, almost immediately, I felt at home. My young coworkers—I was older than virtually all my colleagues by many years, some by decades—became close associates and good friends. It was a special gift that during this, my last "real job," I was constantly challenged and stimulated, never bored.

The PNNL's Global Change Group concentrated on international climate change—causes, likelihood, and impacts on the one hand, and approaches for mitigation or adaptation on the other. My initial reaction to this ambitious effort brought back memories of Alvin Weinberg's climate change admonition to Dr. Frank Press, President Carter's science adviser, twenty years before. Much work had been done on the global climate issue since that 1977 meeting early in Carter's tenure by university and government establishments as well as by Weinberg's own institute. Nonetheless, the surface had hardly been scratched.

The Global Change Group was under Associate Lab Director Gerald Stokes, an accomplished astronomer and atmospheric scientist. Lab Director William Wiley's decision to provide an adequate number of researchers and nontrivial funding was an earnest of the PNNL's readiness to reach out well beyond its original mission, research on environmental problems posed by military and civilian nuclear waste. Our project soon became an ambitious, multidisciplinary, international effort. In a few years it was funded by both the United States and foreign governments and by private-sector establishments in America and abroad. It is now a world leader in the field.

*   *   *

Questions could well be asked about my role in this enterprise. It was by no means a secret that, by training, experience, and inclination, I was hardly equipped to deal with such technical subjects as meteorology, physics, biochemistry, economic modeling, and statistics. (After all, that is why I had parted company with MIT many decades ago.) The rationale for my employment can be found in the full title I selected for myself—deputy director for special projects. Once the scientists, engineers, and modelers have had their say (or, at least, have removed some of the guesswork), addressing the global climate change challenge takes on a wide array of public policy issues: institutional arrangements, intergenerational equity, political costs, economic tolerances, international cost sharing, and human behavior patterns are among the nontechnological considerations that come into play. At this point the team of social science and public policy buffs was yanked off the bench and were flung into the game.

To provide the PNNL in general and the Global Change Group in particular with a broader disciplinary and geographically more diverse perspective on global climate change, I launched a "special project"—an International Advisory Board. The board consisted of a dozen or so prestigious experts from eight countries who had government, academic, and think tank experience in a variety of fields. We met for three days, twice a year, to review the work of my colleagues and to suggest new lines of inquiry. Among the board members were Robert McNamara (then retired from the presidency of the World Bank), Lord Meghnad Desai (London School of Economics), George Golitsyn (Russian Academy of Sciences), Richard Odingo (University of Nairobi), and Francisco Barnes (rector, National Autonomous University, Mexico). Aside from various venues on America's East and West coasts, the board met in Korea, England, and Mexico.

The board fared well and did well during the tenure of Lab Director William Wiley. After he passed away, however, the board languished and then died. Wiley's successor came to the lab from Battelle, Columbus, where he was a senior vice president. He moved in a narrower circle populated by DOE officials, a few members of Congress, and his longtime Battelle colleagues. He was a scientist who had spent his working life in Battelle's womb and seemed uncomfortable when dealing with prestigious public policy experts and intellectuals from the outside world. He was a good manager and a genial soul, but issues other than those with a technological content were evidently of little interest to him. He attended one or two meetings and faded away.

*　　*　　*

Another "special project" was a series of dinner seminars which I hosted and chaired. This enterprise had a much longer shelf life than the International Advisory Board. I first embarked upon the notion of working dinners during my London embassy days many years before. The format has remained pretty much the same over five decades: a score of people from disparate but relevant backgrounds are invited for cocktails, dinner, and a structured but informal discussion of a problem or project of current or potential concern to whoever I was working for at the time. At the PNNL, this approach provided our group with an outreach beyond its usual confines. Aside from useful new analytical insights, the "soirees" broadened our professional contacts and enriched our research agenda. (Not to be overlooked is that they recently provided the venue for the courtship and subsequent marriage of two of our more enthusiastic discussants.)

A more ambitious and long-term "special project" for which I was at least partially responsible was the formation, in 2001, of an intellectual and institutional partnership between the PNNL's Global Change Group and the University of Maryland. The establishment of the Joint Global Change Research Institute (JGCRI—a horrible acronym!) presented an opportunity for the PNNL's climate change researchers to move to College Park, Maryland, where they are away, at least geographically, from the suffocating bureaucratic ambience of the Department of Energy.

The joint institute has provided the PNNL researchers with access to university facilities and to faculty and students working on related environmental issues. Several university professors and graduate students are currently working with members of the PNNL staff on global climate change issues. The partnership between the lab and the university is still young, and judgment as to its effectiveness must be suspended for another few years. The early omens bode well.

*   *   *

During my time at the PNNL, life, both at home and at work, had been winding down. Orah and I were truly experiencing the "golden years." Our children—Joan, Susan, Ron, and Tom—were doing well. Our grandchildren—Elizabeth, James, and Annah—were a source of pride and pleasure. (Someone once said that being parents was equivalent to drinking beer, but being grandparents was like drinking champagne.) Our "adopted children," the doctors Bernadine Healy, Willy Walker, Greg Bulkley, and many friends graced and added luster to our family circle.

Except for occasional bouts of asthma, Orah was in good health, and I had fully recovered from the major surgery and accompanying interior redecoration I had undergone in 1994. Of course, as the months folded into years, we walked more slowly and reached for each other's hand in prudence as well as affection. We preferred matinee performances and concerts to those held at night, and we spent cold winter evenings by the fire and fine summer evenings on our terrace. When we traveled abroad we tended to rely on advance reservations, rather than, as we used to do, trust our instincts and luck.

By now, we well knew that we'd never be rich, but we'd never be poor. An anonymous sixteenth-century English proverb summed this up nicely:

> I scorn no poor, nor fear no rich;
> I feel no want, nor have too much.[1]

My responsibilities at the laboratory were sufficiently challenging, but compared to those I had carried a decade or so before, were hardly onerous. I no longer took work home, no longer worked at night or on weekends, no longer worried about problems at the office during vacations. Most of our old friends and colleagues were still alive and mobile, and we shared many of our evenings and weekends with them. We celebrated our fifty-fifth anniversary by joining our children and grandchildren on a two-week tour of Morocco. Our sixty-first was just over the horizon. We had been very fortunate—and we knew it.

Two hundred fifty years earlier, Benjamin Franklin anticipated my mood. In a letter to a friend, he told of his pleasure at the prospect of retiring from his printing business: "I hope soon to be quite a master of my own time. . . . I am in a fair way of having no tasks than such as I shall like to give myself, and enjoying leisure to read, study, make experiments and converse at large with such ingenious and worthy men as are pleased to honor me with their friendship or acquaintance. . . ."[2]

Although I had hoped to soldier on until my eighty-fifth birthday, I, in fact, retired in April 2001, nine months short of that nice round number. But, as my mother would have said, it was "enough already." I was granted emeritus status, an office, secretarial help, and free stationery. Like Franklin, I found it congenial to be, at long last, my own master, picking and choosing the projects I would like to work on at home, at the PNNL, and at the university. Meanwhile, Orah, who had long since retired, became involved in a host of other projects—yoga, German-language classes, tutoring, serving as impresario of a lively speakers program, providing loving care to me and to ours.

*   *   *

We both instinctively realized that time was slipping by, pleasantly but all too quickly. Frequently and spontaneously, we touched and hugged each other. We updated our wills. We still traveled here in America and to Europe and Asia. In January 2002 Orah and I visited Joan, Ron, and our granddaughters in London. In mid-March we went to Vienna for a friend's birthday party. In late April we toured the battlefields at Gettysburg and plodded up the mile-long hill where Pickett had led his charge. I don't think we would have done anything differently even if we had known how little time we still had together.

In early May 2002, Orah died—suddenly, without warning, without pain.

At the hospital we kissed, I waved to her, she winked at me, and off she was trundled into the operating room. The surgeon thought the procedure would take about three hours.

Orah never awoke from the anesthesia. She officially died the next day. Our children, grandchildren, and a few other members of our family gathered with me during her final hours. I hope she knew we were there, but I doubt it. A few days later our small family clung together on our terrace to mourn for the elegant lady who, for more than half a century, presided over us.

In August we arranged a simple remembrance ceremony. Ron officiated. Tom recounted the highlights of Orah's life. Elizabeth, James, and Annah read some excerpts from the flood of consolation letters. I tried to say a few words. Soon after, I flew to England and, in the comforting embrace of Joan, Ron, and my granddaughters, spent a peaceful, recuperative two weeks on the Devon coast.

I write this now, two years later, still in disbelief, still numb, still getting out of bed quietly each morning lest I awaken her. I miss her smile and touch and care; I need all of this and more. Orah's analytical and rational approach to personal or world problems was a healthy counterbalance to my own visceral, often emotional one; we were a good combination of head and heart. I can still see her look up at me with amusement and say, "Chet, you don't *really* believe that, do you?" Now Orah has gone and the house, fireplace, terrace, and all has been sold. It is a very different place, this world without Orah.

NOTES

1. W. Byrd, "Psalms, Sonnets and Songs, 1588," in *The Oxford Book of Sixteenth-Century Verse* (Oxford: Clarendon Press, 1932), p. 243.

2. H. W. Brands, *The First American: The Life and Times of Benjamin Franklin* (New York: Anchor Books, 2000), pp. 189–90.

EPILOGUE

A memoir, by definition, is the product of the writer's memory, which, for its part, tends to be selective and subjective. More than not, one's memory is skewed by nostalgia, wishful thinking, and self-aggrandizement or self-pity.

The obligatory polygraph tests were one of the less pleasant aspects of my CIA experience. I survived them, but I am not sure how I would fare with regard to this, my memoir. What I have recalled here, despite an honest effort, may not be the unvarnished, truly accurate, objective, literal record of a long, checkered career. Looking back, I suspect that frustration, anger, self-righteousness, and petulance have probably colored some of my memories; I may well have been an edgy colleague and subordinate.

Setting such uncertainties aside, I can say with confidence that a major influence on my life, and those of my generation, can be summed up in one ugly word: war.

Among my first memories is one of soldiers returning from occupation duty in Germany as they marched down the main street of the small town where our family spent the summer. Since that "war to end all wars," American forces have fought in many places against many enemies on almost every continent. Hostilities in Iraq, the latest addition to a long train of tragedies, are far from being resolved as I write. Reading the morning's paper, the word "quagmire" and the long, costly struggle in Vietnam come readily to mind.

Comparisons between the two wars are inevitable, but it would be wrong-headed to imply that Vietnam and Iraq have much in common. Every war has its own character—its climate, its terrain, the enemy, the weapons, the raison d'être, the motivation of each side, the "justness" of the cause. Yet in the case of Vietnam and Iraq, there are a few important similarities—similarities that should be a cause for concern if the past is indeed prologue.

Thus, in each case the *causus bellum* was initially supported by most Americans but, not long after, became a source of public distrust. We fought in Vietnam to prevent the "dominoes" from falling. We are in Iraq because Hussein "had, or was about to acquire, weapons of mass destruction." In the event, the non-Communist regime of South Vietnam was defeated, but there was no sound of crashing dominoes. In Iraq, nuclear weapons turned out to be nonexistent. In each case, the cost of these firmly held misconceptions in lives, property, and treasure has been horrific.

In both wars, America went into battle armed to the teeth, but lacking essential knowledge about our enemy—his language, his culture, his military determination. Our ignorance was accompanied by ample dollops of hubris and ideological passion. Indeed, our leaders were so cocky that they did not even know how little they knew.[1] Throughout, uncongenial facts were brushed aside or spun around to be more palatable.[2]

Of all this administration's sins of omission and commission, one of the least forgivable has been the unwillingness of President Bush, his advisers, and his groupies to recognize and learn from the mistakes of Lyndon Johnson and his political and military advisers: avoid reliance on non-American translators and interpreters; beware of a credibility gap in exaggerating progress and burying mistakes; make sure that government contractors are purer than Caesar's wife; don't count prematurely on the ability, loyalty, and motivation of local military and police forces. And, above all, make no false promises, rosy predictions, and politically clever but ill-informed decisions.

*   *   *

The title *In the Shadows of History* may evoke a sense of chill and darkness, but I cannot close these accounts on such a note. Despite my early restlessness, the Great Depression, and the wars, my life has been replete with exciting challenges and fascinating experiences. I have reveled in the sunshine of a warm, caring family, inspiring colleagues, and good friends. And threading its way through virtually all of it has been a wondrous love story.

*   *   *

I am all too aware that time is pushing me toward the edge. Soon enough, the tragedy of Vietnam, the folly of Iraq, the failure to address threats to the global environment will, for me, become moot. But unless my children and theirs (and yours) have learned from the history of our triumphs and mistakes, they will be destined to live in the shadows that I and my peers have been unable to cast away.

NOTES

1. A few who did know were ignored or scorned by their superiors, who did not know.

2. I was not altogether innocent of such folly, until I woke up in 1965.

INDEX

Acheson, Dean, 10, 103, 197
Adenauer, Konrad, 197
Aldrich, Winthrop, 154, 160, 161
Algeria and France, 143, 159, 178
American Academy of Arts and Sciences, 317, 321, 322, 332n1
Amory, Robert, 106, 135, 163, 165, 168
Angleton, James, 291
Anglo-US relations, 124–25, 142, 157, 161–62, 249, 253–54
anti-Americanism, 163, 171, 201
anti-Semitism, 28, 40
antiwar demonstrations. *See* demonstrations
Army (US), 43–55, 86, 97
Aswan High Dam, 143–44, 145
atomic bomb, 77
Aubrac, Raymond, 267–69, 293–94

Bao Dai (emperor), 120, 121
Barbour, Walworth, 161–62, 165
Barnes, Francisco, 342
Batista y Zaldívar, Fulgencio, 193
Battelle, Gordon, 339
Battelle Memorial Insitute, 333, 337, 338–40

Bay of Pigs invasion. *See* Cuba
BBC. *See* British Broadcasting Corporation
Ben-Gurion, David, 155, 158, 159, 165–66, 167, 168
Berlin Wall, 186
Bernstein, Leonard, 26
Bidault, Georges, 121, 124, 126
Billington, James, 306
"Black Mac." *See* Makarios III (archbishop)
Blackwood, Scottie, 66
Blandford, John, 40
Bloch, Felix, 324–25
Bohlen, Charles "Chip," 149, 185
bombing of North Vietnam, 219, 229, 233, 257, 264, 269, 273, 278
escalation of war after Pleiku, 220–21, 288
impact on peace prospects, 238–41, 247
See also cease-fires
Book-of-the-Month Club, 304
Braun, Wernher von, 303
Brezhnev, Leonid, 313
Bride, Walter, 75–77